The Colonisation and Settlement of Taiwan, 1684–1945

The dispossession of indigenous peoples by conquest regimes remains a pressing issue. This book, unlike most other books on the subject, contrasts two different colonial administrations – first the Chinese Qing Empire, then, from 1895, the Japanese. It shows how, under the Chinese legal system, the Qing managed the relationship between the increasing numbers of Han Chinese settlers and the indigenous peoples and refrained from taking actions to transform aboriginal land tenure, and how nevertheless Chinese settlers were able to manipulate aboriginal land tenure to their advantage. It goes on to examine the very different approach of the Japanese colonial administration, which following the Meiji Restoration of 1868 had begun to adopt a Western legal framework, demonstrating how this was intentionally much more intrusive, and how the Japanese modernised legal framework significantly disrupted aboriginal land tenure. Based on extensive original research, the book provides important insights into colonisation, different legal traditions and the impact of colonial settlement on indigenous peoples.

Dr Ruiping Ye is a lecturer in law at the Victoria University of Wellington, New Zealand.

Routledge Studies in the Modern History of Asia

Secularism, Decolonisation, and the Cold War in South and Southeast Asia
Clemens Six

Chinese Middlemen in Hong Kong's Colonial Economy, 1830–1890
Kaori Abe

World War Two Legacies in East Asia
China Remembers the War
Chan Yang

Civil Society and Postwar Pacific Basin Reconciliation
Wounds, Scars, and Healing
Edited by Yasuko Claremont

Korean National Identity under Japanese Colonial Rule
Yi Gwangsu and the March First Movement of 1919
Michael D. Shin

English Language Teaching during Japan's Post-war Occupation
Politics and Pedagogy
Mayumi Ohara and John Buchanan

China and Southeast Asia
Historical Interactions
Edited by Geoff Wade and James K. Chin

Southeast Asian Education in Modern History
Schools, Manipulation, and Contest
Edited by Pia Jolliffe and Thomas Richard Bruce

The Colonisation and Settlement of Taiwan, 1684–1945
Land Tenure, Law and Qing and Japanese Policies
Ruiping Ye

For a full list of available titles please visit: www.routledge.com/Routledge-Studies-in-the-Modern-History-of-Asia/book-series/MODHISTASIA

The Colonisation and Settlement of Taiwan, 1684–1945

Land Tenure, Law and Qing and Japanese Policies

Ruiping Ye

Routledge
Taylor & Francis Group
LONDON AND NEW YORK

First published 2019
by Routledge
2 Park Square, Milton Park, Abingdon, Oxon OX14 4RN

and by Routledge
52 Vanderbilt Avenue, New York, NY 10017

First issued in paperback 2020

Routledge is an imprint of the Taylor & Francis Group, an informa business

British Library Cataloguing-in-Publication Data
A catalogue record for this book is available from the British Library

Library of Congress Cataloging-in-Publication Data
A catalog record for this book has been requested

ISBN 13: 978-0-367-58731-4 (pbk)
ISBN 13: 978-0-8153-9471-6 (hbk)

Typeset in Times New Roman
by Apex CoVantage, LLC

This first fruit of the season is dedicated to The LORD

Contents

Illustrations

Diagram

Maps

Tables

Dates

Qing Dynasty reigns

Chongde	(1–8) 1636–1643
Shunzhi	(1–18) 1644–1661
Kangxi	(1–61) 1662–1722
Yongzheng	(1–13) 1723–1735
Qianlong	(1–60) 1736–1795
Jiaqing	(1–25) 1796–1820
Daoguang	(1–30) 1821–1850
Xianfeng	(1–11) 1851–1861
Tongzhi	(1–13) 1862–1874
Guangxu	(1–34) 1875–1908
Xuantong	(1–4) 1909–1912

Selected Japanese reigns

Meiji	(1–45) 1868–1912
Taishō	(1–15) 1912–1926
Shōwa	(1–64) 1926–1989

When the years are indicated in regnal years, it is shown by the regnal title followed by the year of reign. For example, Kangxi 23 means the 23rd year of the Kangxi reign.

Measurements

Distance:	1 *li* 里	≈ 0.576 km
Area:	1 *jia* 甲	≈ 0.97 hectares
		≈ 11 *mu* 畝
	1 *qing* 頃	= 100 *mu*
	1 *mu* 畝	≈ 666.67 m^2
Capacity:	1 *shi* 石	≈ 103.6 litres
	1 *dou* 斗	= 0.1 *shi*

Notes

Chinese terms and names are rendered in Pinyin, unless an author's preferred spelling of name is known, or a place name has an established English spelling (for example, Taipei).

Where a Chinese language source is cited, if the source provides an English language title, it is shown in round brackets with quotation marks (for articles and book chapters) or in italics (books), otherwise the English translation of the title is included in square brackets.

All primary sources quoted are translated by the author unless otherwise stated.

Acknowledgements

The author wishes to thank:

Law Professors Richard Boast QC and Tony Angelo QC, and Sinologist Duncan Campbell, for generously sharing their knowledge in their respective speciality areas, and their wise guidance and tremendous support;

Professor John Shepherd and Professor Brian Moloughney for suggestions for improvement to an earlier version of this book;

The Institute of Taiwan History, Academic Sinica, the National Central Library of Taiwan, the National Library of Australia, the Australian National University Menzies library, the Harvard Yen-ching Library, the US Library of Congress, the Taiwan Research Institute of Xiamen University and Victoria University of Wellington for use of library facilities and resources;

The Executive Yuan of Taiwan, the Research Center for Humanities and Social Sciences, Academia Sinica and Professor Ka Chih-ming for permission to use maps published or created by them;

Scholars in the field for their work which provided rich sources for me to draw upon and a foundation to build on; and

Colleagues, friends and family for healthy discussion and ongoing support.

Introduction

Taiwan, an island which used to be known by Europeans as Formosa,[1] has been settled for thousands of years by aboriginal Austronesians. From the early 17th century, successive outside forces established administrations in Taiwan. The first three administrations were relatively brief and controlled only small parts of Taiwan – the Dutch East India Company for 38 years (1624–1662) in the southwest, the Spaniards for 16 years (1626–1642) in the north, and the Chinese Zheng family for 22 years (1662–1683), mainly in the southwestern plains. Following these brief periods of overseas control, Taiwan became part of the Qing Empire for over two centuries (1684–1895). This was followed by 50 years of Japanese administration (1895–1945).[2]

During the Qing period some aboriginal groups, mostly those that lived in the plains areas, were exposed to the Chinese culture when Han Chinese settlement spread and became acculturated. They lost their distinctive features as aborigines, and possession and control of their land.[3] By the end of the Qing period, the western plains of Taiwan were fully developed as farmland and were occupied by Chinese settlers.[4] The mountain territories were still largely controlled by the aborigines.

Having taken over Taiwan from the Qing in 1895, the Japanese administration dealt with the aboriginal groups that were still recognisable as aborigines, deprived them of their land and confined them to aboriginal reserves (*yuanzhumin baoliudi* 原住民保留地). The current Taiwan government inherited that system and has only recently started to make slight changes as a result of aboriginal rights movements.[5]

Taiwan's aborigines once occupied and controlled all land in Taiwan, but lost almost all of their land through settlement and colonisation, and aboriginal land tenure was completely transformed. A notable difference between the Qing and the Japanese administrations was the speed of land tenure changes. When the Qing ceded Taiwan to Japan, the aborigines still occupied and controlled two-thirds of the island.[6] In contrast, 50 years of Japanese colonial rule saw most aborigines displaced and confined to small areas of aboriginal reserves, which they did not own, and which measured about one-eighth of their ancestral land.[7] Land loss of the aborigines during the Qing period was a gradual process, at a speed much slower than that during the Japanese period, and slower than that in European colonies.[8] There was no conscious deprivation of land by the Qing government.

Why did the Qing administration have different effects on Taiwan aboriginal land tenure from that under Japanese administration? From a legal point of view, what role did Qing legal system – its legal culture, administrative system and decision-making process, and its property law regime – play in the process? For example, what were the Qing policies concerning expansion to and administration of Taiwan? Was there a consistent policy rationale and if there was, what was the rationale? How did the Qing view the aborigines and their land rights, compared with the Japanese view of the colonised peoples and their land rights? How did the respective property law concepts and practice of Qing and Japan affect the aboriginal land tenure changes in Taiwan? This book explores answers to these questions.

Expansion, colonisation and legal traditions

When surveying the legal traditions of the world, Patrick Glenn raised the question of the role of law in Western expansion.[9] Glenn also observed that the Chinese legal tradition, rooted in Confucianism and supplemented by Taoism and Buddhism, did not favour expansion and therefore "the world has never seen a form of east Asian expansion similar to that of Europe".[10]

Some scholars of the history of the Qing Dynasty have opposed the view that China did not expand, or did not expand as European countries did. In recent decades Qing history scholars have challenged the traditional view that colonialism was largely associated with European countries, and have asserted that the Qing was a "colonial empire".[11] These scholars argued, that similar to the European states, the Qing Empire was engaged in "imperial conquest, migration of people, and cultural and commercial exchange",[12] and that Qing colonialism was "similar to, and partially contemporary with, that of Europe".[13] More specifically, one scholar has argued that the Qing administration in Taiwan was a variety of colonialism,[14] a view that has been accepted by some scholars,[15] although scholars specialising in the history of colonialism tend not to regard Qing rule of Taiwan as colonial.[16]

The different views about Qing colonialism and the Qing colonial rule in Taiwan are to some extent related to the different interpretations scholars attribute to the terms "colonial" and "colonialism".[17] The Qing colonial scholars have rarely defined "colonial" and "colonialism", but the implication is that expansion of territories and subjugation of peoples of different cultures or ethnicities constituted colonialism. One scholar noted that China was "the metropole for colonial initiatives that span centuries and numerous, diverse cultures across a great swath of Central, East, and South-East Asia".[18] Another pointed out that the Qing was a "colonial empire that ruled over a diverse collection of peoples with separate identities".[19] Edward Said's definition that colonialism is "the implanting of settlements on distant territory" has been employed to support the argument of Qing colonialism in Taiwan.[20]

While the terms are capable of narrow or wide interpretation, where the interpretation differs, the substance of the term which one interpretation designates will be different from that designated by another interpretation. The previously mentioned arguments about Qing colonialism have adopted a relatively wide interpretation of the term colonialism, and at times seem to have equated the terms colonisation and colonialism, which are closely related but not always identical.[21]

Colonisation is an activity of human society which denotes "a *process* of territorial acquisition".[22] The Qing acquired Taiwan in 1684. Chinese settlement in Taiwan increased steadily in the subsequent centuries. For most of the time the Qing government tried to contain settlement, rather than to implant settlement. However, the advance of Chinese settlement often resulted in the expansion of Qing jurisdiction. Therefore arguably Qing possession of Taiwan was a form of colonisation.

Different from colonisation, colonialism is "a *system* of domination", domination of "people of another culture".[23] There are three qualifications for such a domination to be colonialism – the external manipulation and transformation of the indigenous society "according to the needs and interests of the colonial rulers"; the dissimilarity between the colonisers and colonised; and the assumption that the colonisers' culture is superior to that of the colonised which led to the imposition of the colonisers' culture on the colonised.[24] In other words, the necessary ingredients for colonialism are self-interest, dissimilarity, assumption of superiority, imposition of culture, and manipulation and transformation of the indigenous society.

The Qing rulers were Manchus and Taiwan's aborigines were Austronesians; there is no question that the rulers and the ruled were dissimilar. Generally the Manchu rulers and the Chinese officials assumed that the Manchu and Chinese cultures were superior to that of the aborigines, as evidenced in some of the official documents and private writings of the Qing period, although at times the aborigines' culture was praised for its antiquity and innocence.[25] It is also arguable that Qing rulers acquired and administered Taiwan according to their own needs and interests. Therefore, the Qing domination of the Taiwanese aborigines satisfied the conditions of dissimilarity in culture, assumption of superiority and self-interest.

What remain in question are the presence, intention, method, and extent of the external manipulation and transformation of the aboriginal society and the imposition of Manchu or Chinese culture on the aborigines by the Qing government. These are the keys to deciding the nature of Qing colonisation of Taiwan. One of the most important aspects of the aboriginal society is land tenure, and the area that caused most of the grievances of indigenous peoples is the taking of land and transformation of land tenure. Land issues most fully evidenced the colonisers' domination of the colonised, not only for the Taiwanese aborigines, but generally for all indigenous peoples.

This study examines the nature of Qing colonisation of Taiwan through analysing Qing policies towards land settlement and aboriginal land rights in Taiwan. The process and system of Japanese colonisation of Taiwan is set as a comparison to that of Qing colonisation. Scholars have more readily accepted that Japanese overseas expansion and its administration of Taiwan was colonialism than they have Qing expansion and administration of Taiwan.[26] This implies that there existed fundamental differences between Qing colonisation and Japanese colonisation of Taiwan. In fact it has been observed that:[27]

> [s]ince Japanese imperialism emulated but also stood apart from Western imperialism, the difference between Japanese and Qing colonial rule in Taiwan might be seen partly as differences within Asian colonialisms and partly as differences between Asian and Western colonialism.

One task of this book is to explore the different colonisation and expansion style of the Qing from that of Japan in the particular area of aboriginal land tenure, and to suggest the reasons for the differences from the perspective of legal traditions and systems.

The subject matter is slightly complicated by the fact that the Qing rulers were Manchus, not Chinese. Using the Manchu language archives, recent scholarship has discovered aspects of the Qing ruling house which had not been revealed in the Chinese language archives of the Qing. Known as the "new Qing history" school, the scholars stressed the Manchu characteristics and identity of the Qing ruling house. They challenged the traditional view that the Qing were sinicised, a view maintained by the "sinicisation" school of scholars.[28] Despite the heated debate and the important differences between these two schools, in effect the findings of the new Qing history school reveal the multi-dimensional characteristics of the Qing ruling house, but do not deny the sinicisation of the Qing as such. That is to say, in some aspects and at some levels the Qing Court was sinicised, while at others it maintained, utilised and stressed its Manchu way.[29] In particular, it is generally accepted that the Qing administrative institutions and legal system were mainly inherited from the previous Ming Dynasty and were largely Chinese.[30] Furthermore, despite the emphasis that the Manchus were not "Chinese" in its traditional sense, it has been noted that, albeit different from "the old Ming concept of an exclusively Han ethnic state", the Qing was China, and the Qing referred to itself as such since the early decades of conquest.[31] It had passed many of its legacies to the polity and society known as "China" today.[32] For the previously mentioned reasons, the discussion of the Qing legal system in this study is in fact an examination of the Chinese legal system, although at places the system had unique Qing characteristics.

Aboriginal land tenure

Scholars supporting the colonial nature of the Qing administration in Taiwan have not examined it from the angle of aboriginal land issues; scholars who study aboriginal land issues in Qing Taiwan have not usually looked at the issues through the lens of colonisation or colonialism. Studies of Japanese colonialism and Japanese aboriginal land policies have also often been separate.

At the turn of the 20th century, the Japanese anthropologist Inō Kanori pioneered the research on Taiwan's aborigines, Chinese land settlement in Taiwan and the Qing administration of Taiwan.[33] Inō observed that the Qing administration in

Taiwan, especially the administration of the aborigines, was largely one of neglect (*xiaoji* 消極 "passive") before 1875, at which time the government turned active and launched campaigns to subjugate the mountain aborigines, a reaction to the Japanese invasion of southern Taiwan in 1874.[34] Similarly land settlement policies changed from restriction to encouragement in 1875.[35] The idea that the Qing were passive about and neglectful of Taiwan continued for decades in later research by Taiwanese scholars and Western scholars.[36]

This previously mentioned view was challenged in 1993, when John Shepherd suggested that the Qing administration of Taiwan was a careful balancing act of revenue and cost.[37] Shepherd argued that the calculation of political economy led the Qing to devote itself to "accommodate" aboriginal land rights, which appears to mean a certain degree of recognition and protection of aboriginal land rights, or to consider the interests of both aborigines and settlers.[38] Shepherd made a compelling case about the Qing policy rationale, but his study concerned only the period up to 1800 – essentially the reigns of Kangxi, Yongzheng and Qianlong (1684–1795) – and only the land rights of the plains aborigines. Further, the Japanese government also had to balance revenue and administrative cost, yet it took action to reform land tenure and increase revenue, rather than to minimise cost and accommodate aboriginal land rights as the Qing did. Some other factors had caused, or influenced, the Qing and the Japanese governments to make different choices, and one of the factors was the different legal cultures and traditions on governance. The Qing applied the Chinese tradition of governance and Confucian legal thought, while Japan adopted modern legal institutions and emulated Western colonial examples. Each legal order shaped the policymaking and ultimately determined the different courses and outcomes of transformation of aboriginal land tenure.

Shepherd also pointed out that the government, the Han Chinese settlers and the aborigines were three major players in the political scene of Qing Taiwan.[39] Ka Chih-ming, focusing on land rights of the plains aborigines before the end of the 18th century as Shepherd did, further developed this concept and argued that Qing aboriginal land policies were a manipulation of ethnic politics.[40] Ka's argument about ethnic politics is consistent with the fact that the Qing rulers were skilful in managing and manipulating ethnic relationships, being minority rulers over China for nearly three centuries and governing a variety of peoples. However Ka attributed the making, implementation and consequences of the Qing aboriginal land policies to a series of experiments and corrections of mistakes because of "contingencies in the course of history" (*lishi de jiyu* 歷史的機遇), before ethnic manipulation became a clear model and policies protecting aboriginal land rights were formed during the mid- to late Qianlong reign.[41] This proposition suggests a lack of consistency and rationale, and is an oversimplification. Not only the Kangxi, Yongzheng and Qianlong governments (1684–1795), but throughout the whole Qing period, there was a central rationale on settlement and aboriginal land policies. The central rationale was to maintain national or regional security and social stability, and the major policy directions were adjusted according to circumstances to ensure the ultimate goal of security and stability. The goal itself, the methods to achieve the goal and the effects of the methods were all dictated by Qing legal culture and governance tradition.

Other scholars have also tried to find the reasons for land loss by the plains aborigines. For example, through a case study on land tenure changes of the aboriginal Anli village, Chen Chiu-kun argued that aboriginal land tenure changes were the combined effect of local officials' ineffective implementation and distortion of government policies on the one hand, and the influence of the dominating Chinese land practice and commercial economy on the other.[42] The experience of the Anli village to some extent represented that of the plains aborigines, but Chen did not turn his attention to the higher level of governance or policymaking.

Most studies on Qing aboriginal land policies have focused on the period before 1800, and few studies have focused on policies after 1800 and about the mountain aborigines. A notable one is by Chang Lung-chih, who examined debates within the government about expanding land settlement beyond the plains areas before 1875 and the policies after 1875.[43] Chang concluded that 1875 signified the turning point of "Qing colonisation".[44] This confirmed the traditional view which had been expounded by Inō and accepted by subsequent scholars. Chang focused on official discussions about whether to expand government administration and allow or encourage land settlement, but did not consider aboriginal land rights as such.

There have also been studies on Japanese colonial rule and land policies in Taiwan, but each with a different focus. Essays edited by Liao and Wang examined Japanese rule in Taiwan from the angles of colonialism and modernity, colonial policy and cultural change, and literary expression, but not aboriginal land tenure.[45] Ka Chih-Ming studied the agricultural development and the colonial economy in Taiwan during the Japanese period, and only touched on land tenure where rice and sugar production was concerned.[46] The Japanese manipulation of aboriginal property rights has also been the topic of research, yet the attention was on Japanese management of the camphor forest, an aspect relating to the mountain aborigines' rights but not otherwise concerned with land tenure as a whole.[47] Where land tenure issues were studied, the focus has been on the system of aboriginal reserves during the Japanese period and the implications and challenges for the current government.[48] A work that documented the evolution of land registration systems under the Japanese and the subsequent Chinese regime had no concern with the wider context of land tenure changes.[49] All in all, none of the previously mentioned studies has given attention to the connection between the Japanese colonial style and its aboriginal land policies.

This book addresses an area that has been neglected by researchers: how the respective styles of colonisation of the Qing and Japan, each shaped by its own legal system, determined their different aboriginal land policies and changed aboriginal land tenure in Taiwan. It examines the whole length of Qing administration of Taiwan and uses Japanese policies as a comparison; it covers policies and land tenure changes about both the plains aborigines and the mountain aborigines. The study of Taiwan aboriginal land policies is put in the wider framework of the administration of Taiwan by governments whose legal systems were quite different, namely the Qing government, which in many respects was a traditional

Chinese imperial regime, and Japan, which by the time it colonised Taiwan had reformed its law along European lines and emulated a modern and European-style regime.

Overview

A central concern of this book is the connection between law and colonial policy, and their effects on aboriginal land rights. More specifically, the major questions are how, under the Qing and Japanese regimes, laws and policies regarding aboriginal land in Taiwan resulted in aboriginal land tenure changes and loss of land; and further, how the respective legal systems and legal cultures of the Qing and Japanese states influenced policymaking concerning colonisation, settlement and aboriginal land.

This book examines Qing policies towards land settlement in Taiwan, the extent of the government's recognition and protection of aboriginal land rights, the changes that the Qing property law regime brought to aboriginal land tenure, and the aborigines' interaction with the government and settlers regarding their land. The Japanese government's attitudes towards the aborigines and aboriginal land, as well as its reforms of land tenure in Taiwan, are then discussed. Ultimately, this book explores the role the Qing legal system played in shaping the policies and in transforming aboriginal land tenure, and how the Japanese legal system, largely Westernised after the Meiji Restoration in 1868, influenced Japanese colonial policies regarding aboriginal land in Taiwan.

The focus of this book is on the Qing period, and the Japanese period is discussed only for comparison purposes. Reflecting this consideration, the first five chapters concern the Qing period, and the last one, Chapter 6, concerns the Japanese period.

Chapter 1 introduces Taiwan's aboriginal groups and their land tenure, and reviews the process of land settlement before and during the Qing period. This chapter introduces the colonial past of Taiwan and forms of knowledge about the aborigines, identifies patterns of land settlement, and considers the impacts of land settlement patterns on the acculturation of aborigines. It sets the scene for later discussion.

Chapters 2 and 3 analyse Qing regulations and imperial decrees, and trace the policy trends of land settlement and aboriginal land rights during the Qing period. Chapter 2 suggests that Qing policies in Taiwan could be divided into three stages, namely the controlling settlement stage between 1684 and the end of the 18th century, the transitional stage from around 1800 to 1875, and the promoting settlement stage after 1875. This chapter argues that at each stage the determining factor for policymaking was consideration for territorial security and social stability, and this was underpinned by Chinese tradition on governance and theories about expansion.

Chapter 3 examines the Qing aboriginal land policies at the three stages identified in Chapter 2. This chapter clarifies the nature of land ownership under the Qing system, in particular the nature of government "ownership" over wasteland; investigates the extents of Qing recognition and protection of aboriginal land rights; and considers the influence of Confucian legal thought on the land policies and their effects. This chapter argues that the Qing constitutional framework and property law regime determined its policies on aboriginal land rights.

Chapter 4 traverses the influences of Chinese customary land practice on aboriginal land tenure. This chapter surveys land reclamation permits and land deeds; analyses the process of land grants by the government and re-grants by permit holders; and discusses the legal natures of land proprietorship, land registration and various forms of land transaction. The typical forms of transaction, *zu* 租, *pu* 贌, *dian* 典 and *mai* 賣, were fluid concepts and they together formed a spectrum of alienating land rights, with short-term lease and permanent sale at its two ends. This chapter argues that it was Chinese customary land practice that changed aboriginal land tenure most, and caused the most loss of land by the aborigines.

Chapter 5 looks into the aborigines' interaction with the settlers and the government regarding land. The aborigines resisted Han settlement, litigated for their land rights, and eventually adapted to the Chinese practice and became acculturated. Over time the aboriginal communities broke down, which further alienated the aborigines from their land. This chapter demonstrates that colonisation was a two-way contest, and the colonised reacted to defend their rights. However this at most slowed down the process of colonisation, and could not reverse the tide.

Chapter 6 discusses Japan's employment of modern international law theories in occupying the aboriginal territories of Taiwan, and its use of Western legal instruments to reform land tenure. It demonstrates how Japan, as a modernising neo-European colonial power, carried out its colonisation of Taiwan and deprived the aborigines of their land under the modernised legal framework.

This leads to the conclusion that the Qing was a coloniser of a different type, and Qing colonisation of Taiwan was different from the later Japanese colonisation of Taiwan and from the Western styles of colonisation. Shaped by its legal culture, constitutional arrangement, administrative system and property law regime, the Qing government had little or no intention and took little action to transform aboriginal land tenure, which was one of the most important aspects of aboriginal society. Rather, the Qing legal framework allowed or enabled Chinese settlers to manipulate aboriginal land tenure and impose Chinese culture on the aborigines, an effect often unintended by the government.

This study of the land tenure changes and legal traditions is grounded in its historical context and comparisons are made to colonial activities of the era concerned, rather than comparing the legal and political orders of the 18th and 19th century with the contemporary awareness of and respect for indigenous peoples' rights. Further, the terms and substance of land rights in imperial China were highly complex, and special care has been taken to distinguish the rights from ownership in the modern law.

Goals and limits of the present study

When considering the various colonial administrations and their impact on aboriginal land tenure around the Pacific, from Australia and New Zealand to Alaska, and others in between, Stuart Banner commented that "[d]ecisions made in the [past] about how to separate indigenous people from their land . . . continue to shape our lives today".[50] This statement is no less true for Taiwan's aborigines. Like most aboriginal groups, Taiwan's aborigines are now the minority in their own country and lost most of their ancestral lands during the colonial past. They are still battling with this past and are trying to gain recognition of and protection for their land rights, among other things.

Ethnically distinct from the majority Chinese population, presently Taiwan's aborigines make up about 2.3% of the total population.[51] As at 2001, aboriginal reserves measured 251,080 hectares, but the aborigines actually used only about half of the reserves. The other half were either located in remote, rocky or reservoir areas and could not be used, or were used by the government, businesses or non-aborigines.[52] After several "return my land" (*huan wo tudi* 還我土地) movements in the 1980s and 1990s, the government established a mechanism to grant aborigines ownership over reserved land if certain conditions are met. However the percentage of aboriginal ownership remains small.[53]

Given the continuing effects of historical events, it is hoped that interpretation of the historical government actions will provide lessons to assist current endeavours.[54] Furthermore, the experience of Taiwanese aborigines is not an isolated case. Their land tenure changes throughout the colonial history and their struggles for recognition of their rights in some aspects parallel similar loss, demands and indigenous politics in other countries, including Canada, the United States and Australia. It is hoped that this research will contribute to scholarly understanding of the international pattern of appropriation of aboriginal land and of colonialism in the age of decolonisation.[55]

This study is not an ethnohistory of the indigenous peoples of Taiwan. A great deal of valuable work has already been done on this important subject.[56] Rather, the focus is on the legal traditions of the Qing Empire and, to a lesser extent, of post-Meiji Japan, and on how these legal traditions impacted on the development of policies relating to Taiwan.

This study adopts a comparative approach. The focus is more on the Qing period than on the Japanese period. There exist rich primary resources for study of Qing Taiwan, including government regulations, imperial decrees, palace memorials, administrative records, local gazetteers,[57] land deeds and officials' private writings. Many of them are collected in the *Taiwan Wenxian Congkan*, a collection of historic records and literature that has been used by scholars in previous studies.[58] Nevertheless given the large collection of the *Congkan* and this work's focus on legal analysis, this book explores details that have not been noted and reinterprets some documents that have been discussed in earlier studies. In addition, other series of primary collections are consulted, such as *Qinding Daqing huidian shili* (regulations),[59] *Huangchao wenxian tongkao* (regulations and decrees),[60] *Ming Qing Taiwan dang'an huibian* (regulations, decrees and memorials),[61] *Dan Xin dang'an* (government archives)[62] and a number of land deeds collections. As government regulations, official memorials and land transaction deeds are numerous and scattered, it is impossible to exhaust all sources and omissions are possible, although one can be confident that the available resources will have established sufficient basis for the analysis of the general trend. Where appropriate, this work uses case studies in certain localities by way of illustration, but it does not specifically study the developments of individual places or tribes.

Land tenure changes in Taiwan during the Japanese period are discussed only briefly for the purposes of drawing the contrast and comparing the effects of the legal traditions. For the Japanese period, some primary sources, where they exist in Chinese records or have been translated to the Chinese language, are consulted. These include legislation, the administrative files of the Taiwan Governor-General's Office (*zongdufu dang'an* 總督府檔案) and other materials compiled by the colonial government. Aboriginal land tenure during the Japanese period warrants more in-depth study and could be the subject of a separate project by scholars who have the advantage of the language.

Another dimension of comparison, one between Qing Taiwan policies and Qing policies on other frontiers, can be made to help better understand patterns of Qing colonisation. As in the case of Taiwan, individual studies have been carried out regarding government settlement policies and land reclamation in other frontiers, such as Manchuria, Mongolia, the southwest provinces of Yunnan and Sichuan, and the Miao territories in Guizhou and Hunan.[63] There have also been works on the spread of land reclamation in China in general, as well as land reclamation activities during the Qing Dynasty.[64] Chapters 2 and 3 of this book make some brief comparisons of Qing Taiwan and other Qing frontiers, but more work can, and should, be done to study Qing settlement and colonisation of various frontiers from a comparative perspective, and to assess the likelihood and extent of any central rationale or common pattern. Similarly, the relationships between the 19th-century changes in the Japanese legal system and its general colonial policies are also worth close examination. For example, Japan's administration of the land of the Ainu (present-day Hokkaidō) before the reforms of the Meiji era bore similarities to Qing administration of Taiwan, both forming a stark contrast with Japan's Ainu policies and Taiwan policies after the Meiji reforms.[65] These potential areas of research will further inform us on the roles of legal systems in colonisation.

Notes

1 Formosa is Portuguese for "beautiful". In this book, Taiwan refers to the island of Taiwan, and does not include other islands or archipelagos under the jurisdiction of the Taiwan government.

2 The Republic of China took over Taiwan in 1945 after Japan's defeat in World War II.

3 The aborigines who lived in the plains areas are referred to in this book as the plains aborigines, or acculturated aborigines. A contrasting term is mountain aborigines, which refers to those who lived in the mountain areas and maintained their culture until after the Japanese occupation. Mountain aborigines are also referred to as non-acculturated aborigines.

4 There were 3.7 million Han settlers and they were the majority of the total population. See Chuang Chi-fa "Qingdai Taiwan tudi kaifa yu zuqun chongtu" [Land Reclamation and Ethnic Conflicts in Qing Taiwan] (2000) 36 *Taiwan shiji* 3, at 27.

5 See Lin Shu-Ya "Jie/chonggou Taiwan yuanzhu minzu tudi zhengce" (De-/Reconstructing the Land Policies for Indigenous Peoples in Taiwan) (PhD diss, NTU, 2007), at 91–101.
6 Yosaburō Takekoshi (trans George Braithwaite) *Japanese Rule in Formosa* (Longmans, Green and Co, London, 1907), at 218.
7 Lin Chiou-mien "Taiwan geshiqi tudi zhengce yanbian jiqi yingxiang zhi tantao" [The Evolution and Influence of Aboriginal Land Policies of Different Periods in Taiwan] (2001) 2 *Taiwan tudi yanjiu* 23, at 32.
8 For example, two-thirds of the Maori land in New Zealand was alienated in the first 20 years after British colonisation. See Richard Boast *Buying the Land, Selling the Land: Governments and Maori Land in the North Island 1865–1921* (Victoria University Press, Wellington, 2008), at 26. In Australia, the continent was seen as terra nullius and the aborigines were deprived of their land upon European settlement. See Stuart Banner *Possessing the Pacific: Land, Settlers, and Indigenous People From Australia to Alaska* (Harvard University Press, Cambridge (MA), 2007), ch 1.
9 H Patrick Glenn *Legal Traditions of the World: Sustainable Diversity in Law* (5th ed, Oxford University Press, Oxford, 2014), at 272–279.
10 At 355.
11 For example, Michael Adas "Imperialism and Colonialism in Comparative Perspective" (1998) 20 *International History Review* 371–388; Nicola Di Cosmo "Qing Colonial Administration in Inner Asia" (1998) 20 *International History Review* 287–309; Peter C Perdue "Comparing Empires: Manchu Colonialism" (1998) 20 *International History Review* 255–262.
12 Perdue, ibid, at 256.
13 Laura Hostetler *Qing Colonial Enterprise: Ethnography and Cartography in Early Modern China* (University of Chicago Press, Chicago, 2001), at 25.
14 Emma Jinhua Teng *Taiwan's Imagined Geography: Chinese Colonial Travel Writing and Pictures, 1683–1895* (Harvard University Asia Centre, Cambridge (MA), 2004), at 8–9.
15 For example, Robert Eskildsen "Taiwan: A Periphery in Search of a Narrative" (2005) 64 *Journal of Asian Studies* 281, at 287 and 290.
16 For example, Jürgen Osterhammel (trans Shelley L Frisch) *Colonialism: A Theoretical Overview* (Markus Wiener Publishers, Princeton, 1997), at 42, notes that Taiwan was "uncolonised" by the Qing.
17 The ambiguity of terms relating to colonisation and colonialism is often commented on, for example, see Osterhammel, ibid, at 4; Robert Aldrich and John Connell *The Last Colonies* (Cambridge University Press, Cambridge, 1998), at 3.
18 Adas, above n 11, at 371.
19 Perdue, above n 11, at 255.
20 Teng, above n 14, at 8, quoting Edward Said *Culture and Imperialism* (Random House, New York, 1994), at 9.
21 For a discussion of these terms, see Osterhammel, above n 16, especially ch 1 and 2.
22 At 4. Emphasis original.
23 At 4 and 15. Emphasis original.
24 At 15–16.
25 See Teng, above n 14, in general, but at 14 and 79 in particular.
26 For example, see Osterhammel, above n 16, at 79. For Japanese colonial empire in general, and Japanese colonial rule in Taiwan in particular, see Ramon H Myers and Mark R Peattie (eds) *The Japanese Colonial Empire, 1895–1945* (Princeton University Press, Princeton, 1984); Hyman Kublin "The Evolution of Japanese Colonialism" (1959) 2 *Comparative Studies in Society and History* 67–84; Liao Ping-hui and David Der-wei Wang (eds) *Taiwan Under Japanese Colonial Rule, 1895–1945* (Columbia University Press, New York, 2006).

27 Eskildsen, above n 15, at 290.
28 For the Qing's retention of its Manchu heritage and identity, see Mark C Elliott *The Manchu Way: The Eight Banners and Ethnic Identity in Late Imperial China* (Stanford University Press, Stanford, 2001); Evelyn S Rawski "Reenvisioning the Qing: The Significance of the Qing Period in Chinese History" (1996) 55 *Journal of Asian Studies* 829–850; Pamela Kyle Crossley "Thinking About Ethnicity in Early Modern China" (1990) 11 *Late Imperial China* 1–35. For scholarship on the Qing's sinicisation, see, in particular, Ping-ti Ho "In Defence of Sinicization: A Rebuttal of Evelyn Rawski's 'Reenvisioning the Qing'" (1998) 57 *Journal of Asian Studies* 123–155; Pei Huang *Reorienting the Manchus: A Study of Sinicization, 1583–1795* (Cornell University, Ithaca, 2011).
29 A theme that runs through Elliott, ibid. In particular, at 3, "the Qing dynastic enterprise depended both on Manchu ability to adapt to Chinese political traditions *and* on their ability to maintain a separate identity". Emphasis original.
30 For example, see Mark C Elliott "Review of Pei Huang *Reorienting the Manchus: A Study of Sinicization*" (2011) 54 *Journal of the Economic and Social History of the Orient* 584, at 585. For the Qing's inheritance of its legal system from the Ming, see, in particular, Zhang Jinfan *Qingchao fazhishi* [Legal History of the Qing Dynasty] (Zhonghua shuju, Beijing, 1998).
31 William T Rowe *China's Last Empire: The Great Qing* (Belknap Press of Harvard University Press, Cambridge (MA), 2009), at 210.
32 At 287.
33 Inō's most notable works include *Taiwan banjin jijō* [Notes on Taiwanese Aborigines] (Taiwan Sōtokufu, Taipei, 1900), *Taiwan Banseishi* [A History of Aboriginal Management in Taiwan] (Taiwan Sōtokufu, Taipei, 1904) and *Taiwan bunkashi* [A History of Taiwan's Civilisation] (Tōkō Shoni, Tokyo, 1928). For an evaluation of Inō's contribution and lasting influence, see Paul D Barclay "An Historian Among the Anthropologists: The Inō Kanori Revival and the Legacy of Japanese Colonial Ethnography in Taiwan" (2001) 21(2) *Japanese Studies* 117–136.
34 Inō Kanori (trans Taiwan Historica) *Taiwan wenhua zhi* [A History of Taiwan's Civilisation] (Chinese trans Rev ed, Taiwan Shufang, Taipei, 2011), vol 3, at 284 and 300.
35 Part 14 "Tuozhi yange" [The History of Land Settlement], ch 1 and 2.
36 Examples of Taiwanese scholars that expounded this view are Tai Yen-hui "Qingdai Taiwan xiangzhuang zhi shehui de kaocha" [An Investigation of the Local Society in Qing Taiwan] (1963) *Taiwan yinhang jikan* 198, at 198; Song Tsêng-chang "Qingdai Taiwan fuken cuoshi zhi chengxiao jiqi yingxiang" [The Consequences and Influences of the Qing's Land and Aboriginal Policies in Taiwan] (1979) 30(1) *Taiwan Wen Hsien* 142, at 155. For Western scholars who follow the same view, see John Robert Shepherd *Statecraft and Political Economy on the Taiwan Frontier, 1600–1800* (Stanford University Press, Stanford, 1993), at 3.
37 At 5.
38 This theme recurs throughout Shepherd's discussion. For example, at 5, 13, 242, 306 and 396.
39 At 7 and 8.
40 Ka Chih-ming *Fantoujia: Qingdai Taiwan zuqun zhengzhi yu shufan diquan* (*The Aborigine Landlord: Ethnic Politics and Aborigine Land Rights in Qing Taiwan*) (Academia Sinica, Taipei, 2003).
41 See ibid, in particular, at 364, 370–373, and 378.
42 Chen Chiu-kun *Qingdai Taiwan tuzhu diquan: guanliao, handian yu Anlishe ren de tudi bianqian 1700–1895* (*Taiwan's Aboriginal Proprietary Rights in the Ch'ing Period: Bureaucracy, Han Tenants and the Transformation of Property Rights of the Anli Tribe, 1700–1895*) (2nd ed, Academia Sinica, Taipei, 1997), in particular, at 132 and 218–219.
43 Chang Lung-Chih "From Quarantine to Colonization: Qing Debates on Territorialization of Aboriginal Taiwan in the Nineteenth Century" (2008) 15(4) *Taiwanshi yanjiu* 1–30.

44 In particular, at 4–5 and 23.
45 Liao and Wang (eds), above n 26.
46 Ka Chih-Ming *Japanese Colonialism in Taiwan: Land Tenure, Development, and Dependency: 1895–1945* (Westview Press, Boulder, 1998).
47 Antonio C Tavares "The Japanese Colonial State and the Dissolution of the Late Imperial Frontier Economy in Taiwan, 1886–1909" (2005) 64 *Journal of Asian Studies* 361–385.
48 For example, Yen Ai-ching and Yang Guo-zhu *Yuanzhu minzu tudi zhidu yu jingji fazhan* [Land Tenure and Economic Development of the Aborigine Groups] (Daoxiang, Taipei, 2004); Lin, above n 5.
49 Li Zhi-yin "Taiwan tudi dengji zhidu bianqian zhi yanjiu" [The Evolution of Taiwan Land Registration System] (LLM diss, Taiwan National Chengchi University, 2010).
50 Banner, above n 8, at 320.
51 Total indigenous population is about 546,700 as of December 2015. See *The Republic of China Yearbook 2016* (Executive Yuan, Taipei, 2016), at 45.
52 Lin, above n 5, at 84 and 110.
53 As at 2001, aborigines had ownership of 50,435 hectares of reserved land, about 20% of the total reserves. See ibid, at 110 and 136.
54 The current Taiwan president, Tsai Ing-wen, recently apologised to the aborigines for the colonial past. See Austin Ramzy "Taiwan's President Apologizes to Aborigines for Centuries of Injustice" *New York Times* (Online ed, New York, 1 August 2016), Sinosphere.
55 For example, Richard Boast *For the Good of the Natives: Land and Society in the Pacific 1860–1940* (book manuscript) presents the broad picture of the land tenure changes in the Pacific Rim in the late 19th and early 20th centuries.
56 The Japanese administration instigated the study of Taiwanese aborigines and published a series of work, including the works of Inō Kanori, noted in above n 33. More recently, Taiwan Historica published *Taiwan yuanzhumin shi* [History of Taiwanese Aborigines] (Taiwan Historica, Nantou), which includes one title on prehistory (Liu Yi-chang 2002); three titles on government policies (Fujii Shizue 2001, Peter Kang 2005 and Wen Chen-hua 2007) and two titles on the history of the plains aborigines (Chan Su-chuan and Chang Su-fan 2001, Liang Chih-hui and Chuang Yu-lan 2001).
57 Gazetteers (*zhi* 志) are formal records of an administrative unit, such as a county, prefecture or province. They were compiled by local governments from time to time, and include official records as well as selected private writings about the administrative unit concerned.
58 *Taiwan Wenxian Congkan* [Taiwan Literature and Documents Collection] (Taiwan yinhang, Taipei, 1957–1975). The Collection contains 309 titles, and in this thesis they are indicated as TWWX followed by the series number of the title.
59 *Qinding Daqing huidian shili* [Imperially Approved Precedents of the Great Qing Institutes, 1886] (Chinese Text Project, www.ctext.org).
60 *Huangchao wenxian tongkao* [Comprehensive Collection of Important Documents of the Qing Dynasty, 1797] (Chinese Text Project, www.ctext.org).
61 Taiwan Shiliao Jicheng Bianji Weiyuanhui *Ming Qing Taiwan dang'an huibian* [Collection of Historic Documents Concerning Taiwan During the Ming and Qing Dynasties] (Yuanliu, Taipei, 2004–2009) 110 vol.
62 Wu Mi-cha (ed) *Dan Xin dang'an* [Administrative Files of Danshui and Xinzhu Counties] (NTU, Taipei, 1995–2010).
63 For example, Robert HG Lee *The Manchurian Frontier in Ch'ing History* (Harvard University Press, Cambridge (MA), 1970); James Reardon-Anderson "Land Use and Society in Manchuria and Inner Mongolia during the Qing Dynasty" (2000) 5 *Environmental History* 503–530; C Patterson Giersch *Asian Borderlands: The Transformation of Qing China's Yunnan Frontier* (Harvard University Press, Cambridge (MA) and London, 2006); Robert Entenmann "Sichuan and Qing Migration Policy" (1980) 4(4) *Ch'ing-shih wen-t'I* 35–54; Donald S Sutton "Violence and Ethnicity on a Qing Colonial

Frontier: Customary and Statutory Law in the Eighteenth-Century Miao Pale" (2003) 37 *Modern Asian Studies* 41–80.

64 For example, Tang Qiyu *Zhongguo de kenzhi* [Land Reclamation and Colonisation in China] (2nd ed, Yongxiang, Shanghai, 1952); Peng Yuxin 彭雨新 *Qingdai tudi kaiken shi* [History of Land Reclamation During the Qing Dynasty] (Nongye, Beijing, 1990).

65 For the history of Japanese colonisation of the Ainu land, see Takakura Shinichiro (trans John A Harrison) *The Ainu of Northern Japan* (The American Philosophical Society, Philadelphia, 1960). Also see Tomonori Sugimoto "The Yellow Man's Burden: The Politics of Settler Colonialism in Hokkaidō and Taiwan" (MA thesis, University of California, San Diego, 2013).

1 Land settlement

Progression and pattern

Although Taiwan is situated close to the coastal provinces of China, the first colonisers of Taiwan were the Europeans, namely the Dutch East India Company and the Spaniards, both for trade purposes and each competing with the other. The subsequent Zheng regime had intended to use Taiwan as a foothold in its mission to resist the Manchus and restore the Ming governance over China.[1] It was the Zheng's opposition that led the Qing government eventually to annex Taiwan in 1684.

The Dutch, the Spaniards, the Zhengs and the Qing all had encounters with the aborigines, and their understanding and records of the aborigines were empirical in nature. It was not until the Japanese period that anthropological research about the aborigines was carried out, the research itself signalling a different approach to colonisation. Archaeologists and ethnohistorians have since found that Taiwan is the ancestral homeland of the Austronesian peoples and of the Austronesian languages, which spread between Madagascar in the west and Easter Island in the east.

Land settlement in Taiwan began with the arrival of the Dutch, and the spread of settlements in subsequent centuries unavoidably affected the aborigines. The history of land reclamation[2] in different localities and historical periods has been the subject of in-depth study, and much has been discovered about the spread of Han settlement in Taiwan.[3] This chapter establishes that land settlement throughout the 17th to 19th centuries was a slow but continuous expansion. The varying degrees of acculturation of the aborigines followed the spread of land settlement. The various statuses of the different aboriginal groups in present-day Taiwan, as recognised by the government, were the result of varying degrees of acculturation in the history.

Taiwan: stages in history

Early contacts

Taiwan measures about 35,808 square kilometres, being about 400 kilometres from north to south, and about 145 kilometres from west to east at its widest. Converting to the measurement that was used during the Zheng, the Qing and most of the Japanese periods, the total land area is just over 3.7 million *jia* 甲. Central mountain ranges run from the north to the south, occupying about half of the island. West of the mountain ranges are fertile plains, and east of the mountains are scattered lowlands (Map 1.1).

Being separated from its nearest neighbour, the mainland of China, by the Taiwan Strait at about 130 kilometres at its narrowest and 220 kilometres at its widest, and being about 1,100 kilometres south of Japan, Taiwan was relatively isolated and the aborigines were their own masters until the 17th century. Chinese records of as early as the 3rd and 7th centuries referred to Taiwan,[4] but the Chinese had shown little interest in acquiring the territory. The Song Dynasty (960–1279) established administration on the Pescadores archipelago (*Penghu* 澎湖), which lie between Taiwan and mainland China, but control was intermittent during the subsequent Yuan (1271–1368) and Ming (1368–1644) dynasties.[5] Chinese merchants were present in Taiwan by the 1340s. In 1430, the Ming Dynasty admiral Zheng He visited Taiwan during one of his voyages, but apart from taking back with him some native herbs, nothing ensued from the visit.[6]

By the second half of the 16th century, fishermen and merchants from coastal Fujian Province sailed to Taiwan regularly and some settled there, although the number was small.[7] During the late Ming period, Chinese and Japanese pirates also used Taiwan as a base for their activities. The Japanese government sent envoys to Taiwan to demand tributes and request trade in 1593 and 1609, and sent 13 boats in 1615 with the intention of invading Taiwan, all without success.[8] Japan soon entered a period of self-imposed isolation called *sakoku* (Ch *Suoguo* 鎖國) in 1633, and as a result abandoned any effort to assert a Japanese presence in Taiwan.

European occupation

The lack of interest on the part of the late Ming government and the changed policy in Japan gave the Dutch East India Company (Vereenigde Oost-Indische Compagnie, the "VOC") an opportunity to become the first colonisers of Taiwan. In fact it was Chinese officials who induced the Dutch to settle in Taiwan.[9] To obtain a trade relationship with the then Ming China, the Dutch forcefully established themselves on the Pescadores in 1622, which was then under Chinese administration. After some battles and negotiation, Chinese officials persuaded the Dutch to settle in Taiwan by promising to send goods to Taiwan for trade. In 1624, the Dutch landed on Tayouan. Tayouan was a small isle that was an arrow shot away from the south-west end of the main island.[10] The Dutch built Fort Zeelandia on Tayouan. Later they purchased a piece of land from the aboriginal village of Saccam on the main island, just opposite Fort Zeelandia, where they built Fort Provintia.

To the Dutch, Taiwan was valuable not in itself but as a potential base for establishing commercial relationships with China.[11] However eventually the Dutch became involved in the local politics of the aboriginal groups and were able to exercise influence and control over the nearest five villages, with many villagers converting to Christianity.[12] As for the more distant aboriginal villages that subsequently surrendered, the Dutch had clergymen live in a small number of

Map 1.1 Taiwan: geography and current administrative units
Source: *Republic of China Yearbook 2016*

villages and set up schools there, and held an annual assembly of village headmen. Other than these, it does not seem that the Dutch established any administration or exercised effective control over them.[13]

In an effort to compete with the Dutch, the Spaniards occupied northern Taiwan in 1626. This was part of the world-wide commercial and economic conflict between Spain – which at this time included Portugal and the Portuguese possessions in Asia – and the Protestant Dutch Republic.[14] The Spanish built two small fortresses, one at the entrance to the Jilong Harbour, the other at the mouth of the Danshui River. Extensive research has been done on the brief Spanish era in Taiwan, which shows that Spanish activities in Taiwan were limited.[15] At any time there were no more than a few hundred Spaniards present, and the trade with the aborigines was confined to provisions for the soldiers.[16] The lack of trading opportunities led to neglect of the fortresses, which resulted in the Dutch successfully ousting the Spaniards in 1642. The Spanish era left no permanent mark on Taiwan or its aborigines.

Chinese administration

At about the same time, China experienced a major dynastic change. In 1636, the Manchu Khan Hung Taiji announced the formation of the Qing Dynasty in the northeast of China. In 1644, two years after the Dutch ousted the Spaniards from northern Taiwan, the Ming Dynasty collapsed under peasant rebellion. Within a few months the Manchus entered Beijing, drove out the rebels and established their rule over China.[17] This event was one of the most important turning points in Chinese history, and was to have significant impact on Taiwan.

Some remnant Ming forces continued to resist the Qing. The most powerful force was that of Zheng Chenggong (known to the West as Koxinga) in south China. Zheng's father was a pirate turned Ming official, using his large fleets to guard the Chinese coast against pirates. Zheng's father eventually defected to the Qing, but Zheng continued to fight against the Qing in south China and tried to restore the Ming regime.[18] Hard-pressed by the Qing, in late 1661 Zheng's army attacked the Dutch in Taiwan, with the purpose of obtaining an overseas foothold to continue his resistance against the Qing. After five months of siege, the Dutch in Fort Zeelandia surrendered in early 1662, following the surrender of Fort Provintia earlier.[19]

The Zheng regime used Taiwan as a military base for recovery of mainland China from the Qing. Viewing themselves as the preservers of Ming legitimacy and governing Taiwan as a part of the collapsed Ming China, the Zhengs established their central government as a prefecture of the deceased Ming Empire, Chengtian 承天 Prefecture, with two counties below it, Tianxing 天興 and Wannian 萬年. The administrative centre was at Tayouan, and Zheng renamed it Anping 安平. Zheng Chenggong soon died and was succeeded by his son Zheng Jing, who carried on the mission in fighting against the Qing. Three years after Jing's death in 1680, the Zhengs surrendered to the Qing.[20] The Zhengs ruled Taiwan for 22 years. Although the history of the Zheng resistance to the Qing is well known, there is little information available on their administration of Taiwan.[21] Nonetheless, Zheng rule marks an important stage in Taiwanese history, as it established the first Chinese-style government on Taiwan, albeit as part of a rump Ming loyalist state fighting a losing battle against the Qing.

Qing annexation

In 1684, the Qing annexed Taiwan, making it a prefecture under Fujian Province with the new name Taiwan Prefecture. The prefecture capital remained in the same place, and a new county named Taiwan was established on the prefecture capital, as was the custom of the Qing. The two Zheng counties were renamed Zhuluo 诸罗 and Fengshan 凤山 counties, respectively (Map 1.2). Fengshan was

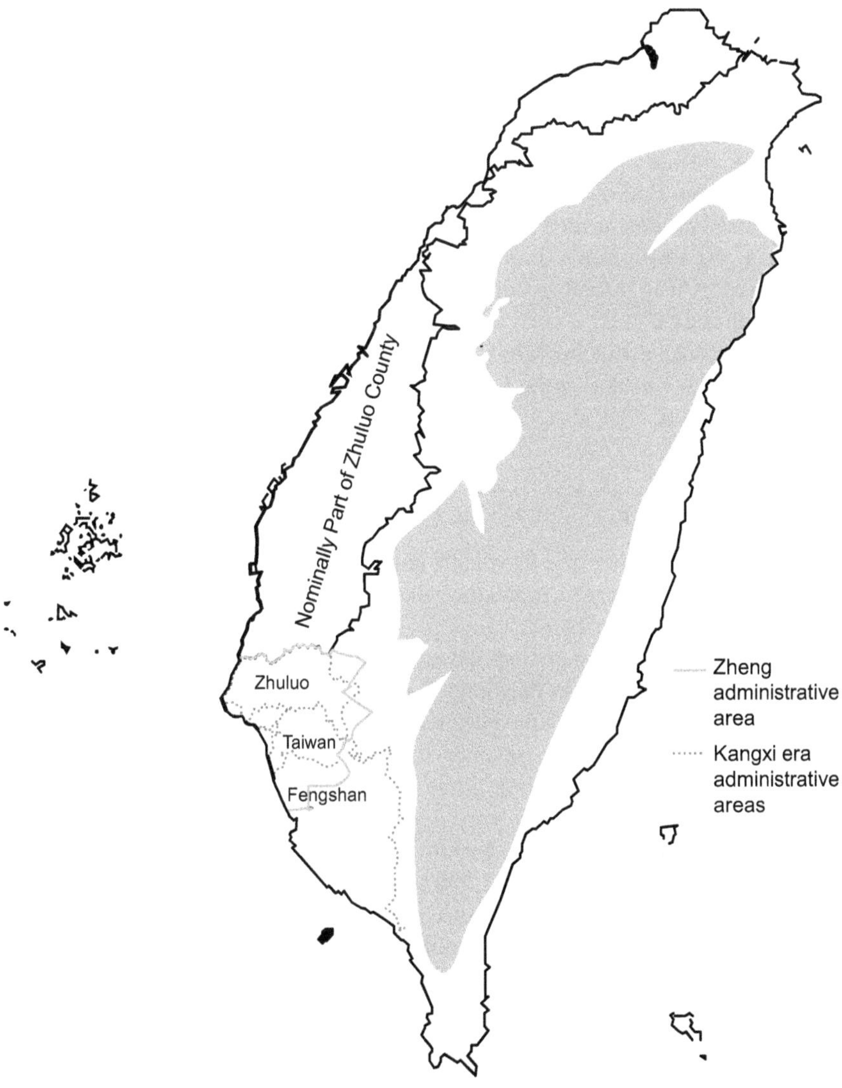

Map 1.2 Zheng and Qing Kangxi administrative areas

situated to the south of Taiwan County and Zhuluo to the north. The administration in Taiwan did not experience any dramatic changes for nearly two centuries, until the last 20 years of Qing rule of Taiwan when the government suddenly expanded control over the whole island. Taiwan was made a province in 1887, signifying its growing importance in the eyes of the Court by this time. Modernising efforts were made, including building infrastructure and establishing mining and trade. But the efforts were not consistent and were short lived. Within a few years the Qing surrendered Taiwan to Japan, ending its 211 years' administration of Taiwan.

The aborigines: forms of knowledge

The Taiwanese aborigines are Austronesian-speaking peoples. Austronesian, meaning "southern islands", is a large language family which consists of at least 10 primary subgroups, nine of which are present only in Taiwan.[22] The 10th is the widely dispersed Malayo-Polynesian languages, spoken by peoples in Southeast Asia and the Pacific Islands, including mainland Southeast Asia, the Philippines, Indonesia, Micronesia, Melanesia, Polynesia and Madagascar.[23] It is therefore believed that Taiwan is the originating place for all Austronesians.[24]

The knowledge about the Taiwanese aborigines increased as contact with them increased, but it was during the Japanese period that anthropological study of the aborigines started.

Empirical knowledge

The earliest records about the Taiwanese aborigines were made before Dutch colonisation. Many travellers recorded their observations of the Taiwanese aborigines in the subsequent centuries.

Two brief eyewitness accounts about some "barbarian" peoples (*fan* 番) of *pisheye* 毗舍耶, written in the Song Dynasty (960–1279) and Yuan Dynasty (1271–1368), respectively, have been recognised as describing the aborigines of Taiwan.[25] In 1603 a Chinese traveller, Chen Di, published a relatively detailed description of the Taiwanese aborigines in the western plains areas.[26] The record notes that the aborigines were "very diverse in kinds" (*zhonglei shenfan* 種類甚繁), and dwelt together in groups known as "villages" (*she* 社). Village sizes varied from 500 or 600 to around 1,000 people, and there was no political leader. The aborigines knew basic agriculture, made a fermented beverage from rice, kept limited types of domesticated animals, were engaged in deer hunting, and traded deer products for other commodities with merchants from mainland China. The people practised head hunting, went about naked, but had commonly observed laws and etiquettes, such as prohibition against thieves and etiquette regarding death and marriage.[27] Although the record mentions that the aborigines were scattered at different locations which extended "over a thousand *li*", the author spent most of his time in the Bay of Tayouan, where the Dutch later built their power base. Therefore it is likely that the author was describing the aborigines around that area.

After the Dutch arrived in the southwest of Taiwan in 1624, they eventually established contacts with the villages near its base, Tayouan. The Dutch found the eight aboriginal villages near Tayouan shared the same customs and language, but were independent from one another.[28] The Dutch records are more elaborate than Chen Di's record, but they show no material difference from Chen's observations about the aborigines.[29] The Dutch missionary work bore fruit mostly among the aboriginal villages near Tayouan, namely Sinkang, Bakloan, Soulang, Mattau and Tavakan.[30] From the Dutch these aborigines acquired a Romanised written form of their language, which they used till at least mid-Qing.[31] The Dutch later encountered more aboriginal villages in other parts of the island, and found them to differ in size, custom, language and political organisation. The size of the aboriginal villages varied from a few hundred to a few thousand inhabitants, and some of them had no chief while others did.[32] At the southern end of Taiwan, in the area of Longkiau (*Langqiao* 瑯嶠), the Dutch agent found 15 villages under one chief.[33] In about the middle point of the western plains, around the villages of Darida (*Dadu* 大肚), a chief called "the King of Darida" (*Daduwang* 大肚王) controlled large areas, and enjoyed tribute from other villages as well as judicial authority.[34] A census carried out by the Dutch in 1650 recorded over 68,000 aborigines in the 315 villages that had submitted to Dutch authority.[35] A rough estimation of the aboriginal population in 1654 was 100,000.[36]

The Spaniards were established in Tamsui (*Danshui* 淡水) and Quelang (*Jilong* 基隆) at the northern tip of Taiwan between 1626 and 1642. There they encountered a people now known as Basayans. The Basayans were not farmers or head hunters. They were craftsmen and traders, going through the villages and trading with the Chinese and other aboriginal groups, and often served as intermediary between those two communities.[37] After the Dutch replaced the Spaniards in the north, they found some natives who could read Spanish.[38] However in general the Spaniards had few dealings with the natives in the Taipei Basin,[39] or those in the Kavalan area at the northeast of Taiwan,[40] which was on the maritime route between Jilong and Manila.[41]

The Zhengs left little record about the aborigines during their brief rule over Taiwan, but it is known that the Zheng government divided the aborigines who came under its administration into four districts and appointed 10 officers to administer these districts.[42] By the time the Qing traveller Yu Yonghe visited Taiwan in 1697, he found that the aboriginal villages around Tayouan were similar to villages in mainland China. Yu was told that the villagers of Sinkang, Bakloan, Soulang and Mattau had paid tax and had been educated under the Chinese system since the Zheng period.[43]

As in earlier Chinese records, the Zhengs and the Qing referred to the Taiwanese aborigines as *fan*, which, together with terms such as *yi* 夷, *di* 狄 and *man* 蠻, were used to denote those outside Chinese civilisation. The Qing government continued the Dutch and Spanish method of identifying the aborigines by areas of habitation, rather than by their different ethnolinguistic characteristics. A study of the aborigines conducted in 1722 by an inspecting censor for Taiwan (*xun Tai yushi* 巡臺御史), Huang Shujing, classified the aborigines as "the northern route aborigines" (*beilu fan* 北路番) and "the southern route aborigines" (*nanlu fan* 南路番), according to their geographic locations in relation to the prefecture capital.[44] There were 10 clusters of the northern aborigines and three clusters of the southern aborigines. Each cluster had a group of villages, and in total 151 villages were recorded, with some big villages containing a number of small villages. It appears that the recorded villages were those that were under government administration, although the degree of government control and the burden of tax varied among the villages. The arrangement of clusters, apart from being based on geographic locations, was probably also related to tax collection. Huang seemed to recognise that the villages within a cluster shared the same culture and language. He described the culture of each cluster as a whole, under six headings – housing, food, costume, marriage, burial, and household objects and tools. Included in each cluster were also lyrics of the aborigines' folk songs, which suggested that the villages within each cluster shared a common language.[45] Modern research shows that Huang's grouping of some of the clusters was consistent with later ethnolinguistic classification of some aboriginal groups.[46]

By 1742 when the revised gazetteer of Taiwan Prefecture was compiled, 244 villages were recorded by name.[47] The number was increased to 299 within a few years.[48] The increase in number was a mixture of factors, including different recording methods, increased knowledge about the aborigines and expanded government control, as well as subdivision of some villages. For example, traditionally 36 villages dwelt in Gamalan (噶瑪蘭 Kavalan). Huang Shujing noted the 36 villages, but only counted them as one Gamalan village.[49] Similarly, traditionally there were 18 villages in the southern areas of Langqiao. While Huang listed the 18 villages within the Langqiao cluster, the 1741 revised gazetteer only recorded Langqiao as one village, and the subsequent 1747 revised gazetteer reverted it back to 18 villages.[50]

This knowledge about the aborigines acquired before and during the Qing period was through observation by travellers or officials who came into contact with the aborigines. This form of knowledge changed during the Japanese period. The Japanese government organised systematic modern anthropological studies on the aborigines, which is an example of the different style of Japanese colonisation from Qing colonisation.

Anthropological study

Modern anthropological study of the Taiwan aborigines started soon after Japan took over.[51] The Japanese anthropologist Inō Kanori, dispatched by the colonial government, conducted research on the aborigines and classified the aborigines of Taiwan into eight main groups: Atayal 泰雅, Bunun 布農, Tsou 鄒, Tsalisen (later known as Rukai 魯凱), Paiwan 排灣, Puyuma 卑南, Ami 阿美 and Pepo 平埔.[52] The first seven groups were mountain aborigines, while the group of Pepo (*pingpu* 平埔, literally "flat land") was in fact the generic term for the aborigines on the plains area.

The seven mountain groups, together with the Yami 雅美of Orchid Island (an island off the southeastern coast of the main island of Taiwan), and the group of Saisiyat 賽夏, which was later identified as mountain aborigines, were the "traditional nine groups" recognised as the aborigines of Taiwan by the Japanese government and the subsequent Chinese Kuomintang (國民黨 "national party") government.[53] The Japanese administration also established a committee for investigation of aborigines (*Taiwan Sōtokufu Banzoku Chōsakai* 臺灣總督府蕃族調查會), which organised systematic research on the aboriginal groups between 1909 and 1912. The committee compiled detailed research reports on the aboriginal groups and their languages and customs.[54] This was in itself part of the "modern" Japanese administration – conducting historical and anthropological research on the colonies, like Britain or France did.[55]

Inō identified 10 different groups within the Pepo group.[56] Later scholars proposed slightly different numbers or groupings, but most of the differences seem to be whether a certain group was an independent group or a subgroup of another group, rather than identification of new groups.[57] A recent study by a Taiwanese linguist proposes that, from a linguistic perspective, the plains aborigines could be classified into six groups, which contain eight previously well-recognised groups: Baburan 巴布蘭 (including subgroups of Taokas, Papora and Babuza), Kavalan 噶瑪蘭, Ketagalan 凱達格蘭 (including Basay, Luilang and Trobian), Hoanya 洪雅, Pazeh 拍宰海 and Siraya 西拉雅 (including Siraya, Makattao and Taivoan).[58] Scholars disagreed on whether the seventh group, Thao 邵, was a plains or mountain aborigine group.[59] Recent scholarship seems to lean towards the opinion that it was a mountain group.[60] The classification of the various plains aboriginal groups as one Pepo group by the Japanese administration signifies that the plains aborigines had by then lost their distinctive culture but, from an administrative point of view, were still distinguishable from the Han Chinese after 200-odd years of contact with the Chinese migrants.

Although there has been no complete agreement on the numbers and grouping of the Taiwan aborigines, a recent ethno-language report is helpful in giving an overview of the Austronesian languages spoken in Taiwan and their current status.[61] According to this report, at least 21 Austronesian languages have been spoken in Taiwan. These 21 languages belong to 14 language families, and each has some dialects.[62] Of the 21 languages, four are now extinct, two have no known first language speakers, and five more have fewer than 100 speakers.[63] The plains aboriginal groups' languages are now extinct or nearly extinct, and the people are all sinicised (Table 1.1).[64]

Table 1.1 Taiwan aboriginal language groups

Languages	*Plains/mountains*	*Language/cultural status*	*Government recognition**
Amis	Mountains	Developing	Yes
Amis Nataoran	M	Nearly extinct	Sakizaya 2007
Atayal	M	Developing	Yes
Bunun	M	Developing	Yes
Kanakanabu	M	Nearly extinct	2014
Paiwan	M	Developing	Yes
Puyuma	M	Shifting	Yes
Rukai	M	Developing	Yes
Saaroa	M	Nearly extinct	Hla'alua 2014
Saisiyat	M	Threatened	Yes
Taroko	M	Educational	Sediq 2008 Truku 2004
Thao	Mountain/plain	Nearly extinct	2001
Tsou	M	Vigorous	Yes
Yami	On Orchid Island	Threatened	Yes
Babuza	Plains	Dormant. Sinicised	
Basay	P	Extinct. Sinicised	
Kavalan		Nearly extinct. Sinicised	2002
Ketagalan	P	Extinct. Sinicised	
Kulon-Pazeh	P	Extinct. Sinicised	
Papora-Hoanya	P	Extinct. Sinicised	
Siraya	P	Dormant. Sinicised	

Source: table created according to Lewis, Simons and Fenning (2015)

* The groups that are marked "Yes" are the "traditional nine groups" noted since the Japanese period and were recognised by the Ministry of the Interior of Taiwan in 1954. See Pan (1998), at 94.

Currently the Taiwan government recognises 16 language groups as the aborigines of Taiwan (see Table 1.1 and Map 1.3). The official recognition is not a static process and it is possible that new groups may be recognised in the future. The 16 groups were recognised at different stages, and in addition about 14,500 people identified themselves as aborigines but as not belonging to any of the 16 groups.[65] The recognised aboriginal groups all live in the mountain areas or in eastern Taiwan – "at the back of the mountains" (*houshan* 後山), as the Qing officials would call it. All are classified as mountain aborigines except Kavalan. The aboriginal groups that are not recognised have acculturated to the dominant Han culture and lost their distinctive languages and culture, a consequence of Chinese settlement.

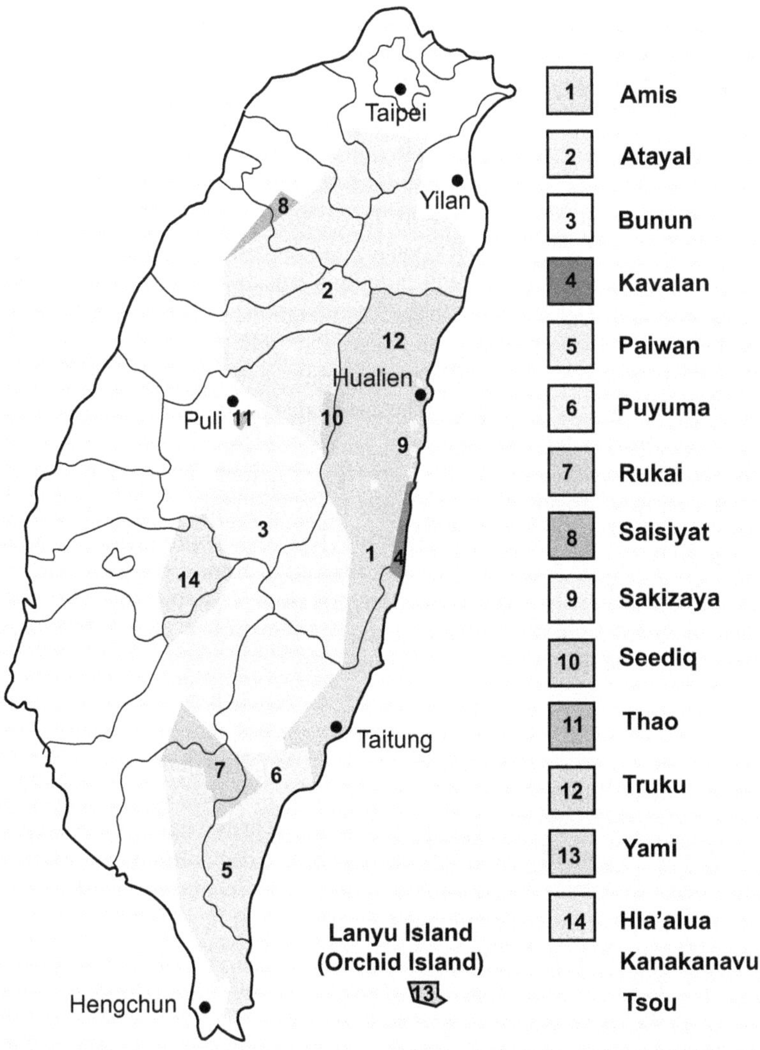

Map 1.3 Distribution of indigenous peoples

Source: *Republic of China Yearbook 2016*, at 45

Progression of land settlement

Aboriginal land tenure

The Taiwanese aborigines' principal means of livelihood was deer hunting, as well as gathering, small-scale fishing and limited farming.[66] Chinese travellers before the Dutch time recorded primitive horticulture activities by the aborigines.[67] Their way of farming was to burn the vegetation on a piece of land and rotate the fields for planting. The slash-and-burn style of farming was a typical type of cultivation in Southeast Asia, but the Taiwanese aborigines only planted in small areas, and the fires they built to clear the land were limited in scale.[68]

Before the Dutch arrival, the aborigines planted limited types of crops, vegetables and fruits, such as rice (on dry land), soybeans, sesame, Chinese pearl barley, spring onion, ginger, sweet potato, taro, sugarcane, coconut and Taiwan persimmon. They also kept cats, dogs, pigs and chickens, but did not have ducks, geese, horses, donkeys, cows or sheep.[69] Although the land was fertile, they did not cultivate more than necessary, and every day only prepared enough food for the day's consumption.[70] The closer to the mountain areas the aborigines dwelt, the fewer types of crop they planted. The mountain aborigines did not grow grains, and only had sweet potato and taro.[71]

Land tenure practised by the plains aborigines before outside contact was not recorded. Scholarly attempts to reconstruct their land tenure system before colonisation show that the plains aborigines had land ownership patterns similar to one another, although detailed arrangements varied from group to group.[72] The villages arranged their settlements in concentric rings, from the inner to the outer: the enclosed village, farmland, hunting and fishing grounds, and distant hunting grounds. Within the enclosed village were central areas, shrines and other facilities which were common property, and house sites which belonged to kin groups semi-permanently. Farmlands belonged to kin groups that had exclusive rights of usufruct during each cropping rotation, but the fallow fields belonged to the clan or the village. Hunting and fishing grounds usually belonged to clans or the whole village collectively. Villages also claimed exclusive rights to the outer ring of distant hunting grounds, but the rights might have been difficult to enforce.[73] It is believed that the plains aborigines recognised property claims by investment of labour in reclaiming the land, and thus had the concept of private ownership and owners could alienate their private land to the Chinese.[74] However it is likely that alienation to people outside the villages, or even the concept of private ownership, was developed after contact with the Chinese.[75]

The mountain aborigines mostly practised collective ownership, although there were variations among different groups.[76] Village common areas were public land, collectively owned by all members. Ownership of hunting grounds and fishing grounds varied among different aboriginal groups, some belonging to the village as a whole, some the clan, and some the hunting or fishing confederations (*lietuan* 獵團, *yutuan* 漁團).[77] Farmland usually belonged to the clan or kin groups. Two mountain aboriginal groups, Paiwan and Rukai, practised an ownership system different from the others. In these two groups, all land was owned by the hereditary chiefs, with the exception of the village common areas and facilities, which were collectively owned.

Overall, the plains aborigines and most mountain aborigine groups practised common ownership of land, and very little private land ownership was recognised.

Land tenure under the Dutch

Although initially the VOC only intended to use Taiwan as an entrepôt, the interaction with and submission of the aborigines tied the Dutch more closely with the land than was initially planned. The VOC required each submitting village to sign a treaty, which specified that the aborigines were to "give [the VOC] the sovereignty over their country", or "surrender their country and their possession to the States of Holland".[78] Therefore not only sovereignty, but also property rights, were transferred to the VOC as the representative of the States of Holland. It is questionable how well the aborigines understood the terms and consequences of the treaties, but the presentation of native betel-nut and coconut trees to the governor as required by the treaty was seen by the Dutch "as a symbol that the sovereignty of their country had now been given to the [United Provinces]".[79]

Under the Dutch administration, the number of Chinese migrants increased and agriculture was developed. The Dutch granted monopoly to selected Chinese merchants to trade with the aboriginal villages, collected residency-permit tax and trade duty from Chinese residents and traders, but the most important aspects of Dutch colonisation were licensing the Chinese to hunt deer and developing agriculture through Chinese peasants. Licences were issued to Chinese migrants to hunt deer on grounds which were "previously native-controlled" or near aboriginal villages.[80] The aborigines reacted by attacking the Chinese deer hunters and tearing or stealing hunting licences.[81] It is clear that the aborigines were not only defending their livelihood of deer hunting and deer skin trade, but also guarding their land rights by trying to exclude the outsiders from their traditional hunting grounds.

The Dutch recruited Chinese migrants to reclaim land for farming. Areas were demarcated and noted as "ample and empty" for the Chinese to reclaim and farm.[82] At the time of Dutch arrival, about 1,500 or more Chinese lived or sojourned in southwestern Taiwan.[83] The Chinese adult male population under Dutch control increased to about 25,000 in 1650, compared with 68,657 aborigines in the same year.[84] The Chinese population in Taiwan continued to rise, and reached about 35,000 in 1661.[85] By then they had reclaimed just over 10,000 morgen of land for agriculture.[86] Most of the land was used for growing rice and sugarcane, which together with deer products were the main exports of the VOC. Only a very small portion was for vegetables and other use.[87] The lands were mostly situated in present-day Tainan, especially in and around Tayouan and the nearby villages.[88]

The land tenure adopted by the Dutch is less than clear, and it probably varied in different circumstances. Although the extent is unclear, records show cases of the Chinese paying annual rent to the aboriginal villages, which was collected by the VOC and distributed to the aborigines.[89] Overall, likely the Dutch recognised aboriginal land rights to the extent that the land was being occupied and used by the aborigines, such as village sites and farm lands. The Dutch possibly also recognised certain land as aboriginal land when the land was adjacent to the village centre and of which the aborigines had clear control.[90]

The Chinese peasants played a significant role in the Dutch economy, through providing products for exports from their work in both deer hunting and agriculture. For this reason one scholar has argued that the Chinese were co-colonisers with the VOC.[91] What is in dispute in the literature is the Chinese peasants' title to land. Qing records show that the Dutch provided seeds, draft oxen and farm implements for the Chinese to work on the land, the land being "Crown land" (*wangtian* 王田 "king's land") and the Chinese peasants tenants of the Dutch.[92] Although earlier scholars have accepted this view,[93] recent scholarship has revealed that the VOC planned to bestow or had bestowed on the Chinese peasants property rights over the land that they farmed, rights equal to "full ownership rights for them and their descendants".[94] The recent scholarship has the backing of new information found in the VOC archives, which presumably are more reliable than the later and scant records of the Qing which, incidentally, also misused the term "king's land", since the Netherlands was a republic at that time. But questions remain, as other evidence against Chinese ownership existed.

Some clues could be found through the Dutch-Zheng transition of administration and the tax/rent (as the case may be) burden over the land. After the Dutch surrendered, the Dutch and the Zhengs signed a treaty. The treaty contained 18 clauses, with detailed provisions about transfer of property. The Dutch were required to provide a list of debtors and leaseholders, but no list of land owners or land register was mentioned.[95] After the transition, the Zhengs, even though they recognised private land ownership, took over the "king's land", managed it as "government land" (*guantian* 官田), and continued charging the same amount of produce per *jia* ("unit charge") from the Chinese peasants. The unit charge was about five times the unit tax of private land, and roughly equalled the combination of the unit tax and unit rent of private land. Compared with the burden on the land during the Qing period, it was more than double of the unit tax of private land, and at about the same level of unit rent over government-owned *tundi* 屯地.[96] This suggests that the VOC received the produce as rent, rather than as tax. In other words, the peasants were tenants of the VOC, not private land owners.

Considering the VOC archival records, it is likely that private ownership over land was discussed during the Dutch period and was even implemented in limited cases, but it had not been implemented systematically or in large scale before the end of the Dutch administration.

Overall, although the number of Chinese settlers increased during the Dutch period, as the land was vast and the aborigines still outnumbered the Chinese, the impact of the Chinese farming activities on aboriginal land tenure was little, while the competition in deer hunting and the intrusion into the traditional hunting grounds provoked aboriginal protest.

Land reclamation under the Zhengs

In some respects the Zheng administration maintained continuity from the Dutch administration. The VOC surrendered all company property to the Zhengs, including its rights to collect debts and rents.[97] As mentioned previously, the Zheng government continued receiving the same rent for the 10,000 *jia* "king's land", and called this category of land "government land". The village monopoly and tax system introduced by the Dutch also continued, but with minor alterations.[98]

Chinese migration accelerated during the Zheng period, as did land reclamation. Because of the Zhengs' encouragement, during 1662–1664 six waves of migrants arrived from coastal China to Taiwan.[99] The Han Chinese population increased by about 70,000 during the Zheng period to about 120,000.[100] Settlements extended from southwestern Taiwan to many areas of the western and northern lowlands.[101] Land reclamation by Zheng clan members, officials and migrants was encouraged, and private land ownership was granted over reclaimed land.[102] In total 20,270 *jia* of private land was reclaimed during the Zheng period.[103] Most of the areas reclaimed by officials were near the administration centre (in present-day Tainan and Gaoxiong); only one or two were in central western or northwestern plains (in present-day Jiayi or Taipei).[104] About 22 major areas were developed into farms by other settlers, 16 of which were in present-day Jiayi (central western plains), four in Gaoxiong (south), and two in Yunlin (northwestern plains).[105]

To provide for the troops, the government also established military colonies, where the soldiers were required to reclaim lands and to farm them for their own upkeep. Lands reclaimed by the soldiers were called "military farms" (*yingpan tian* 營盤田), and there were 40 military farms during the rule of Zheng Jing (1662–1680).[106] The military farms mostly lay in the south of the island, in present-day Tainan and Gaoxiong.[107] The total area of military farms is not clear, but it was the "most extensive and systematic" land reclamation during the Zheng period.[108]

From the few records available, the Zhengs respected aboriginal land rights only to the extent of farm lands in active use. Regulations encouraged land enclosure by officials and reclamation by settlers, but strictly forbade encroachment on "land currently cultivated by aborigines and settlers", which seems to be the only restriction on land enclosure and reclamation.[109] The Zhengs also allocated lands in the aboriginal villages to their officials,[110] but no record of compensation for taking the land has been found.[111] Despite this, the relationships between the government and the plains aborigines were said to be "generally peaceful".[112] The absence of conflict suggests that a mechanism for using the plains aborigines' land might have been in place. The operation of the military farms was probably more aggressive, and encroached on aboriginal hunting grounds, which caused resentment from the aborigines. The government had to use armed force to repress the aborigines' revolts.[113] Against the mountain aborigines, the government built earthen boundaries, called "earthen oxen" (*tuniu* 土牛), to separate the settlement areas from the mountain areas .[114] This strategy was adopted by the Qing in later years.

During the brief Zheng era, Chinese settlement increased and spread to further north and further south of the western plains. Agricultural land in Taiwan eventually was divided into areas called *bao* 堡. During the Zheng period, reclamation of about 80% of the *bao* in Anping, 73% of those in Fengshan, 67% in Jiayi, 50% in Danshui and 43% in Yunlin was started, but each reclaimed area was relatively small, and reclamation of most of the *bao* was not complete till the Qing period.[115] Therefore reclamation concentrated in the southwest but some scattered pockets along the western plains were started, and most parts of the western plains were still occupied by aborigines. The pockets were expanded during the Qing period. The reclamation pattern suggests a lack of coordinated or organised reclamation, as the government did not have a scheme to systematically reclaim the land other than the military farms. As such, and evidenced by the generally peaceful ethnic relations, the impact of land reclamation on the aborigines remained relatively small.

Spread of settlement during the Qing period

Chinese settlement continued to expand during the Qing period, but it was limited to the plains areas. After the Zhengs surrendered, the Zheng soldiers and many farmers were repatriated to the mainland, and more left voluntarily. The population dropped sharply. At the time of transition to Qing rule, the government counted 12,724 tax-paying adult males in Taiwan, just over half of the Zheng record of 21,320.[116] Although the figure of tax-paying adult males did not equal the total settler population and was not always a reliable source to calculate the settler population, the extent of decrease indicates the degree of population reduction. Much farmland became waste because of the fall in population. Registered land in 1684 (Kangxi 23) was 18,453 *jia*, a decrease from a total 30,052 *jia* of government land and private land in the Zheng record.[117] The military farms no doubt became derelict with the Zheng army being disbanded and soldiers repatriated to the mainland.

The 18,453 *jia* of registered land in 1684 included 8,561 *jia* in Taiwan County, 5,048 *jia* in Fengshan County and 4,843 *jia* in Zhuluo County. Population growth and land reclamation activities were slow in the first few years of Qing administration. Zhuluo and Fengshan Counties remained so deserted that for 20 years the county magistrates based their offices in Taiwan County.[118] In 1685 (Kangxi 24), 2,565 *jia* of new land was registered, but most of this was very likely to be land already reclaimed under the Zhengs and then registered by Qing officials following annexation. A significant example is that the Fujian maritime commander, Shi Lang, who had conquered Taiwan and acted as the ambassador to take over Taiwan, owned dozens of estates and was often criticised for land grabbing.[119] From 1685 to 1702, newly opened land continued to be registered, ranging from as much as 969 *jia* in one year and as little as 52 *jia* in another. It took nearly 40 years for the registered land in the whole prefecture to be brought back to about 30,000 *jia*, the total recorded agricultural land area during the Zheng period.[120] The slow progress in land reclamation shows the lack of active colonisation.

While land registration indicates a slow increase of newly reclaimed land, travellers of the Kangxi years saw a fast spread of settlement. In 1697 (Kangxi 36), when Yu Yonghe travelled from the south (Anping) to the north (Danshui), he did not see many Han settlers along the way, and saw no evidence of human activity for about 90 *li* in the north, from Zhuqian 竹塹to Nankan 南崁.[121] This suggests that there were few, if any, land settlements in the northern part of the western plains in the one or two decades following Qing annexation. By 1713 (Kangxi 52), a travelling officer Ruan Caiwen wrote in a poem that from Banxian 半綫, which was about the central point of the western plains, to Zhuqian in the north, "half of the deer hunting grounds have been reclaimed by settlers".[122] The Gazetteer of Zhuluo County, which was first published in 1717 (Kangxi 56), also recorded that "in the past 30 years, there has been much land reclamation around the county. Deer hunting grounds turned into farm lands, and deer are few now".[123] The first inspecting censor for Taiwan, Huang Shujing (1722), also noted that "in the past years the foothills were all aborigines' deer grounds. Now the Han reclaimed the land and cultivate it. All one could see are fine farms".[124]

These writings showed the transformation of landscape from aboriginal deer hunting grounds to Han agricultural farms. They pictured a speedy development of land reclamation and provided a contrast to the seemingly slow increase of registered land. Both should be interpreted with caution, and a more or less accurate situation could be discovered through balancing the two types of sources. On the one hand, land registration was not necessarily a reliable source of the actual area of land having been reclaimed, as "hidden land" (*yintian* 隱田) was a major problem during the Qing Dynasty, not only in Taiwan, but also across the empire, for tax purposes. Hidden land was farmland that should have been, but was not, registered, or in other words, taxable but un-taxed land. Because of the hidden land problem, the actual area of reclaimed land was usually larger than that was on government register. On the other hand, the travel writings recorded their authors' impression and sentiment, rather than a careful calculation of areas of reclaimed land. For example, Ruan disapproved of the spread of land reclamation, and lamented for the aborigines whose living space was intruded upon or taken over by Han settlers.[125] Research reveals that what Ruan saw were limited areas in Zhuqian, and the reclamation was small in scale.[126] Reclamation in Zhuqian was started in about 1711 (Kangxi 50) and advanced during the Yongzheng reign, but much land remained unreclaimed even during the Qianlong years.[127] The slow pace of land reclamation, the existence of hidden land and the officials' disapproving attitude towards the spread of land settlement evidenced the fact that settlers were more proactive in colonisation than the government and its officials.

During the Kangxi reign, reclamation activities were mainly in Fengshan and Zhuluo Counties, including the northern part of Zhuluo which became Zhanghua County in 1722 (Yongzheng 1).[128] In the Yongzheng era land reclamation expanded north to the Danshui area and to areas in the south of the island. An early Yongzheng period officer noted that "before, Fengshan and Zhuluo were dangerous unhealthy lands, even their county magistrates dared not go there. Nowadays settlers flooded in to as far south as Langqiao and as far north as Danshui and Jilong".[129] Most of the Taipei basin and the areas of Lower Tamsui (*xia Danshui* 下淡水, in Fengshan County) were reclaimed during the Yongzheng reign.[130]

Reclamation of the Taipei basin was completed by 1755 (Qianlong 20), about seven decades after the annexation. Most of the reclamation during the Qianlong years was in the foothills, pressing the mountain areas.[131] Thus the areas west to the central mountain ranges were mostly reclaimed, but areas over the mountains were little ventured into.

After the Qianlong years, a breakthrough occurred during the Jiaqing reign, when settlers crossed the mountains in the northeast and reclaimed land in Gamalan (present-day Yilan), a triangular plains area, two sides bordering mountains and one side the sea. Han settlers reclaimed about 2,400 *jia* of land over a period of about a decade, which resulted in the establishment of administration by the Jiaqing government in 1810 (Jiaqing 15). Reclamation continued until Gamalan was fully developed into farms.

By 1840 the only unreclaimed lands that were suitable for agriculture, in the eyes of the Qing officials, were strips of land south of Gamalan along the eastern coast, Langqiao in the southern tip of Taiwan, and some parts of Puli in central Taiwan, which was surrounded by mountains.[132] These areas remained largely unreclaimed until the last 20 years of Qing administration, and even in those 20 years the reclamation was limited. In southern Taiwan, by 1888 (Guangxu 14), the newly established Hengchun County recorded 4,266 *jia* of reclaimed land.[133] No advance seemed to have been made after 1888, since in 1892 (Guangxu 18) the area of registered land was smaller than that in 1888, because not only was no new land added to the register, but also some lands were damaged due to flooding and were then removed from the register.[134] In eastern Taiwan, officials claimed that about 2,000–3,000 *jia* of land was reclaimed by 1880 (Guangxu 6), but in 1891 (Guangxu 17) registered land area was only 2,255 *jia*.[135] Therefore it appears that land reclamation did not advance well in the east or far south.

Japanese surveys amply revealed that land reclamation did not reach the full potential of the land even by the end of Qing rule. The Japanese government investigated arable land to plan for Japanese migration and settlement in 1908 (Meiji 41). What they found to some extent represents the status of land settlement at the end of the Qing administration. In the western plains, 344 areas were found to be suitable for new settlement, with a total area of over 90,000 *jia* of unreclaimed land. In eastern Taiwan, the Japanese found 15 suitable areas measuring over 27,000 *jia*.[136] Together the unreclaimed land was more than a quarter of the total recorded area of agricultural land of 432,009 *jia*, a figure which was obtained in 1890 after a thorough land survey by the late Qing government, and which was the result of over 200 years of land settlement.[137] The areas in the western plains measured about 261 *jia* on average, which means that unreclaimed land was fragmented or marginal. Eastern Taiwan consists of a long thin strip of low land, and compared with the west there is not much arable land. However the areas on average measured 1800 *jia*, which proves that land settlement in eastern Taiwan in the last 20 years was small scale. This accords with findings from land registration records that reclaimed lands in eastern Taiwan were mostly small and fragmented.[138]

The Japanese findings show that, after over 200 years of Qing administration, although land settlement expanded to the whole western plains and to some areas in the eastern coast, land reclamation did not cover all areas. The view of Qing officials that not much land was left for reclamation, in contrast to the detailed and accurate findings of the Japanese, also shows that the Qing was indifferent to colonisation, while Japan was more industrious and proactive.

Land settlement pattern and acculturation of aborigines

Land settlement shows a pattern of spreading from southwestern Taiwan to the whole western plains, and finally to the eastern side of the mountains.

As summarised in Table 1.2 and reflected in Map 1.4, land settlement started from around the Dutch administration centre of Tayouan, which was renamed but remained the administration centre of successive governments in the next two centuries. Land settlement spread southward and northward in subsequent years. When most of the fertile lands were reclaimed by the end of the Yongzheng reign, reclamation pushed eastward towards the foothills. By the late Qianlong reign, territories west of the central mountains were mostly reclaimed.

Reclamation of Gamalan, in the northeast corner of the island, during the Jiaqing reign was a breakthrough in that it went over the mountains. After that, not much land settlement was advanced until the last 20 years of Qing rule of Taiwan. During the Guangxu reign reclamation of the residual areas of arable land commenced, in particular in eastern and southern Taiwan. However the reclamation was late in time and on a small scale.

Table 1.2 Progression of land settlement

Period	*Areas of land settlement*
Dutch (1624–1662)	Near Tayouan in the southwest.
Zhengs (1662–1683)	Same as previous period, but small areas scattered along the western plains.
Qing (1684–1895)	The plains areas, including those in the west, east and south, but not all arable land was reclaimed. The mountain areas were not settled.
Kangxi (1684–1722)	Recovering farm lands that were left to waste after Qing annexation, and enlarging areas that had been reclaimed during the Zheng period.
Yongzheng (1723–1735)	Reclamation accelerated and advanced to further south and north.
Qianlong (1736–1795)	Western plains mostly reclaimed, and advanced to foothills.
Jiaqing (1796–1820)	Gamalan at the northwest corner settled.
Daoguang, Xianfeng, Tongzhi (1821–1874)	No significant advance, but reclamation of land at the margins of settlement areas and borders of the mountain territories continued.
Guangxu (1875–1895)	Eastern Taiwan, southern Taiwan and the Puli area in central Taiwan.

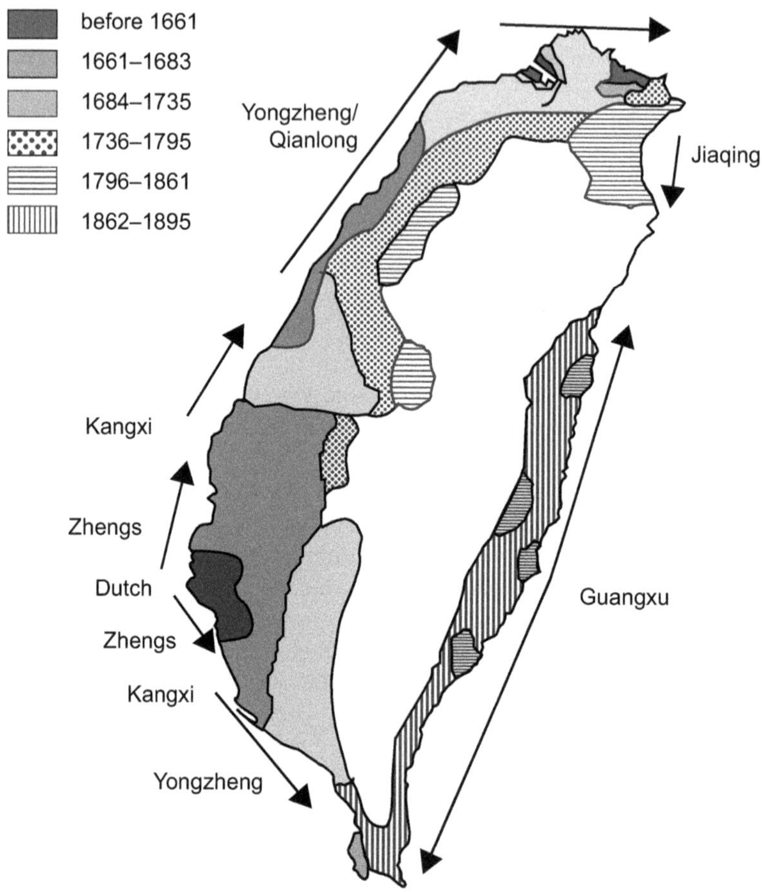

Map 1.4 Spread of settlement

Source: Map adjusted from Ka (1998), at 15

The Han settlements hence started from the administrative centre and pushed outwards to the north, south and east in a pattern resembling ripples. The whole process took over 200 years. The pattern and speed of reclamation testify to the lack of organised colonisation or proactive expansion by the government.

Furthermore, even by the end of Qing rule, more than half of the island was not settled by Han Chinese migrants, despite a huge increase in Han population. Throughout the Dutch, Zheng and Qing periods, Han population continued to increase. By 1790 (Qianlong 55), the Han population reached nearly 950,000.[139] By the end of the Qing period, the number increased to about 2.5 million, more than doubling that of a century earlier. Nevertheless, Han settlement mostly spread around the coast and in the plains area. The mountain areas and forest remained under the aborigines' occupation and control till the end of Qing administration. This shows that there was a strong constraint on Han settlement. As will be discussed in the next chapter, the Qing government's settlement policies restrained the Han settlement from entering the mountain areas.

With the spread of the Han settlement, aborigines were exposed to Han culture and eventually became acculturated. Like the four aboriginal villages under the Zheng administration, other aborigines of settled areas were exposed to Han culture and eventually became acculturated. An example can be seen from the Qing perspective of Taiwan in the late Qing period. In a map drawn in 1880 (Guangxu 6), no aboriginal village was marked in the western plains, as they had lost their distinctiveness in the government's eyes (Map 1.5). In contrast, scattered

Map 1.5 Spread of aboriginal villages (as recorded in 1880)

Source: *Academia Sinica, Taiwan History and Culture in Time and Space*, 1st Edition (Taipei, Academia Sinica, September 2003)

aboriginal villages along the eastern coast were recorded by Qing officials. The number of aboriginal villages known to the government increased in later years as the government strengthened its administration over the mountain territories. However, given the slow progress of settlement and land settlement, the aborigines in eastern Taiwan and in the mountains remained un-acculturated until the Japanese period. The facts that 15 out of 16 aboriginal groups recognised by the current government are mountain aborigines, and that the only plains aboriginal group, Kavalan, also situates over the central mountains in eastern Taiwan, testify to the direct and close link between settlement and acculturation.

The correlation between land settlement and the disappearance of the aboriginal groups' identities highlights the long-lasting effects of land settlement during the Qing period on the aborigines. In turn, the land settlement pattern during the Qing period was largely shaped by government policies, as is demonstrated in the next chapter.

Notes

1 History repeated itself almost 300 years later, when the Chinese National Party (Kuomintang) was defeated by the Communist Party and moved the Republic of China administration to Taiwan, with a hope that one day it would "recover" control over the mainland and reunite the country.

2 Land reclamation (*kaiken* 開墾; *tuoken* 拓墾) refers to the development of non-agricultural land into agricultural land, to bring land into production, as agriculture was the single most important way of land use in traditional Chinese culture. A person who reclaimed land is referred to as a reclaimer.

3 For example, Song Tsêng-chang *Taiwan fuken zhi* [History of Aboriginal Management and Land Reclamation in Taiwan] (2nd ed, Taiwansheng wenxian weiyuanhui, Taizhong, 1997) documents land reclamation in Taiwan; Sheng Ch'ing-I "Xinzhu, Taoyuan, Miaoli sanxian diqu kaifashi" [The History of Reclamation in the Three Counties of Xinzhu, Taoyuan and Miaoli] (1980) 31(4) *Taiwan Wen Hsien* 154–176 (Part I); (1981) 32(1) *Taiwan Wen Hsien* 136–157 (Part II) explores the history of land reclamation in certain areas.

4 Albeit under different names. See Inō Kanori (trans Taiwan Historica) *Taiwan wenhua zhi* [A History of Taiwan's Civilisation] (Chinese trans Rev ed, Taiwan Shufang, Taipei, 2011), vol 1, Section 1 "Qingdai yiqian zhongguoren suozhi zhi Taiwan" [Taiwan as Known by the Chinese Before the Qing Dynasty].

5 At 20, and 23–24.

6 At 25–26.

7 William Campbell *Formosa Under the Dutch* (Kegan Paul, Trench, Trubner, London, 1903), Part 1.

8 As there was no unified political unit in Taiwan, the envoy found no one to receive the letter in the 1593 attempt. In the second attempt conflicts occurred with the aborigines. It is not clear what happened to the last attempt. See Inō, above n 4, at 28–34.

9 Dutch record acknowledged that Taiwan belonged to the Chinese emperor who "granted" Taiwan to the VOC. See Campbell, above n 7, at 27, 32 and 36.

10 *Dayuan* 大員, present-day Anping, near Tainan. Because of geographical changes, the isle has become connected to the main island and is part of it.

11 Part 1 ch 3 "History of the Dutch Trade".

12 At 180 and 212.

13 See ibid, Part 2 in general. Also see I-Shou Wang "Cultural Contact and the Migration of Taiwan's Aborigines: A Historical Perspective" in Ronald G Knapp (ed) *China's*

Island Frontier: Studies in the Historical Geography of Taiwan (University Press of Hawaii, Honolulu, 1980), at 35.

14 See José Eugenio Borao Mateo *The Spanish Experience in Taiwan 1626–1642: The Baroque Ending of a Renaissance Endeavor* (Hong Kong University Press, Hong Kong, 2009), especially ch 1, for Dutch-Spanish rivalry in Southeast Asian and the Taiwan Strait.

15 Borao Mateo, ibid, so far is the most complete work on Spanish occupation of Taiwan.

16 At 155.

17 For the late Ming history and the collapse of the Ming, see William Atwell "The T'ai-ch'ang, T'ien-ch'i, and Ch'ung-chun reigns, 1620–1644" in Frederick W Mote and Denis Twitchett (eds) *The Cambridge History of China Volume 7: The Ming Dynasty, 1368–1644 Part One* (Cambridge University Press, Cambridge, 1988), at 585–640. For the rise of the Qing and the entry to China, see Gentraude Roth Li "State Building Before 1644" and Jerry Dennerline "The Shun-chih Reign" in Willard J Peterson (ed) *The Cambridge History of China Volume 9: The Ch'ing Dynasty to 1800 Part One* (Cambridge University Press, Cambridge, 2002), at 9–72 and 73–119.

18 See Lynn A Struve "The Southern Ming, 1644–1662" in Mote and Twitchett (eds), ibid, 641–725, in particular, at 710–725 for Zheng Chenggong's missions.

19 See Campbell, above n 7, Part III "Chinese Conquest of Formosa", for accounts of the Zheng conquest of Dutch Taiwan. For a more colourful narrative of the events, see Tonio Andrade *Lost Colony: The Untold Story of China's First Great Victory Over the West* (Princeton University Press, Princeton and Oxford, 2011).

20 See Kawaguchi Choju *Taiwan Zhengshi jishi* [Chronicles of the Zhengs of Taiwan, 1828] (TWWX 5) for the rise and fall, and the battles, of the Zhengs in Taiwan.

21 For a recent discussion on the Zhengs in Taiwan, see Peter Kang *Taiwan yuanzhumin shi zhengce pian: He Xi Mingzheng shiqi* [History of Taiwan Aborigines: The Policy Chapter: The Dutch, Spanish and Zheng Periods] (Taiwan Historica, Nantou, 2005), ch 15.

22 Robert Blust *The Austronesian Languages* (revised ed, ANU, Canberra, 2013), at 30. Also see David Blundell "A Century of Research: Austronesian Taiwan, 1897–1997" in David Blundell (ed) *Austronesian Taiwan: Linguistics, History, Ethnology, Prehistory* (revised ed, Shung Ye Museum of Formosan Aborigines, Taipei; Phoebe A Hearst Museum of Anthropology, Berkeley, 2009), at 8–9. For the history, cultures and societies of the Austronesians, see Peter Bellwood, James J Fox and Darrell Tryon (eds) *The Austronesians: Historical and Comparative Perspective* (ANU E Press, Canberra, 2006).

23 Blust, ibid; Darrell Tryon "Proto-Austronesian and the Major Austronesian Subgroups" in Bellwood, Fox and Tryon (eds), ibid, at 37–38.

24 Robert Blust "The Prehistory of the Austronesian-Speaking Peoples: A View From Language" (1995) 9(4) *Journal of World Prehistory* 453, at 458 and 460.

25 The two works are Zhao Rugua *Zhufanzhi* [Accounts of Various Barbarians] (TWWX 119), and Wang Dayuan *Daoyi zhilüe* [Brief Accounts of the Island Barbarians, 1349], an appendix to Zhao *Zhufanzhi*. Both descriptions are brief. See Laurence G Thompson "The Earliest Chinese Eyewitness Accounts of the Formosan Aborigines" (1964) 23 *Monumenta Serica* 163 for English translation of the latter record.

26 Chen Di *Dongfanji* [Accounts of the Eastern Barbarians, 1603], Collected in Shen Yourong *Minhai zengyan* [Words of Praise From the Fujian Sea] (TWWX 56), at 24–27. See Thompson, ibid, for English translation.

27 Ibid.

28 Campbell, above n 7, at 9 and 15.

29 See Part I ch 2 "Account of the Inhabitants".

30 At 179–180. The aborigines of these villages are now known to belong to the Siraya group.

31 There exist bilingual land deeds, in the Sirayan and Chinese languages, that the Sirayan concluded with the Chinese during the early to mid-Qing period.

32 Campbell, above n 7, at 15 and 137. At 180 it indicates that one of the villages had at least 3000 people.

33 At 137. These villages are now known to belong to the Paiwan group.

34 These aboriginal villages are now known to belong to the Papora group. See Kang, above n 21, at 27–28.

35 See Chuang Sung-lin "Helan zhi Taiwan tongzhi" [Dutch Administration in Formosa] (1959) 10(3) *Taiwan Wen Hsien* 1, at 3.

36 Campbell, above n 7, at 64.

37 See Borao Mateo, above n 14, ch 3.

38 Campbell, above n 7, at 231.

39 Now known as the Ketagalan group, of which Basay is a subgroup.

40 Now known as the Kavalan group.

41 Borao Mateo, above n 14, ch 3, in particular at 60 and 63.

42 Hung Chien-Chao "Taiwan under the Cheng Family: Sinicization after Dutch Rule" (PhD diss, Georgetown University, 1981), at 132. The four districts likely refer to the four villages of Sinkang, Bakloan, Soulang and Mattau.

43 Yu Yonghe *Bihai jiyou* [Small Sea Travelogue, 1697] (TWWX 44), at 17.

44 Huang Shujing *Taihai shichalu* [Records of a Tour on Duty Over the Taiwan Seas, cir 1722] (TWWX 4). After a major Han uprising in 1721, inspecting censors regularly visited Taiwan to inspect the situation there and report it to the emperor.

45 Ibid. The volume on the aborigines study is called "Fansu liukao" [Examination of the Aborigines' Customs From Six Aspects].

46 Pan Ying *Taiwan yuanzhu minzu de lishi yuanliu* [History of the Taiwanese Aboriginal Groups] (Taiyuan, Taipei, 1998), at 75–76.

47 Liu Liangbi *Chongxiu Fujian Taiwan fuzhi* [Revised Gazetteer of Taiwan Prefecture, Fujian, 1741] (TWWX 74), at 80–91.

48 See Fan Xian *Chongxiu Taiwan fuzhi* [Revised Gazetteer of Taiwan Prefecture, 1747] (TWWX 105), at 69–73.

49 Huang, above n 44, at 141.

50 Ibid, at 155–156; Liu, above n 47, at 81; Fan, above n 48, at 70.

51 See essays in Blundell (ed), above n 22, for accounts of the study of the Taiwanese aborigines in various aspects, including linguistics, history, ethnology and archaeology.

52 James W Davidson *The Island of Formosa: Past and Present* (MacMillan, London and New York, 1903), at 561; Yosaburō Takekoshi (trans George Braithwaite) *Japanese Rule in Formosa* (Longmans, Green and Co, London, 1907), at 219.

53 For a thorough survey of the study and classification of the Taiwan aboriginal groups, see Pan, above n 46, in particular, ch 3.

54 *Banzoku chōsa hōkokusho*蕃族調查報告書 [Investigation Reports on the Savage Peoples] and *Banzoku kanshū chōsa hōkokusho*蕃族慣習調查報告書 [Investigation Reports on the Customs of the Savage Peoples], respectively, Chinese translated versions are *Taiwan fanzu diaocha baogaoshu* (Academia Sinica, Taipei, 2007) and *Taiwan fanzu guanxi diaocha baogaoshu* (Academia Sinica, Taipei, 1996–2003).

55 See Yao Jen-To "The Japanese Colonial State and Its Form of Knowledge in Taiwan" in Liao Ping-hui and David Der-wei Wang (eds) *Taiwan Under Japanese Colonial Rule, 1895–1945* (Columbia University Press, New York, 2006), at 37–71 for the extensive research the Japanese administration conducted on Taiwan and its inhabitants. For the correlation between anthropology and colonialism, see Akitoshi Shimizu "Colonialism and the Development of Modern Anthropology" in Jan van Bremen and Akitoshi Shimizu (eds) *Anthropology and Colonialism in Asia and Oceania* (Curzon Press, Surrey, 1999), at 115. Also see Bernard S Cohn *Colonialism and Its Forms of Knowledge: The British in India* (Princeton University Press, Princeton, 1996).

56 Davidson, above n 52, at 580–581.
57 See Pan Ying *Taiwan pingpuzu shi* [History of the Taiwanese Plains Aborigines] (Nantian, Taipei, 1996), at 35–36.
58 Paul Jen-kuei Li "Taiwan pingpuzu de zhonglei jiqi xianghu guanxi" [The Classification of Taiwanese Plains Aborigines and Their Inter-Relationships] in Zhang Yan-xian, Li Xiao-feng and Dai Bao-cun (eds) *Taiwanshi lunwen jingxuan* [Selected Essays on Taiwan History] (Yushan, Taipei, 1996), at 46 and 61.
59 At 46. Also see Paul Jen-Kuei Li "Formosan Languages: The State of the Art" in Blundell (ed), above n 22, at 52; Pan, above n 46, at 118.
60 See Kang, above n 21, at 30, note 1.
61 M Paul Lewis, Gary F Simons and Charles D Fenning "Ethnologue: Languages of Taiwan" in *Ethnologue: Languages of the World* (18th ed, online ed, SIL International, Dallas, 2015).
62 At 11–23.
63 Ibid.
64 Ibid. Also see Blundell "A Century of Research", above n 22, at 8.
65 *The Republic of China Yearbook 2016* (Executive Yuan, Taipei, 2016), at 45.
66 See Ming-tu Yang "Going Back Into a Future of Simplicity: Taiwan Aborigines' Sustainable Utilization of Natural Resources" in Chia-ju Chang and Scott Slovic (eds) *Ecocriticism in Taiwan: Identity, Environment, and the Arts* (Lexington, London, 2016), at 3–15.
67 See Chen, above n 26.
68 Yang, above n 66, at 8–9.
69 Chen, above n 26.
70 Campbell, above n 7, at 10.
71 See Huang "Fansu liukao", above n 45.
72 For more details of the reconstruction described in this paragraph, see John Robert Shepherd *Statecraft and Political Economy on the Taiwan Frontier, 1600–1800* (Stanford University Press, Stanford, 1993), at 240–242.
73 This could be what was later regarded as "wasteland".
74 Shepherd, above n 72, at 242.
75 Since Shepherd used materials from the Qing period and after to reconstruct the land tenure system. See ibid, at 240.
76 For more details of the land tenure discussed in this paragraph, see Huang Ying-kuei "Taiwan tuzhuzu de liangzhong shehui leixing jiqi yiyi" [The Two Types of Taiwan Mountain Aboriginal Societies and Their Significance] and Wei Hue-lin "Taiwan tuzhu shehui de buluo zuzhi yu quanwei zhidu" [The Tribal Organisation and Power System in the Taiwanese Mountain Aboriginal Societies] in Huang Ying-kuei (ed) *Taiwan tuzhu shehui wenhua yanjiu lunwenji* [A Collection of Research Essays on the Society and Culture of the Taiwanese Aborigines] (Lianjing, Taipei, 1986), at 13 and 125–126, respectively.
77 The hunting or fishing organisations could be within the village or across villages. See Wei, ibid, at 121–122.
78 See the treaties recorded in Campbell, above n 7, at 119 and 129.
79 Tonio Andrade *How Taiwan Became Chinese: Dutch, Spanish and Han Colonization in the Seventeenth Century* (Columbia University Press, New York, 2008), at 72 quoting a Missionary's letter to the directors of the Amsterdam Chamber of the VOC, 5 September 1636.
80 At 136 and 139.
81 At 140. For the aboriginal resistance of Chinese hunting on their grounds, see ch 7.
82 At 123.
83 At 42 and 116. However, Campbell, above n 7, at 8, records that over 10,000 Chinese resided in Tayouan at the time of Dutch arrival.
84 See Campbell, ibid, at 36; Chuang, above n 35, at 3.

85 Yang Yan-jie *Heju shidai Taiwan shi* [The History of Taiwan Under Dutch Occupation] (Lianjing, Taipei, 2000), at 170. The estimation of the Chinese population differs in different sources, ranging from 35,000 to 100,000. For example, see Shepherd, above n 72, at 8; Wen-Hsiung Hsu "From Aboriginal Island to Chinese Frontier: The Development of Taiwan Before 1683" in Knapp (ed), above n 13, at 17; Hung Chien-Chao *A History of Taiwan* (Cerchio Iniziative Editoriali via Gambalunga, Rimini, 2000), at 18, each presents a different figure.

86 Yang, ibid, at 178. Morgen is a unit of measurement of land under the Dutch system, and is understood to be the same size as *jia*, the measurement unit that was commonly used after the Dutch period.

87 At 175–177.

88 At 180.

89 Chiu Hsin-hui *The Colonial "Civilizing Process" in Dutch Formosa, 1624–1662* (Brill, Leiden and Boston, 2008), at 152. Also see Kang, above n 21, at 223.

90 Shepherd, above n 72, at 87 also notes that the Dutch recognised some aboriginal land claims but did not recognise the bulk.

91 Tonio Andrade "Pirates, Pelts, and Promises: The Sino-Dutch Colony of Seventeenth-Century Taiwan and the Aboriginal Village of Favorolang" (2005) 64 *Journal of Asian Studies* 295–321.

92 See Zhou Xi *Zhanghua xianzhi* [Gazetteer of Zhanghua County, 1830] (TWWX 156), at 162.

93 For example Lian Heng *Taiwan tongshi* [A Comprehensive History of Taiwan, 1918] (TWWX 128), at 168; Hsu, above n 85, at 16 and 18.

94 Governor of Formosa, letter, 11 July 1647, quoted in Andrade, above n 79, at 123. Also see Chiu, above n 89, at 152.

95 Clause VII. See the treaty in Campbell, above n 7, at 455–456. The exact meaning of the term "leaseholders" is not clear – it could mean leaseholders of land, or the merchants who held monopoly trading licences, or both.

96 See Lian, above n 93, at 188–194, for the various rent and tax rates during the Dutch, Zheng and Qing periods.

97 Clauses II and VII of the treaty, in Campbell, above n 7, at 455.

98 See Kang, above n 21, at 271–272.

99 Hung, above n 85, at 59.

100 Shepherd, above n 72, at 96.

101 Wang, above n 13, at 39.

102 This category of land was called "Officials' Land" (*wenwu guantian* 文武官田), but there were in fact private land. See Zhou, above n 92, at 161.

103 Jiang Yuying *Taiwan fuzhi* [Gazetteer of Taiwan Prefecture, cir 1689] (Taiwansheng wenxian weiyuanhui, Nantou, 1993), at 80.

104 Song, above n 3, at 46.

105 At 47–50.

106 Hung, above n 85, at 78.

107 Song, above n 3, at 43–45.

108 Hsu, above n 85, at 25.

109 "不許混圈土民及百姓現耕田地". See the regulations in Yang Ying *Congzheng shilu* [Veritable Records of Zheng Chenggong's Expeditions] (TWWX 32), at 189–190.

110 Ruan Minxi *Haishang jianwenlu* [Things Seen and Heard Over the Seas] (TWWX24), at 39.

111 Shepherd, above n 72, at 94. See Ts'ao Yung-ho *Taiwan zaoqi lishi yanjiu* [A Research on the Early History of Taiwan] (Lianjing, Taipei, 1979), at 255–293 "Zhengshi shidai zhi Taiwan kenzhi" [The Zhengs' Colonisation and Land Reclamation in Taiwan] for more discussion on the Zheng's colonisation activities in Taiwan.

112 Shepherd, ibid. Also see Ts'ao, above n 111, at 266.

113 Shepherd, ibid, at 102; Hung, above n 85, at 78–79.

114 Hung, above n 85, at 79.
115 Li Ju-ho and Chuang Chin-Teh (eds) *Taiwansheng tongzhi* [A Comprehensive History of Taiwan Province] (Taiwansheng wenxian weiyuanhui, Taizhong, 1972), vol 10, at 119; Chuang Chin-Teh "Qingdai chuqi Taiwan tudi kaifa daoyan" [An Introduction to Land Reclamation in Taiwan During the Early Qing Period] (1971) 15 & 16 *Taipei Wen Hsien* 166, at 166.
116 Jiang, above n 103, at 77.
117 At 80. The Qing gave private land ownership to the tenants of the Zheng period government land.
118 Inō, above n 4, vol 1, at 179.
119 The first magistrate of Zhuluo County, Ji Qiguang, complained to Shi himself that wherever he went, he was told that the land belonged to Shi and the people Shi's tenants. See Ji's letter to Shi Lang in Taiwan Shiliao Jicheng Bianji Weiyuanhui *Ming Qing Taiwan dang'an huibian* [Collection of Historic Documents Concerning Taiwan During the Ming and Qing Dynasties] (Yuanliu, Taipei, 2004–2009), vol 9, at 105–106. Inō also mention criticisms against Shi in ibid, at 140–141.
120 See the statistics in Liu, above n 47, at 129–134.
121 Yu, above n 43, at 22. Zhuqian and Nankan are at present-day Xinzhu and Taoyuan counties, respectively.
122 "鹿場半被流民開". The poem of Ruan, "Zhuqian", is recorded in Zhou Zhongxuan *Zhuluo xianzhi* [Gazetteer of Zhuluo County, 1717] (TWWX141), at 267–268.
123 Zhou, ibid, at 298, "三十年來附縣開墾者眾，鹿場悉為田".
124 Huang, above n 44, at 65, "昔年近山皆為土番鹿場；今則漢人墾種，極目良田".
125 Ruan, above n 122, "鵲巢忽爾為鳩居，鵲盡無巢鳩焉徙？"
126 Sheng, above n 3, at 159.
127 Shih Tien-fu *Qingdai Taiwan de diyu shehui: Zhuqian diqu de lishi dili yanjiu* [The Local Society in Qing Taiwan – A Research on the Historical Geography of the Zhuqian Area] (Xinzhuxian wenhua ju, Xinzhu, 2001), at 125, 233–240 and 249.
128 Chuang, above n 115, at 172.
129 Lan Dingyuan *Ping Tai jilüe* [Brief Accounts of the Pacification of Taiwan, 1723] (TWWX 14), at 30.
130 Peng Yuxin *Qingdai tudi kaiken shi* [History of Land Reclamation During the Qing Dynasty] (Nongye, Beijing, 1990), at 247; Chuang, above n 115, at 170.
131 Peng, ibid; Chuang, ibid, at 170 and 172.
132 See *Tai'an huilu jiaji* [Taiwan Documents Collection A] (TWWX 31), at 164.
133 Tu Jishan *Hengchun xianzhi* [Gazetteer of Hengchun County, 1894] (TWWX 75), at 114.
134 At 114 and 118.
135 Hu Chuan *Taidongzhou caifangce* [Draft Gazetteer of Taidong Department, cir 1892–1895] (TWWX 81), at 42.
136 Li Wen-liang "Linye zhengli shiye yu dong Taiwan tudi suoyouquan zhi chengli xingtai, 1910–1925" [The Forest Land Investigation Project and Methods of Establishing Land Ownership in Eastern Taiwan, 1910–1925] (1997) 2 *Dong Taiwan yanjiu* 169, at 171.
137 See the statistics in *Liu Zhuangsugong zouyi* [Memorials of Liu Mingchuan] (TWWX 27), at 318–319.
138 Lin Yu-ju "You yulin tuce kan Qingmo houshan de qingfu shiye yu diquan fenpei xingtai" [The Land Survey Project and the Pattern of Land Rights Distribution in Eastern Taiwan During the Late Qing Period as Seen From the "Fish-Scale" Land Register] (1997) 2 *Dong Taiwan yanjiu* 131, at 152.
139 See Chuang Chi-fa "Qingdai Taiwan tudi kaifa yu zuqun chongtu" [Land Reclamation and Ethnic Conflicts in Qing Taiwan] (2000) 36 *Taiwan shiji* 3, at 5.

2 Settlement policies

Reluctant expansion

As discussed in Chapter 1, for most of the Qing period, land settlement largely occurred in the western plains, and apart from the settlement of Gamalan, it was only after 1875 that there were sizeable settlements by Han Chinese in eastern Taiwan. The mountain areas remained under aboriginal control. This settlement pattern was determined by the settlement policies of the Qing government.

For nearly 200 years the Qing government controlled migration to Taiwan, and established aboriginal boundaries along the central mountain ranges to segregate the Han settlers and plains aborigines from the mountain aborigines. The government forbade settlement beyond the boundaries and made no attempt to extend government administration over the mountain territories, which made up about half of the island of Taiwan. This restrictive stance of the Qing government is referred to in the literature as the "quarantine" (*fengjin* 封禁) of Taiwan and especially of the mountain aboriginal territories.[1] This approach came to an abrupt end when the Guangxu government abolished the quarantine policies in 1875, launched campaigns to "open the mountains and subjugate the aborigines" (*kaishan fufan* 開山撫番),[2] and eventually expanded administration over the whole of Taiwan. It is widely accepted that 1875 was the watershed of Qing administration in Taiwan, as is suggested by an apparently abrupt change from a policy of quarantine to expansion.

This chapter examines the Qing government's settlement and land reclamation policies in Taiwan and analyses the rationale that underpinned these policies. To inform discussions in this and later chapters, the chapter starts with introducing the Qing Empire and its administrative and legal systems. This is followed by examination of the Qing policies at three different stages: the restricting settlement stage, the transitional stage and the promoting expansion stage. During the century-long "High Qing" period under the Kangxi, Yongzheng and Qianlong reigns (1684–1795), the Qing Empire expanded its territory and experienced economic prosperity, yet the government refrained from expansion in Taiwan, and generally discouraged or tried to prevent migration to and settlement in Taiwan. Since the late 1700s and early 1800s, the empire started to decline. In responding to internal turmoil and external threats, the Qing government and officials considered expanding government control in Taiwan and opening up mountain territories for settlement. The most salient examples were the expansion of administration over

Gamalan and the recurrent debates and attempts to open up inner Shuishalian 水沙連 for settlement. Contrary to the common belief that Qing policies changed abruptly in 1875, the period between 1795 and 1874 was in fact a transitional stage in terms of settlement policies concerning Taiwan. The pressure under the general climate of foreign threats to the Qing Empire climaxed in Taiwan as Japan invaded southern Taiwan in 1874, and the third stage saw the Qing government engaged in active expansion and settlement activities, although not without set-backs. At each stage the government either refrained from expansion or expanded only reluctantly. The policy trend was dictated by the paramount consideration for security of the regime and social stability, and fit with Qing policy shifts in other frontier areas such as the inner Asian regions (Manchuria, Mongolia and Xinjiang) and southwest China. This was heavily influenced by the Qing tradition, including Confucian legal thought and Manchu apparatus. The Western social and political thoughts to a limited extent also influenced officials' thinking in the late 19th century.

Qing regime

The rise and fall

The Qing Empire was "one of the largest and longest-lived multinational empires of the early modern world".[3] The empire was created by the Manchus and originated in northeast China, known as Manchuria.

The Manchus belonged to the ethnic group known as Jurchen. Jurchen is a name that emerged in the early 10th century, although the people possibly dated back to the 6th century BC.[4] The Jurchen people were seen by the Chinese during the Ming Dynasty as "wild people" (*yeren* 野人), who practised hunting and gathering, and used Chinese and Korean slaves whom they captured at the borders to engage in agriculture.[5] Some Jurchen chiefs acknowledged Ming suzerainty, as well as having interaction with Korea and the Mongols. One of the three major Jurchen groups, the Jianzhou 建州 Jurchen confederation grew in power under Nurhaci (1559–1626), the forefather of the Qing rulers.[6] In 1616 Nurhaci ascended to the throne and declared his reign to be "Heavenly Mandated" (*tianming* 天命), a title after the Chinese fashion.[7] This signified independence from the Ming. The term "Manchu" appeared during Nurhaci's time, but it was formally adopted only in 1635.[8] In 1636 Nurhaci's son Hung Taiji (r 1626–1643) announced a new name, "Qing", for the Manchu entity, and thus started the Qing Dynasty. The Manchus' sinicisation process started during Nurhaci's time, when Nurhaci recruited Chinese scholars to translate Chinese literature and the Ming laws. By 1638, the Qing Court completed the central bureaucracy on the Ming model, and adopted Ming laws with some adjustments.[9] Therefore the Chinese legal system was a cornerstone of the foundation of the Qing.

Qing forces entered Beijing in 1644, and in subsequent decades the Qing defeated remnant Ming resistance forces and consolidated their rule over the rest of China.[10] The Shunzhi government conquered northern China and lower Yangtze valley before taking control of the south and west of China.[11] The Kangxi government pacified the rebellion of the Three Feudatories (*sanfan* 三藩) in southern China,[12] defeated the Zhengs and annexed Taiwan, settled borders with Russia in the northeast, and launched military campaigns in the northwest.[13] Known as the High Qing stage, the Kangxi, Yongzheng and Qianlong reigns have been seen as the golden age of the Qing Dynasty, when the empire continued to expand and consolidate its control. By the 1750s, the Qing Court controlled Mongolia, Xinjiang and Tibet, in addition to China proper, Manchuria, Taiwan and southwest China.[14] Yet this prosperous High Qing deliberately refrained from expansion in Taiwan.

As the High Qing drew to a close, the dynasty started to decline because of secular changes as well as dynastic cycles, while the Qing tried to cope with internal rebellions as well as foreign threats.[15] The White Lotus Rebellion lasted nearly a decade (1796–1804), a "multifaceted disaster" that seriously crippled the Qing's financial capacity.[16] In 1840 the first Opium War with Britain was fought and lost, and subsequently the Qing government was forced to open treaty ports for trade after signing a series of treaties with Britain, France, the United States and Russia.[17] Economic depression in the 1840s was followed by the Taiping Rebellion (1850–1864) and the second Anglo-Chinese War of 1856–1860. Surviving near collapse at the end of the Xianfeng reign (1851–1861), the Qing Court made efforts to revive the regime, and entered a period of self-strengthening and industrialisation under the Tongzhi emperor (1862–1874), known as the Tongzhi Restoration.[18] The internal turmoil and external pressure were to have effects on the Qing's Taiwan policies.

Added to Western imperialism was the ambition and threats of China's close neighbour, Japan. In 1874 Japan invaded southern Taiwan, and occupied the Kingdom of Liuqiu, which had been a vassal of the Chinese Ming then the Qing. The realisation of the threats Japan posed and the real risk of losing Taiwan, which was a shield protecting coastal China, changed the Qing's Taiwan policy dramatically. In 1894 Japan declared war against the Qing, over matters concerning another Qing suzerainty, Korea. The war resulted in the Treaty of Shimonoseki, by which Japan gained Taiwan and other valuable prizes. Efforts were made to revive, reform and prolong the Qing regime, but the last dynasty in Chinese history ended when revolutionaries overthrew the Qing Court and replaced it with the Republic of China.

With each turn of the Qing history, from prosperous and strong to dynastic decline, and then to heightened crises and threats to Taiwan, the Qing settlement policies in Taiwan shifted.

The administrative and legal systems

Being an ethnic minority ruler over China, the Qing Court had two foundations for its rule – "neo-Confucian legitimacy" and "ethnic sovereignty". That is, the Qing embraced Confucian culture and political norms on the one hand, and retained Manchu identity and culture on the other.[19] The early to mid-Qing government particularly showed "zealous adherence" to Confucian values.[20] Confucian norms underpinned the Qing legal tradition, while the unique Manchu identity adjusted the legal system where necessary. An example of the adjustment was the creation of the Board for Governing Outer Territories (*Lifanyuan* 理藩院), to govern Mongolia, Xinjiang and Tibet,[21] and the implementation of dual legal systems in those areas.[22] A unique feature of Qing organisation was the banner (*qi* 旗) system, which was a way of organising fighting forces as well as the society of Manchus and their close allies. However in general the Qing administrative and legal systems were largely Chinese in character, and followed long-established Chinese precedents.

The Qing administrative structure was largely inherited from the preceding Ming Dynasty. In the central government, six ministries administered six areas of national affairs. The Ministry of Households (*hubu* 戶部) was responsible for taxes and revenues, as well as regulation of other civil matters such as marriages and inheritance;[23] the Ministry of Justice (*xingbu* 刑部) for criminal law matters; the Ministry of Personnel (*libu* 吏部) for official appointments; the Ministry of Works (*gongbu* 工部) for construction matters; the Ministry of War (*bingbu* 兵部) for military affairs; and the Ministry of Rites (*libu* 禮部) for ceremonies, including the reception of foreign guests.[24] At the local government level, the Qing divided its empire into provinces (*sheng* 省), provinces into prefectures (*fu* 府), and prefectures into counties (*xian* 縣) and sometimes sub-prefectures (*ting* 廳). A governor headed each province, and a governor-general oversaw or coordinated the administration of two or three provinces. Governors and governors-general reported directly to the emperor, and served as the channel between local and central government.[25]

Taiwan was incorporated as a prefecture under Fujian Province. The Taiwan prefect was the civil head of the prefecture, while the regional commander (*zongbing* 總兵) was the military head. A special Taiwan-Xiamen military defence circuit intendant (*Fenxun Taiwan-Xiamen bingbeidao* 分巡臺灣廈門兵備道), later changed to Taiwan circuit intendant (*Taiwan dao* 臺灣道), oversaw the civil and military affairs of Taiwan. The circuit intendant was subordinate to the governor, although they were given direct access to the emperors from 1788 (Qianlong 53) on.[26] Under the Taiwan Prefecture were counties, the lowest level at the formal administrative structure. Each county was headed by a magistrate. The process for appointing officials to Taiwan followed the regular process, but officials were appointed for a term of no more than three years to avoid their gathering too much power in the former base of opposition.

The Qing legal system also largely followed the traditional Chinese style. Underpinning the Chinese legal tradition were Confucian norms, which emphasised *li* (禮 "rite", "propriety") as the governing force of human behaviour.[27] The formal law governed only criminal and administrative matters, and *li* as the "moral law" and "customary, un-codified law" governed other aspects of society.[28] This meant that there was little distinction between law and social norms. The formal law had an authoritarian structure and a public character, and it was "primarily directed not to the people, but to administrative officials".[29] Criminal law guided officials in adjudicating cases, and administrative law regulated officials' behaviour. Reflecting this Chinese legal tradition, the major Qing legislation was the *Great Qing*

Code (*Daqing lü* 大清律) and the *Great Qing Institutes* (*Daqing huidian* 大清會典), constituting a criminal law code and an administrative code, respectively. Both codes were based on Ming Dynasty models and were relatively stable.[30]

Other than the law codes, *li* (例 literally "precedents", in effect regulations) was the most important form of legislation. Although understood to be subordinate legislation, *li* had the same legal status as law codes, and they were revised regularly.[31] Two sets of important regulations were the *Imperially Approved Precedents to the Great Qing Institutes* (*Qinding Daqing huidian shili* 欽定大清會典事例) and the *Regulations of the Six Ministries* (*Liubu zeli* 六部則例).[32] These regulation series were made up of single-entry stand-alone regulations, which were made at different times to address specific issues. Typically officials raised issues and made recommendations on certain matters, and the emperor would refer important recommendations for discussion by the Grand Council (*Junjichu* 軍機處) or central government officials.[33] Important recommendations were made into regulations after imperial approval.

Imperial decrees, and the emperor's endorsement or annotation on the official memorials which made the original recommendations, were not recorded in formal regulation books, and probably should be classified as policies. However, the Confucian legal tradition emphasised the authority of the emperor, who enjoyed legislative, executive and judicial powers in one person.[34] Because of this absolute authority of the emperor and because laws were directed at officials, in reality anything the emperor pronounced became enforceable by officials, and had the effect of law. Therefore there was little distinction between law and policy. Further, decrees and notices issued by local officials also had the effect of law within the jurisdiction of the issuing officials.

Given the lack of distinction between law and policy, Qing laws and policies towards land settlement in Taiwan at various stages were manifested in regulations, imperial decrees, official recommendations and administrative action.

Restricting settlement during the High Qing period (1684–1795)

Despite the different personalities and governance styles of the Kangxi, Yongzheng and Qianlong emperors, over the century of these three reigns, the government deliberately restricted land settlement and refrained expanding government administration in Taiwan. There were two layers of quarantine, the first being the whole island of Taiwan, enforced through controlling migration, and the second the mountain territories in Taiwan, achieved through segregating settlers and the aborigines.

Minimal expansion

The Kangxi era

The Qing Court was not interested in acquiring an overseas territory. The purpose of the attack on the Zhengs in Taiwan was to quash the last Ming stronghold and to eliminate an enemy,[35] and the annexation after the Zhengs' surrender was primarily the result of security considerations.

After the Zhengs surrendered, one option of the government was to withdraw all Chinese subjects and abandon the island.[36] However, the then Fujian maritime commander, Shi Lang, who had led the successful expedition to Taiwan, argued for the retention of the island on the basis of defence and security. Shi argued that Taiwan was the shield for the coastal provinces; if abandoned, it could become a bandits' lair or be re-occupied by the "red-hair" (the Dutch), which could threaten the empire's security.[37] Recognising that Taiwan was strategically important, the Kangxi emperor adopted Shi Lang's view and formally annexed Taiwan in 1684.[38]

The fact that no consideration was given to Taiwan apart from for security was illustrated clearly in the administrative system in Taiwan. Military forces of 8,000 soldiers were placed to guard important ports.[39] In contrast, civil administration was maintained at a minimum level with few changes from the Zheng period, and by a handful of civil officials. The Kangxi government maintained the Zhengs' administrative structure in Taiwan, that is, a prefecture with two counties, and added only one county at the prefecture capital (see Map 1.2). Nominally the three counties – Taiwan, Fengshan and Zhuluo – covered the whole western plains. In reality administration did not effectively extend to all parts of the territory, and settlers needed a government permit to go beyond Dajia River at about the mid-point of the western plains.[40]

The Kangxi emperor was not interested in colonisation of Taiwan. When the Fujian-Zhejiang governor-general recommended in 1715 (Kangxi 54) that the Court encourage land reclamation in Taiwan, the emperor was reluctant to approve the recommendation and expressed the view that to encourage land reclamation in Taiwan was short-sighted, as this would only cause major trouble in the future.[41] By major trouble, the emperor certainly had in mind conflicts and instability in Taiwan. This attitude of the emperor partly accounted for the insignificant advance of land settlement during the Kangxi era.

The Yongzheng era

The Yongzheng government has often been seen as pro-colonisation, mainly because it extended the government control over the whole Western plains.[42] In fact the government did so to strengthen the administration, in order to better control the settlers and maintain security, and the existing policies of quarantine largely remained in place.

In the first year of the Yongzheng reign, Zhuluo County was subdivided to create a new county, Zhanghua, above the middle point of the western plains. In addition, a Danshui sub-prefect was posted in the north. This change effectively extended government control from the southwest to the far north (see Map 2.1). Although this has been seen as expanding Qing territory, the government's intention was not colonisation. Before the subdivision, Zhuluo County covered a vast territory that extended "east to the mountain ranges, west to the sea, south to Fengshan Country, southwest to Taiwan Country, and north to the Jilong Mountain [in the

Map 2.1 Expansion of administrative areas

far north]".[43] From the south to north it extended 919 *li*, and the total area was more than three times larger than the second largest county Fengshan.[44] Despite the restriction on going beyond Dajia River during the Kangxi reign, illegal crossing and unauthorised land reclamation in the northern part of Zhuluo County had continued to occur. To tighten control on law and order in the north, and to eliminate security risks, as early as 1717 (Kangxi 56), the Zhuluo County magistrate had recommended subdivision of the county, arguing that the district was too vast to be effectively controlled, which allowed the disorderly to hide from the law.[45]

The government finally decided to strengthen control in the north after a major settler uprising, the Zhu Yigui uprising, broke out in 1721 (Kangxi 60). An inspecting censor for Taiwan repeated the recommendation of subdividing Zhuluo in 1723 and this was accepted by the Court.[46]

An often-cited strong advocate for expansion and land reclamation of that time was Lan Dingyuan, an advisor to Lan Tingzhen, the Fujian maritime commander who led troops to suppress the uprising. Yet Lan's focus was on law and order. Having played an important role in pacifying the settler uprising, Lan's expansionist advocacy was the recommendation to strengthen government control in areas of strategic importance, so as to better control the Chinese settlers. Lan's call for land reclamation aimed at reducing settler-aborigine conflicts. He argued that in order to reduce trouble caused by aborigines, it was better to fill the land with settlers and have the land developed into agricultural land. This would in turn expose the aborigines to Han culture and transform them into the Empire's subjects.[47] Security was therefore the determining factor for Lan's advocacy, as well as the Yongzheng government's expansion.

The Qianlong era

The administrative structure as adjusted by the Yongzheng government remained unchanged during the Qianlong reign, and scholars have seen the Qianlong era as reversing from the Yongzheng government's "pro-colonisation" approach.[48] In reality, while the emperors might have different views on how to maintain effective governance of Taiwan, the ultimate objective of security remained the same.

Like the Kangxi emperor, the Qianlong emperor was concerned that Chinese land settlement could cause disturbances on the island. When officials recommended allowing settlers to reclaim land in Taiwan in 1744 (Qianlong 9), the Qianlong emperor dismissed the recommendations and reasoned that the government "should not . . . seek trivial benefit and encourage land reclamation", lest trouble would ensue.[49] This was despite the fact that, since the Yongzheng era, Taiwan had become the granary of Fujian Province and regularly exported rice to relieve the food shortages there.[50] However, at the outbreak of another major Han uprising in Taiwan, the Lin Shuangwen uprising, in 1786 (Qianlong 51), the emperor saw wisdom in Lan's strategy. The emperor agreed with Lan that leaving fertile lands to the non-acculturated aborigines, who did not cultivate them, only attracted settlers to reclaim them illegally, resulting in conflicts and trouble.[51] The emperor repeatedly emphasised to his officials that Taiwan was the "important coastal frontier territory" (*haijiang zhongdi* 海疆重地) and "the important fence line of the five [coastal] provinces" (*wusheng fanli zhongdi* 五省藩籬重地).[52]

Therefore, in the first century of Qing administration of Taiwan, the only expansion occurred during the Yongzheng reign. No matter whether to annex Taiwan, to expand or to restrict settlement and limit government control, the policy rationale was security and social stability.

Administration of aborigines

The Qing government made little effort to administer the aborigines. The government rarely tried to subjugate the aborigines or to impose cultural change.

Qing officials classified the aborigines into two general types – acculturated aborigines (*shufan* 熟番) and non-acculturated aborigines (*shengfan* 生番), according to the level of acculturation.[53] The concepts of *shu* and *sheng* were used by earlier Chinese dynasties to classify different groups of less developed ethnic peoples in mainland China. "*Sheng*" is a word to describe uncooked food, unworked land, un-ripened fruit, unskilful hands or strangers. "*Shu*" is the opposite of "*Sheng*".[54] To the Qing officials, *shufan* were those who paid tax, performed corvée and to some degree adopted Han Chinese culture.[55] *Shengfan* who submitted to Qing rule paid a token tax, were exempted from corvée and were left to continue with their old ways of living.[56] This type of *shengfan* was called *guihua shengfan* (歸化生番 "submitted non-acculturated aborigines") or *huafan* 化番 for short. The classifications of "*shu*" and "*sheng*" aborigines were evolving, as the "*sheng*" eventually became more acculturated, and gradually transformed to "*shu*".

At the time of the Qing annexation, in total 46 aboriginal villages were subject to the Qing administration – 12 in Fengshan and 34 in Zhuluo.[57] These were likely to have been inherited from the Zheng regime. The Kangxi government was not interested in changing the status quo in Taiwan, and there is no record of the government trying to subjugate the aborigines, although some aboriginal villages submitted themselves to the Qing government.[58] In the case of submitted aborigines, the government was happy to charge only a token tax and to otherwise leave them in the state as they were, without any disturbance or additional administration.[59] During the Yongzheng reign, the Taiwan regional commander, Lin Liang, encouraged and enticed aboriginal submission, resulting in the submission of 108 aboriginal villages during the 13 years of the Yongzheng reign.[60] The Qianlong government preferred not to encourage submission of the aborigines. In fact the emperor expressly forbade the enticement of aborigines to come under the regime, for fear of future conflicts.[61] Nevertheless, as Han settlements expanded, more aboriginal villages submitted themselves to Qing rule. It can only be conjectured whether this might have been the aborigines' way of seeking government protection from settler aggression as settlement expanded.

In the early Qianlong reign, local officers identified at least 299 aboriginal villages by their names.[62] Records show that 93 aboriginal villages paid village tax (*shexiang* 社餉) and 61 aboriginal villages paid token tax.[63] The 93 villages were seen as acculturated aborigines by the government. The classification seemed to stabilise after that, and the number of recognised acculturated aborigines remained at 93 till the end of the Qing period. The fact that for over a century the number of acculturated aborigines did not increase signifies that the government was relaxed in transforming the aborigines' culture, and that settler-aborigine interaction slowed down because land settlement progressed little after the Qianlong period.

The settler-aborigine disputes over land caused the government to appoint two aboriginal affairs sub-prefects (*lifan tongzhi* 理番同知) to manage aboriginal affairs in 1766 (Qianlong 31).[64] The two sub-prefects, one in charge of the areas in the north and one in the south, focused on the plains aborigines. To those mountain aborigines, the government was content to keep them out of the settlement areas through building aboriginal boundaries. Thus while the settlers drove the colonisation and acculturation, the government made every effort to contain settlement and maintain status quo of aboriginal villages. To a great extent, the aborigines, especially the mountain aborigines, were protected by the government's efforts, most notably the migration control and segregation policies, which reduced the impacts of settlers on the aborigines.

Migration control

By means of a permit system, the government controlled the number and types of people to enter Taiwan.

The first recorded regulation on the subject of the permit system was made in 1712 (Kangxi 51), but evidence suggests that it was introduced before 1711, probably soon after formal annexation in 1684.[65] There were two main considerations for a permit system. The first consideration was to reduce pressure on land; the rationale being that Taiwan was not able to support too large a population which could lead to conflict.[66] Therefore regulations forbade migrants to bring families with them, presumably to reduce the size of population and to prevent the settlers from taking root in Taiwan. The second, and the more important consideration, was to exclude unruly persons from Taiwan, thus threatening the stability of the society. To this end, officials often recommended that only those who had property in mainland China or those who had relatives in Taiwan were allowed to enter Taiwan.[67] A Taiwan prefect in 1729 (Yongzheng 7) argued that "the migration of good subjects" (*liangmin zhi du* 良民之渡) "definitely should not be forbidden" (*bi buke jin* 必不可禁), while "the migration of villains" (*jianmin zhi du* 奸民之渡) "must definitely be forbidden" (*bi buke bujin* 必不可不禁).[68] Wanderers, who had no family or property attachment, were believed to be prone to cause trouble and were thus excluded from receiving a permit. Consequently, a 1730 (Yongzheng 8) regulation stipulated that people who did not have property or family in Taiwan, or who had property or family but committed certain criminal acts, were to be repatriated from Taiwan.[69] A 1751 (Qianlong 16) regulation reiterated the same law in slightly different terms.[70]

Scholars have argued that the government "tightened" or "relaxed" the migration control at different times.[71] But in fact, over the century, the regulations were largely consistent, and any changes were superficial. The official regulation collection, *Qing huidian Taiwan shili*, recorded 15 regulations concerning migration to Taiwan made in the High Qing era, one during the Kangxi reign, three during the Yongzheng reign and 12 during the Qianlong reign (Table 2.1). The Kangxi and early Yongzheng regulations stressed the good character of permit receivers, while the later regulations mostly reiterated implementation measures, such as patrolling and punishment. The government repeatedly warned against and tried to curb illegal crossing. The policy trend continued into the Jiaqing era. The only changes over the years were on whether or not to allow migrants to bring families to Taiwan, as the government considered how better to manage the settlers, whether to keep

Table 2.1 Imperial regulations concerning migration to Taiwan*

Year	*Law*
1712 (KX 51)	Permit needed to go to Taiwan. Officials not to issue permit in an irresponsible manner. "Good subjects" (*liangmin*) could apply to reside in Taiwan.
1729 (YZ 7)	Policing illegal crossing. Officials to be punished if negligent.
1730 (YZ 8)	Those settlers in Taiwan who did not have a family to be expelled from Taiwan, those who had family and property but engaged in unruly activities to be punished according to law.
1734 (YZ 12)	Boat owners/operators to be punished if illegally taking passengers.
1736 (QL 1)	Policing illegal crossing. Officials to be punished if negligent.
1737 (QL 2)	Tightening up the permit system, and details of boats to Taiwan and the crews to be recorded. Taiwan local officials to record details of local residents.
1740 (QL 5)	Where boats took passengers illegally, boat owners/operators and illegal passengers to be punished.
1745 (QL 10)	Migrants could only apply for wives and children to go to Taiwan, and no other relatives.
1747 (QL 12)	Procedures prescribed for bringing families to Taiwan, and officials to be punished if issuing permits irresponsibly.
1761 (QL 26)	Permit needed to go to Taiwan, and the only port of departure was Xiamen. Policing illegal crossing. Officials to be punished if negligent and to be rewarded if diligent. Family reunion migration closed.
1770 (QL 35)	Policing illegal crossing. Officials to be punished if negligent and to be rewarded if diligent; boat owners and passengers to be punished for breaches.
1772 (QL 37)	To punish a range of people if involved in the illegal crossing business, including organisers, boat crews and passengers.
1784 (QL 49)	Taiwan settlers were allowed to go back to reside in their place of origin in mainland China without a permit. They could only depart from Lu'ermen 鹿耳門 port. Other ports must be strictly policed against boats arriving and departing.
1788 (QL53)	To open another port in Taiwan so as to reduce illegal crossing (prompted by the Lin Shuangwen uprising).
1789 (QL54)	Officials not to extort from applicants going to Taiwan so as to reduce illegal crossing.
1800 (JQ 5)	Policing illegal crossing. Officials to be punished if negligent and to be rewarded if diligent. Settlers who were in Taiwan could apply for residency if they had family and property, otherwise would be expelled back to their place of origin.
1801 (JQ 6)	Policing illegal crossing. Officials to be punished if negligent.

* Table created according to *Qing huidian Taiwan shili*. These were all government regulations. Other recommendations that might have been approved by the emperors but not made a regulation are not included.

KX = Kangxi, YZ = Yongzheng, QL = Qianlong, JQ = Jiaqing

their families in the mainland as de facto hostages so that they dared not misbehave, or whether to let them enjoy family life so that they would not cause trouble.[72] The central principles of controlling what kind of people could migrate and of monitoring the movements of people through the permit system never wavered. This was designed to ensure the social order on the island and the security of Qing rule, which were always the prime considerations.

Segregation

Another measure of controlling Han settlement was segregation. Policies of segregation included building boundaries to separate settlements from aboriginal territories, as well as forbidding interaction between settlers and the non-acculturated aborigines, in particular marriage.

The policy to segregate settlement areas from the aboriginal territories was introduced in 1722 (Kangxi 61). This was the direct response to the 1721 Zhu Yigui uprising, an event that aggravated security concerns. Fifty-four stelae were erected at crucial points to mark boundaries between settlement areas and aboriginal territories (Map 2.2). The areas west of the boundaries – the settlement

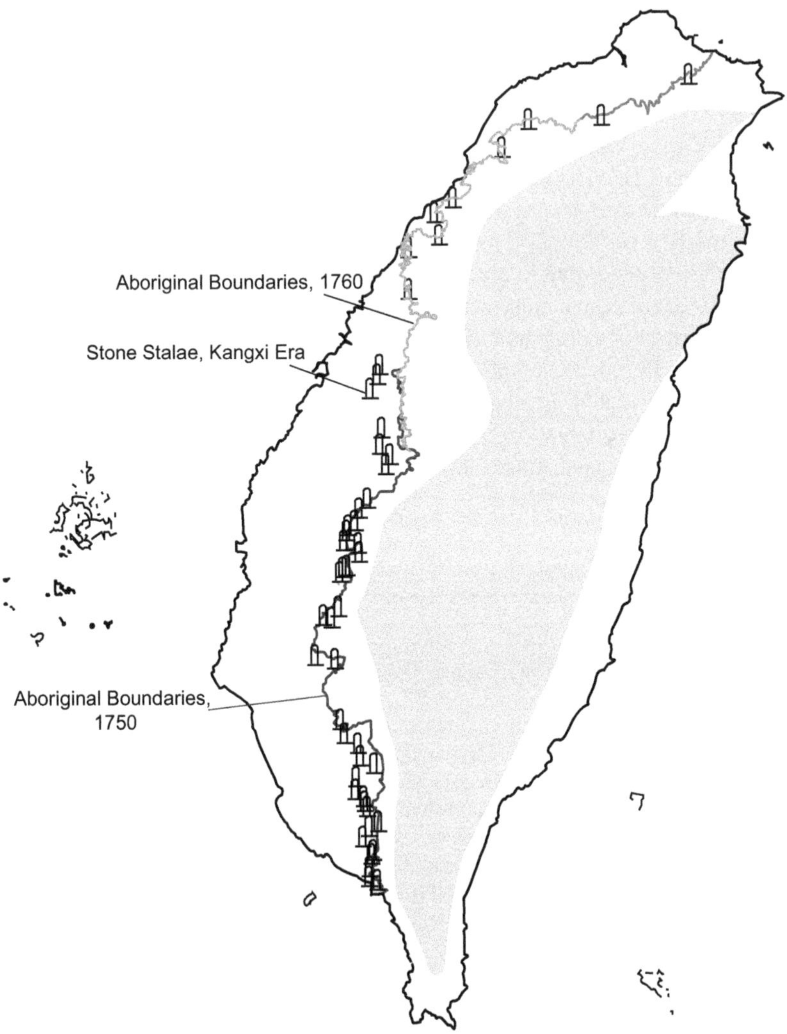

Map 2.2 Aboriginal boundaries

areas – were called “within the boundaries” (*jienei* 界内), and the areas east of the boundaries – the aboriginal territories – were called “beyond the boundaries” (*jiewai* 界外). Han settlers were confined to the western plains and were forbidden to cross the boundaries.[73]

The subsequent Yongzheng government made at least one, and the Qianlong government made at least four, regulations to reiterate the ban against entering the mountain territories (Table 2.2). Because of settler encroachment, the Qianlong government four times, in 1750, 1760, 1784 and 1790 (Qianlong 15, 25, 49 and 55, respectively), investigated the border areas, and clarified and rebuilt boundaries.[74] Each time the boundary lines were marked on maps in colours, being red, blue, purple and green in the respective years. Settlement expansion pushed the boundaries towards the foothills, but the government was determined that boundaries must remain to separate the settlers from the non-acculturated aborigines. The government’s resolve to some extent slowed down the settlers’ advance towards aboriginal territories.

Another type of segregation policy was forbidding inter-marriage between Han Chinese and the non-acculturated aborigines. This was stipulated in a regulation of 1737 (Qianlong 2).[75] The ban had in fact been in place during the Kangxi reign, as an inspecting censor for Taiwan recorded in the late Kangxi era that if Han people secretly married (*daoqu* 盜娶) aboriginal women, the consequence was divorce and punishment according to law.[76] The government was keen to keep the peoples separate to reduce ethnic conflicts and cultural assimilation.

The “quarantine” policy had the effect of slowing down settlement. Migration control served to reduce the influx of settlers from mainland China, and aboriginal boundaries isolated the aboriginal territories and made them unavailable for settlement or land reclamation. The law against inter-marriage to some extent also protected aboriginal land, since marrying aboriginal women was one of the means

Table 2.2 Imperial regulations concerning aboriginal territories (1684–1795)*

Year	*Law*
1722 (KX 61)	Local officials to be punished if settlers crossed the aboriginal boundaries.
1730 (YZ 8)	Those Han settlers who entered the aboriginal territories and squatted aboriginal land or were engaged in other illegal activities to be punished.
1737 (QL 2)	Settlers who entered the aboriginal territories to be punished. Officials to be rewarded or punished according to their achievements in apprehending settlers who entered the aboriginal territories.
1746 (QL 11)	Those who entered the aboriginal territories to reclaim land to be punished.
1754 (QL 19)	Officials to be punished if non-acculturated aborigines killed settlers (caused by settlers entering the aboriginal territories).
1794 (QL 59)	As the 1737 regulation.

* Table created according to *Qing huidian Taiwan shili*. These were all government regulations. Other recommendations that might have been approved by the emperors but not made a regulation are not included.

by which Han settlers obtained their land. Migration control and segregation both had the actual effect, if properly carried out, of restricting colonisation of Taiwan, reducing pressure for land, and thus protecting aborigines from being deprived of their land. They were often seen as the government's anti-colonisation and anti-development stance, and the relaxation on their implementation or the wavering of policies were often seen as a change of direction towards expansion.

The reality was, throughout the Kangxi, Yongzheng and Qianlong reigns, policies to control settlement remained largely consistent and wavered little. The family reunion aspect of the migration policy was tightened or relaxed at times, and the boundaries were redrawn a few times. However, essentially the "quarantine" policies remained in place and were many times reiterated. Even the Yongzheng government, which was said to be "pro-colonisation", was vigorous in regulating illegal crossing and monitoring the integrity of the aboriginal boundaries, which were the essence of "quarantine". Furthermore, despite the practical effects of restricting colonisation, the migration and segregation policies were only a means to achieve the government's ultimate objective. The purpose of migration control was to preclude trouble-makers from settling a land that at one time had harboured pirates and rebels. The rationale of segregation was to minimise contacts between Han settlers and non-acculturated aborigines, and to prevent conflicts or alliance between these two groups.[77] Therefore although the policies might serve to reduce settlement and land reclamation, colonisation was not part of the consideration in the policy design; rather security of the regime and social stability in Taiwan were the prime concerns.

This fundamental policy trend of "quarantine" continued until 1875, when the government formally abolished restrictions on migration. However, in responding to new situations that arose in the late 1700s and early 1800s, the government began to implement or attempt measures to expand administration and settlement. There was an undercurrent for expansion.

An undercurrent for expansion in the years of decline (1796–1874)

In the early 19th century, the Qing Court and officials, although they continued with previous policies of migration control and segregation, subtly changed their attitude towards aboriginal territories.

The overarching policies of "quarantine" were maintained. The Jiaqing government in 1800 and 1801 (Jiaqing 5 and 6) twice made regulations to hold officials responsible for illegal crossing and to require deportation of wanderers who had no family or property in Taiwan. Another regulation prohibiting Han settlers from entering aboriginal territories and interacting with aborigines was made in 1807 (Jiaqing 12).[78] The Daoguang government (1821–1850) approved "twenty guidelines on Taiwan affairs", which included provisions on controlling illegal migration from the mainland and policing the aboriginal boundaries.[79] Therefore there was continuity in policymaking. However a new trend that pushed for changes also emerged at this time.

From the early 1800s, local officials repeatedly pressed for the colonisation of aboriginal territories. The two salient cases were Gamalan and inner Shuishalian. Although the only visible outcome was the incorporation of Gamalan into the realm, the repeated recommendations concerning Gamalan and the debates over inner Shuishalian both evidenced a turn towards a policy of expansion. Such a desire for expansion was provoked by growing threats to Taiwan and coincided with the decline of the empire.

Over the mountains: Gamalan

Being separated from the plains in the west and the Danshui Sub-prefecture at the northwest by mountains, Gamalan was situated "beyond the boundaries". About 60–70 *li* from north to south and about 30 *li* from east to west, it is surrounded by mountains on all but the east side which faces the sea.[80] Traditionally 36 aboriginal villages were located in the area. The Gamalan aborigines started paying tax to the Qing government during the Kangxi reign, which meant that technically they were submitted aborigines, but they remained non-acculturated (hence they were *guihua shengfan*).[81] The Gamalan aborigines continued to live without disturbance until a century later, when the Han Chinese started to settle the area and subsequently government administration was established.

Chinese settlers pioneered the settlement of Gamalan, but not without the local officials' support. In 1787 (Qianlong 52), a Han settler, Wu Sha, attempted to reclaim land in Gamalan, but was defeated by the aborigines.[82] The next year, the then Danshui sub-prefect persuaded the Taiwan prefect, Yang Tingli, to support Wu Sha. Yang recommended that the Fujian governor should subjugate the aborigines and open up Gamalan for settlement, which the governor refused to do for fear of the aborigines' retribution.[83] In 1797 (Jiaqing 2), a new Danshui sub-prefect issued a permit and provided financial support for Wu to recruit people to reclaim the land.[84] As Gamalan was out of bounds, this step was in fact against the regulations. Subsequent efforts by Wu's successors to register reclaimed land on the government register were declined.[85] Clearly local officials favoured land reclamation, but they were bound by government regulations against land settlement in the aboriginal territories. Consequently the officials chose to acquiesce in the reclamation, although they could not expressly recognise it.

In the meantime, local officials continued to press for the extension of the administration to Gamalan. They probably would not have succeeded had it not been for pirate activities in Taiwanese waters. In 1806 (Jiaqing 11), the then Fuzhou garrison general, Saichong'a, reported to the emperor that a notorious pirate Cai Qian was prowling the fertile land of Gamalan. The emperor ordered officials to investigate the situation.[86] The next year the Taiwan Prefect Yang, in an audience with the emperor, recommended opening up Gamalan, reasoning that it was "not advisable to abandon it and leave a cause for trouble in the frontier".[87] Later when another pirate band attempted to occupy Gamalan, Yang again recommended to the Fuzhou General Saichong'a to establish administration and start surveying the land in Gamalan. Saichong'a refused again, but for some reason he soon changed his mind and sent a memorial to the emperor in early 1808 (Jiaqing 13), recommending incorporation of Gamalan.[88]

Saichong'a's memorial was discussed by the central government officials. One official reasoned that "if [Gamalan was] incorporated into the realm, it could not only end pirates' prowling, but also [allow the government to] benefit (*li* 利 'profit') from the land in the overseas frontier".[89] This was the first known incident that acquiring a territory was associated with "profit" in a positive sense in the history of Qing administration of Taiwan. This was not surprising, since after the prosperity and peace of the earlier reigns, the Jiaqing government was under great demographic pressure – the population of China had more than doubled in the previous century to over 300 million, and pressure on land had greatly increased.[90] Southwest and central China were flooded with land hungry migrants. Likewise, the population in Taiwan had also increased dramatically. By 1811 (Jiaqing 16), the settler population had reached 1,944,737, one million up from 943,414 in 1790 (Qianlong 55).[91]

The pressure on land accounted for the local officials' growing desire to expand, but it was the pirate threat that pushed the Court to finally incorporate Gamalan into the realm. In early 1809 (Jiaqing 14), the emperor ordered the then Fujian-Zhejiang Governor-General Alinbao to start working on incorporation of Gamalan. The emperor reasoned that the land was fertile, which made it the object of coveting by robbers and rebels, and for this reason became the source of troubles in Taiwan.[92] The emperor shied away from economic gains, and justified the expansion on security grounds. In 1810 (Jiaqing 15) an imperial decree was issued to formally incorporate Gamalan, and a Gamalan sub-prefect was subsequently appointed.[93]

Thus after over a century's quarantine, for the first time the government expanded administration over the central mountain ranges. Even before the pirate threats became an issue, local officials in Taiwan supported or acquiesced in settlers' reclamation, and attempted to persuade their superiors to incorporate Gamalan. This displayed a new interest in expansion and colonisation, which likely had grown out of the need to ease population pressure in the western plains and to increase tax revenue, as well as reflecting an anxious mentality caused by the events across the empire. Specifically, security threats remained the main driving force for the government action.

In the mountains: inner Shuishalian

Unlike the case of Gamalan, debates on inner Shuishalian resulted in the continuing close-off of the area. Nevertheless the fact that the matter was repeatedly discussed signifies a changing attitude within the government.

Shuishalian refers to the upstream areas of two rivers in central Taiwan – the Wu River and the Zhuoshui River. The historical records sometimes refer to different localities in the wider area.[94] The locality at issue here was the "inner mountain area of Shuishalian" (*Shuishalian neishan* 水沙連内山).[95] Traditionally 24 aboriginal villages lived in this locality, and six of them occupied the basin area, which was flat and fertile. It was this basin that was the subject of an incident during the

Jiaqing reign, and which was the cause of much debate in 1823, 1841 and 1846 (Daoguang 3, 21 and 26).

Initial reclamation and government "quarantine"

Like Gamalan, inner Shuishalian was located beyond the aboriginal boundaries, and the land was fertile. The aborigines had submitted themselves to the Qing government, some villages submitting as early as 1693 (Kangxi 32).[96] As the area was located among the mountains, the people remained non-acculturated aborigines.

Settlers coveted this fertile land and had tried to reclaim it even though it was clearly a forbidden area. In 1814 (Jiaqing 19), some settlers had obtained land reclamation permits through fabricating the aborigines' request to lease the land to settlers. The settlers subsequently reclaimed over 1,200 *jia* of land in inner Shuishalian, causing serious armed conflicts with the aborigines.[97] As a result, in 1816 (Jiaqing 21) the government sent troops to destroy the settler strongholds, expelled the settlers and erected stelae with inscribed decrees forbidding reclamation of the land by Chinese settlers.[98]

The contrast between the Jiaqing government's approaches towards Gamalan and inner Shuishalian demonstrates the weight of security on government decision-making, since Gamalan was faced with pirate threats while inner Shuishalian was not. Furthermore, the settler leaders in inner Shuishalian ruthlessly killed many aborigines and caused a great deal of bloodshed. While the settlement of Gamalan also met aboriginal resistance, the settlers' leader, Wu Sha, was more prudent and was said to have helped the aborigines to defeat outside intrusions and to have saved the aborigines' lives when an epidemic struck.[99] Thus the lack of external threat and the presence of settler-aborigine conflicts determined the different outcome for Shuishalian under the Jiaqing government.

Attempts to open up for settlement

The 1816 government quarantine did not put the matter to rest and officials of the Daoguang government several times recommended opening up inner Shuishalian for settlement, the first time being in 1823 (Daoguang 3) by the aboriginal affairs sub-prefect for the Northern Circuit, Deng Chuan'an, whose chief responsibility was, ironically, to protect aborigines from settlers' advancement. After a visit to inner Shuishalian, Deng found that the land could be developed into thousands of *qing* 頃 of good farms,[100] but the aborigines were not good at farming, not even the plains aborigines who had migrated there.[101] Deng lamented that the land was situated beyond the aboriginal boundaries, and recommended to his superiors to open up Shuishalian.[102] The Fujian governor was interested, but then Gamalan Sub-prefect Yao Ying discouraged them, citing administrative costs issues and the unwillingness of the aborigines.[103]

The same issue was brought up again nearly two decades later, but this time the consideration extended to all land that could be and had yet to be reclaimed in Taiwan. In 1841 (Daoguang 21), the Daoguang emperor, at the recommendation of a central government official, decreed that the Fujian-Zhejiang governor-general investigate unreclaimed land in Taiwan with the objective of increasing revenue to help with maritime defence.[104] The wider context of this was the decline of the empire, as the Daoguang Court was faced with a silver reserve drain, eroding army strength and weakening government control.[105] Yet the immediate cause for concern was the Opium War between China and Britain, which commenced in 1840, highlighting the need for maritime defence and triggering the search for more revenue.

The plan was again shelved after the revenue and cost were weighed, and still the central consideration was security. The former Gamalan sub-prefect, Yao Ying, was by then the Taiwan circuit intendant, the highest ranking official based in Taiwan. In his letter to the governor-general, Yao discussed unreclaimed land in the whole of Taiwan, including inner Shuishalian and the eastern coast.[106] Yao reasoned that Shuishalian was not by the coast, and therefore there was little risk of foreign possession of it. Yao then weighed up the risk of foreign possession of eastern coastal areas and the costs to open up those areas for settlement. To open up the areas would involve either sending troops to subjugate the aborigines or spending money and material to appease them, and both options were costly. Yao pointed out that in the administration of Taiwan costs had always been larger than revenue (which fact itself was an indication that security consideration outweighed economic gains), and that it was false to hope that allowing land reclamation could raise revenue for maritime defence. Since there was no imminent threat, and given the costs that would be involved, the matter was again put to rest.[107] The deciding was, yet again, security, or the lack of it.

Population and revenue pressure continued to mount, and within a few years local officials had renewed their interest to colonise inner Shuishalian. In 1846 (Daoguang 26), a new Fujian-Zhejiang governor-general, Liu Yunke, argued that opening up inner Shuishalian would eliminate five evils and bring five benefits, the evils being causes to social instability, and the benefits being increased revenue and increased social stability.[108] Liu was careful to centre his argument on social order, but central government officials were conservative and were not convinced. The emperor ordered Liu to travel to Shuishalian and investigate the situation in person, which Liu did, before furnishing a detailed report about the aborigines and their land, and urged the Court to open up the land for settlement.[109]

The central government in the end refused to open up the area. As in the 1841 discussion, it was thought that the administrative cost would be significantly higher than the revenue, and because foreign occupation of that area was unlikely. Traditionalists also argued that the benefits that might come with land reclamation would become a cause of other trouble, especially conflicts and foreign coveting, and that the best way was to observe the precedents established since the Qianlong era.[110] The cost of colonisation was seen as unnecessary when there was no imminent security risk, and was to be avoided if there were perceived conflicts.

That was the final decision on inner Shuishalian, although local officials still tried to find opportunities to open up the land. In 1848 (Daoguang 28), a new Taiwan circuit intendant, upon arriving at the post, recommended establishing aboriginal colonies (*fantun* 番屯) in inner Shuishalian. An aboriginal colony was a model under which the aborigines were organised in units and allocated land, which they could lease to the settlers.[111] The suggestion for Shuishalian was a way to circumvent the central government decision and to have inner Shuishalian land reclaimed.[112] No response to this suggestion is recorded.[113]

Thus, the Qing government and officials gave serious consideration to colonising the aboriginal territories, and gave up the plan after considering the low risks of foreign occupation and the cost of administration. The major consideration was once again security. Revenue and costs were part of the calculation, but they were used as arguments against colonisation, the rationale being that there was no need to spend more money if security was not an issue.

Changes and continuity

The cases of Gamalan and inner Shuishalian manifested an emerging desire for expansion in the early 1800s. During the first century of Qing administration of Taiwan, Lan Dingyuan of the early Yongzheng years was the only "pro-colonist" who advocated expanding government control and land settlement. Since the early 1800s, there appeared to be an undercurrent of support for expansion, as successive government officials envisaged or argued for opening up the aboriginal territories and extending government control to the whole island. Among such officials were the circuit intendant, who was the highest official stationed in Taiwan, and the aboriginal affairs sub-prefect, who was supposed to restrict settlement and protect the aborigines.

Yao Ying, the Gamalan sub-prefect (1821) and later Taiwan circuit intendant (1838–1842), who several times had argued against opening up Shuishalian, expected that not only inner Shuishalian, but also the whole eastern territories, would be incorporated into the empire within the next hundred years.[114] Yao preferred a gradual strategy, which was to acquiesce in Han settlement and for the government to reap the benefits when the time was right. Others, however, were more radical than Yao. In 1867 (Tongzhi 6), an official in Fujian argued that following the incorporation of Gamalan the government should extend control over inner Shuishalian, and eventually over the remaining portion of the aboriginal territories.[115] This official directly recommended that "the back of the mountains [the aboriginal territories] should be opened, and the aborigines should be subjugated".[116] A long-term Taiwan official, Ding Yuejian, who was posted to Taiwan under the successive Daoguang, Xianfeng and Tongzhi governments, compiled a book to advise on "administration of Taiwan" after concluding his term as the Taiwan circuit intendant (1864–1865).[117] The collection started with Lan Dingyuan's writings, proceeded with documents and writings on Gamalan and Shuishalian, and was followed by discussions on opening up aboriginal territories and defence against foreigners. The book illustrates the strategic thinking of some Qing officials of the early to mid-19th century, and their desire for expansion. Similarly, the Danshui Sub-prefecture Gazetteer, compiled in 1871 under the leadership of the sub-prefect, recommended opening up the mountains and subjugating the aborigines as the option for the empire.[118] Therefore after the incorporation of Gamalan, colonisation of the remaining aboriginal territories was a topic of continuing discussion, and strategic thinking about "opening the mountains and subjugating the aborigines" had already emerged at least a decade before 1874 and continued to be advanced by officials. It had not adopted simply because there was not significant security issue to prompt the government to act.

This undercurrent for expansion was part of the reaction of the literati and officials concerning the dynastic decline and foreign intervention. Across the empire literati searched for ways to reform and revive the regime, and produced voluminous work on statecraft. Among them was a close study of Europe, *Haiguo tuzhi* (海國圖志 Illustrated Gazetteer of the Maritime Nations, meaning the European countries), published in 1844.[119] In subsequent years the study of the West intensified, and a Translation Bureau (*Tongwenguan* 同文館) was established to study European science and politics.[120] The rise of the European nations would have provided some valuable lessons to ponder on, if not copied outright.

At a time of imminent outside threats, the security issue provoked the government to extend control over the aboriginal territories as a means to resist threats, and to find ways of raising revenue to fund defence. There were different opinions in officialdom, and in the end the traditionalists won the day. The fact that Gamalan was incorporated, while inner Shuishalian or other aboriginal territories were not, was because Gamalan faced direct pirate threats, while the government did not perceive any imminent security risks in the other areas. Therefore the decisions about expansion and colonisation during this transitional period differed according to the changing situations, while the primary consideration of security continued to be the overarching principle. The arguments for expansion were adopted in 1874 when the threats against Taiwan materialised.

Promoting expansion in reaction to crises (1875–1895)

Although 1875 has been seen as the turning point of Qing policies in Taiwan, in fact there were two stages of colonisation efforts, both of which were in response to foreign threats. The first one commenced in 1874 after the Japanese invasion of southern Taiwan, and the second in 1885 after French occupation of Jilong in northern Taiwan. Both efforts diminished within a few years after the foreign threats subsided, reflecting the usual Qing pattern of expansion only for security reasons.

Reaction to Japanese threat (1874)

In 1874 (Tongzhi 13), Japan invaded the aboriginal territory in southern Taiwan. This is known as the Mudanshe Incident (*Mudanshe shijian* 牡丹社事件). For over six months Japanese soldiers occupied southern Taiwan, which, Japan argued, was not part of the Qing Empire. The background to this incident and the arguments of both parties is discussed in Chapter 6. Here it needs only be pointed out that the incident resulted in the Qing Court paying an indemnity to Japan in return for the Japanese army's withdrawal from Taiwan. The Qing Court keenly realised that Taiwan as a whole could be lost if any part of it was not brought under government control, and losing Taiwan meant exposing the coastal provinces to foreign threats.

The imperial commissioner to Taiwan (*Qinchai Taiwan shiwu dachen* 欽差臺灣事務大臣), Shen Baozhen, who also happened to be the director of the Fuzhou Arsenal (*Fuzhou zaochuanchang* 福州造船廠) and an important figure in the late Qing self-strengthening movement, argued for colonisation of the aboriginal territories. Shen argued that "the reason that Taiwan is being coveted by [Japan] is that the land is too empty; the land is empty because the people are few",[121] and recommended to "open the mountains and subjugate the aborigines" and populate the aboriginal territories with Chinese settlers.[122] Following Shen's recommendation, administration in Taiwan was expanded, and campaigns to colonise the aboriginal territories were launched.

The administrative structure was adjusted to strengthen control. A new prefecture, Taipei Prefecture, was created. The Gamalan Sub-prefecture was raised to the status of county, and renamed Yilan. Over the territory of Danshui Sub-prefecture two new counties, Danshui and Xinzhu, were established. A new county at the far south, Hengchun, was created. Further, the two aboriginal sub-prefects, formerly based in Taiwan County and Danshui Sub-prefecture, respectively, were moved to the aboriginal territories of inner Shuishalian (Puli) and eastern Taiwan (Beinan), the new focus points for colonisation (see Table 2.3 and Map 2.1). Formal administration was thus extended to the inner mountains, east of the mountain ranges and the far south of the island.

The "opening the mountains and subjugating the aborigines" campaigns started in 1874 and continued into the early Guangxu reign. "Opening the mountains" included building roads across the mountains to make the region accessible, and "subjugating the aborigines" meant bringing the mountain aborigines into formal submission to the Qing regime. In 1874 (Tongzhi 13) and 1875 (Guangxu 1), troops were sent to build roads across the mountains, connecting the area "at the back of the mountains" (*houshan* 後山, meaning the east) to that "in the front of the mountains" (*qianshan* 前山, meaning the west). There were three major road-building projects: in the north, the middle and the south of the island, respectively. Five roads cut through the mountain ranges, totalling nearly 900 *li*.[123] The government tried to subjugate aborigines wherever the road-building troops advanced to. In many cases aborigines resisted government troops, and armed conflicts occurred frequently.[124]

Another important aspect of "opening" was the opening of Taiwan for Chinese settlement. In the first year of the Guangxu reign (1875), the emperor proclaimed that the two-century-old ban on crossing the Taiwan Strait was lifted, with the objective of encouraging settlement:[125]

> After the whole island of Taiwan, Fujian, entered the realm, because the aboriginal villages at the back of the mountains had different customs, [the government] has forbidden the mainland people from migrating to Taiwan and entering the aboriginal territories (*fanjing* 番境), so as to prevent trouble. Now

Table 2.3 Changes of local administration in Taiwan

Year	*Prefecture*	*County*	*Sub-prefecture*	*Sub-prefect (position only)*
1684 (KX 23)	Taiwan	Taiwan Fengshan Zhuluo		
1723 (YZ 1)		+Zhanghua	+Danshui	
1812 (JQ 17)			+Gamalan	
1875 (GX 1)	Taiwan	Taiwan Fengshan Jiayi (Zhuluo) Zhanghua +Hengchun		Aboriginal Affairs; established in 1766 but moved to the aboriginal territories of: – Beinan – Puli
	+Taipei	Xinzhu (formerly Danshui Sub-Prefecture) Yilan (Formerly Gamalan Sub-Prefecture) +Danshui		
1887 (GX 13) Taiwan Province	Tainan (formerly Taiwan)	Anping (formerly Taiwan) Fengshan Jiayi Hengchun		
	+Taiwan	Zhanghua +Taiwan +Yunlin +Miaoli	Puli (1889)	
	Taipei	Danshui Xinzhu Yilan	+Jilong (1889) +Nanya (1895)	
	+Taidong (department)			

> Shen Baozhen and other officials have opened up the territories at the back of the mountains, and the vacant land needs to be reclaimed urgently. All rules should be changed as situations change. All previous regulations that forbid people from migrating to Taiwan are now abolished. The control on sale of iron and bamboos are loosened.[126] This is to encourage migration and settlement.

As typical of the Qing's law-making, the decree was less than precise, since it did not explicitly abolish regulations that forbade Han settlers from entering the aboriginal territories. This was only implied in the decree, given that the ultimate goal was to have people settle in the aboriginal territories and reclaim the land.

Shen Baozhen was appointed to posts unrelated to Taiwan in 1875, before much progress in Taiwan was made. The Fujian Governor Ding Richang, who was also committed to promoting settlement in the aboriginal territories, also left the post shortly after issuing "21 guidelines for subjugating the aborigines and opening the mountains" in 1877 (Guangxu 3).[127] Ding's guidelines were implemented for a short time, as the government established agencies in coastal cities in the mainland and in Hong Kong to recruit settlers to Taiwan; arranged for transportation of the recruits to Taiwan; provided them with seeds, draft oxen and other tools, plus a living allowance for one year; and gave a three-year tax grace period for land reclaimed.[128] Yet very soon the opening and subjugating campaigns virtually ceased.

The colonisation efforts in the late Tongzhi and early Guangxu years were provoked by the Japanese challenge, with the clear purpose of avoiding any similar incidents and strengthening the Qing government's ability to defend its territory. Shen Baozhen made it clear that "our strategies to the areas at the back of the mountains are for preventing troubles, not for gaining profits".[129] He went on to state that:[130]

> everyone knows that today we open the mountains to subjugate the aborigines, but not everyone knows that subjugating the aborigines is for maritime defence; everyone knows that preparing for maritime defence is crucial to the safety of Taiwan, but not everyone knows that it is crucial to the whole situation of the south and north seas.

Security being the paramount consideration, it is not surprising that when the foreign threats appeared to have passed, government efforts relaxed. It took another crisis to revive government efforts to promote settlement in Taiwan.

Reaction to the Sino-French War (1885)

The same scenario repeated after another foreign threat occurred a decade later.

In 1883 the Sino-French War broke out, and in 1884 the French army occupied Jilong in northern Taiwan and threatened Taipei.[131] Subsequent to the cease-fire agreement and the withdrawal of the French army from Taiwan in 1885, Liu Mingchuan, the Taiwan defence commissioner (*Taiwan fangwu dachen* 臺灣防務大臣) and Fujian governor, renewed the efforts to "expand territory and encourage reclamation" (*kuojiang zhaoken* 扩疆招垦) in the aboriginal territories. The administrative system was further expanded and strengthened.

Administering Taiwan became the sole focus of the Fujian governor in 1885 (Guangxu 11), while the administration of the Fujian Province was entrusted to the governor-general. Taiwan finally became a separate province in 1887 (Guangxu 13). The administrative units were reorganised and local administration was further expanded in 1888 (Guangxu 14). Another prefecture in the middle of the western plains (Taiwan Prefecture; the former Taiwan Prefecture was renamed Tainan) and three new counties (Taiwan, Yunlin and Miaoli) were established through subdividing the existing administrative units. The eastern part of Taiwan, which was supervised by the Beinan sub-prefect, was governed through a newly created Taidong Department (*Taidong zhou* 臺東州 "eastern Taiwan department"), which worked directly under the provincial government. In the next few years, the government continued to make adjustments to the administrative structure, adding the Sub-prefectures of Puli (the base of the former aboriginal affairs sub-prefect), Jilong (far north) and Nanya (south of Danshui). By that time, Taiwan had changed from a prefecture with three counties at the beginning of the annexation to a province with three prefectures, 11 counties, one department and three sub-prefectures (see Table 2.3 and Map 2.1).

To facilitate the pacification and reclamation work, a Taiwan Pacification and Reclamation Head Office (*Taiwan fuken zongju* 臺灣撫墾總局) was established, heading eight pacification and reclamation bureaus. Seven of the eight bureaus were located in the aboriginal territories: four in eastern Taiwan, two in Puli (inner Shuishalian) and one in the far south. The only one in the west was also close to the mountain areas. In total 18 branches at various crucial spots operated under the eight bureaus.[132] By 1887 (Guangxu 3), nearly 500 aboriginal villages with about 90,000 aborigines had formally submitted, which would enable reclamation of tens of thousands of *jia* of land.[133] Within a few years this number had increased to over 800 villages with 148,479 aborigines.[134] The colonisation effort was at its strongest in the Qing period, and the number of villages and aborigines who submitted themselves to the Qing authority appeared impressive.

Yet criticisms soon followed and problems surfaced. The government usually used materials to induce the aborigines into submission, and paid village heads monthly allowances once the aboriginal communities had submitted. The cost was high, but the government was not always able to exercise effective control over the aborigines. Furthermore, after years of promotion and facilitation, the progress of land reclamation was slow. By 1891, only 2,255 *jia* of land was reclaimed and registered in eastern Taiwan, and the situation was not much better in southern Taiwan.[135] Many reasons were attributed by researchers for this failure, such as that most labourers at that time were attracted to Southeast Asia and few went to Taiwan, that the few settlers were intimidated or attacked by aborigines, that the areas to be settled were too remote, or that the climate was harsh and few settlers survived.[136]

The reality was that, as the security threats seemed to have subsided, the calculation of revenue and costs re-surfaced. Governor Liu was criticised for the high cost of and little gain from the opening and subjugating activities. Liu resigned in 1891 (Guangxu 17), and colonisation efforts ceased. Although administrative units expanded, the government could not maintain effective control over the non-acculturated aborigines, and much of the reclaimed land returned to "waste". It was likely that even without the cession of Taiwan to Japan in 1895, the Qing government would not have made much progress in colonising the aboriginal territories.

The post-1874 development was the extension of the self-strengthening movement across the empire. It again shows that security was the single most important factor that drove the government to expand. Revenue and control costs were cited to dissuade or criticise expansion when security threats subsided.

Taiwan policies and the Qing tradition

Over the two centuries of Qing administration in Taiwan, the underlying policy rationale was consistently security, whether the policy was to control or promote settlement. When the central government was strong, it tightly restricted colonisation to reduce social conflicts. When the government grew weak and faced security threats, it tried to defend the realm through expansion. The more imminent the external threats were, the more aggressive the colonisation efforts became. When threats diminished, the desire to expand disappeared and the focus became that of avoiding costs. The three stages, from controlling settlement to tentative expansion and then to promoting settlement, showed a clear correlation to the dynastic trend of prosperity, decline and crises.

The methods the government adopted for Taiwan had parallels in other Qing frontiers, and the policy rationale had its root in the Chinese tradition of governance. "Quarantine" was the usual approach used by the Qing government in the frontiers to preserve social order and security, and the usual methods of quarantine were migration control and segregation of peoples. The same happened in Taiwan as in other frontiers, including Manchuria, Mongolia, Xinjiang and southwest China. In other words, Taiwan was not unique, but typical.

Migration control tried to stop movement of people and prevent Chinese settlement, as well as to screen migrants to prevent perceived trouble-makers from going to the frontier areas. There were parallels to the migration control in other Qing frontiers. Manchuria was closed to settlement, mainly because of its status as the Qing ruler's native place.[137] Mongolia was also closed off from settlement until the late 1800s. Despite the government's encouragement of land settlement in Xinjiang and the southwest frontier, regulations imposed restrictions on people's movement to these areas similar to those for Taiwan.[138]

The aboriginal boundary in Taiwan was partly an inheritance from the Zheng regime, which had built boundaries to separate the settlement areas from the aboriginal territories, and partly an extension of the Qing's own practice. In 1623 Nurhaci implemented policies to segregate the Han from the Manchus within his realm after serious conflicts between the two peoples had occurred.[139] This tradition had continued to be used to ensure peaceful relations between different ethnic groups.[140] In Xinjiang, the government segregated different ethnic groups, containing them in Manchu quarters, Han quarters and Hui (Muslim) quarters, respectively.[141] Although the Qing encouraged land settlement in Xinjiang after the conquest in 1759, the Hui areas were not opened for settlement.[142] In the southwest frontier of Yunnan, there was a division of "inner" and "outer" territories, the outer territories including those that were occupied by "barbarian subjects", who were similar to the non-acculturated aborigines in Taiwan.[143] In the Miao area in the Hunan and Guizhou provinces (southwest China), Han settlers were banned from entering into Miao land.[144] The Qing also built willow palisades to exclude Manchuria from Han settlement and encroachment. Therefore it was the Qing's own tradition of segregating different ethnic groups which sustained the policy for nearly 200 years.

There were also similar policies against inter-marriage between Han Chinese and minority ethnic groups such as the Manchus, the Hui in Xinjiang and the Miao in the southwest.[145] In fact regulations forbidding inter-marriage and entrance to Taiwan's mountain aboriginal territories specifically cited the Miao regulations as precedents.[146] This again shows the consistency of Qing policies in frontier regions.

At times when external threats overshadowed the potential risk of internal conflicts, it was also a Qing pattern to populate frontiers with settlers in order to strengthen border defence. This occurred at different times, but mostly during the late Qing period when the empire was under increasing foreign threats from various directions. In the early Qing period, the government had waged wars against the Zunghars in central Asia for decades, and finally pacified the area in 1759.[147] To consolidate government control, the Qing Court encouraged and organised settlements in the area.[148] In the mid-19th century, the Qing government faced serious threats from foreign states such as Russia, France and subsequently Japan. In particular northeastern Manchuria was lost to Russia in 1860. The northern frontier of the Qing Empire, from Manchuria to Xinjiang, was opened to Russian influence.[149] In response the government opened Mongolia and Manchuria for Chinese settlement in the late 1800s, the purpose being to "populate the frontier with settlers to strengthen frontier defence" (*yimin shibian* 移民實邊).[150] The Qing took exactly the same approach when encouraging Chinese settlement in Taiwan, especially eastern Taiwan, after 1874.

Overall, Qing policies in Taiwan were consistent with those in other frontiers, although the exact timing was not always the same. The variations in timing can be explained by the different local situations. No matter whether quarantine or colonisation, the purpose was always to maintain social stability and security. It has been said that "there was nothing that the [Qing] wanted from [inner Asia] but peace".[151] The same could be said of Taiwan, or any other frontiers of the Qing.

Putting the policies into their historical context, it is clear that colonisation corresponded with the perception of external threats. When there was no external threat, the Court focused on preventing internal conflicts, and preserved the status quo of the conquered land through "quarantine" policies. When the dynasty started to decline and faced external threats, the minds of officials and literati were motivated to search for means to strengthen and defend the empire, expansion being one of the means. When crisis struck, the government quickly acted to guard frontier areas against foreign invasion. The typical way of guarding frontiers was to fill them with people, that is, settlers from the heartland. Thus the weaker the empire grew, the more aggressive it was in promoting settlement.

The focus on security and social order was largely because of the Chinese tradition on governance. Two principles of Confucian legal thought were monarchism (*junzhu zhuyi* 君主主義) and people-centredness (*min benwei* 民本位).[152] The Confucian tradition saw the monarch as a boat and the people as water, and the most important task of statecraft was to keep the boat afloat; that is, to preserve the monarchy.[153] Therefore the principle of monarchism in essence put the monarch in the centre of the constitutional framework, and the principle of people-centredness was a way to preserve the rule by the imperial house. The governing of the empire revolved around ensuring the ruling authority of the monarch over the masses. The Manchu house as a conquest elite and minority ruler was particularly mindful of the need to maintain the security of their rule. Therefore security was placed in a paramount position in the Qing Court's decision-making regarding the periphery, and hence its security-paramount approach towards the colonisation of Taiwan.

Furthermore, in Chinese tradition, the purpose of managing peripheries was to "defend against enemies", since "to expand the territory and reclaim the land to extract [resources] was not what a sage king would do", as was aptly summarised by a Taiwan official.[154] Therefore expansion was a means to defend the borders, and the emperors and officials mostly shied away from extracting resources or revenue from the land, as the Qianlong emperor repeatedly warned against. This tradition was deep rooted, yet in the 19th century when the Qing was exposed to Western threats and tried to "self-strengthen", the Western social and political thoughts, as well as Western science and technology, also played a part in shaping the thinking of officials and literati.

Notes

1 Shepherd is the first to use the term "quarantine" to describe the Qing's restriction of migration to Taiwan and forbiddance of settlement in the mountain areas, and to contrast it with "colonisation". The term is used throughout in John Robert Shepherd *Statecraft and Political Economy on the Taiwan Frontier, 1600–1800* (Stanford University Press, Stanford, 1993). For example, the title of Part II is "Ch'ing Quarantine Policies and the Spread of Han Settlement".

2 *Kaishan fufan* is usually translated as "open the mountains and pacify the aborigines", but "pacify" implies the use of military force (which corresponds to the Chinese word *jiao* 剿, meaning to send armed forces to suppress an opposing force), while the word *fu* means to bring to surrender, usually by offering rewards. Since the Qing government used both *fu* and *jiao* to bring the aborigines under control, "subjugate" seems to be the more appropriate term to describe the campaigns.

3 R Kent Guy "Who Were the Manchus? A Review Essay" (2002) 61(1) *Journal of Asian Studies* 151, at 151.

4 Gentraude Roth Li "State Building Before 1644" in Willard J Peterson (ed) *The Cambridge History of China Volume 9: The Ch'ing Dynasty to 1800 Part One* (Cambridge University Press, Cambridge, 2002), at 10.

5 At 10 and 21. Nicola Di Cosmo "The Extension of Ch'ing Rule Over Mongolia, Sinkiang, and Tibet, 1636–1800" in Willard J Peterson (ed) *The Cambridge History of China Volume 9: The Ch'ing Dynasty to 1800 Part Two* (Cambridge University Press, Cambridge, 2016) 111, at 112, notes that only one of the three major Jurchen groups was called *yeren*.

6 Li, ibid, at 11–51.On Nurhaci, see also Frederick W Mote *Imperial China 900–1800* (Harvard University Press, Cambridge (MA), 1999), at 786–790.

7 Li, ibid, at 37.

8 At 27.

9 At 35 and 60–61. Also see Zhang Jinfan *Qingchao fazhishi* [Legal History of the Qing Dynasty] (Zhonghua shuju, Beijing, 1998), at 22.

10 See Mote, above n 6, at 801–810.

11 See Jerry Dennerline "The Shun-chih Reign" in Peterson (ed), above n 4, at 83–97; Mote, ibid, at 821–824.

12 The Three Feudatories were three highly autonomous Han generals who were rewarded with large domains for their service during the course of Qing conquest.
13 See Jonathan D Spence "The K'ang-hsi Reign" in Peterson (ed), above n 4, at 136–156.
14 See Peter C Perdue *China Marches West: The Qing Conquest of Central Eurasia* (Harvard University Press, Cambridge (MA), 2005) for an analysis of Qing expansion in the northwestern territories.
15 See William T Rowe *China's Last Empire: The Great Qing* (Belknap Press of Harvard University Press, Cambridge (MA), 2009), ch 6 "Crises" in general.
16 At 156 and 185.
17 See John K Fairbank (ed) *The Cambridge History of China Volume 10: Late Ch'ing 1800–1911 Part One* (Cambridge University Press, Cambridge, 1978), in particular ch 3, Susan Mann Jones and Philip A Kuhn "Dynastic Decline and the Roots of Rebellion" 107–162; and ch 5, John K Fairbank "The Creation of the Treaty System" 213–263.
18 See Rowe, above n 15, ch 8 "Restoration".
19 Mark C Elliott *The Manchu Way: The Eight Banners and Ethnic Identity in Late Imperial China* (Stanford University Press, Stanford, 2001), at 13.
20 William T Rowe "Social Stability and Social Change" in Peterson (ed), above n 4, at 562.
21 Xiao Yishan *Qingdai tongshi* [Comprehensive History of the Qing Dynasty] (Shangwu, Taipei, 1963), at 503, 525, 547–558. *Lifanyuan* has traditionally been translated as "the Court of Colonial Affairs". In fact the term itself does not contain the meaning of "colonial", and Di Cosmo, above n 5, at 123–124, argues that "the Board for Governing Outer Territories" is a more appropriate translation.
22 See Dorothea Heuschert "Legal Pluralism in the Qing Empire: Manchu Legislation for the Mongols" (1998) 20 *International History Review* 310–324; Tian Huan "Governing Imperial Border: Insights From the Study of the Implementation of Law in Qing Xinjiang" (PhD diss, Columbia University, 2012).
23 Charles O Hucker *A Dictionary of Official Titles in Imperial China* (Stanford University Press, Stanford, 1985) translates *hubu* as Ministry of Revenue. This is the widely accepted translation. However, although tax and revenues were the major function of the Ministry, given that the Ministry also regulated other household matters, and the character *hu* 戶 means household, it is felt that "Ministry of Households" is more appropriate.
24 See Xiao, above n 21, for a comprehensive examination of the Qing decision-making bodies and administrative departments.
25 At 524–542. Also see R Kent Guy *Qing Governors and Their Provinces: The Evolution of Territorial Administration in China, 1644–1796* (University of Washington Press, Seattle, 2010).
26 *Qing Gaozong shilu xuanji* [Selected Veritable Records of the Qianlong Emperor] (TWWX 186), at 613 ("*Gaozong shilu*"). See Lian Heng *Taiwan tongshi* [A Comprehensive History of Taiwan, 1918] (TWWX 128), at 145–150 and 337 for the civil and military hierarchy and positions in Taiwan.
27 See H Patrick Glenn *Legal Traditions of the World: Sustainable Diversity in Law* (5th ed, Oxford University Press, Oxford, 2014), ch 9, in particular at 326–339 for a discussion of Confucian ways and *li*.
28 At 326–328; Yang Jingfan et al *Zhongguo falü sixiangshi jianbian* [A Brief History of Chinese Legal Thoughts] (Guangxi shifan daxue, Guilin, 1988), at 7–8; Derk Bodde and Clarence Morris *Law in Imperial China: Exemplified by 190 Ch'ing Dynasty Cases* (Harvard University Press, Cambridge (MA), 1967), at 5.
29 Glenn, above n 27, at 322; Hyung I Kim *Fundamental Legal Concepts of China and the West: A Comparative Study* (Kennikat Press, New York, 1981), at 117.
30 See Zhang, above n 9, at 165–168.
31 At 170.

32 At 165–181.

33 John K Fairbank and Ssu-yu Teng "On the Types and Uses of Ch'ing Documents" (1940) 5 *Harvard Journal of Asiatic Studies* 1–71 discusses the process of dealing with official memorials and recommendations in the central government.

34 Yang et al, above n 28, at 24.

35 See the Kangxi emperor's comments in *Qing Shengzu shilu xuanji* [Selected Veritable Records of the Kangxi Emperor] (TWWX 165), at 129 ("*Shengzu shilu*"), "臺灣屬海外地方, 因從未向化, 肆行騷擾, 濱海居民迄無寧日, 故興師進繳".

36 Lian, above n 26, at 59.

37 See Shi Lang's memorial to the emperor, "Gongchen Taiwan qiliu shu" [Some Humble Opinions on Whether to Retain or Abandon Taiwan] in Shi Lang *Jinghai jishi* [Records of Pacifying the Seas] (TWWX 13), at 60–61.

38 *Shengzu shilu*, above n 35, at 131.

39 At 165.

40 Huang Shujing *Taihai shichalu* [Records of a Tour on Duty Over the Taiwan Seas, cir 1722] (TWWX 4), at 134.

41 "臺灣地方多開田地，多聚人民，不過目前之計而已。將來福建無窮之害，俱從此生". See the Kangxi emperor's rescript in Taiwan Shiliao Jicheng Bianji Weiyuanhui *Ming Qing Taiwan dang'an huibian* [Collection of Historic Documents Concerning Taiwan During the Ming and Qing Dynasties] (Yuanliu, Taipei, 2004–2009), vol 9, at 308–309 ("*Ming Qing dang'an*").

42 For example, see Shepherd, above n 1, at 195 and 236. Another reason for seeing the Yongzheng government as pro-colonisation is because of its policies on land reclamation, but this point will be discussed in Chapter 3.

43 Zhou Zhongxuan *Zhuluo xianzhi* [Gazetteer of Zhuluo County, 1717] (TWWX141), at 5.

44 Ibid, at 6; Chen Wenda *Fengshan xianzhi* [Gazetteer of Fengshan County, 1719] (TWWX 124), at 15.

45 Zhou, above n 43, at 50.

46 *Qing Shizong shilu xuanji* [Selected Veritable Records of the Yongzheng Emperor] (TWWX167), at 3–4 ("*Shizong shilu*").

47 See Lan Dingyuan *Ping Tai jilüe* [Brief Accounts of the Pacification of Taiwan, 1723] (TWWX 14), in particular at 30–32, 56 and 69; Lan Dingyuan *Dongzheng ji* [Collection of Records of the Eastern Expedition, 1732] (TWWX 12), in particular at 60 and 87.

48 For example, Shepherd, above n 1, at 151 and 236.

49 "不應聽奸匪之浮言，圖目前之微利，遽議召[招]墾；或致將來別生事端，甚有關係。" *Gaozong shilu*, above n 26, at 39.

50 In 1729, the Yongzheng government decided to transfer 49,000 *shi* of grains from Taiwan to Fujian, and this was made a precedent to be followed in later years. See *Shizong shilu*, above n 46, at 28. Also see John Robert Shepherd "Taiwan Prefecture in the Eighteenth Century" in Peterson (ed), above n 5, at 101–102.

51 *Gaozong shilu*, above n 26, at 401–402.

52 For example, ibid, at 38.

53 There are a few possible translations for *shufan* and *shengfan*, and the most commonly used translations are "cooked aborigines" and "raw aborigines", respectively. See Magnus Fiskesjö "On the 'Raw' and the 'Cooked' Barbarians of Imperial China" (1999) 1 *Inner Asia* 139 for a discussion of the use of "raw" and "cooked". In this book, *shufan* is referred to as "acculturated aborigines", and *shengfan* "non-acculturated aborigines".

54 Emma Jinhua Teng *Taiwan's Imagined Geography: Chinese Colonial Travel Writing and Pictures, 1683–1895* (Harvard University Asia Centre, Cambridge (MA), 2004), at 123, explains it this way: "*Sheng* and *shu* express a host of binary concepts, not only raw and cooked, but also unripe and ripe, unworked and worked (as metal or stone), wild and tamed, unplowed and plowed, strange and familiar".

55 Liu Liangbi *Chongxiu Fujian Taiwan fuzhi* [Revised Gazetteer of Taiwan Prefecture, Fujian, 1741] (TWWX 74), at 101.
56 Ibid, at 517; *Shengzu shilu*, above n 35, at 162.
57 Gao Gongqian *Taiwan fuzhi* [Gazetteer of Taiwan Prefecture, 1694] (TWWX 65), at 5–6.
58 For example, in 1693 (Kangxi 32), six aboriginal villages in Zhuluo County submitted. In 1716, 10 villages in the south and five in the north submitted. See Liu, above n 55, at 516–517.
59 Ibid. The 10 southern villages had 1,385 people and the five northern villages had 3,368 people. The tribute was 50 deer skins each year from each of the south and the north clusters.
60 Lan Dingyuan *Luzhou chuji* [First Collection of Lan Dingyuan's Writings], vol 8 (Chinese Text Project, www.ctext.org).
61 See the emperor's comment in 1737 in *Gaozong shilu*, above n 26, at 8, "嗣后各社生番似應聽其自便，嚴飭通事等不必誘其來歸，致啓日後釁端".
62 See Fan Xian *Chongxiu Taiwan fuzhi* [Revised Gazetteer of Taiwan Prefecture, 1747] (TWWX 105), at 69–73.
63 See Liu, above n 55, at 191–192. Village tax applied to acculturated aborigines, and was usually calculated in grain and paid in silver. Token tax applied to non-acculturated aborigines, usually was a certain amount of deer skins over the whole village. The burden of village tax was higher than the token tax.
64 See more on the aboriginal affairs sub-prefects in Chapter 3.
65 See *Qing huidian Taiwan shili* [Great Qing Institutes, Precedents Concerning Taiwan] (TWWX 226), at 30, for the regulation ("*Taiwan shili*"). A report dated 1711 (Kangxi 50), by Zhou Yuanwen (Taiwan prefect 1707–1711), indicated that policing of illegal crossing without a permit had been reiterated by the authorities a few times. See Zhou Yuanwen *Chongxiu Taiwan fuzhi* [Revised Gazetteer of Taiwan Prefecture, 1718] (TWWX 66), at 325. *Ming Qing dang'an*, above n 41, vol 9, at 56–58, attributes (in estimation) two regulations of the Ministry of Wars against illegal crossing without a permit and against family migration to Taiwan to 1684 (Kangxi 23).
66 See Zhou, ibid, at 325. Also see a report by the Fujian-Zhejiang Governor-General Jueluo Manbao in 1724 (Yongzheng 2), in *Ming Qing dang'an*, ibid, vol 10, at 108–111: "臺灣無此田畝供耕種，爲治安隱憂".
67 Ibid.
68 Taiwan Prefect Shen Qiyuan's essay in about 1729 (Yongzheng 7), in *Ming Qing dang'an*, ibid, vol 13, at 220–223.
69 *Taiwan shili*, above n 65, at 168.
70 At 171.
71 For the policy shifts between "tightening" and "relaxing" over time, see Chuang Chin-Teh "Qingchu yanjin yanhai renmin toudu lai Tai shimo" [An Account of the Prohibition of Migration From Coastal China to Taiwan in the Early Qing Period] (1964) 15(3 & 4) *Taiwan Wen Hsien* 1–20 (Part 1), 40–62 (Part 2); Ji Yunfei "Tongzhi jiaxu qian Qing zhengfu Taiwan yimin zhengce zhi tanxi" [An Analysis of the Qing Government's Policies Concerning Migration to Taiwan Before 1874] (1998) 5 *Xueshujie* 64–68.
72 For example, see discussion by the Taiwan Prefect Shen Jinsi (1721) in *Ming Qing dang'an*, above n 41, vol 9, at 343–344, and the memorial of Fujian Governor-General Hao Yulin (1733) in Liang Chih-hui and Chung Yu-lan (eds) *Taiwan yuanzhumin shiliao huibian di qi ji* [A Collection of Historic Records Concerning the Taiwanese Aborigines, vol 7] (Taiwansheng wenxian weiyuanhui, Nantou, 1998), at 202. Evidence cited in Chuang and in Ji, ibid, to prove relaxation or tightening up of migration was mainly about whether or not to allow migrants to bring families to Taiwan.

73 See a regulation of the Ministry of Wars in about 1722 (Kangxi 61), in *Ming Qing dang'an*, above n 41, vol 9, at 376–77.

74 See Lin Yu-ju and Wei Dong "Lin Shuangwen shijian qian de Taiwan bianqu tuxiang: yi Qianlong 49 nian Taiwan fanjie zixiantu wei zhongxin" [Frontier Areas in Taiwan Before the Lin Shuangwen Uprising: An Investigation Centering on the 1784 Purple-line Aboriginal Boundaries] (2012) 19(3) *Taiwanshi yanjiu* 47, at 73.

75 *Taiwan shili*, above n 65, at 27.

76 Huang, above n 40, at 170.

77 This was so in Taiwan as well as other frontiers. See Robert HG Lee *The Manchurian Frontier in Ch'ing History* (Harvard University Press, Cambridge (MA), 1970), at 21.

78 *Taiwan shili*, above n 65, at 167–168.

79 臺湾善后章程二十条. See *Qing Xuanzong shilu xuanji* [Selected Veritable Records of the Daoguang Emperor] (TWWX 188), at 161–165.

80 Ke Peiyuan *Gamalan zhilüe* [Brief Records of Gamalan, 1837] (TWWX 92), at 177.

81 Different records had the timing in 1695 (Kangxi 34) or the late Kangxi era. See Chen Shujun *Gamalan tingzhi* [Gazetteer of Gamalan Sub-prefecture, 1852] (TWWX 160), at 3; Ke Peiyuan *Gamalan zhilüe* [Brief Records of Gamalan, 1837] (TWWX 92), at 9.

82 Ke, ibid, at 9–10.

83 Yao Ying *Dongcha jilüe* [Records of My Appointment to the East, 1829] (TWWX 7), at 72.

84 Ke, above n 81, at 174; Chen, above n 81, at 330.

85 Ibid. Wen Chen-hua *Taiwan yuanzhumin shi zhengce pian: Qingzhi shiqi* [History of Taiwan Aborigines: The Policy Chapter: The Qing Period] (Taiwan Historical, Nantou, 2007), at 74, also indicates that Wu did not obtain the rights of *yezhu* (業主 registered proprietor), which meant the land was not registered.

86 Yao, above n 83, at 73.

87 Ibid, "不宜棄置貽邊患".

88 At 74. For Saichong'a's memorial, see *Ming Qing dang'an*, above n 41, vol 46, at 489–494.

89 "若收入版圖，不特絕洋盜窺伺之端，且可獲海疆之利". Yao, ibid, at 74.

90 See Jones and Kuhn, above n 17, at 108–110.

91 Sheng Ch'ing-I, Wang Shi-lang and Gao Shu-fan *Taiwan shi* [History of Taiwan] (Taiwansheng wenxian weiyuanhui, Taizhong, 1977), at 297; Chuang Chi-fa "Qingdai Taiwan tudi kaifa yu zuqun chongtu" [Land Reclamation and Ethnic Conflicts in Qing Taiwan] (2000) 36 *Taiwan shiji* 3, at 5.

92 See Yao, above n 83, at 74.

93 See *Qing Renzong shilu xuanji* [Selected Veritable Records of the Jiaqing Emperor] (TWWX 187), at 165–166; *Taiwan shili*, above n 65, at 9.

94 See Chen Zhe-san "'Shuishalian' jiqi xiangguan wenti zhi yanjiu" [A Research on Shuishalian and Related Issues] (1998) 49(2) *Taiwan Wen Hsien* 35–57.

95 At 50.

96 At 40.

97 See Yao, above n 83, at 34–35.

98 Ibid.

99 Ibid, at 70; Ke, above n 81, at 89–90.

100 One *qing* is 100 *mu*, and 1 *jia* is about 11 *mu*. So thousands of *qing* is the equivalence of tens of thousands of *jia*.

101 See Deng Chuan'an *Lice huichao* [Measuring the Sea With a Calabash, 1830] (TWWX 9), at 6.

102 Ibid; Yao, above n 83, at 36.

103 Yao, ibid, at 36–38.

104 See *Tai'an huilu jiaji* [Taiwan Documents Collection A] (TWWX 31), at 164, at 161, "據奏該處[臺灣]地多遼闊，未墾之田極多，如果認真墾種，即以每歲所入爲福建海防，可潛消英夷覬覦".

105 Jones and Kuhn, above n 17, at 146.
106 See Yao's letter in *Tai'an huilu jiaji*, above n 104, at 163–167.
107 At 161–163.
108 See Liu's memorial in Ding Yuejian *Zhi Tai bigaolu* [A Collection of Must-read Documents on Governing Taiwan, 1868] (TWWX 17), at 207–212.
109 At 212–228.
110 See Grand Councillor Muzhang'a's memorial in ibid, at 227–228.
111 Aboriginal colonies will be discussed in Chapter 3.
112 See the intendant's recommendation in ibid, at 272–281.
113 Scholars have suggested that it was not adopted. For example, see Wen, above n 85, at 81.
114 Yao, above n 83, at 36.
115 See the letter to the Fujian-Zhejiang Governor-General in Luo Dachun *Taiwan haifang bing kaishan riji* [A Journal of Maritime Defence and Mountain Opening in Taiwan] (TWWX 308), at 65–68. The author of this letter did not identify himself, but at 88 it is indicated that it was an official in the Fujian Province.
116 Ibid, at 66, "後山 . . . 宜開，生番 . . . 宜撫".
117 Ding, above n 108.
118 "上策開闢內山招徠番族". Chen Peigui *Danshui tingzhi* [Gazetteer of Danshui Sub-Prefecture, 1871] (TWWX 172), at 19.
119 See Rowe, above n 15, at 158–162.
120 At 202–204.
121 "臺地所以為彼族眈眈者，病于土曠；土曠之病，由於人稀", quoted in Luo, above n 115, at 38.
122 See Shen's memorial in *Fujian Taiwan zouzhe* [Memorials on Taiwan] (TWWX 29), at 11–13.
123 Inō Kanori (trans Taiwan Historica) *Taiwan wenhua zhi* [A History of Taiwan's Civilisation] (Chinese trans revised ed, Taiwan Shufang, Taipei, 2011), vol 3, at 198.
124 For example, see records in *Liu Mingchuan fu Tai qianhou dang'an* [Historic Documents Before and After Liu Mingchuan's Governorship in Taiwan] (TWWX 276) ("*Fu Tai dang'an*").
125 *Qing Dezong shilu xuanji* [Selected Veritable Records of the Guangxu Emperor] (TWWX 193), at 3: "福建臺灣全島自隸版圖以來, 因後山各番社習俗異宜, 曾禁內地民人渡臺及私入番境, 以杜滋生事端. 現經沈葆楨等將後山地面設法開闢, 曠土亟須招墾; 一切規制, 自應因時變通. 所有從前不准內地民人渡臺各例禁, 著悉與開除; 其販買鐵竹兩項, 著一律弛禁, 以廣招徠". This was made a regulation, see *Taiwan shili*, above n 65, at 44.
126 The previous control on sale of iron and bamboos was to prevent the people from keeping weapons.
127 "抚番开山善后章程21条", in *Fu Tai dang'an*, above n 124, at 7–9.
128 See Linshi Taiwan Jiuguan Diaochahui *Taiwan sifa fulu cankaoshu* [Private Law of Taiwan Reference Book] (Taipei, 1910), vol 1A, at 9–12.
129 Luo, above n 115, at 60, "臣等經營後山，為防患計，非為興利計".
130 At 59, "人第知今日開山之為撫番，固不知今日撫番實以防海也；人第知預籌防海之關係臺灣安危，而不知預籌防海之關係南北洋全局也".
131 The Sino-French War was over Vietnam, which was under Qing suzerainty at that time. For the Sino-French War Taiwan zone, see Lian, above n 26, at 405–414.
132 At 457–458.
133 See details in *Liu Zhuangsugong zouyi* [Memorials of Liu Mingchuan] (TWWX 27), at 220.
134 Inō, above n 123, vol 3, at 311. Inō thinks the actual number was about one-tenth of that. The difference probably lies in procedural submission and actual control.
135 Hu Chuan *Taidongzhou caifangce* [Draft Gazetteer of Taidong Department, cir 1892–1895] (TWWX 81), at 42.

136 See Linshi Taiwan Jiuguan Diaochahui *Taiwan sifa* [Private Law of Taiwan], vol 1 (Chinese translation, Taiwansheng wenxian weiyuanhui, Taizhong, 1990, original first published in 1910), at 47; Inō, above n 123, vol 3, at 2014; Sheng Ch'ing-I "Qingdai Taiwan Tong-Guang zhiji kaishan fufan shishi biannian" [Chronicles of the "Opening the Mountains and Subjugating the Aborigines" Campaigns During the Tongzhi and Guangxu Years] (1979) 30(3) *Taiwan Wen Hsien* 1, at 11; Lian, above n 26, at 447.

137 Lee, above n 77, at 20.

138 See Yang Jun *Qingdai Xinjiang diqu falü zhidu jiqi bianqian yanjiu* [A Research on the Legal System and Its Evolution in Qing Xinjiang] (Minzu, Beijing, 2012), at 46; C Patterson Giersch *Asian Borderlands: The Transformation of Qing China's Yunnan Frontier* (Harvard University Press, Cambridge (MA) and London, 2006), at 132 and 211. Also see, in general, Zhang, above n 9, ch 7.

139 Li, above n 4, at 48.

140 Elliott, above n 19, at 99.

141 Yang, above n 138, at 45.

142 At 310.

143 Giersch, above n 138, at 61.

144 Donald S Sutton "Violence and Ethnicity on a Qing Colonial Frontier: Customary and Statutory Law in the Eighteenth-Century Miao Pale" (2003) 37 *Modern Asian Studies* 41, at 62; Zhang, above n 9, at 518.

145 Yang, above n 138, at 46; Sutton, ibid, at 62; Rowe, above n 20, at 508.

146 See *Taiwan shili*, above n 65, at 27.

147 See Di Cosmo, above n 5, in general.

148 Tang Qiyu *Zhongguo de kenzhi* [Land Reclamation and Colonisation in China] (2nd ed, Yongxiang, Shanghai, 1952), at 54.

149 See Joseph Fletcher "Sino-Russian Relations, 1800–1862" in Fairbank (ed), above n 17, at 332–348.

150 Tang, above n 148, at 16–17 and 47; Joseph Fletcher "The Heyday of the Ch'ing Order in Mongolia, Sinkiang and Tibet" in Fairbank (ed), ibid, at 357.

151 Joseph Fletcher "Ch'ing Inner Asia c 1800" in Fairbank (ed), ibid, at 106.

152 Yang et al, above n 28, at 24.

153 "The lord is the boat; his subjects the water. It is the water that sustains the boat, and it is the water that capsizes the boat". See John Knoblock *Xunzi: A Translation and Study of the Complete Works* (Stanford University Press, Stanford, 1988), vol 2, at 97.

154 "古之善籌邊者，卻敵而已。開疆闢土，利其有者，非聖王所欲爲". Ke, above n 81, at 168.

3 Aboriginal land

Recognition and protection

Studies of Qing aboriginal land policies in Taiwan have largely focused on the plains aborigines and on the period up to about 1800, that is, the High Qing period. Scholars argue that the Qing government was protective of the aboriginal land rights but that the protection was ineffective, either because of poor policy or inadequate measures of protection,[1] or poor implementation by corrupt officials.[2] These interpretations, however, have been made on the basis of restricted case studies, rather than by analysing Qing aboriginal land policies. While the standard interpretation appears to be true in some cases, it is an oversimplification of the situation as a whole.

Researchers that examined land issues over the High Qing period from a policy perspective have reached quite different conclusions. Shepherd proposed a shift of policies, in land issues as well as in other aspects of governance, from "quarantine" during the Kangxi era to "pro-colonisation" in the Yongzheng era, and then a reversal to limiting Han encroachment of aboriginal land in the early Qianlong era, finally to policy fluctuation in the late Qianlong era.[3] Shepherd recognised that the land policies were guided by considerations of reducing ethnic conflicts and by Mencian paternalism.[4] The High Qing policy did experience shifts, to a certain extent as Shepherd described, but the Yongzheng policies were due to an attitude of *laissez faire* rather than of pro-colonisation. This could be seen more clearly when the government's conducts in the 19th century were added to the picture. The considerations that Shepherd identified were valid reasons for the High Qing policies, but the next question is the reasons behind such considerations, inherent in the legal tradition under which the Qing operated.

In contrast to Shepherd, Ka proposed a division in the mid-Qianlong era. Before the mid-Qianlong era the Qing implemented passive quarantine policies, and after that the government formed an alliance with the plains aborigines, using the plains aborigines to suppress Han rebellions and to contain the mountain aborigines in the mountains.[5] As such, active protection of aboriginal land rights emerged only in the mid-Qianlong era, became mature in the late Qianlong era and was redundant soon afterwards because Han settlement spread towards the territories of the mountain aborigines, rendering the deployment of plains aborigines as the barrier between settlers and mountain aborigines unworkable and unnecessary.[6] Ka's conclusion on the different periods of protection was drawn less from land policies per se than from his theory concerning the construction and maturation of the three-zone ethnic division (*sancengzhi zuqun fenbu* 三層制族群分佈), being the Han settlers, the plains aborigines and the non-acculturated aborigines who occupied the west plains, the middle grounds and the eastern mountains, respectively.[7]

This chapter re-examines the Qing policies regarding aboriginal land, extending the coverage to the whole Qing period, identifies policy trends regarding recognition and protection of aboriginal land rights, and discusses the effects of the Qing legal tradition on recognition and protection. To put the discussion in context and to assist understanding the Qing's land policies, the chapter starts with a discussion of the Qing land tenure, in particular the notion of the emperor's "ownership" over land, especially wasteland. It clarifies that the emperor's "ownership" over land was a public power, not a property right. Corresponding to the Qing settlement policies in Taiwan, the Qing government's recognition and protection of aboriginal land rights in Taiwan went through some shifts: the gradual emergence of the concept of aboriginal land and the commencement of protection during the Kangxi reign, the relaxation of restricting aboriginal land reclamation during the Yongzheng reign, the vigorous protection of land rights during the early to mid-Qianlong reign, the establishment of aboriginal colonies during the late Qianlong reign, the proactive approaches during the Jiaqing and Daoguang reigns to aboriginal land in the newly or to-be-acquired territories of Gamalan and inner Shuishalian, and finally the post-1875 land policies. The government's recognition of aboriginal land rights, its ebbing and flowing efforts in protecting aboriginal land rights, and the effectiveness or ineffectiveness of such efforts were all shaped by the Qing property law regime and Confucian legal principles.

Qing land tenure

Title to land

Chinese tradition assumed that "all land under Heaven belongs to the king", meaning that the "king" owned all land once a territory entered the realm.[8] It is important, however, to clarify what exactly constituted the king's ownership, especially the "ownership" over wasteland.

During the Western Zhou period (1059–771 BC), land tenure was feudal. Similar to the feudal land tenure in English history, the king granted fiefs to the lords, who owed allegiance to the king. The lords granted smaller fiefs to lesser lords, and at the bottom of the ladder were commoners who worked on the land.[9] Under a system called "*jingtian*" (井田, 井 *jing*-shaped fields), the lords divided land into nine-plot pieces as shown in the character 井 (*jing*), and allocated one piece to every eight households. Each household occupied and cultivated one plot, and all eight households worked on the plot in the middle which yielded produce for the lord. The households usually rotated occupation of the plots, and did not have rights to dispose of the land.[10] There was no private land ownership under the feudal arrangement. That arrangement was the origin of the saying "all land under Heaven belongs to the king".

The feudal system of land tenure broke down in the Warring States period (476–221 BC), during which time the Qin state abolished the *jingtian* system. The unification of the warring states in China by the Qin Dynasty (221–207 BC) saw the formal establishment of new administrative and land systems.[11] Hereditary feudal lords were replaced by appointed administrative officials, and the "king" who "owned" all land was no longer necessarily the person of the king or the emperor, or the government which the emperor presided over. It is a concept akin to the "Crown" in the British constitution, which could refer to the sovereign or the government in different contexts. Common people were given private proprietary interests over land. The government allocated land to households (*shoutian* 授田), which then had their land registered and paid land tax. Land became inheritable and alienable, although the system fluctuated and evolved over the millennia that followed.

Scholars are generally of the opinion that private land ownership emerged in China during the Qin Dynasty,[12] but some scholars argue that there was no private land ownership in imperial China, because of the concept that the "king" owned all land.[13] The latter view appears to have confused the king's ultimate title with ordinary land ownership. Ancient China was not alone in having the concept of the king "owning" all land. That the king owned all land within his realm was the characteristic of the feudal world. In England the Norman Conquest saw the introduction of feudal tenure, and it became "a fundamental maxim" of English tenures that "the king is the universal lord and original proprietor of all the lands in his kingdom".[14] Therefore all lands in England were "held mediately or immediately of the king".[15] Despite this, English legal scholars do not regard the king "as being in any meaningful sense owner of all the land in England".[16] At most the king had an ultimate property right, in the sense that "the lord had once had the land, and might have it again if the tenant's interest ceased".[17] As the English tenure developed, tenants' interests were fully alienable and became a "full property right".[18] This estate in land, called fee simple, is "the totality of ownership",[19] even though the notion of holding land of the Crown continues to exist, somewhat as a "mere fiction".[20] In other words, fee simple denotes private land ownership, but the traditional concept that the Crown is the original proprietor continues to exist in a non-substantive sense.

Similarly, the feudal tenure of the Zhou Dynasty evolved, and land became alienable and inheritable in imperial China. People who were granted land held full property rights over land, subject only to land tax. The notion that the "king" owned all land persisted, but the nature of such "ownership" changed. Given the alienability, inheritability and fullness of land rights, which were the key characteristics of private ownership, arguably private land ownership existed in imperial China, in a form analogous to the fee simple estate in the English land tenure.[21] As such the substance of the "king's ownership" changed from proprietary rights to an underlying title that represented public law power.

Government's "ownership" over wasteland

In Chinese land tenure, there is a concept of "wasteland" (*huangdi* 荒地). As China was mostly an agrarian society, land that was not in cultivation generally fell into the category of wasteland. Even scholars who recognised private land ownership in imperial China were of the view that the government owned wasteland.[22] However the nature of the government's "ownership" is worth examining. There were usually two types of wasteland, virgin land (*yuanhuang* 原荒 "originally waste") and cultivated land that became waste (*paohuang* 拋荒 "left to waste", abandoned land), usually because of war. *Yuanhuang* land remained in the government's hands and was subject to grant. *Paohuang* land could revert to government control and became available for grant if the original owners or cultivators did not claim it back. Virgin land and *paohuang* land that reverted to government control were referred to as "land without an owner" (*wuzhudi* 無主地, *bona vacantia*), although occasionally it was also called "government's land" (*guandi* 官地).[23] Anyone could work wasteland into agricultural land and apply for a grant after the reclamation had been completed, usually free of charge and sometimes even with government subsidies as an incentive for land reclamation.[24]

Therefore the government's "ownership" was not a proprietary interest, instead it was an administrative power to make or not to make grants, and to decide to whom to grant the land. Before wasteland was reclaimed and claimed, there was no recognition of "ownership" and hence no notion of property. This land system led to the ignoring of aboriginal land rights at the beginning of the annexation, but also assisted in the government's readiness to recognise aboriginal land rights once it was accepted that the aborigines had claims over the land.

The government could be a land owner in the sense of a private land owner, when it appropriated land to itself, an equivalent to the European law concept of dominium. A typical type of land owned by the government was official estates (*guanzhuang* 官莊) – the land was leased by the government and the rental income set aside for various types of official use, depending on the purposes and circumstances of establishing the estates. This was in contrast to the government's rights over "wasteland", which were limited to the power to make grants.

Therefore in imperial China the sovereign or the government did not own the land, not even wasteland, in the sense of possessing propriety rights, except in cases where the government owned cultivated land in the same manner as private land owners did. The "king" exercised his "ownership" in the area of public administration. The Qing Dynasty inherited this system, but it retained certain wasteland as *guanhuang* (官荒 wasteland owned by the government), which was reserved land that was not to be granted for reclamation.[25] In this case the government in fact granted the land to itself.

Land grants

During the Qing Dynasty, land grants were made after land reclamation was completed. After the Qing Court was established in Beijing, although the government made regulations to encourage land reclamation, no procedure was set out for reclamation. Land reclaimers were only required to report to the local government after the reclamation was completed. The local government then surveyed the land and recorded the relevant information on the land register.

Land registers were kept for taxation and other administrative purposes.[26] A "fish scale register" (*yulin ce* 鱼鳞册), devised during the Southern Song Dynasty (1127–1279 AD), recorded the location of each piece of land, the total area, boundaries, the registered proprietor's name, the tenant's name and the proprietors of adjacent lands.[27] Another register, the "yellow register" (*huang ce* 黄册), recorded each household's land holding. Both registers functioned as the basis for tax collection. The "fish scale register" focused on land information, and the "yellow register" focused on household information. Because these registers, which the Qing Dynasty inherited from earlier dynasties, were not always updated when transactions or subdivision occurred, the Qing government created a transaction register (*tuishou ce* 推收册) to record changes of land holdings.[28] The purpose of these registers was to provide the government with correct information for taxation, but upon registration, a grant was deemed to have been made. In contrast, wasteland was not surveyed or registered.[29] As such, the register formed the basis for claim of proprietorship.

The Qing government was concerned only with registering reclaimed land, and for many decades did not regulate the reclamation process at the central government level. Because disputes arose over whether land being reclaimed had prior owners or reclaimers, in 1661 (Shunzhi 18) an inspecting censor for Henan Province recommended that reclaimers be required to apply for land reclamation licences in advance, listing relevant details including the reclaimer's name and the land in question.[30] This was approved but probably it was applied only in Henan, as regulations made by the Yongzheng government still required reclaimers to "reclaim and report on their own account" (*ziken zibao* 自墾自報) and "report as soon as reclaimed" (*suiken suibao* 隨墾隨報).[31] A 1734 (Yongzheng 12) regulation required local officials to publish information about land that was reported by reclaimers and give a five-month notice period, so that other interested parties could object to registration by the current reclaimer.[32] It was not until 1737 (Qianlong 2) that the government required prior application before reclamation (*ying xian chengbao* 應先呈報).[33] The freedom to reclaim land without prior government approval was further evidence that the government did not assert property rights over wasteland, and the eventual improvement in regulating the reclamation process was to avoid disputes among the people.

Different from the general practice in mainland China, a reclamation permit system was applied in Taiwan, which was likely to have been inherited from the Zheng period. Zheng regulations required prior government approval for land reclamation, officials to apply to Zheng himself and ordinary people to the prefecture government.[34] The reason of this requirement is unclear, but it appears that the local Taiwan government continued this practice after Qing annexation.[35] Land reclamation permits recorded the permit holder's details and the location and boundaries of the land, but as in the empire-wide practice, the land was not surveyed until after the permit holder "reported for survey and taxation" (*baozhang shengke* 報丈升科) when the reclamation was completed.

It was in the process of issuing land permits that aboriginal land issues emerged and were eventually dealt with.

Aboriginal land: an emerging concept (the Kangxi era)

Ignorance about aboriginal land rights

The concept of aboriginal land did not emerge in the years immediately after annexation. Because of the traditional concept that all land within the realm belonged to the "king", after annexation Qing officials acted on the assumption that, once the aborigines submitted, the government gained an ultimate title over the land. There was no notion of property over wasteland, and therefore the aborigines' ownership over uncultivated land was not noted.

In the early years of annexation local officials encouraged land reclamation in Taiwan. The first Taiwan prefect, Jiang Yuying, encouraged land reclamation and agricultural activities.[36] The first Zhuluo County magistrate, Ji Qiguang (Kangxi 23–24), called for land reclamation by settlers, saying that "as one could see [from] the south to the north, grasslands are wild and vacant [*huangwu* 荒蕪]. If [we] have people to reclaim them, they will become fertile lands".[37] Ji recommended recruiting peasants from the mainland, and providing settlers with land and draft oxen, which was the usual approach of the Qing to encourage land reclamation. Driven by his belief, Ji "worked hard to solicit [settlers], so that population on the register could be increased, and new farmland could be opened in the wilderness".[38]

A few years later, another Zhuluo County magistrate, Zhang Fa (Kangxi 29–33), encouraged land reclamation, as he "saw that the county was newly established, and [there was] much vacant land".[39] The encouragement of land reclamation was because much land had been abandoned or had reverted to waste in Taiwan due to the change of dynasty, and because of the general policy of the empire to encourage land reclamation.[40] Local officials bore personal responsibility for implementing such policies, as their competency was judged according to their achievements in terms of local land reclamation and their diligence in tax collection.[41] Given China's agrarian tradition, among officials there was also an inherent desire to turn wild land into production.

At first local officials issued land reclamation permits without paying any attention to aboriginal land rights, possibly because no occasion arose to challenge the traditional concept that wasteland was subject to government grant. The Taiwan magistrate, Ji, stated in an essay about Taiwan affairs that "once [the territory] is annexed . . . every inch of field is the king's land and every person is the king's subject".[42] Although the context was collecting land tax and poll tax from Han settlers, Ji's statement had a general application given the call for land reclamation. Since all land titles must flow from the emperor, some Qing officials assumed that even land occupied by aborigines was on the basis of a grant from the emperor. An early Taiwan prefect, Zhou Yuanwen (Kangxi 46–52), expressed the view that "because the aborigines did not know agriculture, [the emperor] granted land to the aborigines for deer hunting".[43] There was of course never any such grant, but Zhou's statement assumed all land titles must flow from the emperor's grant, since the emperor "owned" all land within the realm. This was therefore a kind of fictional grant, as in English law.

Another reason for the lack of understanding of aboriginal land rights was that, in the first few decades of Qing rule, land reclamation was mainly on formerly cultivated land that had reverted to wasteland when the Zhengs surrendered. Consequently the aborigines did not demonstrate strong claims over such land as they did with their deer grounds.

As discussed in Chapter 1, during the Kangxi era land reclamation advanced slowly and it took nearly 40 years for the area of registered land to increase to the level of the Zheng period. The government and local officials were not aware of the issue of aboriginal land rights because, in the absence of settler-aborigine conflicts and aboriginal protest against land reclamation, the traditional belief that all land "belonged" to the "king" was not challenged. As land reclamation became more widespread, aboriginal land rights started to become an important issue.

Beginning to recognise aboriginal land rights

As land reclamation advanced, officials became aware of the effects of settlement on the well-being of the aborigines. Officials were sympathetic towards the aborigines and attempted to protect them, seeing them as the weaker people having to withstand the invasion of the Han migrants. Some officials issued decrees forbidding exploitation of the aborigines, and made efforts to relieve their hardship.[44] Eventually the issue was focused on land. A Zhuluo County magistrate, Zhou Zhongxuan (Kangxi 53–55), complained that the aborigines were being oppressed and exploited by Han settlers and officials, and that aboriginal hunting grounds had become settlers' farmland, leaving aborigines with only a small proportion of their land on which to maintain themselves.[45] A travelling military officer, Ruan Caiwen, also criticised the settlers for displacing the aborigines.[46] Although the officials were Han people, their ethnicity did not stop them from speaking in support of the aborigines and condemning Han settlers' land grabbing.

In about 1704 (Kangxi 43), Taiwan Circuit Intendant Wang Minzheng (Kangxi 42–48) issued a decree concerning aboriginal land rights:[47]

> If the Han people and acculturated aborigines make agreements freely between themselves (*renyi qiyue* 任意契約), and the aborigines give up their wasteland (*huangpu* 荒埔) for [settlers to] reclaim, they [the settlers] should first apply to the government [for a reclamation permit]. Local officials shall investigate all details of the transaction and the relationship between the settlers and the aborigines, and decide whether to approve the application. Those [settlers] who are granted a permit must fulfil the contractual obligations (*qiyue tianjian*契約條件) with the aborigines, and report the land for taxation according to law.

This decree reveals that the aborigines and settlers had been making arrangements regarding aboriginal land without the government's authority, or even knowledge. In the absence of clear government policy, settlers were left free to contract with aborigines and reclaim aboriginal land. The decree probably intended to bring "hidden land" onto the government register, but clearly it also purported to safeguard the aborigines' financial interest in the settler-aborigine transactions, and to generally protect the aborigines from Han exploitation. Although not expressly stated, this policy implied government recognition of aboriginal ownership over wasteland. Wang's decree was observed, as existing land reclamation permits from this time on often recorded that the land subject to grant did not encroach on aboriginal land.[48]

A late Kangxi period circuit intendant, Chen Bin (Kangxi 49–53), was the first to expound aboriginal rights over uncultivated land. Chen argued that each aboriginal village had its own boundaries that other villages could not violate. All land within the boundaries was the village property, and the villagers could use it as they liked.[49] For a culture that put agriculture over any other industry, a system that only recognised rights over cultivated land, and a deep-rooted tradition that all uncultivated lands were the government's "wasteland", Chen's opinion was well ahead of the common understanding of the time. Nevertheless, the government fully endorsed Chen's recommendation to "permanently forbid reclamation of *fandi* [番地 aboriginal land]".[50]

Correlating with the new awareness of aboriginal land rights and efforts to protect them, land grants decreased from a few hundred *jia* per year before 1703 (Kangxi 42) to a few dozen *jia* every year between 1703 and 1722 (Kangxi 61), with the exception of 1716 and 1717 when 102 and 129 *jia* of land was registered, respectively.[51] During the 20 years between 1703 and 1722 only 840 *jia* of new land was registered, compared with 2,565 *jia* in 1685, and 7,669 *jia* in the 17 years from 1686 to 1702 (Kangxi 25–41). The decree indicates that the government measures were effective in reducing land reclamation activities.

Given the ban against reclamation of aboriginal land, the fact that new lands were reclaimed and registered, albeit in small amounts, in the late Kangxi years suggests that the recognition of aboriginal land had at least some limits. Regulations never defined the term *fandi*. Despite his advocacy for aboriginal land rights, Chen at first did not think that all land belonged to the aborigines. Initially he called for settler reclamation of "vacant land" (*kuangdi* 旷地), and stated that:[52]

> Zhuluo County in the north covers over 2,300 *li*, Fengshan in the south covers over 600 *li*, and in the middle Taiwan County is over 50 *li* from the east to the west. In between there is much vacant land [*kuangdi* 旷地], and it is a pity to leave it untouched. Residents in Zhangzhou and Quanzhou are only at the other side of the [Taiwan] Strait, and should be accommodated in the idle and vacant land.

Chen's statements suggest that while he recognised land that was actively controlled and used by aborigines was aboriginal land, he considered land that aborigines did not actively control to be wasteland belonging to the government. After a few years of observation, however, Chen seemed to have concluded that all uncultivated land in Taiwan was in fact controlled and used by aborigines. In 1715 (Kangxi 54), Chen told the Kangxi emperor that "there is no wasteland in Taiwan. Although there is much vacant land in the south and in the north, this is all aboriginal deer grounds".[53] In this way Chen extended his recognition of aboriginal rights over all land. The government's recognition was not necessarily as extensive, given that small amounts of land were granted in the late Kangxi years.

Thus the government's recognition of aboriginal ownership over wasteland in Taiwan went from implicit to explicit, and the attitude towards land reclamation went from allowing free contracting to forbidding reclamation. The extent of aboriginal land became clearer, but was not defined. Because of the lack of definition, officials relied on aboriginal claims to ascertain aboriginal land. If aborigines could control their territory and enforce their rights over the land, their claims would be upheld. If no aborigine came forward to claim a piece of land, that land was not subject to protection against Han claims and fell into the category of government "wasteland". This method was imprecise. On the one hand, as the Taiwan intendant, Chen Bin, noted, each aboriginal village had its own boundaries. Although it may seem lacking clarity, the players in the scene of the frontier knew the owner of any piece of land concerned. On the other land, the clarification of aboriginal land was dependent on the peoples and events involved, and the ambit of aboriginal land could be fluid and subject to manipulation. There was room for the settlers and the aborigines to reach under-the-table agreements, where the settlers paid a price and the aborigines presented statements to declare that a piece of land did not violate aboriginal boundaries. That was why, despite the entrenchment of the aboriginal land, new land was reclaimed and registered. This lack of precision was typical of the Chinese legal tradition. Overall, the Kangxi era saw an emerging and growing awareness of aboriginal ownership over wasteland and the government's eventual recognition of it.

Relaxing the restriction (the Yongzheng era)

The ban against reclaiming aboriginal land was removed in 1724 (Yongzheng 2), when the Yongzheng emperor decreed:[54]

> If Taiwan aborigines' idle and vacant (*xiankuang* 閑曠) deer grounds are suitable for agriculture, order the local officials to publish notice that, the aborigines are free to lease (*zu* 租) [them] to settlers for cultivation.

The decree was then made a regulation (*li* 例). This decree has been seen as opening the floodgates to land reclamation by settlers, and hence as showing a shift from "quarantine" to a pro-colonisation policy. It was true that the decree gave settlers the licence to reclaim aboriginal land, but it is important to note that the recognition and protection of aboriginal land rights were not withdrawn at this time.

The issue of the decree accorded with the Yongzheng government's changing policy focus, which was not limited to Taiwan. The Yongzheng government initiated some important policies at both imperial and local levels, including expanding the agricultural base and major fiscal reforms to increase revenue for the central government.[55] One of the important policy initiatives concerning land was encouraging land reclamation.

The emperor regarded land reclamation as vitally important:[56]

> The country has for long been peaceful, and the population is growing. The produce [of the land] is just enough [to support the people]. If there is a famine or bad harvest, people will have difficulty finding enough food. In the future

> when the population continues to grow, what can people's livelihood be? Only land reclamation will benefit the people most.

Thus the emperor extended the tax grace period for dry land to 10 years, and "several times decreed to encourage people to reclaim and cultivate land".[57] Millions of acres of land were reclaimed during the Yongzheng reign, extending from the economic heartland of China to the distant provinces, as Han settlement was extended to the northwest and southwest of the empire.[58]

Against this background, it is not surprising that the government would have searched for ways to promote land reclamation in Taiwan as well. Once again, the lack of any Taiwan-specific policy is apparent.

The argument of Lan Dingyuan, the advisor to the Fujian maritime commander who pacified the 1721 Han uprising in Taiwan, may have also influenced policy change. Lan evaluated benefits of reclamation of aboriginal land, and suggested that the government require the aborigines to reclaim their vacant land, failing which the land should be opened to settlers.[59] Although often seen as pro-colonist, Lan did not deny the aborigines' prior ownership. He conceded that "if we talk about aboriginal land, the whole of Taiwan was taken from the aborigines", and suggested that settlers who reclaimed aboriginal land should assume the aborigines' tax burden as a kind of rent.[60] Thus Lan accepted that compensation should be paid for land used by settlers. Although the suggested amount was very small, paying compensation in principle recognised the aborigines' property rights.

The 1724 regulation was a lot more restrictive than Lan's suggestions. The wording of the regulation was neutral. It allowed but did not force or encourage the aborigines to open up the land. Further, although it appeared to be pro-colonisation if compared with the Kangxi government's ban, by allowing only lease but not sale, the regulation preserved, or at least intended to preserve, a safeguard for the aborigines. In fact, by making existing under-the-table arrangements between settlers and aborigines more transparent, it may have provided better protection to the aborigines.

The Han aggression in reclaiming aboriginal land and the concern that the aborigines could lose all their land was noted again in 1727, as it was during the Kangxi era. To facilitate land reclamation as well as to set boundaries for reclamation, two inspecting censors to Taiwan, Solin and Yin Qin, jointly wrote a memorial to the emperor, and recommended that the government reserve 500 *jia* of land for each large aboriginal villages, 400 *jia* each for medium-sized villages, and 300 *jia* each for small villages, and open up the rest of land for reclamation (*zhaoken* 召墾).[61] The memorial did not specify any detailed plan for opening up – whether it was simply to open the land for reclamation and allow settlers and aborigines to negotiate terms of use, or whether the government would actively take the land (with or without compensation) and let settlers reclaim. As no plan was recorded (and likely none had been made), the scheme could either protect the aborigines through entrenching certain amounts of aboriginal land or deprive the aborigines of their land through government taking of land.[62] The emperor commented that "this might be workable", but did not make any order for it to be implemented.[63] This discussion shows that the government continued to recognise aboriginal land ownership, and was still in the process of working out how best to achieve a balance of advancing land reclamation without impinging the aborigines' livelihood. The fact that the scheme was not further developed or implemented indicates that the government was reluctant to be involved in taking of land or to coerce the aborigines to part with their land, but preferred only to give policy directions and let the private parties carry out the transactions according to their needs.

The policy direction did prompt land reclamation to advance, as the Yongzheng era saw increasing land grants. In 1728 (Yongzheng 6), the area of newly registered land in Taiwan suddenly rose sharply to 16,337 *jia*, compared to 156 *jia* in 1724 (Yongzheng 2) and 129 *jia* in 1727 (Yongzheng 5).[64] Over the next two years new land registration remained high, with 3,351 *jia* and 1,736 *jia* of land being added to the register in 1729 and 1730 (Yongzheng 7 and 8), respectively. The sharp increase in registered land was not seen in any other period of the Qing administration, and corresponded with the taking effect of the regulation.[65]

Another factor that contributed to the increase in registered land was an imperial decree of 1727 (Yongzheng 5), which called for land registration, forgave past breaches of not registering land if land reclaimers "confessed" (*zixing chushou* 自行出首) and reported the reclamation within one year, gave a tax grace period till 1729, and imposed heavy penalties for those who did not report past reclamation within one year.[66] This policy was not directed at Taiwan only, but rather was part of the Yongzheng government's efforts to address hidden land issues across the whole empire.[67] Among the 22,222 *jia* of land that was added to the register during the Yongzheng era, just over a quarter (5,667 *jia*) was previously reclaimed and registered under the 1727 decree on registration, including 4,812 *jia* of land that reclaimers reported, and 855 *jia* that the government managed to get on the record.[68] Because of the 1727 decree, compounded with incentives to register provided by reduced land tax rate in 1729,[69] the amount of land under cultivation during the Yongzheng period was more accurately reflected in the records than it was in the decades before and the century after it. Comparing the 22,222 *jia* of newly registered land under the Yongzheng government with the 11,074 *jia* of newly registered land under the Kangxi government, and taking into consideration the 5,667 *jia* of land that was registered during the Yongzheng era but was previously reclaimed, the amount of land reclaimed during the 13 years of the Yongzheng reign was about the same as that during 40 years of the Kangxi reign. This signifies the effect of withdrawing the ban on reclamation of aboriginal land.

Looked at objectively, the Yongzheng government continued to recognise aboriginal land ownership, and afforded a degree of protection to the aborigines. However, the removal of the reclamation ban meant that protection was less vigorous, and the increased reclamation activities did have adverse effects on the aborigines' lives. The government was reluctant to be actively involved in land reclamation matters except to provide general policy direction; this indicates both an unwillingness to actively deprive the aborigines of their land and a slowness in protecting aboriginal land ownership. This attitude was better described as *laissez faire* than as pro-colonisation. Neither was it passive maintenance of the status quo. Rather it was a deliberate decision to achieve a balance between imperial objectives of increasing revenue and minimum disruption to aborigines' livelihood. As land reclamation advanced and the aborigines' living space was increasingly encroached by Han settlers, the following Qianlong government strengthened protection of aboriginal land.

A return to restrict reclamation (the Qianlong era)

Protection: efforts and results

The Qianlong government continued to encourage land reclamation at the imperial level. By the mid-Qianlong reign, land reclamation in the empire was mostly taking place at the margins of existing reclaimed land.[70] In the hilly province of Fujian, provincial regulations made in 1759 and 1760 (Qianlong 24 and 25) encouraged reclamation of marginal land and exempted pieces of land smaller than one *mu* 畝 from tax, relying on imperial decrees issued in 1740 and 1741 (Qianlong 5 and 6).[71] However, in Taiwan, the government reverted to the Kangxi government's stance and tightened the protection of aboriginal land. A regulation of the Ministry of Households stipulated that:[72]

> Han villains in Taiwan who *pu* (贌 lease)[73] acculturated aborigines' wasteland are punishable according to the law of 'theft of land through unauthorised cultivation'; those who reclaim land in the non-acculturated aboriginal territory are punishable according to the law of breach of border control. The land is to be returned to the aborigines.

The regulation book did not note the year this regulation was made, but there is little doubt that it was made in 1746 (Qianlong 11), as the wording of the regulation was almost identical to a report of the ministry in that year.[74] This regulation shows that both the settlers and the government treated acculturated aborigines' land and non-acculturated aborigines' land differently. Clearly the settlers' usual method of reclaiming acculturated aborigines' land was to lease it, but they probably did not accord the non-acculturated aborigines such courtesy and might have simply encroached on the land. The government protected acculturated aborigines' land through applying domestic law relating to agricultural land, but treated non-acculturated aborigines' land as land beyond the border of the realm. This distinction between lands of the two groups of aborigines persisted in laws and policies of the Qianlong government, as did the principles of restricting reclamation.

Acculturated aborigines' land

The Qianlong government regulations repeatedly forbade settler reclamation, cultivation, lease or purchase of aboriginal land. In addition, efforts were made to identify and return to aborigines land that had been illicitly occupied, leased or purchased by settlers. Between 1737 and 1766 (Qianlong 2–31), the emperor approved seven proposals by the Fujian provincial government or the inspecting censor, in 1737, 1738, 1746, 1750, 1758, 1760 and 1766, respectively (see Table 3.1).[75] The proposals

Table 3.1 Laws/policies protective of aboriginal land rights (1684–1795)

Year	*Law*	*Law-making body*	*Source*
About 1704 (KX 43)	Officials to investigate whether aboriginal land would be encroached upon and details of aborigine-settler transactions before issuing a land reclamation permit.	Taiwan Circuit Intendant Wang Minzheng	No direct record.
By 1722 (KX 61)	Reclamation of aboriginal land not allowed.	Likely to be central government law	No direct record
1724 (YZ 2)	Aborigines allowed to lease land to settlers for reclamation.	Imperial decree; was made a regulation	*Taiwan shili*, at 43
1737 (QL 2)	Purchase of aboriginal land forbidden; settlers to return aboriginal land that they illicitly reclaimed. Land that settlers purchased and registered for tax before this to be surveyed and compiled into a special record. Demarcate boundaries of aboriginal land and settlers' land.	Imperial approval of Taiwan censor's recommendation	*Gaozong shilu*, at 9
1738 (QL 3)	To recognise previous sales and allow registration of those not yet registered. Land reclaimed without support of a land deed to be returned to aborigines. Demarcate boundaries between settlers' land and aboriginal land. Reiterate the ban against lease and purchase.	Imperial approval of governor-general's recommendation	*Chongxiu Taiwan fuzhi*, at 483
1746 (QL 11)	Aboriginal land to be cultivated by aborigines only; settlers who leased aboriginal land to return land to aborigines and be subject to punishment; those who reclaimed land in non-acculturated aborigines' territories to be punished; clarify boundaries between aborigines' and settlers' lands.	Imperial approval of governor-general's recommendation; was made an imperial regulation.	*Taiwan shili*, at 44. Also see *Gaozong shilu*, at 51
1750 (QL 15)	To clarify non-acculturated aboriginal boundaries and police illegal reclamation; acculturated aborigines' land to be cultivated by aborigines only. To punish breaches.	Imperial approval of governor-general's recommendation	*Gaozong shilu*, at 79–80
1758 (QL 23)	To clarify and demarcate boundaries between lands belonging to aborigines and settlers.	Imperial approval of governor-general's recommendation	*Gaozong shilu*, at 118
1760 (QL 25)	To clarify non-acculturated aboriginal boundaries; to apply the 1746 regulation and order return of land to aborigines, but Han settlers who leased aborigines' land were allowed to continue as tenants and pay rents to aborigines; unreclaimed aboriginal land to be reclaimed to support border guards; land situated beyond aboriginal boundaries returned to aborigines.	Imperial acknowledgement of provincial regulation	*Gaozong shilu*, at 126–127

(*Continued*)

Table 3.1 (Continued)

Year	*Law*	*Law-making body*	*Source*
1766 (QL 31)	To investigate and demarcate boundaries between aboriginal land and settlers' land; encroached aboriginal land returned to aborigines; land that was illegally leased against regulations returned to aborigines; to compile records of land belonging to aborigines; future sale or lease of aboriginal land would result in confiscation of land and punishment of purchaser/leasee (settlers); forbade reclamation near non-acculturated aboriginal boundaries.	Imperial approval of governor-general's recommendation	*Gaozong shilu*, at 147–149

were in similar terms. Three of them explicitly forbade purchase or lease of aboriginal land (1737, 1738 and 1766), two stated that aboriginal land was to be cultivated by aborigines only (1746 and 1750), and five ordered the return of aboriginal land to aborigines that had been leased to, illegally occupied by or otherwise illicitly reclaimed by settlers (1737, 1738, 1746, 1760 and 1766). Three proposals even prescribed punishment for breaches (1746, 1750 and 1766), showing the government's resolve to curb squatting, leasing or purchasing aboriginal land. On five occasions the government decided to investigate and demarcate boundaries between settlers' land and aboriginal land (1737, 1738, 1746, 1758 and 1766) (see Table 3.2). Some recommendations in the 1746 proposal were made a precedent to the Qing Institute and others made a regulation of the Ministry of Households, indicating the importance of the policy measure in imperial eyes.[76] The repeated attention demonstrates the government's determination to protect aboriginal land rights.[77]

As was the Qing tradition, there was no clear distinction between law and policy, and they were made largely through recommendations of officials and acknowledgement or approval by the emperor. There was no definition of key terms or attention to conflicting regulations. As such the laws and policies were not always consistent and sometimes sent mixed messages. The 1737 and 1738 provisions, although they forbade leasing and purchase of aboriginal land, nevertheless recognised previous land transactions and allowed registration of aboriginal land that had already been sold to settlers. The 1746 and 1750 provisions both specified that aboriginal land was to be cultivated by aborigines only, and the 1746 regulation specifically required settlers to return land that they leased to the aborigines. The 1760 provision cited the 1746 regulation as a precedent, yet it somehow twisted the intention of the 1746 regulation and only required returning land for the aborigines to manage, which meant the aborigines continued in the capacity of landlords. In such cases the lease relationship was one in which the aborigines received a set amount of rent but lost any substantive rights over the land.[78] Only land beyond the non-acculturated aboriginal boundaries was actually returned. The 1760 policy

Table 3.2 Key measures of land policies of the Qianlong government

Year	*No sale/ lease*	*Cultivation by aborigines*	*Clarify boundaries*	*Return land*	*Punishment*	*Non-acculturated aborigines' land*	*Other provisions*
1737	√		√	√ (illicitly reclaimed)			To survey and record leased aboriginal land
1738	√		√	√ (those with no lease agreement)			Allowed registration of aboriginal land sold in the past
1746		√	√	√ (leased land)	√	√	
1750		√			√	√	
1758			√				
1760				√ (land beyond boundaries)		√	Allowed current lease to continue
1766	√		√	√ (leased and encroached land)	√	√	Compile record of aboriginal land

was self-contradictory because the 1746 regulation explicitly required cultivation by aborigines, not just management by aborigines. Hence the 1760 policy relaxed the requirement, and rectified illicit reclamation of 20 pieces of land, which were mostly leased by aborigines to settlers.[79]

The 1766 policy overrode the 1760 provision and required return of land to the aborigines. However, as the method of law-making was not systematic, the 1760 provision was not revoked in 1766. A 1767 provincial decision continued the 1760 approach, and allowed the lease of aboriginal land at the "large rent" rate of 4 *shi* 石 and 8 *shi* per *jia* for dry land and wetland, respectively.[80] The Taiwan circuit intendant, Zhang Ting, issued a decree in 1768 to implement the 1767 decision.[81] This approach was directly contrary to the newer and stricter 1766 policy, and shows the deficiencies in the law-making and implementation mechanisms.

The 1766 policy, as the 1737 one, required compilation of records of land belonging to aborigines. The record was different from land registration, as it was for keeping track of aboriginal land rather than for tax purposes. To ensure the policies were implemented properly and aboriginal land issues were dealt with effectively, two positions of aboriginal affairs sub-prefects were created. These sub-prefects had full responsibility for all aspects of aborigine-settler interactions. Their duties included investigating unfair settler-aborigine land transactions and ensuring return of aboriginal land to aborigines, attending to cases where settlers married aboriginal women and occupied aboriginal property, and impeaching government officials or clerks who oppressed aborigines.[82] The government's intention was to protect aboriginal land rights and prevent Han settlers and government agents from oppressing the aborigines.[83]

No further imperial law, policy, proposal or discussion concerning acculturated aboriginal land was recorded after 1766. Given the reactionary nature of government laws and policies, this indicates that the aboriginal affairs subprefects performed their duties well enough, and no further aborigine-settler disputes reached the provincial or central government level that required government response.

Overall, the Qianlong government was determined and vigorous in protecting acculturated aboriginal land rights, but because of the inherent defect in the mechanism of law-making, the regulations were not always consistent, and sometimes left room for misinterpretation and errors in the implementation.

Non-acculturated aborigines' land

As discussed in Chapter 2, the purpose of the aboriginal boundaries was to segregate the settlers and acculturated aborigines from the non-acculturated aborigines. The intention was to keep the setters out of the aboriginal territories, rather than to keep the aborigines in. In 1746 and 1766 the Qianlong government twice forbade Han reclamation of land near or beyond aboriginal boundaries, and in 1760 it required settlers to return land reclaimed beyond the boundaries (see Tables 3.1 and 3.2).

The ban against reclamation beyond the boundaries applied only to Han settlers, and did not apply to acculturated aborigines.[84] The government targeted the Han settlers because they were the main culprits who reclaimed land beyond the boundaries. It is also possible that the government viewed the aborigines as the original owners of all land in Taiwan, and consequently it restricted land reclamation by Han settlers who were intruders, but was less concerned with the fact that different areas of land belonged to different aboriginal groups. Because of the exception made for acculturated aborigines, there was no complete ban against reclamation in the non-acculturated aboriginal territories. This in practice gave Han settlers the opportunity to reclaim land near or beyond the boundaries.

As Han settlement expanded, the de facto boundaries between the settlement areas and the aboriginal territories were pushed towards the foothills. Consequently, the government four times clarified and adjusted aboriginal boundaries (1746, 1750, 1760 and 1766) (see Table 3.2). Each time, when the government considered whether to place an area within the boundaries and acquiesce in reclamation, or to place it beyond the boundary lines and return the land to the aborigines, the principal consideration was the distance of that area from non-acculturated aborigines' activity centres. This arose from the government's policy of reducing conflicts, which were usually caused by the non-acculturated aborigines being irritated by Han encroachment and then killing settlers in retaliation.[85]

Where there was no such security threat, the government acquiesced in illegal land reclamation or transactions and allowed those lands to be registered for taxation.[86] For example, in 1755 (Qianlong 20), the Ministry of Households discussed the Fujian-Zhejiang governor-general's report concerning some land in two mountain territories, Shuishalian and Quantoumu. Both had formerly been marked as settler-forbidden areas, but as they were about 30 *li* away from the non-acculturated aboriginal villages, the central government approved registration of the illicitly reclaimed lands, and allowed reclamation of the remaining land, measuring about 1,104 *jia*.[87]

Similarly, in 1788 (Qianlong 53), following extensive investigation, the government discovered 11,204 *jia* of land near or beyond the aboriginal boundaries, which had been purchased or leased from the aborigines and reclaimed by settlers. The government retrospectively approved the illegal transactions between settlers and aborigines, and allowed the settlers to register the lands.[88] Some lands were apparently illicitly reclaimed (*siken* 私墾) without any consent from aborigines. The government nevertheless decided to allow registration of these lands, presumably because the reclamation was uncontested by aborigines.[89]

The government's inconsistent policies can be explained by two main factors. The first factor was the absence of any clear definition of aboriginal land. Although the Qianlong government made significant efforts to protect aboriginal land rights, and regulations often forbade reclamation of aboriginal land, there was never any attempt to define the term "aboriginal land". The concept remained quite elastic. The second factor was that the government's overriding concern was order and security, not a concern for aboriginal land rights as such. Where reclamation of land did not cause protest from the plains aborigines, or would not provoke retaliation by the mountain aborigines, the government was quite happy to exclude the land from the category of "aboriginal land". Protection of aboriginal land rights was a means to an end, and the government accordingly did not always adhere to its own policy.

Despite the inconsistent policies concerning both acculturated and non-acculturated aboriginal land, the Qianlong government's efforts restored political relationships between the government and the aborigines, which had deteriorated during the Yongzheng reign. During the Qianlong reign, the 93 villages of acculturated aborigines never rebelled,[90] and the number of non-acculturated aboriginal villages that submitted themselves to the government authority increased to over 200. This to some extent illustrates the effectiveness of aboriginal land protection.

Aboriginal colonies

No significant land policy was made after the appointment of the aboriginal affairs sub-prefect, until 1788 (Qianlong 53) when the system of aboriginal colonies (*fantun* 番屯) was created. This was an important event during Qing rule of Taiwan. Its importance lay in the government's willingness to trust the aborigines over Han settlers, and in the system's lasting effects in preserving aboriginal society, which had an indirect effect on preserving aboriginal land tenure.

The tuntian *system*

Tuntian 屯田 was a land reclamation system used throughout Chinese history where the government organised military soldiers to reclaim land, or organised labourers in a quasi-military structure to reclaim large areas of land.[91] The system of *tuntian* originated in the Western Han Dynasty (202 BC–8 AD). After Emperor Wu of the Han Dynasty defeated the nomads in the northwest of China, he sent military forces to guard the borders as well as to reclaim and farm the land.[92] It was not only a method for the soldiers to support themselves, but also an organised and efficient way to reclaim land and guard against invasion.[93] *Tuntian* was used by subsequent dynasties to varying extents, and became a common approach to manage frontiers in the Chinese imperial tradition. As the system developed, its application was not limited to soldiers and the purpose went beyond guarding borderlands. At times *tuntian* involved civilians and focused more on land reclamation than on border defence. For example, the military farms in Taiwan during the Zheng period were a form of *tuntian*, and their main purpose was to support the soldiers.

The Qing Dynasty continued with the tradition of *tuntian*. To increase land reclamation and agriculture activities in Xinjiang, the Qing government organised five types of *tuntian*: by military forces, Han civilians, the local Hui people, bannermen and exiled criminals.[94]

The difference between *tuntian* and ordinary reclamation lay in that *tuntian* was a state-organised land reclamation system where people belonged to military or quasi-military structures. It usually occurred in frontier areas, and involved mobilising people from the heartland to the frontiers, organising them into regiments and allocating them a certain amount of land.

Aborigines as military reserves

The aboriginal colonies in Taiwan were a type of *tuntian*, but the purpose was the special one of building aboriginal military reserves, and the organisation had certain Qing characteristics.

It has been argued that the aboriginal colony system was a design using the plains aborigines to form a kind of baffle zone to separate the settlers and the mountain aborigines, forming a structure of three ethnic zones: the Han settlers in the western plains, the mountain aborigines in the central and eastern areas, and the plains aborigines in between.[95] In fact, the three-zone structure may be the consequence of the aboriginal colony system, but it was not the design.

The establishment of aboriginal colonies was prompted by the Lin Shuangwen uprising, which broke out in 1786 (Qianlong 51). This was the second large-scale Han uprising in Qing Taiwan, following the first uprising in 1721. However the 1721 uprising was suppressed within a month, while the 1786 uprising was much more serious and lasted for over a year. Within one month after it broke out, the rebels took Zhanghua and Zhuluo counties, and threatened the prefectural capital. The Qing government sent troops from the mainland to suppress the uprising. Among these troops were *tunlian* (屯練 militia) forces from Hunan, Guizhou,

Guangxi and Sichuan Provinces.[96] The contribution of the *tunlian* forces inspired the creation of aboriginal colonies in Taiwan after the rebellion was crushed.

The rebellion prompted the emperor to restructure the military forces in Taiwan. At first the emperor considered replacing half of the regular military forces with Han Chinese who supported the government during the uprising (*yimin* 義民 loyal/faithful Chinese subjects), and to use some of the confiscated land for their upkeep. However, the grand councillor, Fukangan, who had led the successful suppression of the rebellion, was concerned about the loyalty and discipline of the Chinese, because the uprising itself was triggered by conflicts among settler communities originating from different regions of China.[97] In Taiwan, most settlers were Hoklos (*Fulao* 福佬) from Zhangzhou and Quanzhou of Fujian Province, and the rest were the Hakkas (*Kejia* 客家) from Guangdong Province. Although they were all Han Chinese, the settlers formed diverse sub-ethnic communities, and their rivalries often resulted in communal strife (*xiedou* 械鬥), a phenomenon in the late 18th and early 19th centuries in Taiwan.[98] This rivalry was manifested in the Lin Shuangwen uprising, where settlers originating from Quanzhou and the Hakkas assisted the government to suppress the Zhangzhou-led uprising. The government also mobilised the plains aborigines to help fight the rebels, and the mountain aborigines helped capture Lin Shuangwen in response to the government's promise for a reward. Ethnic relations in Taiwan were a complicated web of competing interests and rivalries, not a simple matter of "Han" versus "aborigines".

Given the complicated rivalry among the different Han groups and the role played by the plains aborigines in the suppression of the uprising, Fukangan proposed that the aborigines be organised into companies[99] to supplement the regular army in Taiwan, utilising the tradition of *tuntian* and following the Sichuan *tunlian* precedent.[100]

Adopting Fukangan's plan, in 1788 the government established 12 quasi-military companies, positioned near the regular armies at either strategic locations or the borders with mountain aborigines. The 12 companies comprised 4,000 strong and brave male aborigines from the 93 plains aboriginal villages. Large villages were used as the bases of the companies, incorporating members from nearby villages. Each company was made up of 300 or 400 members, and was led by a lieutenant (*waiwei* 外委). In addition there were two captains (*qianzong* 千總) and four deputy captains (*bazong* 把總) over the 12 companies.[101] Although the aboriginal warriors were enrolled in the companies, they were not required to relocate to the company's base. There was no centralised training or work. The aborigines performed their tasks based in their own villages, and were mobilised into companies only when necessary.[102] The arrangement indicates that there was no calculated intention to form a three-zone structure.

The choice of the aborigines as military reserves shows that, in Taiwan, not only the ethnic and sub-ethnic relations were complex, but also that the government's attitude towards different ethnic groups was not straightforward. It was not a case of government supporting colonists to the detriment of the aborigines, but rather a matter of choosing the more reliable ally in preparation for times of trouble. The government preferred the aborigines over the Han settlers as its ally; the distrust of the Han settlers partly explained the government's protection of aboriginal land rights.

The land

Since the companies were established as military reserves, it was necessary to find land for the upkeep of the company members, a provision the Qianlong emperor had considered even if the military reserves were chosen from the Han Chinese. As the western plains had been mostly reclaimed by settlers, and the mountain areas were occupied by mountain aborigines, only places near the mountain aboriginal boundaries were available. In 1784 (Qianlong 49), the government had surveyed land near the boundaries, following the surveys in 1750 and 1760 (Qianlong 15 and 25), as part of the clarification of aboriginal boundaries. The survey discovered 11,204 *jia* of illegally reclaimed land, and 5,441 *jia* of vacant land not yet reclaimed. Before the government made a decision about these lands, the rebellion broke out.[103] Following the plan to establish aboriginal colonies, the land was resurveyed. The new survey found an additional 3,735 *jia* of reclaimed land, and a total 5,691 *jia* of unreclaimed land.

The 5,691 *jia* of unreclaimed land was allocated to the 4,000 aboriginal warriors. Depending on the distance from their respective villages, each warrior received one to 1.6 *jia* of land. The lieutenants and captains received slightly more. This land was called "upkeep land" (*yangshan pudi* 養贍埔地), since it was for the upkeep of the company members. The government imposed rents on the reclaimers of the 3,735 *jia* of illicitly reclaimed land, and used the rent to pay the warriors' monthly allowance. As such the government in effect confiscated the land. To distinguish it from the upkeep land, this land was called "company land" (*tundi* 屯地). The 11,204 *jia* of reclaimed land surveyed in 1784 fell outside the aboriginal colony system and was dealt with separately.[104]

The concepts of "upkeep land" and "company land" were quite different. Company land was part of the government estate.[105] The government set rentals, appointed people to collect the rent, and distributed it to company members. The nature of upkeep land was more complicated. One legal scholar has defined it as "inheritable property of the company individuals" (*tunding de shixiye* 屯丁的世襲業), of which the individuals had ownership.[106] This view is worth re-examination. In theory the upkeep land was allocated to individual company members. When they left the company due to old age, health issues or death, the replacing person would inherit the land. Usually the incoming person was chosen from the outgoing member's family or close relatives,[107] but this was different from automatic succession by a member's family or descendants. In reality, aborigines from the same village often managed their land together. Regulations specified that the land was for the aboriginal warriors to "cultivate themselves" (*zixing gengzhong* 自行耕種).[108] If the aborigines *dianmài* (典賣 pledged or sold) the land, the purchaser was liable to return the land to the village to which the aboriginal warrior belonged, along with other punishments.[109] Therefore the upkeep land essentially belonged to the village of the aboriginal warriors, rather than the individual aborigines or the *tun* companies. This collective land holding of the upkeep land was the same as the aborigines' customary land holding. It helped to preserve the aboriginal community structure and land tenure.

Although the aborigines were allocated the land as an aspect of the military design, in the subsequent century the companies were mobilised only 18 times, half of which were to put down Han banditry or communal strife, and half against the non-acculturated aborigines in the late Qing period.[110] The allocation of upkeep land and the distribution of monthly allowance from company land rental were seen by later officials as a reward to the aborigines for their support to the government during the 1786 uprising, as well as a way to guard the aboriginal boundaries.[111] The establishment of aboriginal colonies hence went a step further than protecting the aborigines' ancestral land, as the government allocated to the acculturated aborigines land that they did not have – the land bordered the aboriginal boundaries and likely belonged to the non-acculturated aborigines who had retreated further into the mountains.

To some extent, the organisation of the acculturated aborigines into companies was similar to that of the Qing banner (*qi* 旗) system. Under the Manchu banner system, all Manchus were organised into eight banners.[112] Each banner was a social unit for land distribution, production and governance, as well as the source and management structure of warriors.[113] Therefore the system was a form of organising fighting forces as well as a way of organising Manchu society. The bannermen enjoyed privileged status, and the banner system helped to preserve Manchu identity because of the exclusive membership, unique structure and distinct status.[114] Similarly, under the *fantun* system, although only 4,000 aboriginal warriors were chosen for the companies, the aboriginal families and villages formed a closed pool from which the warriors were drawn, and a basic unit for continuing possession of land. The aboriginal warriors' families and descendants were closely associated with the company units. Just like the banner system had preserved the Manchu identity, the system of aboriginal companies helped to preserve the acculturated aborigines' identity, even after they had lost their cultural distinctiveness. The protection of "upkeep land" was similar to the protection of banner land. In both cases the government forbade alienation and, if the regulations were breached, frequently ordered the return or redemption of land.[115]

By the time the aboriginal companies were established, the Qianlong reign was drawing to a close. In the 111 years of the High Qing period, there was no significant departure from the central principle of recognising and protecting aboriginal land ownership, although the strength and efforts of protection differed at times. The Kangxi government experienced a gradual realisation and recognition of aboriginal land rights and initiated measures to protect aboriginal land; the Yongzheng government promoted land reclamation but most of the time refrained from intervening between settlers and aboriginal, and remained mindful of aboriginal land ownership; the Qianlong government tried to stop Han reclamation of aboriginal land but seemed to be always one step behind the settlers and had to constantly resurvey aboriginal land and redraw boundaries lines. The appointment of aboriginal affairs sub-prefects saw settler-aborigine land issues stabilised, and the aboriginal colony system entrenched the identity and "upkeep land" of the plains aborigines. Yet at the turn of the century, the situation was about to change.

The government becomes proactive (1796–1874)

Corresponding to the government's changing attitude towards settlement in Taiwan since the Jiaqing reign, officials' approach to aboriginal land became proactive. This was demonstrated in the cases of Gamalan and inner Shuishalian. In contrast to previous government's efforts to exclude aboriginal land from settler reclamation, and moving away from a policy of acting as the adjudicator between settlers and aborigines over land disputes, the government took control of land allocation.

Land appropriation in Gamalan

Before Gamalan was incorporated in the realm, the aboriginal village heads, seeking government protection from the settlers' intrusion, had presented their population information and petitioned to be incorporated into the empire when the Fujian-Zhejiang governor-general visited Gamalan in 1810.[116] The government seemed to take this as amounting to a surrender of land rights, and took charge of the land in Gamalan. After establishing its administration in Gamalan, the government distributed the land among settlers and aborigines, even though it recognised that the land was aboriginal land.

The Gamalan plain was divided into two parts by the Zhuoshui River. North of the river was called "the Western Part" (*xishi* 西勢) and south of the river "the Eastern Part" (*dongshi* 東勢). Before government administration was established, Han settlement was concentrated at the Western Part. Settlers had reclaimed all land in the Western Part apart from one area called Shalunpu. The Western Part had 20 aboriginal villages, with 2,277 aborigines. After the government established administration, it recognised that some land had to be reserved for the aborigines' livelihood, and stipulated Shalunpu to be the aborigines' perpetual property. Settlers were not allowed to encroach there. Thus Shalunpu was a kind of aboriginal reserve. The Eastern Part had 16 aboriginal villages, with a population of 3,307. Settlers only reclaimed a small proportion of the Eastern Part.[117] The government stipulated that one *li* of land around small villages and two *li* of land around large villages were reserved for aborigines.[118] The reserves were in addition to land that was already under cultivation by the aborigines.

Although setting aside of the reserves shows that the government did not entirely disregard the rights of the aborigines, the reserves were too small to sustain the aborigines' living. The aboriginal reserves in the Eastern Part measured 1,255 *jia*, averaging less than 79 *jia* per village and 0.38 *jia* per person.[119] The provision for the aborigines in the Western Part was even less. The reserved area in Shalunpu was 625 *jia*, of which only 495 *jia* was available as reserves for the aborigines.[120] This means that the average reserve was less than 25 *jia* of land per village, and less than 0.22 *jia* per person. As a comparison, the inspecting censors of the Yongzheng reign recommended 300–500 *jia* per village, and the aboriginal colonies of the Qianlong reign provided each warrior at least 1.0 *jia* of land, in addition to their ancestral land. The reserves in Gamalan were clearly insufficient for the aborigines.

Furthermore, while the settlers were forbidden to lease land that was under aboriginal cultivation, the government allowed the reserved land to be leased to settlers. In fact, the government allocated the reserved land among the settlers, who were required to pay an annual rent of 4 *shi* of grain per *jia*. In Taiwan, the prevalent large rent rate was 4 *shi* per *jia* for dry land, but once the land was developed into paddy land, the rent rate was increased to 8 *shi* per *jia*. The stipulation of rent rates through government action, as opposed to leaving it to the parties concerned to reach agreements, resulted in the aborigines losing the opportunity to raise the rent in the future when the land was developed into paddy land. Another problem with large rent, as discussed in Chapter 4, is that the lessor retained only the right to receive the fixed amount of rent, and lost any other rights over the land. The total annual rent for the Eastern Part reserves was 5,124 *shi*, averaging 1.55 *shi* per person per year; for the Western Part, in average each person could receive only 0.88 *shi* of grains annually.[121] This was far from sufficient to sustain living. Therefore, although it looks like the government was protective of the aborigines through setting aside reserves and managing the reserves for the unsophisticated aborigines, in effect the government deprived the aborigines of the reserved land permanently, and the compensation to the aborigines was the minimal annual rent.

The government did not stipulate compensation or rent for land beyond the reserved areas. The land that settlers had reclaimed in the Western Part before government intervention measured over 2,400 *jia*. No lease agreement about this area of land is available, although records mention in passing that settlers had leased the land, often unfairly or fraudulently.[122] After the incorporation, the government allowed the settlers to register this land for taxation, and did not concern itself with whether the aborigines had been compensated.

Unreclaimed land in the Eastern Part measured 2,538 *jia*, and this was taken from the aborigines and allocated to the settlers. The emperor's decree of 1820 (Jiaqing 15) only mentioned that "as to those uncultivated lands, investigate the land boundaries. [Define] which part is for which group of settlers to reclaim, and which part is for aboriginal villagers to reclaim. [The land] must be divided fairly so as to avoid disputes".[123] No compensation or rent was mentioned for this land. The fact that the aborigines were paid 4 *shi* per *jia* of rent for the reserved land suggests that land outside the reserves was taken from the aborigines and was given to the settlers with no payment involved.

The government also had a well-thought-out plan to benefit from colonisation. Different from the previous approaches in the western plains where a permit holder might apply for a huge area of land, the government in Gamalan limited the area of each land permit to five *jia*. The purpose of this was to remove the class of large rent owners, so that the land developed could be treated as government estate.[124] Thus there was a new element of calculation for revenue. Interestingly, the ideas of aboriginal reserves and of limiting the area of each permit were both from the Yongzheng era, although neither was adopted then.[125]

The weak position of the aborigines vis-à-vis the settlers might have been one reason of the government's proactive and high-handed approach. As at the time of incorporation, the settler population was over 45,000, and the aboriginal population was under 6,000.[126] The establishment of aboriginal reserves was designed as a kind of protection, and the management of the reserves by the government was thought to be necessary because the aborigines were "ignorant/stupid" (*yu* 愚), and could be deceived by settlers if the government did not intervene.[127] But overall, it was the first time that the government acted not as an adjudicator in settler-aborigine land disputes, but as an actor itself to take away aboriginal land, to distribute it to settlers and to manage the reserves for the aborigines. The government also attempted to benefit from the colonisation. The differences, in particular the adoption of rejected proposals of the Yongzheng era of just a century ago, signify a turning point of the Qing approaches towards aboriginal land.

"Pilot reclamation" in inner Shuishalian

As already discussed, the Daoguang government several times considered opening up inner Shuishalian for settlement and there was a strong push from local officials for opening up (see Chapter 2). Before the central government finally decided to continue closing off inner Shuishalian, local officials had attempted to colonise the land.

The Fujian-Zhejiang governor-general, Liu Yunke, investigated inner Shuishalian in 1746 (Daoguang 26). According to Liu's calculations, the six villages under consideration had 1,020 people, and occupied an area with about 12,000 *jia* of land that could be reclaimed. Liu reported that the aborigines were eager to surrender their land for the government to "manage".[128] The concept of government "managing" aboriginal land had derived from the Gamalan approach.

What the governor-general did not allude to, and not known by the central government, was that local officials had already made detailed plans to have the land reclaimed, and had started to implement them. The aboriginal affairs sub-prefect for the Northern Circuit, Shi Mi, had arranged for "pilot reclamation" (*shiken* 試墾). This meant that the local government had raised money to reclaim the land as a pilot project before opening up the land for settler reclamation.[129] A number of officials, including the Taiwan circuit intendant, the Taiwan prefect, county magistrates and the aboriginal affairs sub-prefect himself, each undertook to provide funds for this venture. The Taiwan regional commander sent a troop of 200 soldiers to be stationed in the area.[130] Probably this troop was there to intimidate the aborigines and to suppress any resistance, even though the sub-prefect reported that the aborigines "seeing that the government took control, were all very happy and at peace".[131] The local government officials, from the provincial governor-general, the Taiwan circuit intendant and the civil and military chiefs of Taiwan, to the aboriginal affairs sub-prefect, all acted in concert. The arrangement showed that they were determined to create a *fait accompli* in case there was any opposition from the central government. It is ironic that the official appointed to protect aborigines and prevent Han reclamation of aboriginal land became the proponent of reclaiming aboriginal land.

Officials in total sponsored reclamation of about 2,000 *jia* of land as government estate. They also secured some wealthy Han settlers' undertaking to reclaim over 7,000 *jia*.[132] The plan was that for each *jia* of land, the aborigines would receive 1 *shi* of grain every year, one-eighth of the usual large rent rate in Taiwan. Since the aboriginal population was small compared with the large area of land that they occupied, the total rent was deemed sufficient for the population at that time.[133] However the plan essentially was a compulsory government action to deprive the aborigines of their land forever without proper compensation.

The local officials were forced to abandon their venture after the central government took the final decision not to open up the land. However, there was no question that if inner Shuishalian had been opened, the government would certainly have taken control of the land and implemented the local officials' plans. Similar to the Gamalan approach, this was inconsistent with the pre-1800 policies.

The need to find additional revenues when the Qing was under financial pressure was only part of the reason for the government and officials' changed attitude towards aboriginal land. There was a strong trend of asserting government ownership and extending government control over land. In the 19th century some Qing officials emphasised the traditional view that the emperor had an ultimate title over all land within the realm. A Taiwan circuit intendant, Xu Zonggan (1848–1853), said "once they submitted, the aborigines are our people, and the land is our land", and suggested that "land reclaimed by aborigines belong to aborigines, land reclaimed by settlers belong to settlers, and the government organise *tuntian* to reclaim the remaining land for rent".[134] In 1871 (Tongzhi 10), in a decree ordering protection of aboriginal land, the aboriginal affairs sub-prefect of the Northern Circuit stated that "the Taiwan aboriginal villages, at the beginning of their submission, were granted land and rental property by the grace of the emperor".[135] These views were based on the old assumption that the emperor owned all land within the realm, and the aborigines surrendered their land once they had submitted themselves to government authority. This line of thinking continued into the post-1875 era.

Increased government intervention (1875–1895)

After 1875, regulations were made to encourage settlement and land reclamation, but none specifically addressed aboriginal land rights. The extent of government recognition and protection of aboriginal land rights can only be gathered from various different sources, and some of the records contradict one another. Overall it appears that the Qing government continued to recognise aboriginal land rights to a certain extent and varying amount of compensation was given by different means, but the aborigines lost the right to decide whether to have their land opened up, and the government followed the Gamalan approach in a number of cases.

Title to land

When the Qing government launched the campaigns to "open the mountains and subjugate the aborigines", it had the clear objective of having the aboriginal territories settled by Chinese settlers. In 1874 (Tongzhi 13), the specially appointed imperial commissioner to Taiwan, Shen Baozhen, reported to the emperor that "behind the mountain ranges, apart from aboriginal villages, it is all vacant land" which must be filled with people and be reclaimed.[136] Shen did not elaborate on whether the Qing tradition of recognising aboriginal ownership over wasteland in Taiwan was being repudiated now that the government was to promote land settlement. The question soon arose, and the answer became more or less clear only in the process of implementing land reclamation policies.

The interim view

A shift of principle emerged in 1875 (Guangxu 1) when the provincial government considered a county magistrate's proposal. The old assertion that the government owned all wasteland in Taiwan, denounced by Chen Bin, was now renewed.

This proposal came from the magistrate of the newly established Hengchun County, who asked for approval of his plans regarding aboriginal land within his jurisdiction. The magistrate stated:[137]

> The forest land and fields have always been managed by the villages according to their boundaries. Now that [the aboriginal villages] have submitted, could it be allowed that they reclaim and farm the forest lands as usual; and those cultivated fields be exempted from tax? The county [government] will order them to specify the land boundaries and also draw pictures and compile ledgers for file. The village boundaries will remain, and [Han] villains (*jiantu* 奸徒) are forbidden from encroaching. . . . Those forest lands that the villages do not have the ability to reclaim and desire to lease to the settlers should be allowed to be leased and registered [with the government].

This proposal clearly recognised aboriginal ownership over all unreclaimed land, as had long been the case. The proposal to allow aborigines to lease their land was a reversion to the Yongzheng government's approach which respected aboriginal freedom of disposal, although more relaxed than the bans under the Kangxi and Qianlong governments. It differed from the Gamalan approach where the government controlled and distributed aboriginal land. The necessity to ask for an instruction reveals the magistrate's uncertainty and points to a changed policy environment. Indeed, the circuit intendant, upon receiving the Governor's direction, answered that:[138]

> [Regarding] the cultivated land . . . [that] each be managed by the villages and exempted from tax is permissible. Those forest lands that the aborigines do not have the ability to farm, the county [magistrate] suggested that [they be]

> leased to the settlers. This may open the gate for later encroachment, and other plans should be made carefully. *And all Taiwan is government land* [*guandi* 官地]. Apart from those reserved for the village upkeep, it should be carefully planned as to how to draw boundaries and recruit reclaimers.

Here the intendant clearly asserted that the unreclaimed land was government land. Since it was government land, the intendant rejected the aborigines' right to lease it. The intendant disguised his answer to appear that it was for fear of settler encroachment on aboriginal land, and he was ambiguous as to what plans should be made for the aborigines. The situation probably was not entirely clear even to the intendant, and his response was only an interim answer. Later guidelines provided a clearer indication on defining aboriginal land and government land.

The 1877 guidelines

Further directions were provided in the "21 guidelines for subjugating the aborigines and opening the mountains", issued by Fujian Governor Ding Richang in 1877 (Guangxu 3).[139] Four of the guidelines related to land. Guideline 4 recognised that village lands were joined together, required clarification of village boundaries and forbade any village to encroach on neighbouring villages' land.[140] Guideline 5 stated that:[141]

> The government's hills that are near the sea and those lands that the aborigines are not able to reclaim can be reclaimed by settlers. Aside from these, the remaining hills, fields and trees that are attached to the [aboriginal] villages should each be managed by its village. Settlers are forbidden to occupy aboriginal property as their own property.

Guideline 16 set out the plan on educating and engaging the aborigines in agricultural work. Guideline 17 stated that "there is much vacant land in the front and at the back of the mountain ranges" and provided mechanisms for recruiting settlers from the mainland.[142] Reading these guidelines together, it is clear that the government encouraged aborigines to reclaim land, and settlers could only reclaim land that the aborigines were not able to reclaim. The reference to "government's hills that are near the sea" in Guideline 5 indicates that the government assumed ownership over land that was not actively controlled by the aborigines.

A decree issued by the Taiwan circuit intendant in 1878 (Guangxu 4) to implement Guidelines 4 and 5 made the previously mentioned principle explicit. The intendant's decree ordered local officials to survey the population and land boundaries of each village, to determine the amount of land that should be reserved for the aborigines and the amount that was beyond the villages' ability to reclaim, and to investigate land "that was distant from aboriginal villages and was wasteland without an owner".[143] Three categories of land were distinguished here: aboriginal land to be reclaimed by aborigines, aboriginal land beyond the aborigines' ability to reclaim which would be reclaimed by settlers, and "wasteland without an owner" which implied government ownership.

On the surface, it appears that the Guangxu government held the same view as that of Chen Bin. That is, land "actively controlled" by aborigines was aboriginal land, but land that was at a distance with less aboriginal control was seen as wasteland and belonging to the government. Two things had changed, though. Firstly, the late Qing government was keen to have all land reclaimed, and was no longer willing to allow the aborigines to leave their land idle. Aborigines who surrendered to the Qing authorities were required to agree on seven conditions, one of which was reclamation of aboriginal land.[144] Land that was recognised as aboriginal land but beyond the aborigines' ability to reclaim would have to be given up for settler reclamation. The Yongzheng era official Lan Dingyuan had articulated such a lone voice, but his proposal was not adopted then. The idea of aboriginal reserves was a continuation of the Gamalan approach. Secondly, Chen regarded all land as controlled by aborigines, but the late Qing government saw distant land as government wasteland. The standard of "control" appears to have changed.

Post-1885 approaches

After 1885, the government continued to recognise aboriginal ownership over wasteland in the aforementioned limited way. Ding's successor Liu Mingchuan, the new Fujian Governor, in his memorial to the emperor in 1885 (Guangxu 11), recognised that "non-acculturated aboriginal territories (*dijie* 地界), each belonged to a village" and recommended that "the military and settlers be not allowed to encroach".[145] Given that Liu vigorously promoted settlement and land reclamation, "non-acculturated aboriginal territories" probably referred only to areas around the aboriginal villages.

In some cases, the government required aborigines to explicitly relinquish their rights. Village heads of surrendering aborigines each gave an "undertaking of surrender" (*toucheng ganjie* 投誠甘結), and promised that "all forests, trees and land shall be open to harvest or reclamation by reclaimers, and [the village] dare not contest [against it in the future]".[146] The government probably regarded this as surrender of the aborigines' title, even though the surrender might not have been voluntary.

A slightly different approach was adopted by the provincial government in 1888 (Guangxu 14). This policy recognised aboriginal rights over their forests and allowed them to cut down and sell the trees, but required the aboriginal villages to reclaim the land. What was not reclaimed within one year would be opened up for Han settlers to reclaim.[147] This was a method suggested 160 years before by Lan Dingyuan in the early Yongzheng era, but it had not been adopted at that time.

Overall, during the "opening and subjugating" stage the government still recognised aboriginal rights over unreclaimed land, but it now restricted this to land over which the aborigines had actual control. Furthermore, the aborigines were forced to open up their land for reclamation. Without the freedom to decide what to do with their land, the aboriginal property rights were greatly impeded. There remains a question of compensation for land that was given up.

Compensation to aborigines

No record has been found to suggest that the government adopted any certain system of taking land from the aborigines or regulated land transactions between settlers and aborigines. Scattered records and references show cases of aborigines receiving rents for land used by settlers.

In some cases, the aborigines retained the power to negotiate terms of use with the settlers, and the government intervened to protect aboriginal rights where necessary. For example, during the late Qing period, the government licensed settlers to cut camphor trees and make camphor products in the aboriginal territories. The government charged a tax for the production, but the aborigines retained property rights over their camphor forest, and received fees from Han settlers who manufactured camphor.[148] Another example was that the Hengchun County made a set of rules regarding settler-aborigine relations, and one of the rules stipulated that settlers were to pay rents and fees to aborigines if they gathered wood and made charcoal in the mountains.[149] This approach was similar to the Yongzheng government's approach, which was to let settlers negotiate use of land with aborigines.

Other records also indicate that aboriginal villages received rent from land reclaimed by settlers, but under government arrangement. A memorial by Liu Mingchuan in 1887 (Guangxu 13) reads:[150]

> I have checked that the seven villages in Daju have fewer than 1,000 aborigines, male and female included. The surrounding land extends over ten *li* and is fertile. Have settlers reclaim the land, and after two or three years, the rent is sufficient to provide grain rations for the seven villages. At the moment the government needs to find funds to feed [the aborigines].

The reference to grain ration (*kouliang* 口糧) suggests that the government assumed responsibility for the aborigines' livelihood. It is likely that the government took control of aboriginal land and in return took care of aboriginal livelihood. This was probably a widespread practice, as records elsewhere show that the government provided aborigines with grain rations and clothing once they submitted to government authority.[151] Although the government appeared to recognise aboriginal land rights, the government went a step further than in the case of Gamalan. In Gamalan, the aborigines still had a lease relationship with the settlers, even though it was imposed by the government; after 1875 the government was in direct control of the land and the people's livelihood. The difference was because the government grew in eagerness to have the land settled and reclaimed.

A different approach was suggested by Taiwan Circuit Intendant Liu Ao in a letter to his superior in 1883 (Guangxu 9). Liu discussed a piece of fertile land in the southern most point in Taiwan, which was suitable for reclamation.[152] In the letter Liu several times mentioned purchasing the land from the aborigines by the government, as an alternative to providing annual financial support to the aborigines. Liu's suggestion of purchase as an alternative solution to grain rations confirms that it was a standard practice to provide grain rations to the aborigines, and the government saw it as a compensation for land taken. Liu's proposal offered a more clear-cut method, but his discussion centred on effectiveness of administration, rather than consideration for land rights.

The previously mentioned examples show varying degrees of government intervention and different patterns of compensation. The prime focus was to have the wasteland settled and reclaimed, but on that basis aboriginal ownership was generally recognised. It is likely that whether compensation was paid depended on whether the aborigines were strong enough to negotiate with the settlers or the government, and whether the aborigines had sufficient living support. Although the government still protected aboriginal rights over land that they cultivated or had the ability to reclaim, the Gamalan approach was preferred over the pre-1800 protection. At best the government took the Yongzheng era approach of letting settlers negotiate with aborigines about use of land. The prevalent approach was close to the Gamalan arrangement, and at times was even more aggressive and authoritarian than the Gamalan arrangement.

The effects of legal tradition

Over the two centuries of Qing rule in Taiwan, the government was largely consistent in recognising the aborigines' ownership over wasteland, although the aborigines' rights over their wasteland and the areas being recognised diminished in the 19th century, especially after 1875. The High Qing governments made reasonable to stringent efforts to protect aboriginal land rights, but in the 19th century the government became a party in organising land reclamation, and the involvement deepened after 1875. At each stage, the legal tradition played a role in shaping the policy shifts, and the Taiwan experience was not unique.

Many parallels of protecting aboriginal land rights could be drawn from other frontiers in the empire. The policies to demarcate land boundaries between aboriginal land and settlers' land, and to order return of aboriginal land to the aborigines, were largely consistent with approaches adopted for other frontiers in the empire. In the first few decades of Qing rule over China, when Manchuria was not strictly closed off, the land was divided into Han Chinese land and Manchu banner land.[153] Regulations strictly forbade sale or lease of banner land to Han Chinese, and provided for return of banner land to the banners if it had fallen into Han hands.[154] Land in Mongolia was also protected from Han purchase and lease, and those who breached the law against lease, purchase or sell the land were to be punished.[155] Similar policies were implemented in Yunnan to protect the Yunnan aborigines' land. Through to the early 19th century, the government tried to prevent indigenous land being mortgaged or leased in Yunnan.[156] It is apparent that there was a general pattern of protecting aboriginal land rights, shaped by the legal tradition, most notably the Chinese land tenure and Confucian legal thoughts.

Land tenure and recognition of aboriginal land rights

The Chinese traditional concepts of the "king's" ownership over all land within the realm and "land grant" (*shoutian* 授田) in some respects were similar to the English doctrine of tenure, whose "two-fold fiction" assumed that the Crown originally owned all land, and that all titles originated from the Crown.[157] There were important differences, however. Chinese tradition focused on agriculture and the system classified land into two broad categories, agricultural land (*tian* 田) and other land (*di* 地) which could be turned into agricultural land through reclamation. Unreclaimed wasteland was seen as "land without an owner". This means the system recognised that the "king's ownership", or in other words, the government's underlying title, over wasteland was not a proprietary right as such, rather it was the power to make grants.[158]

Because of the position of the government in the land tenure system, there was little obstacle to the government's recognising aboriginal ownership over unreclaimed land, while exercising its administrative power to require that the aborigines open up land for reclamation. The High Qing governments refrained from exercising such powers, but the later governments were more aggressive. Furthermore, the financial benefits that the government gained from land grants were not in the grants themselves, but in the annual land tax that grantees paid. Because the government did not have proprietary interests in wasteland, and did not take pecuniary gains from making grants, the government did not need to compete with the aborigines for ownership over unreclaimed land in Taiwan. Since recognising aboriginal land rights did not restrict the government's power to make grants and did not affect the government's financial interests, the Qing government readily recognised aboriginal ownership over wasteland in Taiwan. This was why the recognition was mostly consistent during the Qing period, even though government policies regarding land reclamation had shifted from restriction to promotion.

The recognition, however, was not universal in Taiwan. Some Qing officials had asserted that the government owned all land once the aborigines submitted, but these occasions were rare and they typically arose when the benevolence of the emperor or the public power of the government to make grants was claimed, and usually in the sense of dominion rather than property. The concept of "land without an owner" was still at work in the government's view of wasteland in Taiwan. The government did not see an "owner" over land that the aborigines did not have clear control of, and regarded such land as wasteland which it was free to dispose of.

It was therefore the legal tradition that allowed the recognition of aboriginal land in Taiwan, as well as limiting the recognition.

Confucian legal thought and protection of aboriginal land rights

The most important principles of Confucian legal thought were monarchism (*junzhu zhuyi* 君主主義), familism (*jiazu zhuyi* 家族主義), people-centredness (*min benwei* 民本位) and preference for good officials in maintaining good governance (*zhifa yongxian* 執法用賢).[159] As discussed in Chapter 2, monarchism and people-centredness in fact divided the constitutional actors in imperial China into two major parts, the monarch, who was the absolute authority, and the people, who formed the basis. Familism drew an analogy between governance of the empire and management of a family, emphasising the father-like figure of the monarch, who had authority over as well as responsibility to his subjects. Preference for good officials in maintaining good governance favoured "governing by men" (*renzhi* 人治) and distrusted "governing by law" (*fazhi* 法治).[160] These principles, together with Qing consciousness of the fact that it was a minority ruler, shaped Qing protection of aboriginal land rights in Taiwan.

The monarch and good imperial subjects

Different from Western colonisation where the encounters were often one people against another, that is, the coloniser against the colonised, in Qing Taiwan, as in imperial China, the main relationship was the ruler over the masses. All peoples, settlers and aborigines alike, were equal subjects of the emperor. The objective of the government was to "make good imperial subjects out of the . . . population".[161] To achieve a power balance and maintain social stability in an environment with complex ethnic relations, the ruler suppressed those groups of people that were potential trouble-makers, and protected the groups that could be potential allies. In Qing Taiwan the trouble-makers tended to be the settlers. The Manchus' status as minority rulers likely also influenced the decision to favour the minority aborigines over the Han settlers.

As a result, in Taiwan the Qing Court sought to protect aborigines from settlers. The Court was fully aware of the importance of land, and protecting aboriginal land against Han settlement and encroachment was the most important part of protecting the aborigines. However, protection of aboriginal land rights was not an end itself, rather it was a means to achieve a power balance and social stability. This was the reason why the policy was inconsistent at times, allowing land reclamation provided it did not threaten social stability, and even taking control of aboriginal land and exercising managerial roles when political needs required urgent settlement of the land.

During the Qing's two centuries of rule of Taiwan, the plains aborigines rarely rose against the government. In contrast, Han settlers often rebelled and the government continuously sought to guard itself against the settlers. This illustrates the government's relationships with the aborigines and settlers, respectively, and explains the government's policy orientation and its effects. The mountain aborigines were mostly left alone until the last 20 years of Qing rule, when the government became forceful, partly because settlers were fewer than desired to fill the land for security purposes.

Paternalism

Being the head of the big "family" and the carer of the people, the monarch and his officials had the responsibility for the well-being of the people. The Confucian and Mencian tradition called for a paternalistic approach towards the weaker party, that is, towards aborigines who faced settler aggression.

During the early Qing period, the emperors and many officials took the traditional paternalistic stance and saw the people as *chizi* (赤子 literally "naked child", meaning a helpless baby needing protection). For example, Shi Lang's memorial to recommend annexation of Taiwan argued that "both the aborigines and settlers are [the emperor's] children";[162] Zhuluo County magistrate, Ji Qiguang, pleaded that "now that Taiwan has entered the realm, the aborigines (*tufan* 土番) are [the emperor's] children (*chizi*)".[163] Chen Bin, the circuit intendant who argued for banning reclamation of aboriginal land, asked rhetorically, "Are they [the aborigines] alone not the children of the heavenly dynasty?"[164] The Qianlong emperor also claimed that "both settlers and aborigines are our children".[165] Because of this attitude, Qing officials often voiced their criticism of Han encroaching on aborigines' living space and taking of their land. For the same reason, the government felt an obligation to protect the aboriginal well-being, of which the main component was land.[166]

The limitation of this approach was that the land issue was seen as integral to aboriginal livelihood, but was not an issue of aboriginal land rights as such. Therefore, provided that aboriginal livelihood was secure, protection of aboriginal land did not need to be on the agenda. Believing that the aboriginal livelihood had been taken care of after the reserves were made, the government distributed the remaining land in Gamalan to settlers. The arbitrary design of 1 *shi* of rent for per *jia* of land in Shuishalian was based on the same thinking. Similarly, after 1875, the government took away aboriginal land and in return assumed the responsibility to provide food and clothing for the aborigines on an ongoing basis. Here the government was in the position of an authoritarian father, who had the authority to take away land and the obligation to provide for the "children". There was no parallel to modern law which requires a proper procedure to extinguish aboriginal title to land.

Governing by men, not by law

The Chinese tradition that "governing by men will work, but governing by law will not work" dates back 2,000 years to the Confucian philosopher Xunzi (313–238 BC).[167] The philosophy behind this concept was that "laws cannot stand alone, precedents cannot apply themselves. With suitable persons, [laws and precedents] will be upheld; without suitable persons, [they] amount to nothing".[168] Following this tradition, Chinese rulers believed that "the public enacting of law is not necessary in the ideal state, and . . . government by law should always be kept secondary to government by moral precept and example".[169] Following the Chinese legal tradition, law-making during the Qing Dynasty had two features – a system of administrative law and an emphasis on managing officials.[170] The government focused more on cultivating good officials than making good laws. Laws were made to guide officials' actions, rather than to inform the people. This focus contributed in large part to the inconsistencies of Qing land policies in Taiwan.

The reluctance to make law meant that there was no systematic law-making to address issues. Although during the Qing Dynasty regulations proliferated, they were not coordinated and not always consistent. Individual regulations were made in a piecemeal manner and collectively they had loopholes, and could not address a problem or achieve the goal thoroughly. More often than not, laws were made to deal with a problem, when a situation had deteriorated. As the Yongzheng emperor said, the government "should not change the law unless the change will bring ten-fold benefit, [and] should not change the custom unless the harm caused by the old custom is ten-fold".[171] This was the reason why aboriginal land issues were not dealt with until a few decades after the annexation, and why the Qianlong government had repeatedly to clarify land boundaries and order return of land to aborigines after serious encroachment by settlers.

The emperors' supreme status above the law and the focus on good officials meant that the personal attributes and beliefs of the emperors and officials played an important role in aboriginal land issues in Taiwan. As these attributes and beliefs varied, the policies and their implementation tended to be inconsistent. The Qing system in particular required the emperor to play a part in every important decision, and had a strong characteristic of "personal rule".[172] The Kangxi and Qianlong emperors had strong views against land reclamation in Taiwan, and the protection was more vigorous during their reigns. When the emperor and the central government were weak, as they were during the period 1800–1875, local officials were able to force their views and the protection was weakened. The belief in "governing by men" generated a complex dynamic of clashes of ideas and compromises. It made policymaking and implementation flexible, but inconsistent at times.

Overall, the Qing protective stance towards aboriginal land rights was the result of Qing legal traditions, particularly the government's place in the land ownership system and the Confucian notion of good governance. Confucian tradition stressed the authority of the good monarch, benevolence towards the people, and selection and management of good officials while intentionally neglecting law-making. Furthermore, the fact that formal law focused on administrative and criminal matters also meant that property matters were largely governed by Chinese customary practice. The next chapter discusses how this aspect of the legal tradition allowed Chinese land tenure to influence and change aboriginal land tenure in Taiwan.

Notes

1 For example, Shih Tien-fu "Qingdai Taiwan 'fanli bu'an gengzuo' de yuanyou" [The Reasons Behind the Aborigines Being "Unskilful at Farming"] (1990) 69 *Bulletin of the Institute of Ethnology Academia Sinica* 67, at 77–87; Wu Qi-hao "You Dadushe zai tan Qingdai Taiwan zhi shufan diquan" [A Discussion of the Acculturated Aborigines' Land Rights Through a Case Study on the Dadu Village] (2003) 20 *Taiwan shiliao yanjiu* 34, at 62.

2 For example, Chen Chiu-kun "Shijiu shiji chuqi tuzhu diquan wailiu wenti – yi Anlishe de tudi jingying weili" [The Aborigines' Land Loss in the Early 19th Century – A Case Study on the Land Management of the Anli Village] in Chen Chiu-kun and Hsu Hsueh-chi (eds) *Taiwan lishi shang de tudi wenti* [Land Issues in Historical Taiwan] (Academia Sinica, Taipei, 1992) 29, at 30; Chen Chiu-kun *Qingdai Taiwan tuzhu diquan:*

guanliao, handian yu Anlishe ren de tudi bianqian 1700–1895 (*Taiwan's Aboriginal Proprietary Rights in the Ch'ing Period: Bureaucracy, Han Tenants and the Transformation of Property Rights of the Anli Tribe, 1700–1895*) (2nd ed, Academia Sinica, Taipei, 1997), at 222–223.

3 See John Robert Shepherd *Statecraft and Political Economy on the Taiwan Frontier, 1600–1800* (Stanford University Press, Stanford, 1993), ch 9, in particular at 305–306.

4 At 305–306.

5 See Ka Chih-ming *Fantoujia: Qingdai Taiwan zuqun zhengzhi yu shufan diquan* (*The Aborigine Landlord: Ethnic Politics and Aborigine Land Rights in Qing Taiwan*) (Academia Sinica, Taipei, 2003), ch 2, in particular, at 58–61.

6 See discussions in ibid, at 25–26, and 363–370.

7 The three-zone ethnic division is the central argument of Ka. See, in particular, ch 7 and 9. However, arguably the three-zone ethnic division was more a natural consequence of Han settlement rather than the design of the government, as traditionally the plains aborigines lived in the western plains and the mountain aborigines in the central and eastern mountains, and later the plains aborigines were pushed towards the mountains by the settlers. The government at best made policies according to the situation, rather than establishing such a structure.

8 *Shijing.xiaoya.beishan* [Book of Songs], "普天之下莫非王土" (Chinese Text Project, www.ctext.org).

9 Wang Wenjia *Zhongguo tudi zhidushi* [History of Chinese Land Tenure] (Zhongzheng, Taipei, 1956), at 26–28. It is worth noting that in recent years some scholars have argued that Western Zhou operated a bureaucratic system, as opposed to a feudal system. For example, see Li Feng "Feudalism and Western Zhou China: A Criticism" (2003) 63 *Harvard Journal of Asiatic Studies* 115–144. However the evidence and arguments do not relate to land issues.

10 There exist ancient records about the system. Although there are some doubts as to whether it was a record of practice or a suggestion of design, scholars generally accept that the tenure had existed. See Zhao Gang and Chen Zhongyi *Zhongguo tudi zhidushi* [History of Chinese Land Tenure] (Lianjing, Taipei, 1982), at 1–3; Chen Guyuan *Zhongguo fazhishi* [Legal History of China] (Zhongguo shudian, Beijing, 1988, facsimile copy of Shangwu yinshuguan, 1934), at 326–327.

11 See Zhao and Chen, ibid, ch 1, for the development of the land system since the Qin Dynasty.

12 For example, ibid, at 19; Chen, above n 10, at 327.

13 For example, Linshi Taiwan Jiuguan Diaochahui *Taiwan sifa* [Private Law of Taiwan], vol 1 (Chinese translation, Taiwansheng wenxian weiyuanhui, Taizhong, 1990, original first published in 1910), vol 1, at 52; Wang Tay-sheng *Taiwan falüshi gailun* [Introduction to the History of Laws of Taiwan] (4th ed, Yuanzhao, Taipei, 2012), at 77 and 79.

14 Wayne Morrison (ed) *Blackstone's Commentaries on the Laws of England* (Cavendish, London, 2001), vol 2, at 42 ("*Blackstone's Commentaries*").

15 At 86.

16 For example see John H Baker *An Introduction to English Legal History* (4th ed, Butterworths, London, 2002), at 230.

17 At 229.

18 At 259.

19 At 263.

20 *Blackstone's Commentaries*, above n 14, at 42.

21 For a more in-depth analysis of the legal nature of private land rights in imperial China, see Ruiping Ye "User Rights or Ownership: The Nature of Land Rights in Imperial China – Using Taiwan During the Qing Period as a Case Study" (2014) 20 *New Zealand Association for Comparative Law Yearbook* 169–198.

22 For example, Zhao and Chen, above n 10, at 41.

23 At 52.

24 At 194.
25 At 59.
26 For detailed accounts of the registers mentioned in this paragraph, see ibid, at 81–86.
27 At 81. Pictures of land as drawn on the register often resembled the shape of fish scales, hence the name.
28 At 83. The "yellow register" was adjusted and renamed "red register" during the Kangxi reign.
29 At 81.
30 See *Huangchao wenxian tongkao* [Comprehensive Collection of Important Documents of the Qing Dynasty, 1797] (Chinese Text Project, www.ctext.org) ("*Wenxian tongkao*"), vol 1, at 27.
31 Vol 3, at 1 and 20.
32 *Qinding Daqing huidian shili* [Imperially Approved Precedents of the Great Qing Institutes, 1886] (Chinese Text Project, www.ctext.org) ("*Huidian shili*"), vol 166 (no pagination).
33 Ibid. Also see *Wenxian tongkao*, above n 30, vol 4, at 13.
34 Yang Ying *Congzheng shilu* [Veritable Records of Zheng Chenggong's Expeditions] (TWWX 32), at 190.
35 *Qingdai Taiwan dazu diaochashu* [Collection of Large Rent Documents in Qing Taiwan] (TWWX 152), collects land reclamation permits issued as early as 1685, the year after the annexation ("*Dazu diaocha*"). Land permits will be discussed in Chapter 4.
36 Song Tsêng-chang "Qingdai Taiwan fuken cuoshi zhi chengxiao jiqi yingxiang" [The Consequences and Influences of the Qing's Land and Aboriginal Policies in Taiwan] (1979) 30(1) *Taiwan Wen Hsien* 142, at 145.
37 See Ji Qiguang "Tiaochen Taiwan shiyiwen" [A Discussion on Taiwan Affairs] in Taiwan Shiliao Jicheng Bianji Weiyuanhui (ed) *Ming Qing Taiwan dang'an huibian* [Collection of Historic Documents Concerning Taiwan During the Ming and Qing Dynasties] (Yuanliu, Taipei, 2004–2009) ("*Ming Qing dang'an*"), vol 9, at 228, "南北草地一望荒蕪，得人開墾，可成沃壤".
38 At 107, "多方招徠，因而冊有續增之丁口，野有新辟之田園".
39 Fan Xian *Chongxiu Taiwan fuzhi* [Revised Gazetteer of Taiwan Prefecture, 1747] (TWWX 105), at 137.
40 The Shunzhi and Kangxi governments both provided extended grace tax periods to encourage land reclamation. See the decrees in *Huidian shili*, above n 32, vol 166 (no pagination). Also see *Wenxian tongkao*, above n 30, vol 1, at 16 and vol 2, at 13.
41 See decrees issued in 1644 (Shunzhi 1), 1671 (Kangxi 10), 1724 (Yongzheng 2) in *Huidian shili*, ibid, vol 166 (no pagination); *Wenxian tongkao*, ibid, vol 2, at 12 and vol 3, at 8.
42 See Ji Qiguang "Zaichen Taiwan shiyiwen" [A Further Discussion on Taiwan Affairs] in Chen Wenda (ed) *Taiwan xianzhi* [Gazetteer of Taiwan County, 1720] (TWWX 103), at 232, "既入版圖 . . . 則尺地皆王土，一民皆王人".
43 Zhou Yuanwen *Chongxiu Taiwan fuzhi* [Revised Gazetteer of Taiwan Prefecture, 1718] (TWWX 66), at 316, "因土番不諳耕種，原撥定地土與土番捕鹿".
44 For example, Zhuluo County magistrate, Ji Qiguang, and Xiamen-Taiwan circuit intendant, Gao Gongqian (Kangxi 32–34), both issued such decrees. See *Ming Qing Dang'an*, above n 37, vol 9, at 100–101; Gao Gongqian *Taiwan fuzhi* [Gazetteer of Taiwan Prefecture, 1694] (TWWX 65), at 249.
45 Fan, above n 39, at 478–479.
46 See Zhou Zhongxuan *Zhuluo xianzhi* [Gazetteer of Zhuluo County, 1717] (TWWX141), at 267–8. Ruan's writing is also discussed in Chapter 1 of this book.
47 This quote is taken from a paraphrase in Wen Ji *Taiwan fanzheng zhi* [A History of Aboriginal Management in Taiwan] (translated and adapted from Inō Kanori *Taiwan bansei shi* (Taiwansheng wenxian weiyuanhui, Taipei, 1957), at 68. The original decree is not extant.

48 For example, see land reclamation permits and government notices collected in *Dazu diaocha*, above n 35, at 2–4, issued between 1709 (Kangxi 48) and 1727 (Yongzheng 5).

49 Chen Bin *Chen Qingduangong wenxuan* [Selected Writings of Chen Bin] (TWWX 116), at 16.

50 Ibid. There is no record of laws being made to this effect, but Lan Dingyuan *Ping Tai jilüe* [Brief Accounts of the Pacification of Taiwan, 1723] (TWWX 14), at 54 states that "in the past, reclamation of aborigines' land has been forbidden". Also see Shepherd, above n 3, at 247 and 257.

51 See the statistics in Liu Liangbi *Chongxiu Fujian Taiwan fuzhi* [Revised Gazetteer of Taiwan Prefecture, Fujian, 1741] (TWWX 74), at 129–134.

52 Chen, above n 49, at 13.

53 Ding Zongluo *Chen Qingduangong nianpu* [A Chronological Biography of Chen Bin, 1825] (TWWX 207), at 80, "臺灣原無荒地；南北路荒地雖多，俱是土番鹿場".

54 *Qing huidian Taiwan shili* [Great Qing Institutes, Precedents Concerning Taiwan] (TWWX 226), at 43: "福建臺灣各番鹿場閑曠地方可以墾種者，令地方官曉諭，聽各番租與民人耕種" ("*Taiwan shili*").

55 See Madeline Zelin "The Yung-cheng Reign" in Willard J Peterson (ed) *The Cambridge History of China Volume 9: The Ch'ing Dynasty to 1800 Part One* (Cambridge University Press, Cambridge, 2002), at 183–229.

56 *Wenxian tongkao*, above n 30, vol 3, at 1, "國家承平日久，生齒殷繁，土地所出僅可贍給。倘遇荒歉，民食維艱。將來戶口日增，何以爲業。惟開墾一事，于百姓最有裨益。"

57 At 1 and 29, "是以屢頒諭旨，勸民墾種".

58 Zelin, above n 55, at 215–218; William T Rowe "Social Stability and Social Change" in Peterson (ed), above n 55, at 484.

59 Lan, above n 50, at 54.

60 Ibid.

61 See *Yongzheng zhupi zouzhe* [Memorials With Rescripts of the Yongzheng Emperor] (TWWX 300), at 44.

62 Shepherd, above n 3, at 258, notes that the scheme would limit the aborigines' claim of land.

63 See the emperor's rescript in *Yongzheng zhupi zouzhe*, above n 61, at 44.

64 See Liu, above n 51, at 135.

65 The increase started in 1728 because it usually took a few years for the reclamation to be completed. The Qing tradition was to allow three years for reclamation of virgin land, and one year for *paohuang* land. See *Wenxian tongkao*, above n 30, vol 1, at 16. Also see a land reclamation permit in *Dazu diaocha*, above n 35, vol 1, at 1.

66 See the decree in *Wenxian tongkao*, ibid, vol 3, at 20–21.

67 Ka argued that the policy intended to encourage registration of aboriginal land that the settlers were allowed to reclaim, and would have reclaimed, following the 1724 decree. This was a misunderstanding, as Ka did not cite the original decree, but rather cited a Taiwan official's memorial which mentioned the policy. See Ka, above n 5, at 109–110.

68 See Liu, above n 51, at 135. The record distinguishes between land that was "newly reclaimed" (*xinken* 新墾), previously reclaimed land that was reported by "self-confession" (*zishou* 自首), and government decision according to the regulation.

69 The tax rates were reduced in 1729 to about a quarter of the previous rates. See land tax rates in Lian Heng Lian Heng *Taiwan tongshi* [A Comprehensive History of Taiwan, 1918] (TWWX 128), at 191.

70 Zelin, above n 55, at 215.

71 *Fujian shengli* [Regulations of Fujian Province] (TWWX 199), at 451–454.

72 "臺灣奸民，私贌熟番土地者，依盜耕本律問擬；於生番界內私墾者，依越度關塞問擬，田仍歸番". *Hubu zeli* [Regulations of the Ministry of Households, cir 1865] (Chinese Text Project, www.ctext.org), vol 10, at 30.

73 *Pu* is a type of land transaction; it is discussed in Chapter 4.
74 See the Ministry of Households report in *Qing Gaozong shilu xuanji* [Selected Veritable Records of the Qianlong Emperor] (TWWX 186), at 51 ("*Gaozong shilu*").
75 Ibid, at 9, 51, 79–80, 126–127, 147–149; Fan, above n 39, at 483.
76 See, respectively, *Taiwan shili*, above n 54, at 44; and above discussion on the Ministry of Households regulation.
77 A further often-cited regulation was that in 1744 (Qianlong 9) which required investigation of estates held by military officers and return of "settlers' land to settlers, aboriginal land to aborigines". This concerned aboriginal land and in effect would have protected aboriginal land rights, but the policy direction was not specifically aboriginal land.
78 This type of lease, called "large rent" (*dazu* 大租), will be discussed in Chapter 4.
79 *Gaozong shilu*, above n 75, at 126–127.
80 A case note in *Dazu diaocha*, above n 35, at 648–649 noted that in Qianlong 32 (1767) the provincial government approved such rent rates. Shepherd, above n 3, at 290–291, quotes a fragment of a 1767 decree collected in Taiwan Sōtokufu Rinji tochi chōsakyoku *Taiwan tochi kankō ippan* [Overview of Customary Land Tenure in Taiwan] (Taipei, 1905), vol 2, at 125. The fragment does not indicate who issued the decree, but is likely to be the one referred to in the case note in *Dazu diaocha*.
81 See Zhang's decree in Linshi Taiwan Jiuguan Diaochahui *Taiwan sifa fulu cankaoshu* [Private Law of Taiwan Reference Book] (Taipei, 1910), vol 1A, at 293–294 ("*Sifa cankao*").
82 See a dispatch in Wu Mi-cha (ed) *Dan Xin dang'an* [Administrative Files of Danshui and Xinzhu Counties] (NTU, Taipei, 1995–2010), vol 17, at 189–190. Song, above n 36, at 147, listed 10 responsibilities of the sub-prefects, which cover all aspects of aboriginal affairs.
83 See the Fujian-Zhejiang governor-general's memorial on establishing aboriginal affairs sub-prefect roles in Inō Kanori (trans Taiwan Historica) *Taiwan wenhua zhi* [A History of Taiwan's Civilisation] (Chinese trans revised ed, Taiwan Shufang, Taipei, 2011), vol 1, at 163–164.
84 See the Taiwan prefect's report in 1790 (Qianlong 55) in *Tai'an huilu jiaji* [Taiwan Documents Collection A] (TWWX 31), at 30, "臺灣東界內山，本多荒土，禁民越墾，準令熟番打牲耕種" ("*Tai'an jiaji*").
85 See Lin Yu-ju and Wei Dong "Lin Shuangwen shijian qian de Taiwan bianqu tuxiang: yi Qianlong 49 nian Taiwan fanjie zixiantu wei zhongxin" [Frontier Areas in Taiwan Before the Lin Shuangwen Uprising: An Investigation Centering on the 1784 Purple-line Aboriginal Boundaries] (2012) 19(3) *Taiwanshi yanjiu* 47, at 67.
86 At 73; Shepherd, above n 3, at 279–284.
87 *Gaozong shilu*, above n 75, at 111.
88 At 611.
89 The lands concerned were in Jijipu (in present-day Nantou), Tuzaikeng (in present-day Taoyuan), Sandiao (in present-day New Taipei, next to Yilan) and Langqiao (in present-day Hengchun, in the far south). See ibid.
90 Song, above n 36, at 148.
91 Tang Qiyu *Lidai tunken yanjiu* [A Research on Land Reclamation Through *tuntian* in the Various Dynasties] (Zhengzhong, Shanghai, 1947), at 5.
92 Zhang Junyue *Lidai tuntian kao* [Study of *tuntian* in the Various Dynasties] (Shangwu, Beijing, 1939), at 4.
93 At 2.
94 Yang Jun *Qingdai Xinjiang diqu falü zhidu jiqi bianqian yanjiu* [A Research on the Legal System and Its Evolution in Qing Xinjiang] (Minzu, Beijing, 2012), at 171; Peng Yuxin *Qingdai tudi kaiken shi* [History of Land Reclamation During the Qing Dynasty] (Nongye, Beijing, 1990), at 209–215.
95 See Ka, above n 5, in particular, at 255–275.

96 *Gaozong shilu*, above n 75, at 586.
97 At 603–604.
98 See, in general, Harry J Lamley "Subethnic Rivalry in the Ch'ing Period" in Emily Martin Ahern and Hill Gates (eds) *The Anthropology of Taiwanese Society* (Standard University Press, Palo Alto, 1981), at 282–318; Shepherd, above n 3, at 310–319.
99 Here "company" is in the quasi-military organisational sense, not commercial sense.
100 *Gaozong shilu*, above n 75, at 611.
101 Ibid.
102 *Tai'an jiaji*, above n 84, at 2–3.
103 At 1–2.
104 See ibid, at 8–9. Also see discussed in the previous section.
105 Tai Yen-hui *Qingdai Taiwan zhi xiangzhi* [The Administration at the Town and Village Levels in Qing Taiwan] (Lianjing, Taipei, 1979), at 487, is also of this view.
106 At 490.
107 *Tai'an jiaji*, above n 84, at 18 and 21.
108 *Taiwan shili*, above n 54, at 43.
109 Ibid.
110 Shepherd, above n 3, at 357.
111 For example, see *Liu Zhuangsugong zouyi* [Memorials of Liu Mingchuan] (TWWX 27), at 306.
112 Later there were also Mongolian banners and Han banners.
113 For the Qing banner system, see, for example, Meng Sen "Baqi zhizhu kaoshi" [A Research on the Eight Banner System] (1936) 6 *Zhongyang yanjiuyuan lishi yuyan yanjiusuo jikan* 343–412; Lu Chih-chun "Jin ershinian lai (1989–2009) baqi zhidu yanjiu de huigu yu taolun" [A Review and Discussion of the Research of the Eight Banner System in the Past 20 Years] (2010) 14 *Shiyun* 125–175; Mark C Elliott *The Manchu Way: The Eight Banners and Ethnic Identity in Late Imperial China* (Stanford University Press, Stanford, 2001).
114 See Elliott, ibid, in general.
115 For protection of banner land, see Zhao and Chen, above n 10, at 64; Zhang Jinfan *Qingchao fazhishi* [Legal History of the Qing Dynasty] (Zhonghua shuju, Beijing, 1998), at 247–250.
116 Yao, above n 118, at 75. Yao recorded that the aborigines sought government protection in order to avoid being bullied by the plains aborigines, but in fact the perpetrators were probably mainly Han settlers.
117 See Yao Ying *Dongcha jilüe* [Records of My Appointment to the East, 1829] (TWWX 7), 77–82.
118 Ke Peiyuan *Gamalan zhilüe* [Brief Records of Gamalan, 1837] (TWWX 92), at 141–142. "Small villages" and "large villages" were not defined. The records in Yao, ibid, shows that the village size ranged from just under 100 people to over 400 people.
119 Yao, ibid, at 80.
120 At 79–80.
121 See the statistics on population and rent in Yao, ibid, at 80–82.
122 Ke, above n 118, at 122, notes that the Han cheated the aborigines in the lease. *Qinding pingding Taiwan jilüe* [Imperially Approved Accounts of Pacifying Taiwan] (TWWX 102), at 863, also mentions that the settlers' leader Wusha "leased and reclaimed aboriginal land" (*zuken fandi* 租墾番地).
123 Wang Kaitai *Fujian tongzhi Taiwanfu* [Gazetteer of Fujian, Taiwan Prefecture, 1871] (TWWX 84), at 22.
124 Although there was much discussion, in the end the tax charged by the government did not follow that of government estate as designed. See a survey of the discussions in Ke, above n 118, at 47–50.
125 See *Yongzheng zhupi zouzhe*, above n 61, at 44. Also see the discussion on Solin and Yin Qin's memorial during the Yongzheng period in this chapter.

126 Ke, above n 118, at 43.
127 See the discussion among the officials in ibid, at 47–49.
128 Ding Yuejian *Zhi Tai bigaolu* [A Collection of Must-read Documents on Governing Taiwan, 1868] (TWWX 17), at 208, "獻納各社輿圖，籲懇歸官經理".
129 See Shi's report in ibid, at 252–258, in particular, at 252.
130 Ibid.
131 Ibid, "見官經理, 均極歡忭靜謐".
132 See the Taiwan circuit intendant's report at 233.
133 At 230.
134 See Ding, above n 128, at 279.
135 *Sifa cankao*, above n 81, vol 1A, at 299.
136 *Fujian Taiwan zouzhe* [Memorials on Taiwan] (TWWX 29), at 11 ("*Taiwan zouzhe*").
137 Collected in *Sifa cankao*, above n 81, vol 1A, at 41.
138 Ibid, at 41–42. Emphasis added.
139 "抚番开山善后章程21条", in *Liu Mingchuan fu Tai qianhou dang'an* [Historic Documents Before and After Liu Mingchuan's Governorship in Taiwan] (TWWX 276) ("*Fu Tai dang'an*"), at 7–9.
140 "各番社田地毘連，宜飭派委員酌選誠實通事帶同番目分報各處，為之嚴定界址；不准鄰社恃強侵佔，亦不許該社冒佔他人土地，以杜爭端".
141 "除近海官山及各番耕種力所不能及者聽民開墾外，其餘附社山田樹木，應令各歸各管，不准地方民人將該番所有占爲己業".
142 "前、後除近海官山及各番耕種力所不能及者聽民開墾外，其餘附社山田樹木，山各處曠土甚多，應即舉設招墾局，即日由營務處選派委員前往汕頭、廈門、香港等處招工前來開墾".
143 "離社較遠無主荒地". Ibid, at 10.
144 Other conditions included shaving the heads, registering the population and no killing. See *Taiwan zouzhe*, above n 136, at 47.
145 *Liu Zhuangsugong zouyi*, above n 111, at 200, "生番地界，各歸各業，不許軍民侵占".
146 "所有社内一切山林、樹木、土地，任憑耕人砍伐開墾，不敢爭競". See 18 undertakings collected in *Dan Xin dang'an*, above n 82, vol 13, at 34–39. All recorded undertakings were given in February 1886 (Guangxu 12). It is not clear whether this was required of all villages, or at all times.
147 *Fu Tai dang'an*, above n 139, at 145.
148 Antonio C Tavares "The Japanese Colonial State and the Dissolution of the Late Imperial Frontier Economy in Taiwan, 1886–1909" (2005) 64 *Journal of Asian Studies* 361, in particular, at 370–372.
149 Tu Jishan *Hengchun xianzhi* [Gazetteer of Hengchun County, 1894] (TWWX 75), at 292. The extent of this arrangement is not clear. Inō, above n 83vol 3, at 205, also records that settlers paid aborigines in goods for the use of aboriginal land.
150 *Liu Zhuangsugong zouyi*, above n 111, at 222, "大埧七社，番丁男女不及千人，其地週圍數十里，土壤肥腴，以民墾之，二、三年後，即可以墾租給七社口糧，目前必由官籌資給食".
151 For example, see *Fu Tai dang'an*, above n 139, at 80.
152 Liu Ao *Xun Tai tuisilu* [Reflections on Being a Circuit Intendant in Taiwan] (TWWX 21), at 62–64.
153 Peng, above n 94, at 259.
154 See Zhao and Chen, above n 10, at 58. Tang Qiyu *Zhongguo de kenzhi* [Land Reclamation and Colonisation in China] (2nd ed, Yongxiang, Shanghai, 1952), at 173.
155 Tang, ibid.
156 See C Patterson Giersch *Asian Borderlands: The Transformation of Qing China's Yunnan Frontier* (Harvard University Press, Cambridge (MA) and London, 2006), at 121, and 142–144.
157 Ulla Secher "The Meaning of Radical Title: The Pre-*Mabo* Authorities Explained" (2005) 11 *Australia Property Law Journal* 179, at 243. For the development of the

English land tenure, see Alfred W B Simpson *A History of the Land Law* (2nd ed, Clarendon Press, Oxford, 1986).

158 In the recent decades the Common Law world has found that upon settlement, the Crown acquired only a radical title over the land, but not beneficial ownership. There are still debates about the exact meaning of radical title. Some jurists and scholars believe it to be equivalent to absolute ownership of land, subject to the burden of native title; others argue that radical title is a governmental power, as opposed to proprietary rights. See Secher, ibid, in particular, at 183, 185, 242 and 243. For the judicial pronouncement of radical title, see *Mabo v Queensland (No 2)* [1992] HCA 23, Brennan J, in particular, para 51; *Ngati Apa v Attorney-General* [2003] NZCA 117, Elias CJ, at paras 25–29. Considering that only in the past few decades did Western scholarship and jurists start to recognise the Crown's radical title over aboriginal land as an underlying title rather than beneficial ownership, the Chinese tradition was advanced in regard to aboriginal land. However, it should also be recognised that it was a tradition rather than a well-defined and articulated theory, and as such there could be wavering at times.

159 Yang Jingfan et al *Zhongguo falü sixiangshi jianbian* [A Brief History of Chinese Legal Thoughts] (Guangxi shifan daxue, Guilin, 1988), at 24.

160 Chen, above n 10, at 61.

161 Rowe, above n 58, at 507.

162 See Shi Lang's memorial to the throne, "Gongchen Taiwan qiliu shu" [Some Humble Opinions on Whether to Retain or Abandon Taiwan] in Shi Lang *Jinghai jishi* [Records of Pacifying the Seas] (TWWX 13), at 60, "土番人民均屬赤子".

163 *Ming Qing Dang'an*, above n 37, vol 9, at 79–80.

164 See Chen's arguments for protection of aborigines in Chen, above n 49, at 15–17.

165 *Gaozong shilu*, above n 75, at 6.

166 Shepherd, above n 3, at 20 and 306, also notes that the "Confucian concern to preserve the livelihoods of subject peoples" and "the Mencian strand of Chinese statecraft" were part of the reasons the Qing protected aboriginal land rights.

167 "有治人, 无治法[*fa*]", *Xunzi* [The Works of Xunzi] (Chinese Text Project, www.ctext.org) ch 12 "Jundao" [On the Way of a Lord]. The ordinary meaning of *fa* is "law". An alternative translation is in John Knoblock *Xunzi: A Translation and Study of the Complete Works* (Stanford University Press, Stanford, 1988), vol 2, at 175: "there are men who can bring order about, but there is no model that will produce order".

168 Ibid, "法不能獨立，類不能自行；得其人則存，失其人則亡". Knoblock, ibid, at 176, translates the passage as: "the model cannot be established alone, nor can its categories for analogical extension apply themselves in particular circumstances. If proper men are obtained, then the model will survive; if such men are lost, then it will perish".

169 Derk Bodde and Clarence Morris *Law in Imperial China: Exemplified by 190 Ch'ing Dynasty Cases* (Harvard University Press, Cambridge (MA), 1967), at 18.

170 Zhang, above n 115, at 191–192.

171 "利不什，不變法；害不什，不改制". See *Qing Shizong shilu xuanji* [Selected Veritable Records of the Yongzheng Emperor] (TWWX167), at 20.

172 John K Fairbank and Ssu-yu Teng "On the Types and Uses of Ch'ing Documents" (1940) 5 *Harvard Journal of Asiatic Studies* 1, at 33–34.

4 Chinese practice

Transforming aboriginal land tenure

Despite government efforts to restrict Han Chinese reclamation of aboriginal land, by the late Qianlong reign the western plains had been fully reclaimed and settled by Han settlers. The plains aborigines experienced intense contact with the settlers, and therefore the focus of this chapter is the land tenure changes of the plains aborigines. A number of earlier studies have investigated land rights over the western plains during the Qing Dynasty. In particular, Shepherd devoted a chapter to "the evolution of aborigine land rights", but his focus remained on tracing government actions throughout the High Qing period.[1] Taking one step further, Ka attributed the plains aborigines' land loss to government actions.[2] Ka found three major methods of land loss by the aborigines – the irresponsible issue of land reclamation permits during the Kangxi reign which resulted in aboriginal land being reclaimed and registered by Han settlers; the Yongzheng government's willingness to permit land registration by Han settlers over land leased by aborigines to settlers; and the Yongzheng and early Qianlong governments' encouragement of registration of aboriginal land by aborigines, which enabled aborigines to sell their land.[3] According to Ka, the loophole for land loss by aborigines was not closed until a Taiwan circuit intendant's decree in 1668 (Qianlong 33) to exempt aboriginal land from tax (hence from registration).[4] Ka's view essentially attributes land loss by aborigines to the government's actions, especially the permission or requirement to register aboriginal land before the mid-Qianlong era.

It is the core argument of this book that aboriginal land holdings in Taiwan during the Qing era were reduced not by the state but by means of commercial interaction with Han settlers. In Qing Taiwan, settlers and aborigines made complex and dynamic private arrangements regarding land. These private arrangements were often used to evade government regulations which purported to protect aboriginal land rights. In order to understand how this worked out, it is necessary to explain how the Chinese land tenure system worked, generally and in Taiwan, and the precise ways in which this interacted with aboriginal lands. This chapter examines the consequence of private land transactions for the aborigines, and evaluates the relationship between land registration and land ownership in Qing Taiwan. Close attention is paid to Chinese customary land practice, and reinterprets some land deeds and analyses the legal nature of the major land transaction forms in Taiwan, namely, *zu* (租 "lease"), *pu* (贌 similar to *zu* but with a different origin), *dian* (典 pledge) and sale (*mai* 賣).

The chapter first traces the emergence of *dazu* (大租 "large rent") in Taiwan and analyses the rights and legal status of large rent holders, who were the registered *yezhu* (業主 literally "proprietary owner") on the government's land tax register. As the practice developed, "lease" by large rent in effect became a re-grant of land to the lessee, and registered *yezhu* were not necessarily proprietary owners of land. In other words, Chinese customary land practice, not the government land register, determined land ownership.

Continuing from the point of land ownership in Chinese land tenure, the chapter examines the forms of aboriginal land transactions, and argues that the Chinese customary land transactions and voluntary privatisation of land by the aborigines caused large-scale land loss by aborigines and major damage to aboriginal land tenure. Registration of aboriginal land by settlers or by aborigines did not affect the legal consequence of private land transactions.

The chapter then discusses the lack of material distinction between *pu* and pledge, and pledge and sale. Chinese customary practice exhibited great flexibility but lacked clarity. As such the customary practice often evaded government regulations that tried to protect aboriginal land. The government made efforts to restrict or prohibit land transactions between settlers and aborigines, but there was no systematic property law regulation to address the lack of precision or lack of clear distinction among the terms. Consequently, in general, government actions were not able to control settler-aborigine land transactions.

The overall conclusion is that the slow penetration of Chinese customary practice, rather than government action, changed Taiwan's aboriginal land tenure. However, the government's unwillingness to interfere with land practices, and the manner of interference when it did interfere, contributed to the problem.

The land deeds relied upon in this chapter are mainly from a collection known as *Qingdai Taiwan dazu diaochashu*,[5] and supplemented by deeds from *Sinkang Manuscripts*.[6] There are other series of land deed collections,[7] but *Dazu Diaochashu* represents the most comprehensive collection of land deeds, and *Sinkang Manuscripts* collects the earliest available deeds. As this chapter examines the general trend rather than land transactions in a certain locality or with a certain aboriginal group, these two collections provide the best examples.

Dazu: land grants and re-grants

The ordinary meaning of *zu* is rent, hire, lease or let.[8] Therefore, as with the European and Common Law concept of a lease, it indicates a temporary parting with the use of property for monetary or material return. Like reversion in the English Common Law, the lessor retained ownership of the leased property during the lease, and regained use and control of the property at the end of the lease term. However not all *zu* in imperial China were straightforward leases as the ordinary meaning suggests. The customary practice in Qing Taiwan, which mirrored that of mainland China, was a lot more complicated than the English terms lease or rent indicate. One example is the *dazu* (大租 "large rent") system. "Large rent" stood in contrast to "small rent" (*xiaozu* 小租), and they were related to the "one field, two [levels of] owners" (*yitian liangzhu* 一田兩主) system. This system emerged in the Song Dynasty (960–1279 AD) and was widely practised in mainland China.[9] The emergence of the system was related to land reclamation and subsequent separation of rights over land.[10] Given suitable conditions, the Chinese settlers were able to replicate the system in Taiwan.

Land reclamation permits

As discussed in Chapter 3, permits were needed for land reclamation in Qing Taiwan. Anyone could apply to the government for a reclamation permit, but in reality only a few people had the connection or knowledge to make applications.[11] An application for a permit made to the Taiwan local government in the second year after the annexation (1685) reads:[12]

> Applicant Shen Shaohong is filing this application for the matter of a notice of land reclamation. In the north circuit there is a parcel of wasteland in Luyecao, [which] was an old military farm . . . of the Zheng period. It is a reasonably large area, and no one has applied for reclamation before. [I] petition your honour's approval for me to appoint Li Ying as manager and to recruit tenants to reclaim [the land], and [I] will start paying land tax after the period of three years. [I] further petition your honour to notify the Taiwan Circuit Intendant that within the four boundaries listed [in the permit], Li Ying is authorised to go to Luyecao, build a house there and recruit tenants to reclaim the land as my inheritable property for ever [*yongwei shiye* 永為世業]. Thus is my humble request.
>
> [Boundaries in four directions to hills or river, respectively]
>
> [Date]

Below the application was an annotation of the local official:

> Wasteland reclamation. By order from the superior, it has been approved for a permit to be issued with speed, so that [the applicant] can recruit tenants and make arrangements as soon as possible. Once the land is fully reclaimed, [it] should be registered for tax according to law.

Some aspects of this application need to be emphasised. It only indicated that the land was a large area, but did not mention the number of *jia*. The reason is that land was surveyed only after it had been reclaimed. The document referred to a manager and tenants, which suggests that the applicant was a land investor who did not reclaim the land or manage the tenants personally, and this fact was known to the officials. The application also promised to register the land for tax after the reclamation was completed, this being the major concern of the government.

The person who was issued a land reclamation permit was known as *kenhu* (墾戶 reclaimer). The format of permits might vary, but a permit usually listed the land under application, the boundaries and the name of the *kenhu*, and stipulated that once the land was fully reclaimed, it had to be registered for taxation within the required time. The earliest land reclamation permit available on record, issued in 1708, reads:[13]

> According to *kenhu* Zhan Sheng's application, there is a parcel of wasteland measuring over 10 *jia* at [location and boundaries]. According to the investigation of the interpreter (*tongshi* 通事) Xie Zhang and others, there is no violation [to aboriginal land boundaries],[14] and a permit should be issued. Therefore, giving *kenhu* Zhan Sheng permission to reclaim the land as applied and pay land tax, this permit is issued.
>
> [Date]

Permits conferred only rights to reclaim land and did not confer title over land as such, but they were the prerequisite for land title. Once the land was developed to be suitable for cultivation, the land was surveyed to ascertain the number of *jia* and then registered for taxation, as the government stressed in these two permits. The government's concern was land tax. The registered taxpayer was called "*yezhu*", the owner of *ye*. As will be analysed later, the owner of *ye* does not necessarily mean land owner as known in the modern law.

Land reclamation deeds and "large rent"

As shown in the previous two land permit documents, a land reclamation permit could grant large areas of land to the applicant. The 1685 application covered a "reasonably broad area", the boundaries being rivers and hills. In some cases, a land reclamation permit could relate to substantial areas covering several hundred *jia* of land.[15] Because many grants were quite large, and because of the Chinese way of intensive farming, permit holders usually subdivided the land for others to reclaim, as the applicant in the 1685 document intended to do. The distribution of subdivided land to actual reclaimers was done by separate documents, called "reclamation deed" (*geiken pi* 給墾批). These deeds were private agreements, and did not involve the government. The actual reclaimers were called "tenants" (*dian* 佃), and the annual payment that they had to pay the permit holders was called "rent" (*zu* 租). This type of arrangement was common in Qing Taiwan, and by the late Kangxi reign it was estimated that about 60–70% of land granted to permit holders was given to "tenants" to reclaim.[16]

Three deeds during the Yongzheng reign illustrate the gradual evolution of reclamation arrangements and the increasing rights of the tenants. In order to document the evolving practice with regard to the kinds of conveyances, the three deeds are quoted in full here. The first deed was made in 1725:[17]

> I, Ya, have an estate in Mamingshan. Out of [this estate I] give a piece of wetland, measuring 1.2 *jia*, to tenant Cai Zanheng to reclaim. For the first and second years [the rent is] 15% [of the harvest], and [from] the third year, following precedents,

> [the rent] is eight *shi* per *jia* of winnowed and clean good grain. [The tenant shall] transport the grain to the granary. [The rent] shall not be short [of the stipulated amount]. This deed is made and given as a proof.
>
> *Yezhu* Chen Ya
>
> [Date]

The second deed was made in 1729:[18]

> The person who makes this deed of reclamation, *yezhu* Jian Linfang, has a piece of land that he *pu* from the Southern Dadu aborigines. Now Lin Shengheng is willing to cultivate it with his own draft oxen and seeds. It is agreed that for each *jia* of land [Lin] will pay *litouyin* (犁頭銀 "plough-head money") 50 taels of silver as a contribution to build canals. The silver is paid on this day. The land is surveyed [by the parties] and it measures 10 *jia*. The boundaries are clear. It is agreed that for each *jia* of land the tenant will pay five *shi* of grain in the first year, eight *shi* in the second year, and afterwards eight *shi* per *jia* as a perpetual precedent. After the harvest, the grain must be blown clean and transported to Luzaigang. [The tenant] dare not pay [the rent] short or late so as to affect tax payment. If the rent is in arrears, *yezhu* is free to evict the tenant and recruit other tenants. If in the future the county magistrate surveys the land, the tenant should pay rents according to the actual number of *jia* and shall not dispute. If the tenant is going home [in mainland China], after consulting *yezhu*, he is free to assign [the leasehold], and *yezhu* cannot share [the price of] the labour and capital [that the tenant invested]. . . .
>
> [concluding formalities]

The third deed was made in 1732:[19]

> The person recruiting tenants, *yehu*[20] Li Chaorong, has bought a parcel of green land (*qingpu* 青埔) at Datu,[21] [specific location and boundaries]. Now [*yezhu*] recruited [tenants' names] to take up the lease and reclaim [the land]. [The tenants] offer *puyin* (埔銀 "soil money") 65 taels of silver, are willing to bring their own draft oxen and farm tools and build irrigation canals, and will reclaim and cultivate [the land] as their own perpetual property [*yongwei jiye* 永爲己業]. The annual rent is 15% of the total produce, following local precedents. Once the land is fully reclaimed as paddy land . . . the rent is eight *shi* [of grain] per *jia*. [The tenants will] transport [the grain] to the harbour for payment of rent. [The agreement is reached by] both parties' free will, [and neither party] dares to repudiate in the future, or to request for increase or decrease of rent. [The tenants] will pay the rent in full and on time. If there are any arrears or insufficient payment, [the *yezhu*] will resort to the officials to enforce the payment. Lest oral agreements do not form evidence, a tenancy deed is given.
>
> The *puyin* is received this day and acknowledged.
>
> [Date]
>
> Tenancy deed given by Li Chaorong

These three deeds show increasingly defined and greater rights of the tenants. The first deed shows that at least by 1725 (Yongzheng 3), the annual rent rate of 8 *shi* of grain per *jia* of land had become a commonly adopted precedent. No term of the "lease" or consequence of default was mentioned. In the early stage of land reclamation activities, the necessity of defining property rights probably was not apparent.

The second deed specified that the rate of 8 *shi* was to be perpetual, but in cases of rent arrears, the *yezhu* had the right to evict the tenants and lease the land to other people (*qigeng huandian* 起耕換佃). However, the tenant had the freedom to assign the "leasehold" to someone else after consulting with, or in reality, notifying, the *yezhu*. The anticipated sale of leasehold by the tenants was in the form of recovering labour and capital investments, and the deed specified that the *yezhu* could not claim a share of the sale price. Thus the tenant gained independent property rights, but the *yezhu* retained rights to evict the tenants.

In the third deed, not only the rent was fixed for perpetuity, the contract itself was perpetual, and the tenant was given perpetual rights over the land. In the case of rent arrears, the *yezhu* could resort to the government for enforcement, but did not have the right of eviction. Thus the *yezhu*'s rights to replace tenants were eliminated, while the tenants' permanent rights over the land were guaranteed.

These deeds show the increasing rights of tenants – at first they appeared to be tenants, but eventually they had rights of "perpetual property". In line with the increasing rights of the "tenants", there were subtle changes to the initial lump sum payments. In the second deed quoted earlier the initial payment, *litouyin*, was said to be a contribution for irrigation work.[22] This implies that the parties had agreed that the *yezhu* had the obligation to build the irrigation system. In the third deed, no reason for the initial lump sum payment was mentioned, and it was the tenants who were responsible for building the irrigation systems. This suggests that an initial payment became an accepted norm, and became detached from a specific investment on the land. The payment was called *puyin*, or more commonly, *pudi yin* 埔底銀. *Pudi* literally means "bottom of unreclaimed land". Thus it appeared that the initial payment changed from a contribution to infrastructure work to in effect the purchase price for rights over the sub-soil.[23] Essentially the tenants were purchasing an estate from the *yezhu*.

The deeds were a consolidation of Chinese customary practice. At least over a decade before the deeds quoted earlier, tenants acquired considerable rights over land that they were given to reclaim. A Zhuluo County magistrate of the late Kangxi period complained that *yezhu* were not free to replace tenants, which would result in tenants becoming the property owner (*jiudian cheng yezhu* 久佃成業主) in the future.[24] This was exactly what happened later on – the large rent owners were still called *yezhu*, but the tenants became the real land owners. The magistrate further noted that the tenants enjoyed rights over the "sub-soil" (*tiandi* 田底), which were bought and sold independently from *yezhu*'s rights over "top-soil" (*tianmian* 田面). The distinction of sub-soil and top-soil was artificial, as they did not really relate to the sub-soil or surface. In reality they referred to the different rights enjoyed by reclaiming tenants and *yezhu*. The system has been called "split ownership", "dual ownership" or "one field, two [levels of] owners".[25]

The development of the practice from simple lease to de facto sale was not uniform in time and space. Whether reclaiming tenants acquired independent sub-soil rights or not would have been influenced by local customs, as well as the intention and negotiating power of the parties. However as time went on, the "split-ownership" system matured and became widespread.[26] In most cases the *yezhu*'s only responsibility was to acquire a land reclamation permit, register the land once the reclamation was completed and pay land tax. *Yezhu* became a kind of property investor who obtained their profits from the difference between "rental" income and tax obligations.[27]

Reclaiming tenants often reclaimed more land than they could cultivate themselves. In many instances they further subdivided the land and leased the pieces to third parties who were the actual cultivators. The sub-lease usually was a short-term or periodic tenancy. Since there were two levels of "lease/tenancy", *yezhu* was hence called "large rent holder" (*dazu hu* 大租戶),[28] who received the customary 8 *shi* per *jia* from the reclaiming tenants. The reclaiming tenants, because they sub-let in their turn, were called "small rent holder" (*xiaozu hu* 小租戶). Over the years a three-tier tenurial system developed: the land permit holders as the large rent owners, the actual reclaimers as the small rent owners and the cultivators as the tenants (see Diagram 4.1).

In summary, at its maturity, lease in large rent gave small rent holders independent proprietary rights called "sub-soil" rights, and large rent holders enjoyed "top-soil" rights. Each had an income attached to it and could be alienated independently from the other. Small rent rates were a few times higher than large rents, an indication that sub-soil rights were more valuable than top-soil rights.[29] The system was complex, and was the product of dynamic development.

Yezhu's *rights and nature of large rent*

After land reclamation was completed, permit holders were registered on the government tax book as *yezhu*, which means the owner of *ye*. Theoretically, only when land was fully reclaimed did it become *ye*.[30] In a modern context, the word *ye* has a range of different meanings, with connotations of industry, occupation and property.[31] In the context of land rights during the Qing Dynasty, commentators have pointed out that *ye* means "land in which labour and capital have been invested", "[business] management" and "the object of control and management".[32] In this sense, *yezhu* means the person who invested in the land and had "real control", or cultivation and management rights, over such land or business operation.[33]

However, that was only one aspect of *ye*. The complex land tenure has given the term *ye* a complex and evolving meaning. Under the large rent model, *yezhu* did not work the land themselves. They leased the land rather than investing labour. As time went on, they tended not to invest capital either, as the reclaimers eventually became responsible for building irrigation systems and bringing their own draft oxen and farm tools. Further, large rent holders did not have control over land, and could not raise the rent or terminate the lease.[34] Large rent was fixed in perpetuity, and the rates were largely consistent across Taiwan, unless in exceptional circumstances such as where the land quality was poor.[35]

In contrast, small rent holders had substantial rights over land. They could alienate the leasehold without obtaining the large rent owners' consent, although the sale deed usually set out the large rent obligation, so that large rent owners continued to receive their due. As shown in the 1732 deed, the small rent holder would not lose the leasehold even in cases of default. A later deed recorded that if the *yezhu* seized the land in cases of default, the *yezhu* had to return the land once the rent was recovered.[36] Small rent holders could use the land as they pleased without being interfered with by the *yezhu*. At the late stages of the system, the extent of small rent holders' rights was such that they could lease agricultural land for building a house,[37] or even damage the land so that it was no longer suitable for production.[38] Therefore the rights of small rent holders over land were not restricted in any way, as long as they continued paying rent to the *yezhu* as head lessee.

Thus, small rent holders had independent and unlimited proprietary rights over land. In fact, their rights were "the biggest rights over land".[39] The sale of small rent holders' rights was called "sale of farmland" (*maitian* 賣田), an expression that emerged as early as 1735 (Yongzheng 13).[40] Some Qing officials, who were more clear-minded, also recognised that when large rent holders gave land for reclamation, it was no different from "selling the property" (*maiye* 賣業).[41] Eventually, small rent holders were referred to as "field owners" (*tianzhu* 田主), to distinguish them from *yezhu*.[42] In contrast to "sale of farmland", the sale of large rent rights was called "sale of rent [collection rights]" (*maizu* 賣租).[43] It has been argued, and in my opinion correctly, that large rent holders' rights were merely debt collection rights, or a charge on the small rent rights.[44]

As large rent rights went through an evolutionary process and large rent holders lost their control over land over time, the rights of the *yezhu* and the nature of large rent changed. In the three-tier tenurial system, the government granted land titles to *yezhu*. In relation to the government, *yezhu* had independent rights which were alienable and perpetual. At this stage, *yezhu* had ownership over the land. *Yezhu* were free to reclaim and cultivate lands themselves, or to grant them to reclamation tenants as the tenants' perpetual property. When *yezhu* granted perpetual rights to reclaiming tenants, they passed property rights to reclamation tenants, and the "split-ownership" model was complete. The true connotation of lease in large rent was transfer of land ownership (see Diagram 4.1). The *yezhu*, who was now the large rent holder, no longer enjoyed real control or management rights over land, but only retained rights to collect rents. The initial lump sum payment was in effect the purchase price for property. The annual payment, although in the name of rent, was almost like the service or fee that tenants paid their lords in feudal grants in the English system, although in Taiwan the relationship was contractual rather than feudal, and the parties were on equal footing, at least legally.

It should be noted that the transfer of ownership did not occur in all cases, and could have variations. For example, if a *yezhu* reclaimed and cultivated the land himself, no lease relationship existed. The *yezhu* could also reclaim the land

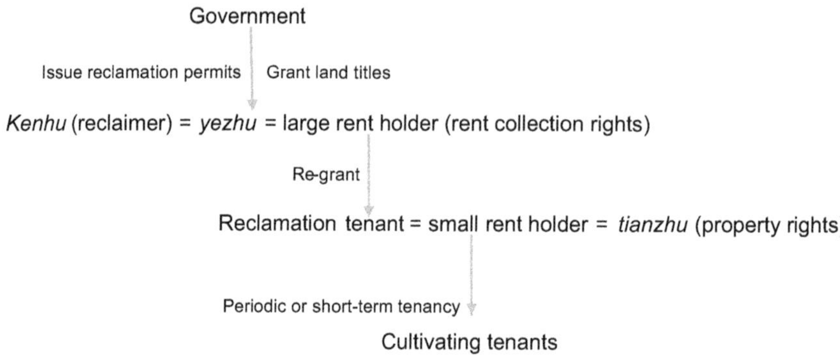

Diagram 4.1 Three-tier land rights system

himself but lease it for periodic tenancy, and theoretically enjoy "large rent" and "small rent" in one person. In the previously mentioned two cases the ownership was not transferred, but remained with the *yezhu*. If a reclamation tenant reclaimed and cultivated the land himself, there was no sub-lease and hence no small rent. However the prevalent practice in Taiwan was the three-tier lease system depicted in Diagram 4.1.

In legal terms, at the maturity of the so-called split-ownership system, a large rent holder's reclamation deed was not a lease, but a grant of land. Although the annual fee was called "rent" (*zu* 租), lease in large rent in effect became permanent alienation of land. A large rent holder was none other than the person who was granted the right to reclaim land, and who in turn granted that right to actual reclaimers. Large rent holders were a special class who used their connections or knowledge to apply for land permits and who lived on rental income which was in reality a fixed annual fee. Small rent holders were the real *kenhu* and the real land owner. This was so not only in the customary practice; it was also recognised by the state law, even though the large rent holders were registered as *yezhu*.

Land registration and proof of ownership

In Chinese customary practice, *yezhu* lost proprietary rights when they re-granted land to reclaimers. In the state law, being registered as *yezhu* did not necessarily mean ownership either.

It had always been the Chinese tradition that the person on the land register should pay tax. Before the Eastern Jin period (317–420 AD), tax was levied according to the actual produce of the land rather than on the land itself. But after the Eastern Jin, tax was levied according to the area of land regardless of how much it produced.[45] In Qing Taiwan, lands were classified into different categories according to their quality and productivity, and each category attracted a different tax rate. The Qing government kept land registers for taxation and other administrative purposes. The "fish scale register" was the main land register. The "yellow register" and the transaction register supplemented the fish scale register through recording household land holding and land transactions, respectively.[46]

The land registers could serve as prima facie proof of title, but they were not the final proof of title. A registered *yezhu* might be the real owner of the land, but there were situations where the *yezhu* was not the real owner. For example, in Fujian province, a practice of "undertaking for tax grain" (*baoliang* 包糧) was prevalent. Land owners did not want to deal with the government on tax issues, and the undertakers got on the register specifically for the purpose of making tax payments on behalf of the land owners. The undertakers' only rights and obligations were to receive a certain amount of grain and pay a part of it as tax.[47] The undertakers made a profit from being on the register, while the land owners were spared tax problems. It was also a common practice in Qing China that land owners surrendered their land to powerful officials or privileged gentry who could provide special protection or enjoyed tax exemption, known as commendation (*touxian* 投獻). The officials or gentry appeared on the land register as the *yezhu* and received a certain amount of annuity from the true owners.[48] For all parties concerned, the undertakers, the officials or the gentry were not the real owners of land. In the case of Taiwan, recipients of land permits registered as *yezhu* when reclamation was completed. There were even cases where some people applied for reclamation permits over land that had been reclaimed by other people. In such cases the people who reclaimed the land ended up becoming the permit holders' tenants and had to pay "large rent" to the permit holders.[49] In this regard, the *yezhu* was not the real owner of *ye*, but the person registered on the land tax register. Their only right was to receive a perpetually fixed amount of rent, and their only obligation was to pay land tax. These practices were another aspect of the complexity and dynamism of the Chinese tenurial system.

In imperial China, land transactions, especially the sale of land, were by deeds, as in English law. Deeds were essentially agreements, but were usually signed by the party giving effect to the land rights (for example, the seller) and by witnesses. They were then given to the party who received the land rights (for example, the purchaser) as proof of transfer of title. A deed would note the origin of the title and the background to the sale, and attach previous deeds relating to that land, known as *shangshou qi* 上手契. The chain of deeds established the title of the latest grantee of deed. A deed was thus a contract and a record of title.

That the deeds constituted proof of title was recognised by the government. A regulation of the Fujian Province clearly states that "according to customs, sale and pledge of property solely rely on the original deeds as evidence [of title]. If [a dispute] is submitted to officials for adjudication, [the officials] also rely on the deeds [to determine land ownership]".[50] This was so even if the parties failed to report and register the transaction as required by law. Regulations required that deeds of land sale had to be reported to the government and the land transaction recorded. This allowed the government to charge a transaction duty (*qishui* 契稅, stamp duty) as well as to keep accurate record of tax obligations. The government affixed a stamp on the land deeds, which were called "red deeds" (*hongqi* 紅契), as opposed to "white deeds" (*baiqi* 白契) which were not reported to the government and did not bear the government stamp. To evade the transaction duty some parties to land transactions did not report the transaction, and the seller remained on the register as the *yezhu*. In cases of dispute, even though they were white deeds, local officials still relied on the deeds to ascertain land ownership,[51] rather than giving effect to the land register and recognising the registered *yezhu* as land owner.

Therefore, land ownership operated independently from the relevant land register. While in modern law, land registration is equated with land ownership, in imperial China they did not necessarily correspond. Land registration was for tax purposes, and it was prima facie proof of title, but not final proof of title. The land tax registers were not title registers. Although the term *yezhu* literally means "proprietary owner", as the tenure evolved it became a term in the tax arena, not one in the property law arena. Being a *yezhu* on the government register was not a real indicator of land ownership, as property rights were determined by Chinese customary practice.

This tenurial system had significant implications for aboriginal land rights in Taiwan, to which this chapter now turns.

Aboriginal land transactions

Pu: *an overall payment for an unspecified area of land*

A term that was closely related to "lease" of aboriginal land but continued to evolve was *pu*. In Taiwan *pu* originated from particular practices concerning aborigines. In the early Qing years the term was predominantly, although not exclusively, used in land transactions involving aboriginal land.[52]

There are two views regarding the origin of the term *pu*. One view is that it originated from the Dutch term *pacht*, which means monopoly.[53] The other view is that *pu* had a Chinese origin, and its southern Fujian dialect form *pak* means "to hire or rent for a long time, to charter or apprentice, to farm as revenue".[54] Both meanings fit with the practice of the *pushe* system which emerged in Taiwan during the Dutch period. The Dutch controlled Han interaction with aborigines, and granted monopoly trading rights in aboriginal villages to Han merchants through auctions. Merchants who paid the highest bids to the Dutch authority won the monopoly to enter and trade in the aboriginal villages that they bid for. This was called *pushe* (贌社; *she* means village).[55]

The Zheng administration continued the *pushe* system, but with some adjustments. The Zheng government imposed a village tax on each aboriginal village that was under its administration. The village tax was paid by the Han merchants who had rights to trade in the villages.[56] Thus *pushe* evolved from paying the price for monopoly trading rights to assuming the village tax by merchants who had monopoly trading rights, essentially tax farming.

The system of village merchants was abolished in the late Kangxi reign, because of complaints that the Han merchants exploited the aborigines.[57] In the meantime, a new practice emerged, where Han settlers paid the village tax on behalf of the aboriginal villages in return for rights to reclaim the villages' land (*daifan naxiang* 代番納餉). This was also called *pu*.[58] Eventually the price for reclaiming aboriginal land increased, and apart from paying village tax, Han settlers paid an additional amount as a "subsidy" (*tie* 貼) which the village could retain for village affairs or the villagers' provision.[59] In some cases, the settlers did not report the reclamation to the authority at all. In other cases, the settlers applied for a land permit, while the aborigines produced a statement to say that the land in question did not violate aboriginal boundaries.[60] In so doing the aborigines in effect relinquished their claims over the land.

Few land deeds of the previously mentioned described form of *pu* are available now. An example of an agreement made in 1723 (Yongzheng 1) reads:[61]

> The people who make this agreement, the village head of Dawujun village, Harou et al, have a piece of grassland, [four boundaries]. The four boundaries are clear. Because we cannot afford to pay the village tax, now [we] recruit Ding Zuozhou to invest in the irrigation and to [develop the land] into wetland. Today we negotiate in front of the Community Compact (*xiangbao* 鄉保) and the interpreter [and reach the agreement that] from the 1st year of the Yongzheng reign, the rent is 50 *shi* each year. . . . This will be the perpetual arrangement, and in the future [the parties] will not be incited by other people to dispute about it. If the tenants do not pay the rent in time or in full, it is Ding Zuozhou's responsibility and should not affect the aborigines. This [agreement is reached] by the two parties' free will, and neither would repudiate it. To have evidence, we sign this agreement.

This document, as did a few others of the same period,[62] commenced with "the people who make this agreement" (*li heyue ren* 立合約人), and was signed by both parties. This is in contrast to deeds between settlers or later aborigine-settler deeds, which were signed by the grantor and usually specified the kind of business transaction by starting with "the person who recruits tenants" (*li zhaodian ren* 立招佃人) or "the *yezhu* who grants reclamation [rights]" (*li zhaopi yezhu* 立招批業主). Having both parties sign the agreement shows that there was probably a mutual distrust between the aborigines and settlers. The reference to future disputes because of third-party involvement indicates that in the early stages of contact settlers and aborigines had different cultural understandings about contract terms which had led to disputes. If this was the case, the problem soon disappeared, as bilateral agreements were replaced by unilateral deeds, following the practice among Han settlers. Further, the parties were either unsure, or deliberately vague, as to what kind of business transaction was involved. The agreement specified the overall annual payment for land, of which the boundaries were recorded but the total area was not specified. Moreover, like the 1725 deed quoted earlier, it tended to be vague on land rights of the parties. The annuity was in perpetuity (*yongyuan dingli* 永遠定例), but no other rights were mentioned.

The terms of deeds indicate that *pu* at this stage essentially meant to pay a perpetually fixed amount of annual grain or money (sometimes with an initial payment), in return for the rights to reclaim a piece of land, which was defined by boundaries but the number of *jia* was not recorded. Since the transaction was a "bulk *pu*", that is, an overall annuity for an unspecified area of land, usually the Han settlers divided and leased the land, and became large rent holders themselves. For example, the 1729 deed of reclamation between Han settlers, quoted earlier, noted that the large rent owner *pu* the land from an aboriginal village. These were the situations which Ka calls "aboriginal rent over large rent".[63] The reference in the previously mentioned agreement to tenants' payment of rent as Ding's responsibility shows that the aborigines were aware that Ding intended to "sub-lease" the land. In essence the transaction was a land grant, but the initial grantor and source of title was the aborigines, not the government.

Aboriginal large rent

Transactions of aboriginal land continued to evolve. An often-quoted Lower Tamsui deed of 1721 (Kangxi 60) depicts the changing relations between the aborigine and settler parties as the transaction evolved over time:[64]

1) The people who make this agreement, Lower Tamsui village head Aremo and [names] et al, had one parcel of grassland. In the 46th year [of the Kangxi reign, 1707], because [sic] He-Zhou-Wang recruited . . . Fu Ruduo et al and reclaimed [the land which is now] the Tonobot estate (*Dunwu zhuang* 頓物莊).
2) Later the people of our village disputed with He-Zhou-Wang. Thanks to the previous county magistrate Song's adjudication, the Tonobot estate was given to the aboriginal people to pay tax (*guiyu fanmin wanke* 歸於番民完課). On that day the aborigines and the tenants made an agreement. The labour and capital investments for building irrigation systems are all the responsibilities of the tenants. After the land was developed into wetland, the *yezhu* . . . 15 *jia*. . . . The annual rent was seven *shi* per *jia*, [and the rent] had been delivered to the village granary without problem.
3) In the 59th year [of the Kangxi reign, 1720], because the population of the village had increased, [the village] requested to the tenants for increase of rent. This was brought before the county magistrate Li, who adjudicated for two *shi* [per *jia*] increase of rent . . . , and the aborigines and tenants both accepted [the decision]. The rents for the Tonobot estate, including the additional rent from the [magistrate's] decision, were being received in full.
4) But now the people of our village had no means to pay for official businesses, and [we] borrowed 700 *shi* of grain from the tenants . . . pay tax . . . are willing to deduct 1.5 *shi* per *jia* each year as interest.
5) On this date the *yezhu* and tenants agreed that each year the rent is 7.5 *shi* per *jia*. The tenants transport [the grain] to our village's granary. This is a perpetual arrangement. In the future if the tenants want to

invest elsewhere or go back to China, they are free to reassign the sub-soil [rights] to recover labour and capital investment, and the *yezhu* should not raise other issue again.

It was standard practice for land deeds to recount the history of earlier transactions, as this deed also exemplifies. Paragraph (1) reveals that at a time before 1707, the aborigines had an agreement with He-Zhou-Wang about the land. The deed does not disclose what arrangement was made between the aboriginal village and He-Zhou-Wang in the first place. Given the customary practice of that time and the statement that He-Zhou-Wang recruited tenants to reclaim the land, very likely He-Zhou-Wang had "bulk *pu*" the land from the aboriginal villages and had then granted a lease in large rent to the tenants.

Paragraph (2) of this deed shows that, after the reclamation was completed, a dispute arose between the village and He-Zhou-Wang as to who was entitled to receive the rent from the tenants.[65] Magistrate Song (1704–1712) adjudicated the land to the aboriginal village and the aborigines became registered *yezhu*, and were responsible for land tax payment, while He-Zhou-Wang lost connection with the land.[66] The rent was fixed at 7 *shi* per *jia*. This was close to the rate of 8 *shi* which became the prevalent large rent rate later on. Together with the fact that the aborigines were registered as *yezhu*, a large rent relationship akin to that between Han settlers was established. However, it is not clear whether the tenants acquired any substantive property rights at that stage.

Paragraph (3) records that in 1720 the aborigines were successful in winning another magistrate's support to increase the rent to a level which was higher than the customary rate. No further rights or obligations are mentioned. Paragraph (4) explains that a loan in 1721 caused the parties to re-negotiate, causing the aborigines to reduce the rent. In later decades the government was alarmed by the grave consequence of aborigines borrowing from settlers and eventually losing their land because of the debt, but this paragraph shows that as early as the Kangxi era such a situation already existed. Paragraph (5) shows that the tenants managed to establish perpetual and independent proprietary rights. The large rent relationship thus evolved to the next step, and transfer of ownership was completed.

This deed depicts that from the initial agreement with He-Zhou-Wang to the agreement in 1721, the transaction evolved from "bulk *pu*" to a large rent relationship without specifying the tenants' property rights, to in the end the tenants acquiring independent property rights. The second and third steps mirrored the large rent model between Han settlers. This deed thus demonstrates the evolving types of transactions by which the aborigines disposed of their land, and the emergence of the aboriginal large rent model.

A 1727 (Yongzheng 5) deed between the aboriginal village of Katin (*Jiateng* 茄藤) and Han settlers had similar arrangements to the 1721 deed. The aborigines promised that the 7 *shi* per *jia* of annual rent was to be fixed for perpetuity, and the Han tenants had the freedom to sell the sub-soil rights.[67] However, a deed of 1732 (Yongzheng 10) between an aboriginal landlord and his tenant still allowed the landlord to replace the tenants where rent was in arrears.[68] This shows that the arrangements were not uniform or clear-cut, as the land reclamation relationships among Han settlers generally were. In general the development of the large rent model between Han settlers and aborigines followed the same pattern as that among Han settlers.

Registration of aboriginal land

Because the Han party of the "bulk *pu*" was essentially the grantee of land, potentially they could become registered *yezhu*, as in the case of land grants from the government. Similarly, when aborigines leased their land in large rent, they were on a similar footing to Han large rent holders and could register their land and become registered *yezhu*. However, because the Qing land register was not a title register, registration of aboriginal land did not have bearing on land loss by the aborigines.

Once the land was on the government register and the Han settlers were recorded as *yezhu*, it does appear that the nominal connection between the aborigines and their land was severed. However, as already demonstrated, land rights generally were defined by contractual arrangements rather than land registration. Aboriginal land rights were no exception. In the *pu* deeds, the aborigines often forfeited all rights over land, except the right to collect an annuity. Despite Han registration of aboriginal land, the annuities agreed upon between aborigines and settlers were observed even with the passing of time and further sale of land. This is shown in many land deeds which recorded that the land in question owed an annual "aboriginal rent".[69] Therefore, private land transactions and government land registration continued to operate in parallel, one determining property rights and the other tax obligations. The key to land loss was the land transactions between settlers and aborigines, not the subsequent land registration by settlers.

By the same token, registration of aboriginal land by aborigines did not facilitate loss of land by the aborigines. It may appear that once aboriginal land was registered, it was no different from Han settlers' land, was no longer subject to the government ban against sale of aboriginal land, and was therefore prone to be sold.[70] While the assumption is correct in modern law where land register is the title register, it was not so for Qing Taiwan. Land registration by the aborigines did not materially affect aboriginal land tenure.

While registration of customary land often caused tenurial changes in countries where the land register was a title register,[71] the situation was different in Qing Taiwan. This was not only because the register was a tax register, but also because of the mechanism of *yehu*. Under the Qing registration system, there was no particular requirement as to the legal personality of a registered title holder. It could be an individual, a firm, a partnership, or any other loose organisation, as long as there was a *hu* (戶, literally "household", but more accurately, an account) on the register.[72] Aboriginal villages could create an account and continue to hold the land as a collective. For example, a public notice, issued by the Zhanghua County magistrate in 1730 (Yongzheng 8) concerning the sale of a piece of aboriginal land, noted that the aboriginal Dongluo village had created an account (*lihu* 立戶) as land title holder, and registered the land in question under the name of the created account.[73] Although the concept of trust was not explicitly developed in imperial China, the created account was analogous to a trust in the Common Law. The operation meant that registration by aboriginal villages did not of itself cause land privatisation among the aborigines.

During the early to mid-Qianlong reign, a system of appointing *fan yehu* (番業戶 aboriginal registered title holder) by the government was established.[74] This means that a *fan yehu* was not only an account or a representative for land registration, but also a person who held office in the village under an established system and procedure. *Fan yehu* were nominated by villagers, checked by officials and appointed by the government.[75] They were the *yezhu* on behalf of the village, and as part of the job they were responsible for granting village land to settlers for reclamation, collecting annual grain from settlers, distributing the grain to villagers and paying land tax.[76] The main reason of appointing *fan yehu* was because interpreters had dominated village affairs and embezzled village rental incomes in many cases.[77] With the system of *fan yehu*, the aboriginal villages registered the land under a representative. From a modern law point of view, the *fan yehu* was the trustee of the aboriginal village, who held the land on trust for the village. As such, the internal operations of the village and the land tenure were not affected. Whether the aborigines created an account and held the land as a collective, or whether they appointed a representative who held the land on behalf of the collective, the registered land continued to be held by the villages and was recognisable as aboriginal land.

A careful examination of available land deeds reveal that registration of land by aborigines did not facilitate alienation of land by aborigines. It was rare for the aborigines to sell their land outright. Sale of aboriginal land was never explicitly allowed, and was in fact explicitly banned in 1737 (Qianlong 2). The prevalent forms of transaction depriving the aborigines of their land rights were land grants through *pu* and large rent, and subsequent sale of large rent collection rights. Whether outright sale of land, land grant or sale of large rent rights, the aborigines transacted them regardless of registration. Existing records show that the aborigines sold their land before 1737, and that in most of these cases the land was not registered. For example, in 1724 (Yongzheng 2), an aboriginal village granted reclamation rights of a piece of land to a settler, who then sold the rights to another person (*zhuanshou* 轉售). Two years later, the village sold the residual rights (rent collection rights) to the new grantee. The deed made by the village was entitled "deed of irrevocable sale" (*dumai qi* 杜賣契). The aborigines allowed the purchaser to register the land for tax, which implies the land had not been registered prior to this. The aborigines also promised that "after the sale all [rights] are forgone" (*yimai qianxiu* 一賣千休).[78] This was a typical example of granting land reclamation rights followed by sale of rent collection rights, but the parties treated it as the irrevocable step of land sale since the aborigines severed the final connection with the land. A "deed of sale" (*maiqi* 賣契) in 1734 (Yongzheng 12) also allowed the purchaser to retain the land "as own property perpetually" and register the land for tax, an indication of no prior registration.[79] Even though called "sale", the purchaser promised to pay an annuity of 40 taels of silver to the village, in addition to the sale price. This indicates a blurred line between sale and *pu*, and the aborigines' reluctance to part with their land entirely. No sale of village collective land after 1737 is recorded, but the aboriginal villages continued to grant leases in large rent through village heads, interpreters or by village assemblies during the Yongzheng and Qianlong reigns, and there is no indication that the practice was replaced by the *fan yehu* system.[80] Further, almost all sale of large rent rights was by village heads or interpreters on behalf of the villages, or by individual aborigines, rather than *fan yehu*.[81] That is to say, the lands were not registered. This was despite the fact that after 1740 (Qianlong 5) *fan yehu* was active in granting leases in large rent.[82]

It is clear that registration of aboriginal land by aborigines operated in tandem with aboriginal customary land tenure, and did not of itself change the actual tenure. After registration the villages still owned the land collectively, and the fact that the registered land was aboriginal land remained identifiable. The aborigines lost proprietary rights when they *pu* or leased land in large rent, and lost the last connection with land and the final income from land once they sold the rent collection rights. Villages *pu* or leased land in large rent and sold rent collection rights regardless of whether the land was registered or not. Land registration did not change aboriginal land tenure; private land transactions did. Furthermore, land registration did not cause privatisation of aboriginal land, which occurred for other reasons and through other means.

Privatisation of land

With the spread of Han settlement and increasing exposure to Han culture, voluntary privatisation of land by aborigines occurred and became widespread.

Available records show that aboriginal private land ownership existed in the early years after Qing annexation. A fragment of a land deed in the early Kangxi years recorded the sale of land by a villager of the aboriginal Mattau village, most likely to another individual aborigine.[83] Mattau was one of the four sinicised villages during the Zheng time, and would have been influenced by the Han concept of private ownership, although the extent of privatisation by that time was likely to be limited.

Throughout the Yongzheng, Qianlong and subsequent reigns, individual aborigines sold or granted their lands to Han settlers for reclamation, and the lands were usually "inherited from forefathers" (*youcheng zufu yixia* 有承祖父遺下).[84] However, the practice of dividing up village land and distributing it to individual households became relatively common only after the mid-1700s.[85] A well-documented example was the experience of the Anli village group.

Privatisation of land in the Anli villages was directly influenced by the interpreter of the villages, who was a Han land investor. The Anli villages were a group of nine villages that occupied the central western plains, and the group was named after the biggest village, the Anli village. In 1716 (Kangxi 55) five of the villages, led by the village head of the Anli village, submitted themselves to the government, and petitioned for a land grant in the plains area.[86] Scholars believe that their interpreter, Zhang Dajing, was the person behind this petition.[87] Zhang was the interpreter of the Anli villages for many decades, as well as the son-in-law of the village head of Anli. Under Zhang's guidance, the villages kept some land as collectively owned, leased the land to settlers in large rent, and used the income to pay village tax and for village affairs. The remaining land was divided up and distributed to individual households.[88] Very often the aborigines simply leased their lands to Han settlers in large rent and lived on the annuity. They then further pledged rent collection rights to settlers, which they were often unable to redeem.[89] This was an example of voluntary privatisation under Han influence.

The Anli villages' experience was but one example. Privatisation of aboriginal land appeared to be widely practised among the acculturated aborigines. For example, most land in the two Dajia villages in the central western plains was privately owned during the Qianlong reign.[90] Once the land was divided, it was likely to be leased, pledged or sold to settlers, since individual aborigines had little means to sustain themselves.[91] Furthermore, while land leased by villages as a collective or by *fan yehu* as the representative of the villages was recognisable as aboriginal land, without the context of the aboriginal community system, individual aborigines' land was more difficult to be recognised as aboriginal land.

Another type of privatisation was to divide up village rent after the land was leased by the village as collective property. This was usually because of complaints that village heads, interpreters or *fan yehu* embezzled village rent, and as a solution individual aborigines were given a share of the rent which they were entitled to collect from the Han tenants.[92] The effect of assigning rights to collect rents from a certain tenant or a certain plot of land to individual aborigines was in effect no different from dividing up land which the aborigine then leased in large rent. Because of difficulties in collecting rents or other financial difficulties, individual aborigines often ended up selling or pledging the rent collection rights. The division of rent collection rights was a means that the aborigines tried to protect their rental income from being squandered by the village office holders, but the end result was fragmentation of land holding. This aggravated the alienation of aboriginal land.

Overall, privatisation of aboriginal land, usually voluntary and without government intervention, sped up land loss by aborigines and caused the most damage to aboriginal land tenure.

Land transaction and loss of land

Land grants by aborigines thus went through a process of development from "bulk *pu*" in return for assumption of village tax or an overall payment, to following the Han large rent model; from no specific definition of the parties' rights and obligations to giving the Han tenants property rights; from allowing land registration by settlers to assuming the status of *yezhu* by aborigines; from land grant by villages under their collective decision-making system to a mechanism of *fan yehu*, and to individualisation of land ownership. No matter whether "bulk *pu*" or lease in large rent, the effect was the permanent alienation of land. The whole process closely followed Han practice, and as in the case of non-aboriginal land, registration did little to change aboriginal land tenure.

The evolution of aboriginal land transactions and land tenure changes demonstrate the increasing awareness of land values by the aborigines. More importantly, it shows the increasing influence of Chinese commerce and land practice. As discussed in Chapter 1, the deer hunting and farming activities of the Taiwanese aborigines were at subsistence level only. Since the Dutch period, the Chinese settlers were "the only bees on Formosa that gave honey", meaning the only source of government revenue.[93] Under the Zhengs, village tax was assumed by village merchants. After the Qing annexation, the aborigines had difficulty affording village tax and living needs, and without deer economy they were content to give up large areas of deer hunting grounds in return for subsidies for tax and living support. With the increasing competition for land and the spread of Han settlement and practice, the aborigines adapted and tried to participate in land reclamation activities. However the Chinese style of farming was intensive and was usually wetland farming, which required capital investment on irrigation systems. This was beyond the aborigines' ability. Therefore they followed the prevalent Han practice and leased land in large rent to settlers. Settlers were responsible for capital and labour investments, and the aborigines became mere receivers of fixed large rent. Privatisation was also a result of cultural influence, as well as pragmatic response to issues within the aboriginal community.

The aborigines lost their substantive land rights through granting "bulk *pu*" or large rent to setters, and retained rent collection rights only. Many further sold or pledged the rent collections rights and lost any connection with the land. As such, land loss by the aborigines was a continuing occurrence, largely unaffected by land registration. There was very little government involvement in the process, and little could the government control the process. In fact, as will be demonstrated later, because of government laws and policies which forbade sale and pledge of aboriginal land, Han settlers and aborigines used other forms of deeds to evade the laws and policies.

Flexible arrangements to evade the law: *pu, dian, mai*

While at times the government allowed the lease of aboriginal land, sale of aboriginal land was never expressly allowed, and regulations usually forbade pledge and sale together (*dianmài* 典賣). Instances of breaching the ban existed, but more often private transactions evaded laws through *zu* or *pu* of their land, which at times had no material distinction from *dian* and sale. The was the case when the aborigines bulk *pu* or leased the land in large rent; it was also the case when *pu* evolved to become periodic tenancy.

Dian *and sale*

Dian 典 was to surrender one's property as a pledge, in return for a loan.[94] In a *dian* transaction, the land was surrendered when the money was delivered, and there was no requirement of paying interest or rent from either side. This was to be distinguished from *tai* 胎, which was also a form of guarantee for loans. In a *tai* relationship the land owner surrendered land deeds as a guarantee while continuing to possess the land, and paid interest on the loan.[95] *Tai* was similar to the concept of mortgage in modern practice, while *dian* was similar to a pledge. *Tai* was a straightforward relationship, although the high interest rates that Han settlers charged sometimes caused government intervention. In contrast, *dian* was a type of conveyance and could be confused with sale at times.

An example of a typical deed of *dian* helps to illustrate the nature of *dian*:[96]

> The person who gives this deed of pledge, Chen Zhou of Xiashuizai village, has a piece of wetland, [location and boundaries in four directions]. Now [Zhou] lacks money for other enterprise, [and he] has asked all relatives [who confirmed that they] would not receive (*chengshou* 承受) it. Through intermediary [Zhou] found Chen Yulin from his own clan, who is willing to accept the pledge (*chengdian* 承典). On this day the three parties [land owner, lender and intermediary] agree that [the land] is worth 150 dollars in silver. The silver is given and received on this day in front of the intermediary; the land is then given to the lender to manage and to recruit tenants to cultivate. There is an annual large rent of one *shi*, and water rent of four *dou*.[97] The land [is pledged] from [1804 to 1814], [after that] Zhou can repay the silver specified in this deed of pledge [meaning the loan amount], and take back the original deed. If Zhou does not have the silver, he will allow the lender to [continue to] cultivate and shall not harass [the lender].

In this deed, the pledger relinquished control and management of the land, and any responsibilities attached to the land, such as paying large rent and water rent, in return for a loan assessed at the value of the land. As in the case of sale, the land owner gave his close relatives right of refusal. During the 10-year period, the pledgee had full control of the land, paid rents and enjoyed the full produce of the land. It was as though the transaction was sale and purchase, the only difference being that the pledger had the right to buy back the land at the original price after the term was due. Therefore to some extent *dian* was "similar to sale with an agreement for redemption when the term was due".[98] As was typical of *dian*, in this deed the pledger was not obliged to redeem after the 10-year term expired, in which case the deal would continue. The term of redemption was to exclude the pledger from redeeming the land within the fixed period of time.[99] The term of *dian* could be very long, and it was not unusual for a contract to omit the term of *dian*. If the contract did not specify the term, or if the debtor could not repay the loan after the term expired, the creditor could continue to possess and use the land until the debtor was able to redeem. Within the term of *dian*, the pledgee could transfer the rights on the land to others, which was called "assigning pledge" (*zhuandian* 轉典).[100]

Therefore, *dian* was a land transaction itself, and when the *dian* relationship was established, the land owner lost the land temporarily, which could become permanent if the duration was too long, or if the debtor did not redeem. In such cases the pledge became a sale.

The problem was exacerbated by the fact that sale was often a temporary and revocable transfer of rights. In Qing Taiwan, as in imperial China, there were two types of sale, irrevocable sale (*juemài* 絕賣) and revocable sale (*huomài* 活賣).[101] Irrevocable sale meant sale in the modern meaning, while revocable sale allowed the seller to request a price top-up (找價 *zhaojia*) or to redeem (*huishu* 回贖) the land at the original price, even though many years or decades had passed.[102] In reality, there were also examples where price top-up was requested and paid in irrevocable sales.[103] Therefore even with sale, there were different degrees of forgoing one's rights on the land. There was no material difference between *dian* and revocable sale, especially when the deed of *dian* did not stipulate a time limit.

Probably because of the similarity between *dian* and sale, the Qing regulations treated both *dian* and sale in similar terms. Early regulations required change of registered title holder (*guoge* 過割) and payment of contract duty in both cases of pledge and purchase (*dianmai* 典買), while also trying to enforce debtors' right of redemption.[104] This was also the reason why *dian* and sale of aboriginal land were banned at the same time.

Consistent with the government ban, available land deeds show that outright sale or pledge of aboriginal land was very rare. More usually unreclaimed land was leased in large rent, and the aborigines may subsequently sell or pledge the rent collection rights.[105] Another way to evade the ban was through taking advantage of the similarity between sale and *dian*, and between *dian* and the evolved *pu*. Often through deeds of *pu* aborigines *dian* their land, which then became sale and led to loss of land by the aborigines. This usually occurred in cases of reclaimed land.

Dian and *pu*

The meaning of *pu* continued to evolve, and later it referred to periodic tenancy, which became the predominant meaning of *pu*. The extension or transformation of the meaning possibly went through a gradual process in customary practice, and the first record of recognising *pu* as periodic tenancy was in the late Qianlong era. As was typical under the Qing system, official usage of the terms often followed, rather than guided, the practice. In 1788 (Qianlong 53), the Anli village petitioned the aboriginal affairs northern sub-prefect and claimed that their land was "temporarily *pu* to Han settlers for two or three years".[106] The sub-prefect endorsed this claim and talked about the expiry and renewal of *pu* contracts.[107] This was the first time the government regulated periodic tenancy,[108] and as a side effect made it clear that *pu* meant, or included the meaning of, periodic tenancy. In 1800 (Jiaqing 5), another local government decree stipulated that where Han settlers *pugeng* (贌耕 "lease for cultivation") aboriginal land, at the end of three years, settlers must return the land to the aborigines who could decide to cultivate it themselves or to lease it to other tenants.[109] This accords with the fact that the term *pu* was used increasingly in periodic tenancy deeds from the early Jiaqing reign.[110] By 1870, it was recorded that where tenants *pu* land from field owners, once the term expired, the field owner could *pu* the land to someone else.[111] This indicates that by then the only meaning of *pu* was periodic tenancy. Periodic tenancy had the feature of giving up use of land for a period of time, a feature shared by *dian*.

The similarity between the actual transactions of short-term *pu* and *dian* is shown in existing deeds. An example of a typical short-term *pu* reads:[112]

> The people recruiting [tenants for] cultivation and giving this deed of *yadi* [money], aborigines of the Meili village, Ponan Weishuo and Qiankun Weishuo, together inherited two adjacent pieces of reclaimed dry land (*shuyuan* 熟園), [location and boundaries]. The four boundaries are clear, and having been measured [by land owner] with the interpreter and the village head, the area is three *jia*. The rent is 12 *shi* of grain per year. Now because the land is far from the village, [the owners] are not able to cultivate it. After consulting relatives in the village, [the aboriginal relatives] could not cultivate it either. Through an intermediary [the owners] found a Han person Yang Congguan [who is willing] to cultivate. [The owners] receive *yadi* money 400 dollars. On this day the money is received, and the land is given to Yang Congguan to cultivate for 20 years. The aborigines are the *yezhu*, and the Han person is the tenant. Every year [the tenant] shall prepare 12 *shi* of grain for the aborigines to take away, and should not be in short or late. When the term is completed, the Weishuos will give back the *yadi* money and take back the original deed, [the tenant] should not make it difficult [for the land owners]. If the money is not returned, [the land] is given to the lender (*yinzhu* 銀主 "money owner") to continue cultivation, and do whatever he wants to do (*rencong qibian* 任從其便), and [the Weishuos] dare not dispute.

In Chinese practice, alienation of land must give the seller's close relatives the first right of refusal, while a tenancy did not have such a requirement. The mention of right of refusal by relatives in this deed suggests that it was not a true tenancy. Another indicator was in the amount of *yadi* money (*yadiyin* 壓地銀), also called *qidi* money (*qidiyin* 磧底銀). *Yadi* money was usually used in short-term tenancies, being a sum paid at the time of agreement and returned when the term concluded. It is commonly understood to be a bond, to guarantee payment of rent, as well as to prevent the landlord from repudiating the agreement.[113] The amount of *qidi* money was often about one year's rent, and on average 70% of annual rent.[114] In the previously mentioned agreement, the *qidi* money was more than 33 times the annual rent.[115] Therefore the transaction was more like *dian* than periodic tenancy. A collection of 12 aborigine-Han tenancy agreements reveals that most of them bear the characteristics of *dian* (see Table 4.1).

Of the 12 deeds in the collection, nine deeds were materially similar to *dian* – the land was given to the "tenants" to manage or cultivate for a period of time in return for a sum of money, and the money owner could continue possessing the land if the landlord could not pay back. In fact the term "redeem" (*shu* 贖), reflecting the nature of the transaction was pledge rather than tenancy, was used in six of the nine deeds. The sum of *qidi* money was usually tens or hundreds of

Table 4.1 Key terms of aboriginal-settler "tenancy" deeds

No.	*Year of deed*	*Qidi money*	*Rent*	*Term*	*Others*
1	1798	400 dollars	12 *shi* of grain	20 years	Can continue cultivation if owner did not pay back *qidi* money.
2	1803	45 dollars	2 *shi*	10 years	As in No 1.
3	1807	120 dollars	1 *shi*	20 years	As in No 1. Mentioned "redemption".
4	1812	75 dollars	0.5 *shi*	5 years	As in No 1. Land owner then *borrowed* 23 dollars in three subsequent occasions, but no other terms changed. Mentioned "redemption".
5	1826	10 dollars	2 dollars	Not specified	Tenant should give the land back if not continuing.
6	1827	30 dollars	Not specified	13 years	As in No 1. Mentioned "redemption".
7	1833				Different from the other tenancy deeds, this land was not developed, and the land owner allowed the tenant five years to reclaim the land. After five years, the land owner would pay the tenant 12 dollars to take back the land. If he did not have the money, the parties split the rental income from the actual cultivator in 40% (aborigine) and 60% (Han) shares.
8	1843	140 dollars	0.2 *shi*	10 years	As in No 1. Mentioned "redemption".
9	1851	7 dollars	0.3 *shi*	Not specified	As in No 1. Mentioned "redemption".
10	1854	10 dollars	0.1 *shi*	7 years	As in No 1. Mentioned "redemption".
11	1883	126 dollars	22 *shi*	10 years	If rent in arrears, land owner could terminate the tenancy; right of renewal.
12	1890	8 dollars	4 dollars	15 years	Parties to return land and money, respectively, when term due.

Source: table created according to *Dazu diaocha*, ch 3.12 *pugeng zi* 贌耕字

times the annual rent – in the 1843 case 700 times. The subsequent borrowing of money from the "tenant" in the 1812 deed was in essence a price top-up in *dian* transactions (*tiandian* 添典). The existence of rent did not necessarily mean the true nature of transaction was lease, since in some deeds of sale the parties also agreed on an annuity. Furthermore, in most of the previously mentioned cases the rent was a token, usually a fraction of 1 *shi*. In the 1827 deed there was no rent at all. Only three out of the 12 deeds appear to be genuine tenancy agreements. The

1833 one was a different arrangement involving land reclamation and cultivation. The 1883 deed gave the landlord rights to terminate the tenancy in case of rent arrears, and together with the 1890 deed there was no provision for continuing cultivation if the landlord could not pay back the *qidi* money. These latter two transactions occurred after the change of policy in 1875, by which time the control on sale and pledge of aboriginal land had relaxed, and there was no need to use *pu* as a disguise for *dian* or sale. The other nine deeds were pledges in disguise, to evade the ban against sale or pledge of aboriginal land.

The deeds show the flexible arrangements in the Chinese customary practice to obtain land rights or credits, which blurred the distinction between different land transactions such as pledge and tenancy. The fact that disputes between aborigines and settlers often broke out about whether certain transactions were *pu* or *dian*[116] showed that the distinction between *dian* and *pu* was elusive. Since *pu* could mean *dian*, and *dian* could mean sale, quite often the aborigines lost their land even through making periodic tenancy agreements, in addition to granting land in large rent.

Government's role

The flexible use of the terms in practice meant that whether *zu*, *pu*, *dian*, or *mài* was used, any of the terms could represent temporary lease or permanent alienation of land. What was important was the content of the agreement, rather than the term used. Furthermore, different forms of alienation of property sat along a spectrum, and their distinctions were a matter of degree – how many rights were given up, rather than a matter of kind. The government was aware of this. Grand Councillor Fukangan succinctly summarised the situation in 1788 (Qianlong 53) in a memorial to the emperor, "settlers rented (*diàn* 佃) land from acculturated and non-acculturated aborigines for cultivation. If the price is low, it is called *zupu*; if the price is higher, it is called *dianmài*".[117] The distinction of high or low price was vague, and it follows that there was no clear distinction between *zupu* and *dianmài*. This provided an opportunity for settlers and aborigines to evade the law.

The dealings with "upkeep" land of the aboriginal colonies was such an example. Despite the awareness of the similarity between *zupu* and *dianmai*, the government did not act to close the loophole. Regulations stipulated that the "upkeep land" was to be cultivated by the aboriginal warriors only, and prescribed consequences for cases of aborigines' *dianmài* the land.[118] The regulation was ambiguous in that, on the one hand, it stipulated cultivation by the aborigines only; on the other hand, it forbade *dian* and sale but did not forbid lease. Within a few years, aborigines started to lease the land to settlers in large rent, sometimes even with the local officials' approval.[119]

Only rarely did the government perceive, or was concerned enough to address, the consequence. The upkeep land of the aboriginal colonies, like other aboriginal land, eventually fell into Han hands. The Jiaqing and Daoguang governments three times investigated the affairs of the upkeep land and company land, and tried to restore upkeep land to aboriginal hands.[120] A decree issued by the Taiwan circuit intendant and published by the aboriginal affairs sub-prefect (Northern Circuit) in 1818 (Jiaqing 23) found that the aborigines *dian* their land to settlers, but to evade the regulation, the deeds were given as deeds of *pu*.[121] The circuit intendant ordered redemption of land by aborigines in the cases of sale and pledge, and return of land in the cases of *pu*. This was to rectify the problem, but no mechanism was devised to prevent further pledge or sale of aboriginal land in the name of lease or tenancy.[122] In 1835 (Daoguang 15), the government decided that any occupation of upkeep land by Han settlers without a deed amounted to encroachment, and settlers had to return the land to the aborigines. If the encroached land had been sold to someone else, the person who encroached and sold the land had to return the price to the purchaser, and the land would revert back to the aborigines. If the land was sold or pledged by the aborigines, as opposed to being encroached upon, the aborigines could redeem the land at half or one-third of the original price. If the original purchaser or pledgee had further alienated the land and the land had new right holders, the aborigines could still claim half of it back.[123] These rectifying measures appeared to be thorough. However, as was the custom, the aborigines usually leased or *pu* their land, rather than sale. Consequently, officials, after investigating the situation of the "upkeep land" in 1838 (Daoguang 18), found that the transactions were lease in large rent (*geiken* 給墾), and not pledge or sale. The finance commissioner of Fujian Province argued that, since the law only expressly forbade pledge and sale, the parties were not guilty of violating the law.[124] Thus the matter was not addressed. This coincided with the post-1800 attitude towards aboriginal land among the officials.

Officials identified the moneylending issue as the root of problems, but the methods adopted fell short of addressing the problem. In 1817 (Jiaqing 22) the Fujian governor looked into the matter and forbade Han settlers from charging interest in *dian* and *tai*, required redemption of land within one year and imposed a penalty on those who refused the aborigines' redemption requests.[125] The circuit intendant's decree of 1818 made similar efforts. As always, the administrative order could not adequately deal with the flexible private arrangements.

Consistent with the Qing's characteristic of maintaining a small civil administration and observing the Confucian value of minimum intervention,[126] the government rarely intervened in private land transactions. When the government did intervene, it did not deal with the root issue of the lack of clarity between the various forms of land transactions.

Property law regime and aboriginal land tenure

This chapter has documented the forms of land transactions between aborigines and settlers. A close analysis on the land reclamation permits and land registration reveals that these requirements were mainly for administrative purposes, and had very little consequence on property. In contrast, *zu*, *pu*, *dian* and sale were flexible and robust forms of land transactions which had determinative consequences on property rights. From periodic tenancy to sale of land there was a continuum transferring ever greater rights in property, often with no clear-cut distinctions. Because of the laws against pledge and sale, lease in large rent and periodic tenancy were often used by Han settlers to obtain aboriginal land. Throughout the whole period of Qing rule, unreclaimed aboriginal land was granted to settlers in large rent by aboriginal villages as a collective, by *fan yehu* as the representatives of the villages and by individual aborigines.[127] Once the land was granted in large rent, the aborigines in effect lost the land ownership and retained only rent collection rights. After the substantive land rights were lost, in many cases the aborigines sold or pledged rent collection rights to settlers, presumably because it was not "sale of land". Further, as most land on the plains was reclaimed by the late Qianlong era, periodic tenancies were used, from the early Jiaqing reign on and mainly for reclaimed land, to evade the law against pledge and sale.

The Chinese customary practice and concepts of land ownership changed aboriginal land tenure in a gradual but dynamic process. The government played very little part in the private land practice. The Qing legal system, following the Chinese tradition, did not concern itself with personal or property law matters unless they were related to social order and security. Property matters were left for customary practice to regulate. Under this system, the Qing government did not interfere with the aborigines' customs, which helped to preserve aboriginal customary land tenure. By the same token, the Qing government did not interfere with the Chinese customary practice which was brought to Taiwan by the settlers. The settlers' land tenure eventually became the dominant practice in Taiwan. It eluded the government's regulations against alienation of aboriginal land, and changed aboriginal customary tenure.

When the government intervened, it was through administrative and criminal law means, but the intervention usually came when the practice had become prevalent and difficult to control. In the late Kangxi years, the Zhuluo magistrate envisaged the emergence of split ownership. In the early Yongzheng years officials recommended limiting the areas of land granted in one permit, so as to eliminate the *yezhu* class, but the government preferred not to interfere.[128] When the problem became widespread and serious, in 1764 and 1765 (Qianlong 29 and 30), the Fujian provincial government made regulations to "forbid and abolish" (*jinge* 禁革) split ownership.[129] Such an administrative order could not control the long-standing and deep-rooted practice among the people, and the practice continued to be prevalent in Taiwan.

Overall, customary land practice existed independently of the formal law, and the government respected it in most cases, but was powerless to change it in others. The government's fault concerning aboriginal land was in its unwillingness or inability to intervene in or regulate the customary practice.

The aborigines were impoverished, and they needed money to sustain themselves, to pay village taxes and for other public expenditure.[130] The land was their only asset. Faced with the powerful commercial economy that the Han brought, they voluntarily or involuntarily participated in land transactions, and lost their land. However this did not mean that they always passively accepted what Han settlers imposed on them. The next chapter explores aboriginal reactions to the spreading Han settlement and the dominant Han culture, and the result of the interactions among settlers, aborigines and the government.

Notes

1 John Robert Shepherd *Statecraft and Political Economy on the Taiwan Frontier, 1600–1800* (Stanford University Press, Stanford, 1993), ch 9.
2 Ka Chih-ming *Fantoujia: Qingdai Taiwan zuqun zhengzhi yu shufan diquan* (*The Aborigine Landlord: Ethnic Politics and Aborigine Land Rights in Qing Taiwan*) (Academia Sinica, Taipei, 2003), ch 4 and 5, and at 316–332.
3 Ch 4 and 5, and at 357.
4 At 220.
5 *Qingdai Taiwan dazu diaochashu* [Collection of Large Rent Documents in Qing Taiwan] (TWWX 152) ("*Dazu diaocha*").
6 Paul Jen-kuei Li *Xingang wenshu yanjiu* (*Studies of Sinkang Manuscripts*) (Academia Sinica, Taipei, 2010).
7 For example, Liu Ze-min *Pingpu baishe guwenshu* [Historic Documents of a Hundred Plains Aboriginal Villages] (Taiwan Historica, Nantou, 2002); Liu Ze-min *Dajia dongxishe guwenshu* [Historic Documents Concerning the Dajia East and Dajia West Villages] (Taiwan Historica, Nantou, 2003); and other collections.
8 Martin H Manser (ed) *Concise English-Chinese Chinese-English Dictionary* (2nd ed, Oxford University Press, Oxford, 1999), at 602.
9 Terada Hiroaki "Tianmian tiandi guanli de falü xing: yi gainianxing de fenxi weizhu" [The Legal Nature of the Customary Practice of Top-soil and Sub-soil Rights: A Conceptual Analysis] in Yang Yifan and Terada Hiroaki (eds) *Zhongguo fazhishi kaozheng* [Research on Chinese Legal History Volume 4 Part 3] (Zhongguo shehui kexueyuan, Beijing, 2003) 344–422 discusses the system in imperial China, and examples given were from various provinces in China. Also see Tai Yen-hui "Qingdai Taiwan zhi daxiaozu ye" [The Large Rent and Small Rent Rights in Qing Taiwan] (1963) 4 *Taipei Wen Hsien* 1, at 2.
10 Tai, ibid, at 2–4.
11 Li Wen-liang *Qingdai nan Taiwan de yiken yu Kejia shehui (1680–1790)* [Land Reclamation and Hakka Communities in Southern Taiwan During the Qing Dynasty] (NTU, Taipei, 2011), at 49.
12 *Dazu diaocha*, above n 5, at 1. Original appended as Appendix 1(1).
13 At 1–2. Original appended as Appendix 1(2).
14 *Tongshi* means "to liaise", "to intermediate". The common translation for *tongshi* is interpreter, because to be a *tongshi* one had to be able to speak both Han and aboriginal languages. Interpreters were chosen by aboriginal villages or appointed by the government to assist with village affairs and official matters. An interpreter usually had the biggest power in the village affairs. After Wang Minzheng's decree in 1704, it was a usual process that before issuing permits government officials would investigate, usually through *tongshi*, whether the land concerned encroached on aboriginal land.
15 Taiwan Prefect Shen Qiyuan's essay "Zhi Tai siyi" [A Private Discussion on Administering Taiwan] in *Taiwan lifan guwenshu* [Historic Documents Concerning Taiwan Aboriginal Affairs] (Chengwen, Taipei, 1983), at 69.
16 Zhou Zhongxuan *Zhuluo xianzhi* [Gazetteer of Zhuluo County, 1717] (TWWX141), at 95.
17 Collected in *Dazu diaocha*, above n 5, at 59. Original appended as Appendix 1(3).
18 At 59–60. Original appended as Appendix 1(4).
19 At 60–61. Original appended as Appendix 1(5).
20 *Yezhu* (the owner of *ye*) was also called *yehu* 業戶(the person who has *ye*).
21 *Qingpu* 青埔 (green land), *huangpu* 荒埔 (wasteland) and *caodi* (草地 grassland) all referred to unreclaimed land, wasteland. It was rare that a *yezhu* would sell the title rather than recruiting tenants. Therefore the purchase referred to here was likely to be from aborigines.
22 *Litou* means "head of a plough", which probably was related to reclamation of land.

23 Tai, above n 9, at 12, does not see the evolution and suggests that no matter what reason was cited, the money was a price for the right of reclamation. This seems unlikely, because if a specific reason was mentioned, the relevant party would have to fulfil the obligation.
24 Zhou, above n 16, at 95.
25 Somehow conveniently but erroneously, because property is a bundle of rights, and ownership is the possession of the totality of property interests, which means that once split, at least one party would lose ownership because of the diminished property interests. See Denise R Johnson "Reflection on the Bundle of Rights" (2007) 32 *Vermont Law Review* 247–272 for a good discussion on property and ownership as a bundle of rights. For want of a more succinct and well-recognised term, this work continues the use of "split ownership".
26 Tai, above n 9, at 23, notes that the complete split of ownership occurred during the Jiaqing reign.
27 Depending on the category of land, land tax varied from 1.71 *shi* to 2.74 *shi* per *jia*, while large rent rates were 4 *shi* and 8 *shi* per *jia* for dry land and wetland, respectively. See Lian Heng *Taiwan tongshi* [A Comprehensive History of Taiwan, 1918] (TWWX 128), at 191–192 for lists for tax rates in Qing Taiwan.
28 The first reference to the term "large rent" appeared in a notice issued by the Zhanghua County magistrate in 1732 (Yongzheng 10), which required tenants to pay large rent to the *yehu*. See Tai, above n 9, at 22. See the notice in *Dazu diaocha*, above n 5, at 8.
29 A deed in *Dazu diaocha*, ibid, at 154, shows that for the same piece of land, the large rent was 12 *shi*, and the small rent was 63 *shi*. Also see Chen Chiu-kun *Qingdai Taiwan tuzhu diquan: guanliao, handian yu Anlishe ren de tudi bianqian 1700–1895* (*Taiwan's Aboriginal Proprietary Rights in the Ch'ing Period: Bureaucracy, Han Tenants and the Transformation of Property Rights of the Anli Tribe, 1700–1895*) (2nd ed, Academia Sinica, Taipei, 1997), at 153.
30 Azuma Yoshio "Qingdai Taiwan zhi tudi suoyou xingtai" [Land Owning System in Qing Taiwan] in *Taiwan jingjishi chuji* [A First Collection of the Economic History of Taiwan] (Taiwan yanjiu congkan 25, Taiwan yinhang, Taipei, 1954) 86, at 95.
31 Manser (ed), above n 8, at 519.
32 Azuma, above n 30, at 95; Wang Tay-sheng *Taiwan falüshi gailun* [Introduction to the History of Laws of Taiwan] (4th ed, Yuanzhao, Taipei, 2012), at 79; Tai, above n 9, at 20.
33 Azuma, ibid. Also see Linshi Taiwan Jiuguan Diaochahui *Taiwan sifa* [Private Law of Taiwan] (Chinese translation, Taiwansheng wenxian weiyuanhui, Taizhong, 1990, original first published in 1910), vol 1, at 52.
34 Tai, above n 9, at 26–27. Terada, above n 9, at 344–422 analyses the arrangements and real meanings of the two-tier ownership system in imperial China.
35 The rent was 15% of the total harvest where a percentage was adopted. If it was by fixed quota, it was usually 8 *shi* per *jia*. This is a well-recognised fact.
36 See the deed of 1893 (Guangxu 19) in *Dazu diaocha*, above n 5, at 128–129.
37 See Taiwan Guanxi Yanjiuhui *Taiwan guanxi jishi* [Records of Customs of Taiwan], vol 1B (Chinese translation, Taiwansheng wenxian weiyuanhui, Taizhong, 1984), at 192.
38 In this case the small rent holders would be obliged to buy out the large rent rights. See ibid.
39 *Taiwan sifa*, above n 33, at 186. But *Taiwan sifa* denies private land ownership in imperial China, and hence did not recognise any rights as ownership.
40 See deeds of sale or mortgage of land in *Dazu diaocha*, above n 5, at 185–266. See the 1735 sale of land deed at 187.
41 See a memorial by Grand Councillor A'gui in *Tai'an huilu jiaji* [Taiwan Documents Collection A] (TWWX 31), at 183, "業戶前已得交犁頭錢，即與賣業無異" ("*Tai'an jiaji*").

42 For example, see Chen Peigui *Danshui tingzhi* [Gazetteer of Danshui Sub-Prefecture, 1871] (TWWX 172), at 88. Also see two land reclamation deeds of 1872 (Tongzhi 11) in *Dazu diaocha*, above n 5, at 162–164.
43 See deeds of sale or mortgage of large rent rights in *Dazu diaocha*, ibid, at 286–316.
44 *Taiwan sifa*, above n 33, at 176–186; Tai, above n 9, at 26.
45 Zhao Gang and Chen Zhongyi *Zhongguo tudi zhidushi* [History of Chinese Land Tenure] (Lianjing, Taipei, 1982), at 180.
46 See chapter 3 of this book for more discussion on these registers.
47 Tai, above n 9, at 3–4.
48 See William T Rowe *China's Last Empire: The Great Qing* (Belknap Press of Harvard University Press, Cambridge (MA), 2009), at 96, about commendation. The practice also occurred in Taiwan, as settlers commended their land to military officers to avoid tax or to gain an advantage over land disputes with aborigines, which resulted in the Qianlong government forbidding military officers getting involved in land investment.
49 Inō Kanori (trans Taiwan Historica) *Taiwan wenhua zhi* [A History of Taiwan's Civilisation] (Chinese trans revised ed, Taiwan Shufang, Taipei, 2011), vol 2, at 329.
50 *Fujian shengli* [Regulations of Fujian Province] (TWWX 199), at 442 "照得民間典賣產業，全以原契為憑。而呈官剖斷，亦以契券為據".
51 Sometimes surrounding circumstances were also considered in determining land titles. See Lin Wen-kai "'Ye ping qi guan'? Qingdai Taiwan tudi yezhuquan yu susong wenhua de fenxi" ["Deed Determines *ye*"? An Analysis on *yezhu* Rights and Litigation Culture in Qing Taiwan] (2011) 18(2) *Taiwanshi yanjiu* 1, at 12 and 41.
52 Most *pu* deeds in *Dazu diaocha*, above n 5, that was made before the early Qianlong reign related to aboriginal land.
53 Peter Kang *Taiwan yuanzhumin shi zhengce pian: He Xi Mingzheng shiqi* [History of Taiwan Aborigines: The Policy Chapter: The Dutch, Spanish and Zheng Periods] (Taiwan Historica, Nantou, 2005), at 199.
54 Shepherd, above n 1, at 474, note 36.
55 A few Qing sources mentioned this system. For example, Yu Yonghe *Bihai jiyou* [Small Sea Travelogue, 1697] (TWWX 44), at 36; Zhou, above n 16, at 102–103 and 168; Huang Shujing *Taihai shichalu* [Records of a Tour on Duty Over the Taiwan Seas, cir 1722] (TWWX 4), at 163–165. For scholarly discussions on the *pushe* system during the Dutch period, see Kang, ibid, ch 12; Wu Tsong-min "Helan tongzhi shiqi zhi pushe zhidu" [The *pushe* System During the Dutch Period] (2008) 15(1) *Taiwanshi yanjiu* 1–29; Wu Tsong-min "Pushe zhidu zhi yanbian jiqi yingxiang, 1644–1737" [The Evolution and Reverberation of the *pushe* System, 1644–1737] (2009) 16(3) *Taiwanshi yanjiu* 1–38 (Wu "Pushe yanbian").
56 Kang, ibid, at 272; Wu "Pushe yanbian", ibid, at 6.
57 It was abolished by 1717 (Kangxi 56). See Zhou, above n16, at 168.
58 Ka, above n 2, at 92.
59 At 280 and 283. Ka classified the arrangements of paying village tax for land and paying subsidies for land as different categories of aboriginal land lease, but the essence of change was price increase, rather than a new type of transaction.
60 At 282. Shepherd, above n 1, at 248–252 discusses "Paying the Tribal Tax in Exchange for Land" in detail.
61 *Dazu diaocha*, above n 5, at 326–327. Original appended as Appendix 1(6).
62 For example, see two other 1723 (Yongzheng 1) agreements and one 1730 (Yongzheng 8) agreement in ibid, at 5–6 and 325–328.
63 Ka, above n 2, at 280.
64 Collected in *Sinkang Manuscript*, above n 6, at 359. The ellipses indicate words missing from the original document. Paragraph break and numbering added. Original appended as Appendix 1(7).

65 The reason for the dispute is unclear. It could be because the reclamation was not consistent with the agreed contractual terms (for example, exceeding the specified boundaries), or the aborigines repudiated the agreement, or the *pu* was a breach of government ban.

66 Shepherd, above n 1, at 252–254, and Ka, above n 2, at 338–341, both discuss this deed. However both neglect the role of He-Zhou-Wang. Consequently, Shepherd finds the passage "difficult to interpret" (at 254). Shepherd is also of the view that subsequent to the dispute a large rent relationship was established between the aborigines and the settlers, but he sees it as Magistrate Song's imposition, rather than as a natural consequence of the aborigines replacing He-Zhou-Wang as the *yezhu* of the land. Ka argues that the tax referred to in the deed was not land tax, and the adjudication was to provide an income to support the aborigines for payment of village tax. However the phase "*guiyu fanmin wanke*" and the reference of *yezhu* suggest that the village was responsible for the land tax and had registered the land for tax after the adjudication.

67 See the deed in *Sinkang Manuscript*, above n 64, at 363.

68 At 376.

69 Many land deeds in *Dazu diaocha*, above n 5, have such a term. For an example, see ch 3.11 "Other deeds".

70 A view held by Ka, above n 2. For example, see 118 and 357.

71 For example, see Richard Boast, Andrew Erueti, Doug McPhail and Norman F Smith *Maori Land Law* (2nd ed, LexisNexis, Wellington, 2004), at 149–150; Ruiping Ye "Torrens and Customary Land Tenure: A Case Study on the Land Titles Registration Act 2008 of Samoa" (2009) 40 *Victoria University of Wellington Law Review* 827–861, in general.

72 For example, the *yehu* Chen-Lai-Zhang that reclaimed the Taipei basin was an account name representing three people whose last names were Chen, Lai, and Zhang, respectively. See Yin Zhang-yi *Taiwan kaifashi yanjiu* [Research on the History of Land Reclamation in Taiwan] (Lianjing, Taipei, 1989), at 65–67.

73 *Dazu Diaocha*, above n 5, at 600–601.

74 *Taiwan sifa*, above n 33, at 207 estimates that *fan yehu* emerged in the early Qianlong years, and Tai Yen-hui *Qingdai Taiwan zhi xiangzhi* [The Administration at the Town and Village Levels in Qing Taiwan] (Lianjing, Taipei, 1979), at 394, states that it emerged in 1757 (Qianlong 22). Ka, above n 2, at 286, refutes the findings of *Taiwan sifa* and Tai because of his view that land registration by aborigines emerged in 1730. However the discussion of those two studies was on *fan yehu* as an office holder (as opposed to a registered title holder who was an aborigine), therefore there is no conflict.

75 Tai, ibid, at 394–395.

76 At 395.

77 At 394.

78 See the deed in *Dazu diaocha*, above n 5, at 328–330.

79 At 330–333.

80 See the deeds in ibid, ch 3.2 "Land grants by aboriginal villages".

81 In the 38 deeds of sale or pledge by aborigines collected in *Dazu diaocha*, ibid, ch 3.10 "Deeds of sale and pledge" concerning aboriginal large rent, only one deed (No 7) was given by a *fan yehu*.

82 See ibid, ch 3.4 "Land grants by *fan yehu*".

83 Since the deed was in Sinkang language only, it is likely that both parties were aborigines. See the deed in *Sinkang Manuscript*, above n 6, at 541.

84 See the deeds in *Dazu diaocha*, above n 5, ch 3.3.

85 Chen, above n 29, at 7.

86 At 26–36. See Taiwan circuit intendant, Zhang Ting, in Linshi Taiwan Jiuguan Diaochahui *Taiwan sifa fulu cankaoshu* [Private Law of Taiwan Reference Book] (Taipei, 1910), vol 1A, at 319–320 for a notice of grant ("*Sifa cankao*").

87 Chen, ibid, at 32; Huang Fu-san "Anli she yu Hanren hezuo kaifa Qingdai Taiwan zhongbu de lishi yuanyuan" [The History of the Cooperation Between the Anli Villages and Han Settlers to Reclaim Central Taiwan During the Qing Dynasty] (1998) 16(2) *Hanxue yanjiu* 61, at 74.
88 Chen, ibid, at 63.
89 At 69–70, and 192.
90 See Liu *Dajia dongxishe guwenshu*, above n 7, at 137.
91 See *Dazu diaocha*, above n 5, ch 3.3 and 3.10 for individual aborigines' lease of land in large rent, and sale or pledge of large rent rights.
92 The details will be further discussed in Chapter 5.
93 Tonio Andrade *How Taiwan Became Chinese: Dutch, Spanish and Han Colonization in the Seventeenth Century* (Columbia University Press, New York, 2008), at 158, quoting a Dutch governor of Taiwan.
94 Zhao and Chen, above n 45, at 24; Wang, above n 32, at 84–85; *Taiwan sifa*, above n 33, at 344.
95 *Taiwan sifa*, ibid, at 367–380.
96 *Dazu diaocha*, above n 5, at 217–218. Original appended as Appendix 1(8).
97 One *dou* 斗 is 0.1 *shi*.
98 Wang, above n 32, at 84–85.
99 Terada, above n 9, at 363.
100 Ibid. Also see *Taiwan sifa*, above n 33, at 350.
101 For explanations of irrevocable sale and revocable sale, see Peter Hoang "Law of Land Tenure in China: A Practical Treatise on Legal Ownership" (Part 1) (1922–1924) 1 *China Law Review* 90, at 93. Also see Terada, above n 9, for an analysis of the real nature of revocable and irrevocable sales.
102 There were cases where the sale did not became irrevocable until after over 70 years. See Mio Kishimoto "Ming Qing shidai de zhaojia huisu wenti" [The Issue of Price Top-up and Redemption During the Ming and Qing Dynasties] in Yang and Terada (eds), above n 9, 423, at 426.
103 See ibid, at 425; Edward Kroker "The Concept of Property in Chinese Customary Law" (1959) Ser 3 vol 7 *Transactions of the Asiatic Society of Japan* 123, at 145–146.
104 See regulations of the Ministry of Households, in *Sifa cankao*, above n 86, vol 1B, at 125.
105 As already discussed. Also see deeds in *Dazu diaocha*, above n 5, ch 3.2, 3.3, 3.4, and 3.12.
106 "暫贌漢人代耕，二三年限滿取回". *Dazu diaocha*, ibid, at 768.
107 Ibid.
108 Ka Chih-ming "Fanxiaozu de xingcheng yu yanbian: Anli xinshe diyu shefan kouliangtian de zudian anpai" ("Formation and Transformation of Aborigine Small-rent Tenure: Land Tenancy of Tribesman's Ration Plot in Anli New Territory") (2008) 15(3) *Taiwanshi yanjiu* 57, at 68, note 35.
109 *Dazu diaocha*, above n 5, at 769–770. The decree was issued also on the Anli village's petition.
110 See land deeds in ibid, at ch 2.2, 3.12, and 656–657.
111 Chen, above n 42, at 297. The Japanese investigation of customs found that *pu* had a fixed term, and that the type of *pu* that gave tenants perpetual rights over land was not real *pu*. See *Taiwan sifa*, above n 33, vol 1, at 96–97 and 106–108.
112 *Dazu diaocha*, above n 5, at 754–755. This deed was made in 1798 (Jiaqing 3). Original appended as Appendix 1(9).
113 Chen, above n 29, at 97.
114 At 97–98, and note 40.
115 The annual rent was 12 *shi*, and the *qidi* money was 400 dollars. The grain price varied over time, but according to Chen, ibid, at 96, the price of 1 *shi* of grain was about one dollar.

116 See ibid, at 167–169.
117 *Dazu diaocha*, above n 5, at 1027, "價輕者謂之贌租，價值稍重者謂之典賣".
118 *Qing huidian Taiwan shili* [Great Qing Institutes, Precedents Concerning Taiwan] (TWWX 226), at 43.
119 For example, see a land deed of 1794 (Qianlong 59), in *Dazu diaocha*, above n 5, at 799, which mentions the Danshui sub-prefect's approval for the lease.
120 In 1810 (Jiaqing 15), 1818–1822 (Jiaqing 23-Daoguang 2) and 1834–1838 (Daoguang 14–18). The government also tried to rectify rent collection issues. See the memorials, decrees and correspondence in *Tai'an jiaji*, above n 41, at 51–74; and a decree of the Fujian-Zhejiang governor-general in *Sifa cankao*, above n 86, vol 1A, at 402–403.
121 *Dazu diaocha*, above n 5, at 771–773.
122 Ibid.
123 *Tai'an jiaji*, above n 41, at 64–65.
124 Ibid, at 68.
125 *Dazu diaocha*, above n 5, at 771–774.
126 Rowe, above n 47, at 32–33.
127 See the deeds in ibid, ch 3.2 (by villages), 3.3 (by *fan yehu*) and 3.4 (by individuals), dated from the early Yongzheng period to the end of Qing rule.
128 See the Taiwan Prefect Shen Qiyuan's recommendation in Taiwan Shiliao Jicheng Bianji Weiyuanhui *Ming Qing Taiwan dang'an huibian* [Collection of Historic Documents Concerning Taiwan During the Ming and Qing Dynasties] (Yuanliu, Taipei, 2004–2009), vol 13, at 224–229.
129 *Fujian shengli*, above n 50, at 445–447.
130 See Shih Tien-fu "Qingdai Taiwan 'fanli bu'an gengzuo' de yuanyou" [The Reasons Behind the Aborigines Being "Unskilful at Farming"] (1990) 69 *Bulletin of the Institute of Ethnology Academia Sinica* 67, in general.

5 Aborigines' efforts

A losing battle

The Qing government, the Chinese settlers and the aborigines were the three major actors in the Chinese settlement of Taiwan.[1] As demonstrated in earlier chapters, in general the government endeavoured to protect aboriginal land rights for the purposes of social stability and security of the reign, but the government and officials subtly changed the attitude towards aboriginal land at the turn of the 19th century. Chinese settlers influenced and transformed aboriginal land tenure through private land transactions. Land transactions were not always the result of fair dealing, and aborigines were often in a disadvantaged position because of their lack of commercial sophistication and financial power. Settlers also employed various other means to obtain aboriginal land, including forceful occupation, encroachment, and "peaceful means" such as marrying into an aboriginal family or building other close personal relationships with aborigines.[2] The aborigines, apart from serving as the government's reliable assistants in suppressing settler uprising and guarding the boundary lines, interacted with the government and settlers regarding land issues in Taiwan.

This chapter examines the Taiwanese aborigines' reactions against land settlement and encroachment by Han settlers. The government's actions in the process are also discussed. The aborigines' first choice against Han settlement was resistance, especially at the early stages of contact when they first felt threatened by settlers. Early stages of contact do not necessarily mean the early annexation years, because new contacts were made as settlements advanced to new areas over time. Resistance was often manifested as violent clashes, but in some cases it took peaceful forms. The government's attitudes and actions concerning the aborigines' armed resistance were manifested in the process. The aborigines also appealed to the government for help when they felt their interests were jeopardised. The disputes brought before the government show changing focuses, and to some extent reveal the tenurial and societal changes of the aboriginal communities over the centuries. Some aborigines adapted to the agricultural and commercial environment which followed Han settlement. The examples of "cession of land for water" (*gedi huanshui* 割地換水) transactions and the establishment of new settlements by the plains aborigines demonstrated the aborigines' adaptation to their new environment and their transformation to be more like Han settlers – a kind of cultural sinicisation. The last section of the chapter looks into the first Taiwan Governor

Liu Mingchuan's land tax reform, which was the last Qing government action that affected aboriginal land tenure.

This chapter depicts the societal and tenurial changes of the aboriginal communities, and demonstrates that the aborigines were the least informed and most disadvantaged actors in the aboriginal land tenure changes during the Qing period. It argues that the aborigines resisted Han settlement on the one hand, and accepted and adapted to Han practice on the other; the government protected aboriginal land against Han encroachment on the one hand, and disregarded aboriginal rights on the other when imperial interests required otherwise. These all worked together for the breakdown of the aboriginal communities and land tenure in a gradual but irreversible manner.

Resisting Han settlement

The aborigines had protested against Han use of their land since the era of Dutch colonisation. They killed those Chinese who entered their land to hunt deer, even though the Dutch authorities had licensed the Chinese to do so.[3] During the Zheng period, violent resistance broke out in localities where the Zhengs attempted to established military colonies.[4] During the Qing period, as land reclamation advanced, the aborigines continued to resist. Resistance mainly took the format of violent conflicts and attacks on settlers, although in some cases more peaceful means of resistance have been recorded. Such conflicts threatened the social order, and the government's maintenance of aboriginal boundaries was strengthened by the establishment of *ai* (隘 guard posts), which were eventually used by settlers to push aboriginal boundaries towards the aboriginal territories and to advance land reclamation.

Armed resistance

At the beginning of the Qing administration, settlers were few and land reclamation mainly took the form of recovering land that had already been reclaimed but left to waste as a result of the change of dynasties. No direct conflict was recorded for this period, even though the Chinese oppression of aborigines certainly occurred.

The Chinese traveller Yu Yonghe, who travelled along the western coast of Taiwan in 1697 (Kangxi 36), had praised the innocence and good nature of the aborigines.[5] Yu noted that the Chinese merchants and interpreters oppressed the aborigines, took advantage of them, and took aboriginal women as wives and concubines, which the aborigines apparently "did not especially resent".[6] However, armed conflicts with Han settlers occurred in the last few years of the Kangxi reign.[7] By the Yongzheng reign, incidents of aborigines attacking settlers had become frequent. The government recognised that these attacks were a result of settlers encroaching on aboriginal territories to reclaim land or acquire resources.[8]

In total, 145 armed attacks by aborigines on settlers throughout the Qing period have been recorded.[9] There was a clear correlation between aboriginal attacks on settlers and the spread of Han settlement, or in other words, between the intensity of reclamation, in both time and space, and the frequency of attacks.

Among the 145 recorded incidents, 71 occurred before the shift of policy in 1874, including 25 attacks on land reclaimers, 11 attacks on settlers who crossed the aboriginal boundaries to cut timber, and 18 cases of attacking villages to kill or wound settlers, burn houses and loot property. In a number of cases settlers were forced to abandon land reclamation.[10] The period that experienced the most frequent attacks was the Yongzheng era, which was the period when land reclamation advanced rapidly after the restriction on reclaiming aboriginal land was removed.

In total 74 cases occurred after the government started to "open the mountains" in 1874; most of these were directed at the soldiers and some at reclaimers and timber cutters.[11] In particular, 1874–1875 and 1886–1887 saw a lot more attacks.[12] This coincided with the periods after the Japanese invasion (Mudanshe Incident) and the Sino-French War, respectively, and when the "opening the mountains" campaigns were promoted vigorously. In addition to the 74 incidents, 31 direct confrontations with government troops, coordinated among a number of villages, were recorded after 1874.[13] The frequency and scale of violence were the result of the forceful opening of the aboriginal territory.

The main locations of aboriginal attacks on settlers during the Kangxi reign were the earliest settled area of Taiwan County. During the Yongzheng era Fengshan, Zhuluo and the newly established Zhanghua County saw most attacks. The Danshui Sub-prefecture became the area of frequent attacks during the Qianlong era, followed by the newly incorporated Gamalan during the Jiaqing period. After 1874 the attacks concentrated at the "back of the mountains" (*houshan* 後山) and the newly established Hengchun County at the southern end of Taiwan.[14] Incidents of aboriginal attacks clearly followed the spread of Han settlement (see Map 1.4).

Conversely, Han settlement spread regardless of aboriginal resistance. One way or another, sooner or later, Han settlements penetrated the aboriginal zone and became established. One well-documented example was the reclamation of Gamalan. The Gamalan aborigines resisted reclamation attempts led by Han settler Lin Hansheng in 1768 (Qianlong 33) and killed Lin.[15] The leader of the successful Han settlement in Gamalan, Wu Sha, was also defeated by the aborigines in the first attempt to reclaim the land in the late Qianlong years, resulting in the death of Wu's brother.[16] In 1796 (Jiaqing 1), Wu built the first stronghold (*touwei* 頭圍) to protect reclamation, and battles occurred on a daily basis with heavy casualties on both sides.[17] Wu managed to befriend the aborigines through providing medication to the aborigines when an epidemic struck, but subsequent reclamation of Gamalan still had to be protected by strongholds around occupied areas, which gradually expanded and advanced. Similarly, in 1815 (Jiaqing 20) some Han settlers entered inner Shuishalian to reclaim land. The first three villages that they encountered were small and could not resist the settlers, but the Puli village armed itself and resisted Han encroachment for over a month, before the settlers tricked them into an unprepared attack and slaughtered the aborigines.[18] The violent resistance of the aborigines against the advancement of Han settlement always ended with the aborigines being overpowered and giving in. The aborigines' resistance might have slowed Han advancement, but could not stop it.

Peaceful resistance

While there is abundant evidence of conflict, resistance also took less violent forms,[19] typically by resisting settlers' attempts to gain title to land.

Some aboriginal leaders were well aware of the risk of Han settlement since the late Kangxi years. In one example, some Han settlers proposed to purchase land from the Shalu village, located in the central western plains. The village head told the villagers that all that their ancestors had left them was that piece of land, which provided for their livelihood and tax payments. If they sold any part to the Han, the Han would occupy and steal the rest, and very soon the whole village would lose their property. The village head told the villagers to resist the proposal, which he could not do in person as he had friendly relationships with the settlers.[20] This incident illustrates that the aborigines were well aware of the importance of land, of the methods used by settlers to acquire it, and of the consequences of land-selling. This same incident also shows the complex relationship between settlers and aborigines in some cases, where they could be friendly towards each other, but pursue competing strategies at the same time.

It is not clear how many aborigines were as insightful as the head of the Shalu village, but as aboriginal land increasingly became lost to Han settlers, more aborigines became aware of ways of Han expansion and formed resolutions to resist it. In 1823 (Daoguang 3), 14 plains aboriginal villages that moved to the Puli basin in inner Shuishalian made a covenant to exclude Han settlers from their land affairs.[21] The covenant recounted that after Taiwan entered the Qing realm, the rights to use and manage the grassland remained with the aborigines (*gui fan zhangguan* 歸番掌管). Further, the government had rewarded the aborigines with the establishment of aboriginal colonies in 1788 (Qianlong 53) and gave them rights to reclaim wasteland beyond the aboriginal boundaries. However their Han tenants, seeing that the aborigines were ignorant, had cheated them or used loans as bait, and the aborigines lost almost all of their land through Han purchase (*maishu daijin* 買贖殆盡). The same document records that the villagers had now found a piece of unreclaimed land, and that they would encourage each other to work hard on the land. They promised each other not to allow Han settlers to reclaim the land, nor employ settlers to work on the land or manage their affairs. Those who breached the covenant would be expelled from the land. The villages were mostly from the central western plains, and they had a clear understanding of the course of land loss and of actions needed. These aborigines flourished in their new settlement.[22]

Actions were also taken to prevent aborigines from pledging or selling their large rent collection rights after the land was granted in large rent to Han settlers. In 1831 (Daoguang 11) the aborigines of Zhonggang village, when signing a covenant about the division of village rent, vowed to punish those who pledged or sold their share of rent.[23] Continuous complaints to the authorities that settlers dwelt among the aborigines and coveted their land and property also evidenced that the aborigines were wary of Han settlers mingling with aborigines to possibly take advantage of them and cheat them out of their lands.[24]

There is little recorded evidence of aborigines forming alliances in their resistance of Han settlement. There are two probable reasons for this. The aborigines were ethnically and linguistically diverse and were rarely united. Furthermore, Han settlement did not occur in all areas at the same time. Rather, it progressed from one area to another, meaning that aborigines were affected by settlement at different times. The settlement pattern and the lack of coordinated resistance resulted in the eventual encroachment on aboriginal land.

Government attitudes and actions

The government had no issue with the aborigines' peaceful resistance. Quite often officials themselves lamented the cunning of settlers and innocence of the aborigines, and condemned the tricks played by the former on the latter. However, officials tended not to intervene in peaceful interactions between settlers and aborigines. The story about Shalu village's refusal to sell land was recorded by the Taiwan censor as a point of interest, and no view was expressed one way or the other. This reluctance to intervene in private affairs evidences the non-interventionist stance taken by the government and the culture among officials at a practical level.

Armed resistance, however, was another matter, as this obviously disturbed social order. In such cases, the government's attitude leaned towards the aborigines, but the solutions, whether intended or not, often facilitated settler advance. This was particularly the case from the early 1800s.

The government was well aware of aborigine-settler conflicts and the reasons behind them, and was often sympathetic towards the aborigines. In 1725 (Yongzheng 3), the Fujian governor reported that during that year three or four cases of mountain aborigines killing settlers had occurred. The reason was that settlers either had encroached upon the aborigines' territory to reclaim land, or had damaged the aborigines' forests by cutting trees.[25] The Yongzheng emperor, even though his reign has been seen as a period of expansion and colonisation in Taiwan, disapproved of retaliation against the mountain aborigines.[26] The government generally distinguished between cases where settlers were killed in aboriginal territories and where aborigines entered settled areas to kill. Encroaching settlers were seen as "villains" (*jianmin* 奸民), and were punished for crossing the aboriginal boundaries and causing social instability.[27] Therefore the primary blame and restraint were placed on settlers.

The government's typical approach prior to 1874 was to strengthen border control.[28] Eventually border control changed from simply marking boundaries by stelae with inscribed warnings, to a system of border posts (*ai* 隘) and guards.

Border guards were first employed by land reclaimers during the Qianlong reign to protect the reclaimers from mountain aborigines' attacks at a time when land reclamation spread to the foothills near aboriginal boundaries.[29] Reclaimers either set aside some land as a reward to the guards who could lease the land for rent, or paid the guards a portion of the harvest as their wages. In both cases what the guards received was called "guard-post rent" (*aizu* 隘租).

During the late Qianlong reign, illicitly reclaimed land beyond aboriginal boundaries was investigated, confiscated and turned into aboriginal "company land" (*tundi*) to support members of the aboriginal companies. Thus the post guards lost the land or rental income from carrying out the guard duty. Because the guards were mostly acculturated aborigines who were good fighters, and because the boundaries still needed to be guarded, the government decided to retain the border guards and pay their wages from the rental of the "company land". Thus the government became involved in the guard post system.[30]

During the Jiaqing and Daoguang reigns, as settlers tried to reclaim land near the mountain aboriginal territories, guard posts became prevalent as a means to protect reclaimers from aboriginal attacks. As such they essentially maintained security along the borders.[31] Because of increasing financial pressure as well as increasing internal and external crises, the government was only too happy to let settlers organise the guarding of borders. Hence a system was established where head guards (*aishou* 隘首) were nominated by the settler community and appointed by the government.[32] Through the government appointment the private guard post system gained an official or semi-official status and authority. The government thus indirectly supported Han reclaimers' intrusion into aboriginal territories.

This coincided with relaxed protection of aborigines' rights after the late Qianlong reign. At times the government allowed or even initiated for settler reclamation of border land in return for policing the boundaries. For example, during the early Daoguang years, in responding to frequent harassment by mountain aborigines, the Danshui Sub-prefecture established a guard post in Shisuilun 石碎崙 and employed 40 guards. The wages were over 1,500 dollars per year, a sum the local government could ill afford.[33] Eventually the local government encouraged settlers to establish the Jin-Guang-Fu 金廣福 guards system, which built 40 guard posts, employed over 200 guards and supported reclamation of thousands of *jia* of land in 25 villages.[34] Thus guard post organisations like Jin-Guang-Fu became a facility to protect advancement of land reclamation into the aboriginal territories. The government, especially during the Jiaqing and Daoguang reigns, knowingly allowed it to progress. The intention was to maintain border peace without using government resources, but the arrangement essentially gave the private organisations power to intrude into the aboriginal territories.

After 1874, the government sent troops to subjugate the aborigines and forcefully required reclamation of aboriginal land, and removed restrictions on Han settlement. The government certainly did not hesitate to quash aboriginal resistance against government troops, but it did not necessarily support settlers in cases of settler-aborigine conflicts. When dealing with a case of aborigines killing Han settlers in 1884, the then Taiwan circuit intendant, Liu Ao, reasoned that "the aborigines do not kill without a good reason. It was all because the settlers attempted to encroach on their [aborigines'] land, and they [settlers] brought death onto themselves".[35] In responding to a recommendation to send troops to punish the aborigines, the intendant retorted that such an action meant that the government and settlers had united to rob aborigines of their land, which had never been the government policy, otherwise it would have been carried out and achieved long ago.[36] Therefore although the government promoted settlement, this did not give the settlers a licence to violate aboriginal land rights. Officials remained of the view that settlers were responsible for aboriginal retaliation.

In summary, at first the aborigines resisted Han settlement when settlers encroached upon their living space and threatened their traditional life style. Their resistance, be it violent or peaceful, might have slowed down Han settlement, but could not prevent it. The government maintained a non-intervention stance if the aborigines' resistance was peaceful, and tried to prevent armed conflicts between settlers and aborigines. The government's attitude was probably harsher towards settlers than towards aborigines, but in reality, the government pursued its own goal of border security, and aboriginal land rights could be sacrificed for security purposes.

Litigating for land and rent

The aborigines who surrendered to government authority had sought the government's protection in cases of disputes and infringed rights. This particularly occurred in Han settlement areas where settlers and aborigines had prior agreements about land use.

Direct sources about aboriginal involvement in litigation are scant, but from the available sources, it appears that although the aborigines brought cases to the authorities regarding substantive land rights, most cases related to rents – rent rates, and collection and distribution of rent. In some cases aboriginal villages protested against settlers' behaviour in general, seeking to exclude settlers from their community and eliminate opportunities of land transactions, loans and other personal contacts so as to protect their land.

Cases on land rights and rent rates

From the early annexation years, aborigines brought disputes over land to the local authority. The 1721 Lower Danshui deed, quoted in Chapter 4, recounted transactions and proceedings regarding the Tonobot estate. In the first instance, the aboriginal village granted a piece of land to Han reclaimer He-Zhou-Wang for reclamation, but afterwards the aborigines brought a case before the county magistrate for the *yezhu* rights over the estate and won the magistrate's support. In another case of the late Kangxi reign, it was the Han *yehu* who petitioned the government for protection of rights. The plaintiff, a Han widow, claimed that she had *pu* a piece of land from the aborigines, but the aborigines, incited by their village merchant, disturbed the settlement and prevented her from exercising management rights and collecting rent. The Taiwan maritime defence subprefect (*haifang fenfu* 海防分府) issued a decree forbidding anyone to incite the aborigines, and asking the aborigines to let the plaintiff observe the terms of the contract.[37]

By the early Qianlong years, even the emperor had become aware that "cases of settlers and aborigines suing each other [regarding land] have been occurring constantly".[38] The emperor noted that settlers often encroached on aboriginal land, and when disputes arose they sought military officers' protection through transferring the land to the officers – this means the officers became the *yezhu* and large rent holders and the settlers became their "tenants".[39] Accordingly the emperor's decree forbade military officers from acquiring estates in Taiwan.[40] The high volume of litigation shows that the aborigines did not hesitate to resort to the authority to resolve disputes and protect their land. The central government's resolution in this case also shows that government policies were responsive to aboriginal complaints. However the order given to military officers was a simplistic approach and did not address the problem of encroachment by settlers.

Existing records show that many land cases were related to rent issues. Many claims requested rent increase, and the grounds for bringing such claims varied. In the 1721 Lower Danshui deed, over a decade after the government adjudicated the Tonobot estate to the aboriginal village, the village petitioned the authorities for an increase of rent because the village population had increased, and the rental income was not sufficient to support the population. Even through the request lacked contractual or legal grounds, the magistrate supported the request. Here the magistrate exercised the "paternal" authority to impose the rent increase, arguably following the Chinese practice of price top-up in sale and pledge cases.

In another case, the ground of the petition arose from changes to the law. A decree issued by the Taiwan circuit intendant, Zhang Ting, in 1768 (Qianlong 33) mentioned that the aborigines could continue to lease the land at the customary rate of 8 *shi* per *jia* for wetland and 4 *shi* per *jia* for dry land, if they were unable to cultivate the land themselves.[41] The aboriginal Dajia and Dehua villages had earlier granted land to Han settlers for reclamation at an agreed rent rate of 6 *shi* per *jia* once the land was developed into wetland.[42] On the basis of the 1768 decree, the aborigines petitioned the aboriginal affairs sub-prefect to increase the rent rate to 8 *shi* per *jia*. The then sub-prefect, Zhang Suoshou (1767–1770), adjudicated for the aborigines and upheld their request. The Taiwan circuit intendant, Jiang Yunxun (1769–1771), overturned Zhang's decision on appeal and the rent rate reverted to 6 *shi*. The aborigines appealed, and the case was referred to the succeeding circuit intendant, Qi Chongge (1771–1774), who supported the aborigines' claim in 1772 (Qianlong 37).[43]

Two points are worth noting in this case. The first is that the two decisions that supported the aborigines' claims relied solely on the 1768 decree which specified 8 *shi* per *jia* of rent. Intendant Qi noted that maintaining the rent rate of 8 *shi* would ensure consistency across the board, and dismissed the settlers' claim of investment in the land, including the construction of irrigation systems, as a valid ground for maintaining a lower rent rate.[44] The 1768 decree to fix rent rates in effect ratified the practice of leasing aboriginal land in the large rent model, and abandoned the earlier policy of forbidding lease of aboriginal land. This essentially relaxed the protection of aboriginal land rights. However, as demonstrated in the previously mentioned case, the decree set a minimum large rent rate for aborigine-settler leases and served to protect the aborigines' income at the practical level, especially when the ban against lease had been ignored.

The second point to note is the government's clear disapproval of court actions. Intendant Qi, despite ruling for the aborigines, believed the aborigines were incited by villains (*shegun* 社棍) and required investigation of the background of the court action. The aborigines were excused from any punishment because their anxiety about their grain rations was understandable, but the village scribe (*sheji* 社記) was punished for drafting the petition for the aborigines .[45] This demonstrates the difficulties the aborigines faced in bringing cases to the authorities. The Chinese legal tradition strove for "no litigation" (*wusong* 無訟) and generally disapproved of court action.[46] This attitude of government and officials aggravated the difficulties that the aborigines already faced because of language issues. A poem by Gamalan Sub-prefect Ke Peiyuan (1835) described the miserable state of the plains aborigines, where they were robbed of their land by Han settlers, and had trouble-making themselves understood when they petitioned the official, who ignored their petitions and flogged and scolded them.[47]

Therefore, although aborigines were able to petition the government for protection of their rights and they often won the support of government officials, litigation was a difficult process for aborigines. The difficulty was not only because of their disadvantaged situation, but also because of the authority's attitude of discouraging law suits, which was rooted in the Chinese legal tradition.

Protest against Han behaviour

The establishment of two aboriginal affairs sub-prefect positions in 1766 (Qianlong 31) was in response to the increasing interaction between aborigines and settlers over land matters and the frequent aborigine-settler disputes. As such one of their main functions was to adjudicate and to prevent settler-aborigine land disputes. The government prescribed that the sub-prefects were to investigate cases where the "villainous and powerful" (*jiangun haoqiang* 奸棍豪强) purchased or accepted pledges of aboriginal land, and to drive out Han "villains" (*tugun* 徒棍) who married aboriginal women and dwelt in aboriginal villages, and so on.[48] These provided grounds for aborigines to bring cases against Han settlers.

Records of aborigines complaining to the government about settler behaviour emerged in the late Qianlong and early Jiaqing reigns. Some well-known decrees of this period, purportedly to protect aboriginal land rights, were in fact a response to aboriginal protests and petitions. In 1788 (Qianlong 53), for example, the interpreter of the Anli village, who was an aborigine, complained to the aboriginal affairs sub-prefect that some Han settlers dwelt in their village, took advantage of the ignorance of the aborigines and had secretly *pu* aboriginal land without permission of the interpreter.[49] A few years later, in 1800 (Jiaqing 5), another Anli interpreter complained that Han settlers had robbed aborigines of their rental income through illegal lending, purposely buried their dead on aboriginal land, entered aborigines' territory to gather rattan and burn charcoal, seduced aboriginal women, and used alcohol and money to lure the aborigines into debt so that they could possess the aborigines' land.[50] Similarly, in 1804 (Jiaqing 9), the interpreter of the Zhuqian village complained that some Han settlers lent money to settlers, charged high interest, accepted pledges of land and refused the aborigines' redemption requests. Moreover they rented houses from the aborigines, seduced their women and eventually robbed aborigines of their houses.[51]

It is likely that these incidents were not isolated, and that settlers carried out the same activities elsewhere in Taiwan, especially moneylending. In response to aborigine-settler disputes and the aborigines' repeated protests, the governor of Fujian Province intervened in 1817 (Jiaqing 22) and set down rules concerning Han moneylending, and pledging and mortgaging land by aborigines.[52]

Settler attempts to take advantage of aborigines did not stop and aborigines continued to protest to the authorities where they could. In 1867 (Tongzhi 5), the lieutenant (*waiwei* 外委) of one of the aboriginal companies complained that Han tenants either tried to steal their land or were not paying rent in full.[53]

These cases all appeared to be based on the government's guiding principle to reduce settler-aborigine interaction, and in particular to prevent settlers from cheating aborigines. The problem with these cases is that they were general complaints and no respondent was named in the complaints or called upon to answer the cases. The typical response of the local government was to issue a public notice to forbid Han settlers from doing the acts that the aborigines complained about. This was the uniform response in all the cases cited earlier. Because the public notices were in response to complaints and the publication was in limited areas, they usually did not achieve any significant result, shown by the fact that protests continued to be made.

Rent distribution

Rent distribution was another focus of litigation, reflecting the societal changes in the aboriginal communities and a new form of conflict between aborigines and settlers.

As most aboriginal villages leased their land as the collective owner, usually the village interpreter or village head, who managed the village affairs, collected rents on behalf of the villages. They also appropriated the rent for various purposes, including paying village taxes, miscellaneous government fees and village expenditure; paying wages and allowances to those who had a role in the village affairs; and distributing grain rations to the villagers. Village heads and interpreters had existed long before the Qing annexation, but during the Qing period they became village office holders whose appointment was ratified by the government. They became the interface between the state and the village community. Because of issues of Han interpreters embezzling village rentals, in 1757 (Qianlong 22) the government started to replace Han interpreters with aborigine interpreters, as by this time aborigines were becoming competent for this role with increasing fluency in the Chinese language.[54] At about the same time, *fan yehu* also became an office holder recognised by the government.[55] Village heads, interpreters and *fan yehu* were recommended by the village, in particular by the educated, the elders or other aborigines who had roles in village affairs. The government checked the ability and integrity of the nominees, made the appointment and issued a seal of office.[56] Despite the safeguards surrounding the appointment of these office holders, complaints about embezzlement of village rents by the office holders continued. Sometimes competitors for appointment to a position brought cases against each other, as they fought for the power to receive and dispose of rents on behalf of the village.[57]

Existing records of individual cases of complaints came mostly from the Guangxu years, but it is known that by the early Daoguang years, cases about embezzlement of rents by interpreters, village heads or *fan yehu* had become "incessant".[58] Village heads and *fan yehu* were aborigines, as were most, if not all, interpreters. Therefore most complaints about embezzlement of rentals were internal affairs in each aboriginal village, but still Han settlers were often involved. For example, in 1878 (Guangxu 4), aborigines of the Tunxiao village complained to the aboriginal affairs sub-prefect that their interpreter embezzled 950 *shi* of their 1350 *shi* annual rent.[59] The aborigines complained that it was a Han individual, Jiang, who conspired with an aborigine, Pan, in making Pan an interpreter, and the rent was in fact received by Jiang. The case reached the Taipei prefect, who removed Pan from the office, and required him to pay tax and village expenditure for that year, but did not require him to repay the residual amount to the village. The prefect further stipulated that from the next year, the aborigines would divide the rent equally among them after deducting village taxes and expenditures. The prefect also mentioned that in most cases the role of interpreter was assumed by aborigines who were manipulated or were in collusion with Han settlers, and that in his previous administration of central Taiwan he had ordered all interpreters to divide the village rents equally among the aborigines.

This case was typical, and it illustrates some facets of aboriginal communities in general and property rights in particular. Firstly, even in the late period of Qing rule, aborigines maintained separate identities and were administered separately through the preservation of aboriginal villages. Further, many aboriginal villages still had collective rental income after 200 years of Qing rule. Tunxiao was under the Qing administration by 1693 (Kangxi 32), and was one of the earliest villages that were subject to Qing authority.[60] By the time of the rental complaints in 1878, the village had 39 households, and by 1888 (Guangxu 14) they still had an annual rental income of 1679 *shi* of grain.[61]

The third facet was the Han involvement in village rent affairs. It is likely that by the Daoguang reign, most, if not all, plains aboriginal villages had lost ownership of land, and large rent income was about the only income the aborigines had and the only connection, albeit a weak one, that they had with their land. Once there was no more land to be taken, Han settlers became involved in rent collection and distribution in most villages, as noted by the Taipei prefect. The reason why Han settlers could become involved in village rental affairs was again related to moneylending. As part of loan arrangements, and possibly to avoid the onerous tasks of official engagements and village affairs, aboriginal leaders let Han creditors take charge of village rents, including to collect rent, deduct interest from the rent, pay tax on behalf of the village, and distribute the residue as grain rations to the ordinary aborigines. Village heads and interpreters entrusted to the Han agents (*baoban ren* 包辦人) their seals of office, which were needed for rent collection. This became a widespread practice, and in the 33 villages in Xinzhu and Danshui Counties, only one did not have a Han agent.[62] The government had tried to prevent Han involvement in aboriginal village affairs, such as replacing Han interpreters with aborigine interpreters and issuing decrees forbidding Han settlers from dwelling in aboriginal villages, but the Han settlers were still able to interfere with aboriginal land and rent issues through acting as their "agents". The government was always one step behind the frontier practice.

Ironically, a major cause of village loans was that aborigines were engaged in litigation, especially litigation with Han settlers over land rights and litigation among aborigines for competition over public offices in the village, such public offices being invested with the power to collect and distribute village rents.[63] The aborigines could not afford the costs of litigation themselves and had to borrow from Han settlers. Therefore it became a vicious cycle – the aborigines litigated for land and rent, and as a result Han settlers had the opportunity to access village rents, which caused more litigation.

The fourth facet about aboriginal communities and property rights, as reflected in the previously mentioned case, was the way aboriginal land and rent became fragmented. Ordinary aborigines suffered from the corrupt village rent collection and distribution process, and they often could not receive their grain rations, which were their only livelihood. To solve the problem, some aboriginal villages chose to divide village rents and assign rent collection rights and obligations to individual households. For example, as early as 1830 (Daoguang 11), the interpreter of the Zhonggang village made a covenant with the villagers, where each person was allocated 5 *shi* of grain per year, and each household was assigned specific tenants from whom they should collect the rent.[64] This solution was adopted by officials, who ordered equal distribution of village rents, as the Taipei prefect did. However the rent available for distribution were the residue once taxes and village expenditures had been deducted, amounts which occupied a substantial proportion of the total rental income. In the case of the Tunxiao village, although an annual rent of 1,350 *shi* of grain seemed a reasonable amount for 39 households, once taxes and village expenditures had been deducted, only about 700 *shi* were left.[65] The amount available for distribution further reduced during the tax reform, as will be discussed later in this chapter. Furthermore, where the rent collection rights were individualised and the aborigines were assigned specific tenants, the collective aspect of village rent became obsolete, and in effect the land became privatised.

Litigation was one method the aborigines resorted to for protection of their land rights, especially as interaction and land transactions with Han settlers increased. Similar to the aboriginal resistance of Han settlement, the Taiwanese aborigines' litigation against Han settlers over land was a process of the aborigines losing ground step by step. Aborigines at first litigated for land, but with increasing land transactions and possibly more elaborate land deeds which reduced ambiguity, the object of litigation soon became rent rates. The government tried to reduce Han-aborigine conflict through preventing Han-aborigine interaction, and aborigines complained that Han settlers tried to steal land from aborigines through mingling with them. The government in general upheld the aborigines' complaints, but the administrative orders made in response to complaints could not have far-reaching effects. Eventually the land all fell into Han hands and the large rent rates fixed, and the problem became collection and distribution of village rent. Aborigines fought to protect their land rights and rent rights through litigation, but litigation added financial burden on the villages, which afforded Han creditors the opportunity to take control of aboriginal rent collection. This in turn caused more litigation. The solution that government officials and aborigines found was to individualise rent collection rights, so as to avoid corruption in and Han interference with the rent collection process. As a result the collective tenure broke down.

Adapting to Han practice

Yet another response was adaptation and acculturation. With increased exposure to Han culture, many Taiwanese aborigines gradually adapted to Han ways, including methods of land use, carrying out land transactions, and even in occupying and seizing land from less sophisticated aboriginal tribes. During the process some aborigines became influential landlords, others moved on to new settlements. Many became acculturated and lost distinctiveness as aborigines. The Taiwanese aborigines' acculturation reflects a common process throughout Chinese history – as ancient China expanded and Chinese culture and civilisation spread, formerly distinct ethnic groups became sinicised, adopted Chinese farming practices and imperceptibly merged into the Chinese world.

The adaptation and acculturation process of the Taiwanese aborigines began with the first contacts. In the early Qing period, travellers found that the aborigines of the four villages close to the administrative centre of Taiwan Prefecture were "hardworking in husbandry" (*qin jiase* 勤稼穡) – denoting Chinese-style farming – because of the Zheng government's education programme and the fact that they were close to the administration centre and Han settlement areas.[66] The aborigines learned to contract with settlers and among themselves. As early as 1684 (Kangxi 22), the first year of annexation, an aborigine of the Mattau village alienated a piece of land for 3,000 dollars.[67] Before the mid-Jiaqing reign, many of the aborigine-settler contracts were bilingual, in Chinese and in aboriginal language – in particular the Sirayan language.[68] These contracts indicate that the aborigines not only participated in land transactions, they were also aware of the necessity and importance of written contracts. By the Jiaqing years, aborigines carried out land transactions with one another, and made deeds in Chinese format even though both parties were aborigines.[69]

To illustrate the process of aboriginal acculturation, this section focuses on aboriginal participation in land investment, using the "cession of land for water" as a principal example. This section also addresses aboriginal mobility, involving searching for and moving to new settlements.

Participation in land investments

A well-documented example of Taiwan aborigines' participation in land investment was the Anli village group.[70] To demonstrate aboriginal participation in complicated commercial transactions and the process by which they became competent in land dealings, this section discusses a series of agreements that the Anli villages formed with Han settlers to "cede land for water" during the Yongzheng years.

As the Chinese style of farming was mainly wetland rice planting, irrigation was very important for farmers. Most of the irrigation systems in Qing Taiwan were built by settlers, rather than by the government. As irrigation systems were complex and expensive projects, the investments usually came from land owners of a certain area jointly, or from wealthy investors who derived their return from charging a water usage fee known as "water rent" (*shuizu* 水租).[71] Water rents were charged on various bases, such as the volume of water used or the area of land irrigated.[72] A widely adopted rate was 3 or 4 *shi* of grain per *jia* of land, the equivalent of the large rent rate for dry land, or half of the large rent rate for wetland.[73]

It was against this background that the Anli villages signed agreements with Han *yehu* to exchange land for irrigation rights. The three available agreements are materially similar, and it is worth quoting the first one in full:[74]

> The people who made this agreement [are] Pan Dunzai, the village head of Anli, Soushu, Wuniulan and Jiushe villages, and [a long list of individual aborigines' names]. Because [sic] the land within the territory of Dun et al is all dry land. [We had] planted crops, but without irrigation there has been no harvest every year and we are helpless. The aborigines assembled and discussed the matter. Through an intermediary we asked the interpreter Zhang Dajing [to find] someone who could invest in labour and capital to build the irrigation system and share the water for land. The villages of Dun et al are willing to [give up] the land [location and boundaries]. This [land] is within the territory of the four villages, and did not encroach on other people's land. [The aborigines] are willing to use this [land] as a compensation for the labour and capital investment, and give it to the *yezhu* to recruit tenants for reclamation. In the future our descendants dare not say otherwise. [We] are willing to give up this dry land, and we humbly request Zhang Dajing to ask *yehu* Zhang Zhenwan to accept the task, [and] self [sic] invest in over 9,300 taels of silver to build the irrigation system and share the water with the aborigines. On this day the three parties agree that Zhang Zhenwan will build the irrigation system. The water is divided into 10 shares. Eight of them belong to Zhang Zhenwan to irrigate his own land, and two shares belong to the aborigines to water aboriginal farms. The land within the specified boundaries is given to Zhang Zhenwan for reclamation, to compensate for the investment in the irrigation building. [Zhang can] register the land for taxation, and have it as perpetual property. We guarantee that the aboriginal assembly is willing to cede this land for water, and Zhang Zhenwan is willing to invest silver to build the irrigation and share water with the aborigines in exchange for land. [This

> is] a mutual agreement. In the future our descendants dare not request for price top-up or redemption. We guarantee that this land is our ancestral land, and does not involve other villages. [Further words of title guarantee]. Each year Zhang Zhenwan [will pay] 200 *shi* of grain, and Dun et al will transport it from [Zhang's] estate. [Concluding with usual contract formalities]
>
> It is noted this day, the aborigines of the four villages received 9,300 taels of silver specified in the agreement.
>
> [List of names who signed the agreement]
>
> In the tenth month of the first year of the Yongzheng Reign[75]

In this deed, Zhang Zhenwan was in fact the business name of the interpreter Zhang Dajing.[76] The total area of land is not specified, but it was a large parcel of land given that the land was across four villages. The deed was less than clear as to whether the 9,300 taels of silver was to be the aborigines' investment in the irrigation system or the total building cost of the system. Scholars usually assume that it was the total building cost, that is, the Han *yehu* Zhang's total investment.[77] However at the end of the deed the aborigines acknowledged the receipt of 9,300 taels of silver. This suggested that the 9,300 taels of silver was the price of the land, which the aborigines had to invest in the irrigation system. Although other examples show that irrigation systems were very expensive to build, no original record exists to suggest the cost of building the system discussed here. Therefore this chapter tentatively adopts the common view that 9,300 taels was the total investment. In any case, the village used the land as an investment to obtain 20% of the water rights, in addition to an annual payment of 200 *shi* of grain. From another perspective, it could also be said that the aborigines sold the land (although they retained some annuity as the aborigines usually did) and used the capital to invest in the irrigation building.

In 1732, because the irrigation system that Zhang built was not sufficient to irrigate the areas required, Zhang together with another five *yehu* treated with the four Anli villages for the construction of another irrigation system.[78] The four villages ceded another piece of land and the six Han *yehu* invested 6,600 taels of silver to build the system.[79] The water rights were divided into 14 shares: the aboriginal villages had two shares and the six Han *yehu* each had two. In addition the aborigines received 600 *shi* of grain per year.

The next year, the interpreter Zhang Dajing found another *yehu*, Zhang Chengzu, to sign a third land-water exchange agreement with six Anli villages, being the original four plus another two.[80] This time the villages gave up four parcels of land for 20% of water right of the new irrigation system, which Zhang would invest 8,300 taels to build. In addition the aborigines received an annuity of 520 *shi* of grain (see Table 5.1). The annotation to the deed noted that Zhang paid an additional 3,200 taels in silver for rights to reclaim some residual land. The large amount of silver involved indicated that large areas of land were ceded.

Many records complained that settlers deprived aborigines of their land by cheating or unfair transactions, and these "land for water" agreements have usually been seen by researchers as a major way by which settlers deprived aborigines of

Table 5.1 Key terms of Anli Village "land for water" agreements

Year	*Aborigines*	*Settlers*	*Land area*	*Irrigation investment (taels)*	*Water rights (Han:Abo)*	*Annuity (shi)*
1723	4 villages	Zhang Zhenwan	Not clear	9,300	8:2	200
1732	4 villages	Zhang Zhenwan and 5 others	Not clear	6,600	6:1	600
1733	6 villages	Zhang Chengzu	Not clear	8,300	8:2	520

their land.[81] There are some good reasons for this view, since all three agreements were arranged by the villages' interpreter Zhang Dajing, who officially represented the aborigines, while at the same time was the leading *yehu* and a party to the transactions. However, in fact the situation is more complex than might appear at first sight.

Examining the agreements themselves, the aborigines were entitled to 20% of the water rights in the first and third agreements, and one-seventh in the second agreement. This means that the lands they gave up were deemed to be the corresponding percentage of the total investment. The aborigines thus changed from land owners to water right owners. To determine whether the transactions were fair, one has to compare the value of the land rights ceded with the value of the water rights gained. This is almost impossible because the area of land is not clear, nor is the designed capacity of the irrigation system. This itself may be an indication that the aborigines were not sophisticated enough to define the key terms of the contract. However looked at from another angle, the total investments of the Han settlers were specified. Hence in effect the ceded lands were quantified in monetary values, that is, 20% of the 9,300 taels, one-seventh of 6,600 taels and 20% of 8,300 taels, respectively. These were in effect the selling prices of the land, and in addition the aborigines were paid an annuity for each parcel of land, as was the customary practice when the aborigines *pu* or sold their land.

It is also important to note that no complaint against Zhang by the aborigines was recorded, and the Anli aborigines several times acknowledged Zhang's contribution of bringing irrigation to their villages, even after decades had passed, in the late Qianlong reign.[82] Furthermore, irrigation building was a costly and time-consuming project, sometimes taking two to three generations to complete.[83] Here the risk of investment failure, additional funding and ongoing maintenance rested on the Han *yehu*. As a matter of fact, one of the six Han *yehu* in the second deed had to sell his share of water rights because he was not able to afford the maintenance.[84] Another reason why the aborigines relied on Han settlers to build irrigation systems was that it was very technical and the aborigines were not able to handle projects of such scale and complexity. Investing in irrigation system carried high risks but gave high returns.[85] Evaluating all the evidence, it appears that these aborigines were able to engage in meaningful negotiations with settlers on investment matters.

Through these processes, the Anli aborigines became active players in land investments and competent landlords. Some lands were developed into wetlands, and the aborigines leased them on periodic tenancy, which meant that they collected higher rent than large rent, and retained property rights over the lands.

As often was the case, usually one or two individuals adapted better than others because of their special position or ability. The head of the Anli village, Pan Dunzai and his family, became powerful and wealthy landlords. Following the example of Han *yehu* like Zhang, the Pan family's investment firm *Dayouren* 大由仁 reached land-water exchange deals with the aboriginal village of Old Anli (*Anli jiushe* 岸里舊社), but this time the village only obtained 10% of the water rights.[86] Pan's family, in association with other investors, invested about 100,000 dollars over 70 years to transform the grassland of the Old Anli village into wetland. Most of Pan's land – 89% of wetland and 54% of dry land – was tenanted for periods fewer than three years.[87] Clearly improved infrastructure enhanced the aborigines' ability to retain ownership over their remaining land.

The Anli case was but one example. The Anli village group were not the only villages that carried out land for water transactions, and the Pan family was not the only aboriginal family that was successfully engaged in land transactions or farming activities. There were cases of aborigines purchasing large areas of land or redeeming land that was granted to tenants, involving thousands of dollars.[88] Some aborigines reclaimed land of aboriginal villages and successfully developed grassland into wetland.[89] Some became pledgees of land from their fellow aborigines.[90] In 1880 (Guangxu 6), a Han *yezhu* reached a "land for water" agreement with an aborigine irrigation system owner, only this time it was the Han who gave up a parcel of land for a share of the water.[91]

The success of the Pan family and other aborigines shows some of the aborigines' ability to participate in commercial activities, how they adapted to Han practice and the positive effects on their land ownership once they became equal market players with Han settlers.

New settlements

Other aspects of aborigines' adaptation were shown in establishing new settlements. As the western plains were fully developed into farms by Han settlers, the acculturated aborigines organised several large-scale migrations to the mountain areas. The migrations were caused by the reduction or loss of the aborigines' traditional living space due to Han settlement,[92] but the process of migration to and settlement in new territories illustrated the aborigines' adaptation and acculturation to Han ways.

There were four major waves of aboriginal migration, each to a new direction. In 1804 (Jiaqing 9), over 1,000 aborigines from eight aboriginal villages in the central to northern parts of the western plains migrated to the newly developed Gamalan area.[93] Subsequently aborigines from another two villages joined the movement, and they settled down in Gamalan.

The second wave was the migration of aborigines of five aboriginal groups, consisting of 32 villages, in central western plains to the Puli area of inner Shuishalian.[94] This occurred because, after the Han encroachment of inner Shuishalian and subsequent government decision to close off the land to Han reclamation in 1817 (Jiaqing 22), the Puli aborigines invited the plains aborigines to move in, to help resist Han encroachment. The aborigines arrived in successive groups from 1823 (Daoguang 3) and they thrived in Puli. Within 20 years, their population increased to over 2,000 people, while just over a score of Puli aborigines survived.[95] By 1877 (Guangxu 3), the population of plains aborigines in Puli reached over 6,000.[96] This shows that migration and resettlement was often a wise strategy.

The third wave was the migration of aborigines from five villages, of the Siraya and Makattao groups, in the southwestern plains. The Siraya group was the first to be exposed to Han culture after the Dutch period, and their retreat to the mountain areas started during the Zheng period. The Makattao group started to retreat to the mountain areas in the mid-Kangxi years. Aborigines from these two groups migrated to further south and to the east of Taiwan in 1829 (Daoguang 9).[97]

The fourth wave was the southward move of the Gamalan aborigines to the present-day Hualian and Taidong in 1840 (Daoguang 20).[98]

These migrant plains aborigines adapted to the Han ways and resembled Han settlers in many ways. The main drive to migrate was to seek new land for agriculture. In the new settlements, they reclaimed land, conducted land transactions with the non-acculturated aborigines, encroached upon their land and provoked conflicts. The aboriginal migrants of the first wave competed for land in Gamalan with Han settlers and held an advantage over the Han settlers, who were not strong enough to contest with the aborigines but eventually managed to appease them and break up their union.[99] The aborigines who moved to Puli (the second wave) *pu* land from the local aborigines. In one case they raised over 5,000 dollars to obtain most of the land in the Puli basin. In total they reclaimed about 2,000 *jia* of land.[100]

The aborigines from the southwestern plains (the third wave) gave the southern aborigines alcohol, meat, tobacco and cloth in return for an agreement to reclaim their land.[101] This was precisely the method by which the Han *kenhu* Chen-Lai-Zhang obtained the Taipei basin for reclamation. After the agreement broke up, these plains aborigines moved further north into the eastern part of Taiwan. They reclaimed land, planted crops, kept buffalo and traded buffalo for land with the local aborigines, recruited their kinsmen from home to reclaim more land, and formed a sizeable settlement group.[102] After the government opened up eastern Taiwan for settlement, usually a small number of Han settlers lived among the plains aborigines or the mountain aborigines, and the relationships between Han settlers and mountain aborigines were more harmonious than that between the plains aborigines and mountain aborigines.[103] This shows that the plains aborigines were resented by the mountain aborigines, because the former had deprived the latter of their land, just as the plains aborigines resented Han settlers for the same reason.

In short, the plains aborigines adapted to the Han way, which was the main reason why they moved to new territories for land. They used the same methods to obtain land from the non-acculturated aborigines as those that the Han settlers had used on them earlier. The pro-colonist Lan Dingyuan had envisaged a process of "acculturated aborigines being transformed to be like the Han settlers (*min* 民), and the non-acculturated aborigines being transformed to acculturated ones".[104] This vision was achieved over a century of interaction between Han settlers and the plains aborigines, and the plains aborigines' settlement in the mountain areas.

Acculturation and the government's role

The plains aborigines on the one hand acculturated to the Han culture, and on the other hand maintained a separate identity. That is to say, although in terms of culture they might have become similar to the Han, in organisation and politics they were still recognisable as aborigines. Government policies helped to preserve the aborigines' identity, until the 1886 (Guangxu 12) land tax reform.

By the late Tongzhi years, most aborigines to the west of the mountains had been acculturated. The aboriginal population decreased, and their everyday life, such as housing, clothing, marriage and burial, mostly followed Han customs. By this time only about 20–30% of the aborigines could speak their mother tongues.[105] This occurred through a long period of interaction with Han settlers, who formed the majority of the population and were culturally dominant.

The government had envisaged acculturation of the aborigines, but played little role in the realisation of it. When some aboriginal villages submitted themselves to the Kangxi government, the preferred treatment of the aborigines was to maintain status quo, and the emperor specifically ordered officials to record the population as reported by the aborigines but not to take a separate census, so as to allow them to maintain their innocent nature.[106] Later the government established schools for the aborigines, and organised teaching of farming to the aborigines.[107] In 1758 (Qianlong 23) the government required male aborigines to shave their heads in the Manchu manner,[108] but this was more than half a century after the Qing annexation, and many tribesmen had adopted the queue long before the government requirement.[109] The government also provided Han-style clothing to the aborigines, and several times bestowed family names or encouraged aborigines to adopt family names, since having family names represented one of the key Confucian values and officials thought it inappropriate that the Taiwanese aborigines lacked family names to carry on family traditions.[110] These steps were about all that the government did to transform the aborigines.

After the change of policy in 1874, the government required that family names adopted by aborigines must bear certain features to distinguish them from Han surnames.[111] Although it may seem discriminatory against the aborigines, the intention was probably to preserve, and it indeed preserved, the separate identity of the newly surrendered mountain aborigines.

The government also helped to preserve the aborigines' separate identity through adopting different administration systems for the Han and the aborigines. Han settlers paid land tax, while the aborigines paid poll tax or village tax, and aboriginal land was in principle exempt from tax. Han settlers were controlled through a household and neighbourhood registration system (*baojia* 保甲), which did not apply to the aborigines.[112] The aboriginal companies (*fantun*), discussed in Chapter 3, helped to preserve the institutional distinctions between the aborigines and settlers and hence the aborigines' identity. Furthermore, aborigines also continued to live and work within their village structure, which was different from Han villages.

An example illustrates both the decline of the aborigines and the government's endeavour to preserve their livelihood and identity. After the plains aborigines moved to inner Shuishalian, the population of the local aborigines continued to decrease. In 1847 (Daoguang 27) the six villages in inner Shuishalian had 1,020 local aborigines, including 27 in the Puli village and 124 in the Meili village.[113] By 1886 (Guangxu 12) Puli had six people left and Meili had one.[114] These aborigines petitioned the government between 1878 and 1886 about non-payment of rent by the migrant plains aborigines. The government supported their claims, and at no time tried to eliminate the category of "Pu-Mei" aborigines.[115]

The aborigines' adaptation and acculturation were the natural consequence of the increased exposure to Han culture and Han practice. The participation in land investments was not only evidence of the aborigines' ability to adapt, but also a catalyst for them to become more acculturated to the Chinese ways. They were forced to leave their ancestral home to search for new land, and after they moved to the mountain areas they repeated the methods of land grabbing which the Han had performed on them. The acculturation had little government input even though officials had tried to educate the aborigines and expected their acculturation.

The aborigines' separate identity, which was still identifiable despite the acculturation, served to maintain the residual links between the aborigines and their land. However, when an extensive land survey and land tax reform was carried out in 1886 (Guangxu 12), the adaptation and acculturation resulted in the government's disregard of aborigines as a separate group, and aboriginal land as a separate type of land, which in turn led to the eventual assimilation of the aborigines and the diminishment of their land rights.

Land tax reform and aboriginal land

Between 1886 and 1890 (Guangxu 12–16), the first Taiwan Governor, Liu Mingchuan, implemented land tax reform in Taiwan, which abolished distinctions between acculturated aborigines and settlers, and aboriginal land and settler land. The reform was the last Qing government action to alienate aboriginal land rights.

Background to the reform

The land tax reform was essentially revenue driven. After the crises of the 1874 Japanese invasion and the 1885 French attack on Taiwan, the Qing government tried to strengthen maritime defence in Taiwan. Recommendations were made and approved for making Taiwan a province, which meant Taiwan could no longer rely on Fujian to provide funds for its administration and military needs.[116] Governor Liu decided to survey agricultural land as one of the means to raise revenue. Liu complained that the land register had not been updated since the Daoguang years, while land reclamation continued and agricultural land had expanded.[117]

As discussed in Chapter 3, the Qing government kept the "fish scale register" (*yulin ce*) to record individual pieces of land with *yezhu* and tenant information, and kept the transaction register (*tuishou ce*) to record changes of proprietary rights, including sales and pledges. The people were expected to report reclaimed land which would then be added to the register, and they could report agricultural land that was damaged, for example by flood, which would then be removed from the register. Much was relied on *yezhu*'s initiative, and land survey was rarely conducted. This was because, in the Chinese tradition, emperors were reluctant to conduct surveys of agricultural land, viewing it as disturbance to the people.[118] The Qing emperors seemed to hold the same view. The problem of "hidden land" was well known by the central government, and although regulations encouraged reporting of land reclamation, there was no desire to uncover "hidden land" through land survey. For example, in 1729 (Yongzheng 7), a Taiwan censor reported that much land was reclaimed but not registered, and weighed the problem against reasons for not surveying the land, being very uncertain as to which course to take. The Yongzheng emperor retorted, "to investigate land for tax is not an urgent matter for the administration of Taiwan. Why did you report it at all?!"[119] Guided by this principle, the Qing government did not systematically survey agricultural land in Taiwan for 200 years.

Another complaint of Liu's was that different types of land had different tax or rental obligations to the government, and it was too complicated for effective administration. Before the reform, the government classified agricultural land in Taiwan into different categories, according to the tax status and categories of tax payers. The first four types of land owners noted in the early Qing were: private owners (*yehu* 業戶), managers (*guanshi* 管事), government (*guanzhuang* 官莊) and aboriginal villages (*fanshe* 番社).[120] These four types of land ownership all referred to cultivated land, as indicated by the use of the term *tianyuan* 田園. The first category, *yehu*'s land, was registered private land, which was subject to the ordinary land tax. "Managers' land" in early Qing Taiwan was in fact also private land. The "managers" represented the local community to liaise with the government on tax and corvée matters, and were given some land by *yehu* as a reward which was exempted from land tax.[121] Since in imperial China land tax was the most important aspect of land that concerned the government, this was listed as a separate type of land.

Eventually other types of private land emerged, such as "education land" (*xuetian* 學田), which was in fact private property owned by educational institutes, and was often given by the government or donated by private land owners. Such lands were also distinguished from *yehu*'s land and recorded separately, although they were not necessarily tax-exempt.[122]

Government estates in Taiwan also were of different types, depending on the purposes of their creation and the use of the rent. What was referred to as *guanzhuang* (官莊 official estate) were first reclaimed by local officials who then leased them and collected rent. In 1725 (Yongzheng 3) rental income from such estates was incorporated into the formal fiscal system and became part of the government income.[123] A second type was called *long'enzhuang* (隆恩莊 soldier-welfare estates), which was started in 1730 (Yongzheng 8), when the government decided to purchase some estates and use the rental to provide for soldiers and their families in case of sickness, death or other unusual occurrence.[124] A third type was forfeited property (*chaofeng chan* 抄封產). Forfeiture of land could be triggered by rebellion, other criminal activities, non-payment of taxes or even civil disputes.[125] The "company land" in the aboriginal colony system was forfeited land, and the rental income was used to pay a monthly allowance to the aborigines of the quasi-military aboriginal companies. These were all government estates, but the receiver of the rents differed and the rents were accounted for differently. Some needed to be accounted for to the imperial coffers; others remained in local government or the military units.[126]

The last type of cultivated land belonged to aborigine villages. The two centuries of settlement changed aboriginal land tenure significantly. Some were registered by *fan yehu* and became taxable, some were distributed among villagers and became individually held land, and the rest were leased in large rent to settlers but were not registered for tax. The establishment of aboriginal companies created the "upkeep land" (*yangshan pudi*), which was a special type of aboriginal land as the land in fact belonged to the villages that made up the companies.[127]

Thus, by the late Guangxu reign, much land in Taiwan was tax-exempt because of the different categories of land, or tax evading because of the inaccuracy of the tax register. Government incomes from land came from different sources, some land tax while others rent, and the incomes were used for different purposes by different levels of the government. The collection and expenditure of incomes were both inefficient and confusing. In search of tax revenues and to streamline the process, Liu embarked on the land tax reform in 1886. The reform measures affected aborigines and their land rights more than those of other land owners. To fully appreciate the changes to aboriginal land rights, it is necessary to survey the situation of land tax over aboriginal land before the reform.

Land tax over aboriginal land

There were two major taxes in imperial China, which the Qing inherited – land tax and poll tax. Land tax applied to cultivated land, and poll tax applied to adult males. The aborigines in principle were not subject to those two taxes.[128] Instead they paid village tax (*shexiang* 社餉), which belonged to the category of miscellaneous tax but was treated by the government as the substitution of land tax.[129] The basis of calculating village tax is unclear; likely the size of the villages and their financial ability were taken into consideration when deciding the tax burden.[130] In 1737 (Qianlong 2), the government converted the village tax of 89 acculturated aboriginal villages to poll tax, which significantly reduced the tax burden.[131] In

1747 (Qianlong 12), the category of poll tax was abolished and the tax burden was distributed to land tax, but this did not seem to affect the aborigines' poll tax payment, since they did not pay land tax.[132]

Although aborigines were not subject to land tax, potentially aboriginal land could be registered by Han settlers when the aborigines *pu* or sold the land to the Han who became the large rent owner; it could also be registered by aborigines when the aborigines leased the land in large rent and stood as the large rent owners.[133] The precise amount or percentage of aboriginal land being registered is unclear, but from the government's policies and the land transaction agreements some understanding of the situation could be achieved.

At the early stage of annexation, as the awareness of aboriginal ownership over wasteland was only emerging, no specific regulation had been developed to deal with the situation of Han reclamation of aboriginal land, and local officials continued the usual practice that Han settlers needed to pay land tax once land was reclaimed. The earliest record about settlers registering aboriginal land is in the decree issued in 1704 (Kangxi 43) by the Taiwan circuit intendant, Wang Minzheng, which required settlers to "fulfil contractual obligations with aborigines, and report the land for taxation according to law".[134] Han reclamation of aboriginal land was soon prohibited. Even if aborigine-settler land transactions continued to occur, such transactions were against the prohibition and the settlers would have difficulty having the land registered. This was reflected in the significantly reduced amount of land being registered in the late Kangxi years.

The Yongzheng government's 1724 regulation that lifted the ban against reclamation of aboriginal land was based on the Fujian governor-general's recommendation that "the aboriginal deer grounds are mostly vacant, and [the government] should let the aborigines lease the land to Han settlers to reclaim and cultivate, and eventually to register for tax".[135] Although the decree as issued by the emperor omitted the requirement of registration for tax, because the purpose of allowing reclamation was to enlarge tax revenue and the government generally encouraged land registration, it is reasonable to expect that the aboriginal land so leased and reclaimed by the settlers were registered for tax, as reflected in the sharp increase of registered land.[136]

At the same time, the aborigines also adopted the large rent model, and could become registered *yezhu* if they wished to. There is no clear record of when the aborigines started to do so or how extensive the practice was. The 1721 Lower Tamsui deed, discussed in Chapter 4, mentioned land tax responsibility on the aboriginal village and referred to it as *yezhu*. This means that registration of aboriginal land by aboriginal villages had started at the latest in 1712 when the county magistrate adjudicated the case. In 1730 (Yongzheng 8), the Zhanghua County magistrate issued a public notice to tenants of a land that was sold by aborigines, which noted that the aborigines had "recruited tenants to reclaim [the land] and registered [it] for tax" (*zhaodian kaiken baosheng* 招佃開墾報升), which was on record (*zai'an* 在案) at the time of sale.[137] Such records were rare. It was likely that in the early years of aborigines adopting the large rent model, no specific attention was given to aborigines acting as large rent owners by the government – as was typical of the Qing administrative and legislative apparatus, being one step behind the actual practice.

In 1730 (Yongzheng 8), the Taiwan circuit intendant, Liu Fanchang, recommended to the emperor that the aborigines be encouraged to reclaim their grasslands and register the land for taxation. The emperor advised Liu to consult with the Fujian governor and Fujian-Zhejiang governor-general and trial the suggestion cautiously,[138] but there is no evidence to suggest that the recommendation was carried out as a mandatory requirement.[139] This shows the emperor's reluctance to systematically change the practice of aboriginal land tenure. Thus, despite the practice among the people and the consideration given to taxing aborigines on their leased land, the state law remained silent on this matter.

The stance taken by the Qianlong government to strictly forbid Han reclamation of aboriginal land render it unnecessary to consider whether aboriginal land should be registered for tax, which the Han had no chance to *pu* or lease, at least not legally.[140] A Taiwan circuit intendant's decree in 1768 (Qianlong 33) reveals the tax status of aboriginal land and clarifies the government's position on this matter. The decree noted that "in Taiwan aboriginal land has not been subject to land tax by law" and that the only exception was in Danshui Sub-prefecture where the sub-prefect required registration by mistake.[141] This statement proves the point that the government had never imposed mandatary registration and tax on aboriginal land. The decree further clarified that all aboriginal land leased to settlers in large rent was exempted from tax. In addition, all aboriginal land cultivated by the aborigines were not taxed.[142] This provision was not changed until Governor Liu's tax reform.

In summary, lacking clear policy guidance, some aboriginal land was registered by Han settlers, especially during the Kangxi era when the concept of aboriginal land was developing, and during the Yongzheng era when the government acquiesced in the registration. Once the large rent model between Han settlers and aborigines was developed and aborigines no longer granted bulk *pu* for Han settlers to act as *yezhu*, there was no more basis for Han settlers to register aboriginal land, and the aborigines started to register land and became *yezhu* themselves. The aborigines' voluntary adoption of Han practice was another aspect of their acculturation. The aborigines also tried to protect their land from Han encroachment and from manipulation by interpreters through land registration.[143] In addition, some officials probably encouraged aborigines to register their land for revenue reasons, or in rare cases required registration, as the Danshui sub-prefect did, despite the silence of state law. There is no clear record of how much land the aborigines *pu* to settlers and were registered by the settlers, and how much land the aborigines leased in large rent and registered for tax. The facts that the government did not require mandatory registration, that for most of the time *pu* and lease of aboriginal land was forbidden by law, and that not many land deeds mentioned the land in question was registered suggest that large amounts of aboriginal land remained unregistered.[144] The situation was about to change under Governor Liu's land tax reform.

Aboriginal land under the reform

Governor Liu was looking for a simple and straightforward solution to solve the tax problems that he identified. The reform was not designed to target aboriginal land, but the reform measures affected aborigines and their land rights more than those of other land owners. All agricultural land in Taiwan was to be thoroughly surveyed and registered for tax. The distinctions between various categories of land, including aboriginal land, were eliminated. To address the problem of "split ownership", reflect the true proprietorship and ensure effective collection of tax, small rent owners were to be registered as *yezhu* and become the taxpayer. Large rent owners were required to give up 40% of large rent to subsidise small rent owners for payment of tax. The government allowed sale of aboriginal land, and removed the separate administrative system for the aborigines by requiring registration of aborigines in the same way as that of Han settlers (*bianji weimin* 編籍爲民). The combined effect of eradicating the category of aboriginal land and breaking down aboriginal society removed aborigines further from their land.

There were different types of land that related to the aborigines – unregistered land held by the villagers in collective (*tongtu kouliang tian* 通土口糧田), land registered by *fan yehu*, land held by individual aborigines, and land associated with the aboriginal companies, namely upkeep land and company land. Company land was government estate but the beneficiaries were the aborigines.

Liu specifically addressed company land and upkeep land, and explained why these lands should be treated as ordinary taxable land.[145] Not long after the aboriginal companies were established, the company business fell into confusion. Collection of rents from company land and distribution of monthly allowances were delegated to company leaders, which were originally the local government's responsibility. Upkeep lands were sold, pledged against the regulations, and lease was approved or rectified by officials.[146] The situation continued to deteriorate, and Governor Liu complained that the companies were not functioning, rent was not collected in full, aborigines received about half of their allowance and the upkeep land had changed hands – some many times.[147] Liu's response to this was his usual straightforward and simplifying method. The rental payment for company lands were changed to tax obligations.[148] Although this essentially changed the company land from government estate to private land owned by the tenants,[149] it also changed the relationship between the government and the cultivators from an ill-managed commercial landlord-tenant rental payment to coercive tax collection.

Upkeep land was aboriginal land, but Liu argued that the land had long been sold or pledged to Han settlers, plus the government had provided for the aborigines for a century, and they had become as equal subjects of the emperor as settlers were. Therefore the aborigines should enter the same household and neighbourhood registration as Han settlers, and all aboriginal land had to be surveyed and registered for tax. The structure of aboriginal companies disappeared and the land that supported the aboriginal warriors and their family lost the tax-exempt status and the special protection.

Liu's initial plan was to distinguish *tongtu kouliang tian* from other aboriginal land.[150] While the latter types were to be treated the same as settler land, the former was not. But the Taipei prefect argued that the former type of land was reclaimed by aborigines in the mountain areas, and that most of it had been controlled by Han settlers.[151] The Taipei prefect's suggestion to include unregistered collective aboriginal land in the reform was approved.[152] Consequently all aboriginal land was to be treated in the same way as settler land.

After a thorough survey, the area of registered land increased to about six times the area before the survey. The area of agricultural land, as last recorded during the Daoguang years, totalled about 70,148 *jia*,[153] compared with 432,009 *jia* after the survey.[154] It is difficult to judge the proportion of aboriginal land in the increase, as the increase included uncovered "hidden land", and other types of land which were previously non-taxable or recorded separately, such as soldier-welfare land, "education land", registered and unregistered aboriginal land, aboriginal companies' upkeep land and one particular official estate.[155] What is known is that the upkeep land and company land were 9426 *jia* in total. The amount of other aboriginal land is less clear. In 1888 the Danshui County recorded 17 aboriginal villages that were receiving rent from unregistered collective land and land registered by *fan yehu*. The total rent was 13,542.7 *shi* of grain. The Xinzhu County recorded 16 villages with total rent of 9,743.5 *shi* of grain.[156] Assuming that the villages received the standard large rent rate of 8 *shi* per *jia*, these numbers converted to 2,910 *jia* of land for the aborigines in the two counties. This does not seem to be a large amount, but Governor Liu had found that 60% of land in the eight coastal counties "belonged" to the aborigines – in the sense that they had large rent rights – while only 40% belonged to Han settlers.[157] Therefore aboriginal land would have accounted for a sizeable proportion of the increase.

Strictly speaking, registration would not have altered the nature of aboriginal land, since the rights of the aborigines over most so-called aboriginal land was to receive large rent only. However under the sweeping policies to eliminate the category of aboriginal land and the distinct identity of aborigines, the reform laid the foundation for the aborigines to further lose the residual rights over their land. This was manifested in two aspects.

Firstly, although registration as *yezhu* did not necessarily convey or prove ownership over land, the reform endeavoured to give *yezhu* rights to the real land owner. This move withdrew government recognition of the legitimacy of the large rent holder class and severed their only connection with land. For those aboriginal lands that had not been subject to tax, the 40% was a net loss. The poll tax, village tax and various fees that the aborigines had to pay before the reform were abolished, but the abolished amount was usually much less than the 40% of rent that they had to give up.[158] As a consequence of the reduction of rent and the marginalisation of large rent owners, the aborigines received less income and experienced more difficulties in collecting rent.

The more damaging aspect was the withdrawal of protection built around aboriginal land; in particular, the emergence of a policy to facilitate alienation of aboriginal land rights. Guided by the principle that aboriginal land was to be no different from settler land, the government's response to the aborigines' petition to redeem pledged upkeep land was that "it is better to allow sale than to allow redemption".[159] This was because sale was more straightforward than redemption, as redemption required clarifying past transactions which often went back a lengthy period of time and involved different parties. This policy was a departure from the Qianlong government's policies of returning alienated land to aborigines, and the Daoguang government's policy to restore sold or pledged upkeep land to the aborigines.[160] Although aboriginal lands were alienated regardless of government bans before Liu's reform, government policies before the reform were often a type of positive discrimination for the benefit of the aborigines. In contrast, Liu's government encouraged sale of aboriginal land, probably for reasons of expediency, but it also reflected the government's growing disregard for aboriginal land rights. As such Governor Liu's action withdrew the protection that was previously afforded to the aborigines, and sped up alienation of the residual aboriginal land.

Liu Mingchuan's policies towards aboriginal land during the land reform were both the result of the acculturation after 200 years of settler-aborigine interaction, and a cause of further breakdown of aboriginal communities, which affected the aborigines' residual land rights. The reform treated aborigines as no different from settlers, and aboriginal land as no different from settler land. Apart from further breaking down aboriginal communities, it strengthened the claims of Han small rent owners over land while weakening those of the aborigines, caused difficulties in rent collection, and accelerated aboriginal land alienation. The reform did not change aboriginal land rights overnight, but rather it set aboriginal land rights on a new path of diminishment and alienation. It laid a foundation for the Japanese rearrangement of aboriginal land.

Three actors: government, settlers and aborigines

The frontier society was dynamic and full of action, reaction and interaction by the three actors in Qing Taiwan's political scene – the government, the settlers and the aborigines. Each, acting in their own interests, played an important role.

Throughout the Qing period, Han settlers had the financial advantage and cultural domination over the aborigines, and their interests were to obtain land from the aborigines, in whatever form that they found to be allowed by the circumstance – but not necessarily allowed by the government.

As one of the important actors, the aborigines actively participated in the frontier development – resisting Han encroachment, litigating for their land ownership and rent rights, and becoming adapted to Han culture, especially agricultural and commercial practices. However pressed by expanding Han settlement, the aborigines retreated step by step. They first lost their land ownership, then much of their rent. Some of them – but not many – adapted and became prosperous; some moved to new settlements and flourished – belatedly, after they had lost their ancestral land. Taiwanese aborigines were fighting a battle that they could not win.

The process of land loss was a long one, due to the Qing government's resolve to protect aboriginal land rights for most of the time. Shepherd's study found that until the Japanese period, the aborigines held large rent rights over large areas in the western coast and enjoyed rental income.[161] Using statistics from Japanese investigations in 1905, supplemented by records from the late Qing period, Ka found that by the late Qing the aborigines still owned 10.55% of large rent income out of the total "large rent" over land in the western plains, and 19.82% out of the total "large rent" west of the central mountain ranges (including areas bordering aboriginal boundaries).[162] This was after Governor Liu's withdrawal of the "quarantine" around aboriginal land and allowing alienation of aboriginal land and associated right, which would have caused the amount of aboriginal large rent to diminish. Considering that Han settlement had been expanding for over 200 years, these percentages, although relatively small, testify that the government's protection policies were not completely ineffective.

Because the government's overriding concerns were security and social stability, when the conflicts were not serious enough to threaten the social stability, the government left the aborigines to fend for themselves and did not try to intervene. When conflicts or complaints became intense, the government was generally supportive of the aborigines. When threats to imperial security came from a different direction and the needs of the government changed, the government became a party to put the aborigines' rights in jeopardy.

The plains aborigines were on the way to completely losing their residual rights over land, even if Japan had not become Taiwan's new master. But Japan took over Taiwan just a few years after Liu Mingchuan's reform, and any residual connections that indicated the aborigines were the original owners of the land were severed in a swift and clear-cut manner by the Japanese administration. In particular, the mountain aborigines' independence and land rights remained largely intact throughout the Qing period. Under the Japanese administration, they were to experience fatal changes.

Notes

1 John Robert Shepherd *Statecraft and Political Economy on the Taiwan Frontier, 1600–1800* (Stanford University Press, Stanford, 1993), at 7 and 243.
2 Wen Ji *Taiwan fanzheng zhi* [A History of Aboriginal Management in Taiwan] (translated and adapted from Inō Kanori *Taiwan bansei shi*, Taiwansheng wenxian weiyuanhui, Taipei, 1957), at 300–301; Huang Fu-San "Qingdai Taiwan yimin de gengdi qude wenti jiqi dui tuzhu de yingxiang" [The Methods of Acquiring Land by Migrants in Qing Taiwan and the Effects on the Aborigines] (1981) 11 *Shih-huo* 72, at 72–75.
3 Tonio Andrade *How Taiwan Became Chinese: Dutch, Spanish and Han Colonization in the Seventeenth Century* (Columbia University Press, New York, 2008), at 140.
4 Wen, above n 2, at 55–56. Also see discussed under "Progression of Land Settlement" in Chapter 1 of this book.
5 See Yu Yonghe *Bihai jiyou* [Small sea travelogue, 1697] (TWWX 44), at 33.
6 At 37, "不甚怨之".
7 Two cases in the late Kangxi years were recorded. See Huang Huan-yao "Qingji Taiwan fanhuan shijian zhi benzhi tantao" [A Discussion on the Nature of Aboriginal Attacks in Qing Taiwan] (1987) 79 *Taipei Wen Hsien* 129, at 133, Table 1.
8 For example, see memorials and the emperor's rescripts in *Yongzheng zhupi zouzhe* [Memorials With Rescripts of the Yongzheng Emperor] (TWWX 300), at 4, 36–37, 41 and 47 concerning several incidents in the years of Yongzheng 3, 4, 5 and 7.

9 See Huang, above n 7, Table 1.
10 Ibid, at 145 and Table 1.
11 At 146.
12 See ibid, Figure 4.
13 See ibid, Table 3.
14 See ibid, Table 1.
15 See Yao Ying *Dongcha jilüe* [Records of My Appointment to the East, 1829] (TWWX 7), at 70.
16 Ke Peiyuan *Gamalan zhilüe* [Brief Records of Gamalan, 1837] (TWWX 92), at 89.
17 Yao, above n 15, at 70, "與番日鬥，彼此殺傷甚眾".
18 At 34.
19 This is also a characteristic of many frontier societies, such as in Australia, Argentina and the United States. See a discussion in Richard Boast *Buying the Land, Selling the Land: Governments and Maori Land in the North Island1865–1921* (Victoria University Press, Wellington, 2008), at 16.
20 Huang Shujing *Taihai shichalu* [Records of a Tour on Duty Over the Taiwan Seas, cir 1722] (TWWX 4), at 128–129.
21 See the covenant in Wen, above n 2, at 317–318.
22 As will be further discussed under "Adapting to Han practice".
23 *Qingdai Taiwan dazu diaochashu* [Collection of Large Rent Documents in Qing Taiwan] (TWWX 152), at 667–670 ("*Dazu diaocha*").
24 Litigation will be discussed later in this chapter.
25 *Yongzheng zhupi zouzhe*, above n 8, at 3–4.
26 See the emperor's rescripts in ibid, at 4, 37and 39.
27 For example, ibid, at 47–48, 72 and 142.
28 Huang Huan-yao "Qingling shiqi Taiwan de fanhuan fangzhi" [The Prevention and Management of Aboriginal Attacks in Qing Taiwan] (1988) 32/33 *Gaoshi wenxian* 21, at 21–29.
29 For the development and functions of *ai*, see Tai Yen-hui *Qingdai Taiwan zhi xiangzhi* [The Administration at the Town and Village Levels in Qing Taiwan] (Lianjing, Taipei, 1979), Part 8; Inō Kanori (trans Taiwan Historica) *Taiwan wenhua zhi* [A History of Taiwan's Civilisation] (Chinese trans revised ed, Taiwan Shufang, Taipei, 2011), vol 3, Part 14, ch 5.
30 Ibid.
31 Tai, ibid, at 537–538.
32 At 543.
33 See Chen Peigui *Danshui tingzhi* [Gazetteer of Danshui Sub-Prefecture, 1871] (TWWX 172), at 50. 1,500 dollars was about the value of 1,500 *shi* of grain.
34 Inō, above n 29, vol 3, at 446; Lian Heng *Taiwan tongshi* [A Comprehensive History of Taiwan, 1918] (TWWX 128), at 858.
35 Liu Ao *Xun Tai tuisilu* [Reflections on Being a Circuit Intendant in Taiwan] (TWWX 21), at 203.
36 At 192.
37 *Dazu diaocha*, above n 23, at 22–23.
38 "民番互控之案，絡繹不休". See *Qing Gaozong shilu xuanji* [Selected Veritable Records of the Qianlong Emperor] (TWWX 186), at 34.
39 Ibid, "有客民侵占番地，彼此爭競，遂投獻 [*touxian*, commend] 武員". Here the blame was placed on the Hakkas (*kemin* 客民), who were settlers from Guangdong province, as opposed to the more numerous migrants from Fujian.
40 Ibid.
41 See the decree in Linshi Taiwan Jiuguan Diaochahui *Taiwan sifa fulu cankaoshu* [Private Law of Taiwan Reference Book] (Taipei, 1910), vol 1A, at 293–294 ("*Sifa cankao*"). This decree was also discussed under "Protection: efforts and results" in Chapter 3.

42 *Dazu diaocha*, above n 23, at 648–649.
43 Ibid.
44 At 649.
45 Ibid.
46 This is a generally recognised fact. For example, see Zhang Jinfan *Qingchao fazhishi* [Legal History of the Qing Dynasty] (Zhonghua shuju, Beijing, 1998), at 628–630.
47 Ke, above n 16, at 191.
48 See the decree recorded in Wu Mi-cha (ed) *Dan Xin dang'an* [Administrative Files of Danshui and Xinzhu Counties] (NTU, Taipei, 1995–2010), vol 17, at 189–190.
49 *Dazu diaocha*, above n 23, at 768–769.
50 At 769–770.
51 *Sifa cankao*, above n 41, vol 1A, at 296–297.
52 See a notice published by the aboriginal affairs sub-prefect in 1818 (Jiaqing 23), in *Dazu diaocha*, above n 23, at 771–774. Also see discussed under "Government's role" in Chapter 4 of this book.
53 *Dazu diaocha*, ibid, at 814.
54 Tai, above n 29, at 389.
55 At 394. See "Aboriginal land transactions" in Chapter 4 of this book for more on *fan yehu*.
56 At 373–374 and 386–396.
57 For example, see cases in *Dan Xin dang'an*, above n 48, vol 13, topics on *Shewu* (village administration) and *Shezu* (village rent).
58 As noted in a covenant between the interpreter and villagers of Zhonggang village in 1831 (Daoguang 11), in *Dazu diaocha*, above n 23, at 667.
59 See case notes about the background and decision of this case in *Dan Xin dang'an*, above n 48, vol 13, file No 17202, at 109–130.
60 See a list of annexed villages in Zhou Zhongxuan *Zhuluo xianzhi* [Gazetteer of Zhuluo County, 1717] (TWWX141), at 31–32.
61 *Dan Xin dang'an*, above n 48, at 126 and 362.
62 At 398.
63 See Tai, above n 29, at 398 and 432–433.
64 *Dazu diaocha*, above n 23, at 667–670. The covenant distributes the rent according to *ding* 丁, which usually meant adult male, but it is likely that in this case it meant each person.
65 *Dan Xin dang'an*, above n 48, vol 13, at 129.
66 Yu, above n 5, at 17.
67 See the deed in Paul Jen-kuei Li *Xingang wenshu yanjiu* (*Studies of Sinkang Manuscripts*) (Academia Sinica, Taipei, 2010), at 330–333. The deed was in Sirayan language only, and the Chinese translation is not coherent, but it is clear that it was about alienation of land.
68 The latest bilingual deed collected in Li, ibid, was made in 1818 (Jiaqing 23).
69 For example, see deeds of pledge ranging from 1818 (Jiaqing 23) to 1882 (Guangxu 8) in Tung Yuan-Chao and Tseng Cheng-ming (eds) *Gamalan Xilaya guwenshu* [Historic Documents of the Aboriginal Groups of Kavalan and Siraya] (NTU, Taipei, 1999), at 84–94 and 96–97.
70 There have been focused studies on land issues of the Anli village groups. For example, Chen Chiu-kun *Qingdai Taiwan tuzhu diquan: guanliao, handian yu Anlishe ren de tudi bianqian 1700–1895* (*Taiwan's Aboriginal Proprietary Rights in the Ch'ing Period: Bureaucracy, Han Tenants and the Transformation of Property Rights of the Anli Tribe, 1700–1895*) (2nd ed, Academia Sinica, Taipei, 1997); Chen Chiu-kun "Shijiu shiji chuqi tuzhu diquan wailiu wenti – yi Anlishe de tudi jingying weili" [The Aborigines' Land Loss in the Early 19th Century – A Case Study on the Land Management of the Anli Village] in Chen Chiu-kun and Hsu Hsueh-chi (eds) *Taiwan lishi shang de tudi wenti* [Land Issues in Historical Taiwan] (Academia Sinica, Taipei,

1992) 29–56; Ka Chih-ming "Fanxiaozu de xingcheng yu yanbian: Anli xinshe diyu shefan kouliangtian de zudian anpai" ("Formation and Transformation of Aborigine Small-rent Tenure: Land Tenancy of Tribesman's Ration Plot in Anli New Territory") (2008) 15(3) *Taiwanshi yanjiu* 57–137.

71 See Chen Zhe-san "Qingdai Nantou xianjing de shuizhen kaizao guanfu yu minjian suo banyan de jiaose" [The Roles of the Government and the Society in Opening Water Channels in Nantou County During the Qing Dynasty] (2007) 15 *Fengjia renwen shehui xuebao* 105–141, in particular, at 128.

72 See Hui Tsun "Qingdai Taiwan zhi zufu" [Types of Rents in Qing Taiwan] (1959) 10(2) *Taiwan Wen Hsien* 91, at 132–137.

73 Ka, above n 70, at 74.

74 See the deed in Wen, above n 2, at 432–434. Original appended as Appendix 2.

75 Most scholars accept that this deed was made in Yongzheng 1. Ka, above n 73, at 127, note 189, argues that the dating of the deed was incorrect and the correct date should be in 1733 (Yongzheng 11). However the 1732 deed, to be discussed later, referred to this project, therefore it could not have been made in 1733.

76 And that was why the agreement noted that the aborigines asked Zhang Dajing "through an intermediary", as was customary for land transactions, even though he was those villages' own interpreter.

77 For example, Chen *Qingdai Taiwan tuzhu diquan*, above n 70, at 38.

78 See the deed in *Dazu diaocha*, above n 23, at 23–26.

79 This deed only mentioned the investment of 6,600 taels of silver, but a subsequent deed, where one of the six *yehu* sold his share, was clear that the total investment was 6,600 taels. See the deed of sale in *Sifa cankao*, above n 41, vol 1C, at 117–118.

80 *Dazu diaocha*, above n 23, at 26–28.

81 For example, Chen "Shijiu shiji chuqi tuzhu diquan wailiu wenti", above n 70, at 34.

82 See the aborigines' acknowledgements in Chen, above n 77, at 45. At 45–46 Chen suggests that Zhang might have been unfairly taking possession of the aborigines' land, but at the same time noting that none of the complaints against Han settlers was directed at Zhang.

83 At 39.

84 This is the deed of sale referred to in above n 79.

85 Chen, above n 77, at 39.

86 Ka, above n 73, at 75–76.

87 Chen, above n 77, at 90–91.

88 See examples in Liu Ze-min *Dajia dongxishe guwenshu* [Historic Documents Concerning the Dajia East and Dajia West Villages] (Taiwan Historica, Nantou, 2003), at 139.

89 For example, see a land deed of 1764 (Qianlong 29) in *Dazu diaocha*, above n 23, at 542–543.

90 For example, a certain Pan A'xiang was the pledgee of several land deeds between 1861 (Xianfeng 11) to 1882 (Guangxu 8). See the deeds in Tseng and Tung (eds), above n 69, at 88–93 and 96–97.

91 See the deed in *Dazu diaocha*, above n 23, at 21.

92 Liang Chih-hui and Chung Yu-lan *Taiwan yuanzhumin shi: Zhong Taiwan pingpu zuqun shi* [History of Taiwan Aborigines: The Central Taiwan Plains Aboriginal Groups] (Taiwansheng wenxian weiyuanhui, Nantou, 2001), at 125.

93 Yao, above n 15, at 71. Also see further details in Liu Ze-min *Pingpu baishe guwenshu* [Historic Documents of a Hundred Plains Aboriginal Villages] (Taiwan Historica, Nantou, 2002), at 7; Inō, above n 29, vol 3, at 495–496.

94 Liu, ibid, at 7–8; Inō, ibid, at 493–494. The five aborigine groups are Pazeh, Babuza, Papora, Taokas and Hoanya.

95 Ding Yuejian *Zhi Tai bigaolu* [A Collection of Must-read Documents on Governing Taiwan, 1868] (TWWX 17), at 229. Also see Inō, ibid, at 494.

96 *Liu Mingchuan fu Tai qianhou dang'an* [Historic Documents Before and After Liu Mingchuan's Governorship in Taiwan] (TWWX 276), at 15 ("*Fu Tai dang'an*").
97 Liu, above n 93, at 8–9; Inō, above n 29, at 494–495.
98 Liu, ibid, at 8; Inō, ibid, at 495.
99 Yao, above n 15, at 71.
100 Liu, above n 93, at 8; Ding, above n 95, at 229.
101 Inō, above n 29, at 494.
102 Ibid.
103 Lin Yu-ju "You yulin tuce kan Qingmo houshan de qingfu shiye yu diquan fenpei xingtai" [The Land Survey Project and the Pattern of Land Rights Distribution in Eastern Taiwan During the Late Qing Period as Seen From the "fish-scale" Land Register] (1997) 2 *Dong Taiwan yanjiu* 131, at 150.
104 "生番化爲熟番，熟番化爲人民". See in Ding, above n 95, at 3.
105 Chen, above n 33, at 306.
106 "順其不識不知之性，使之共樂堯天". See Liu Liangbi *Chongxiu Fujian Taiwan fuzhi* [Revised Gazetteer of Taiwan Prefecture, Fujian, 1741] (TWWX 74), at 517.
107 See Inō, above n 29, vol 3, at 324–377.
108 At 345.
109 Shepherd, above 1, at 379.
110 At 370–375.
111 At 375–376.
112 See Tai, above n 29, in general, for the different administration systems of settlers and aborigines.
113 Ding, above n 95, at 215.
114 See noted by the aboriginal affairs sub-prefect in *Sifa cankao*, above n 41, vol 1A, at 309.
115 See the decrees in ibid, at 305–310.
116 Although there was an arrangement for temporary financial support.
117 *Liu Zhuangsugong zouyi* [Memorials of Liu Mingchuan] (TWWX 27), at 300 and 319.
118 Zhao Gang and Chen Zhongyi *Zhongguo tudi zhidushi* [History of Chinese Land Tenure] (Lianjing, Taipei, 1982), at 71.
119 *Yongzheng zhupi zouzhe*, above n 8, at 43–44, "清查田糧，非現今治臺急務，何必汲汲奏及與此".
120 Zhou, above n 60, at 86.
121 Ibid.
122 For example, see Fan Xian *Chongxiu Taiwan fuzhi* [Revised Gazetteer of Taiwan Prefecture, 1747] (TWWX 105), at 292–293 about "education land".
123 See the evolution of official estates in a memorial of the Fujian governor in 1756 (Qianlong 21), collected in *Tai'an huilu bingji* [Collection of Taiwan Document Series C] (TWWX 176), at 19 ("*Tai'an bingji*"). Also see Hui, above n 72, at 109–112.
124 *Dazu diaocha*, above n 23, at 991. Also see Hui, ibid, at 112–117, for accounts on soldier-welfare estates.
125 Hui, ibid, at 117–123.
126 At 118.
127 See discussion in Chapter 3 of this book.
128 The exception was eight aboriginal villages in Fengshan County. As they were sufficiently acculturated, their adult males and females paid poll tax. See Gao Gongqian *Taiwan fuzhi* [Gazetteer of Taiwan Prefecture, 1694] (TWWX 65), at 113.
129 See Zhou Yuanwen *Chongxiu Taiwan fuzhi* [Revised Gazetteer of Taiwan Prefecture, 1718] (TWWX 66), at 316–317.
130 See ibid, at 161.
131 Liu, above n 106, at 192. The non-acculturated aborigines continued to pay token tax calculated in deer skin.

132 See Yu Wenyi *Xuxiu Taiwan fuzhi* [Revised Gazetteer of Taiwan Prefecture, 1764] (TWWX 121), at 246–248.
133 See discussion in Chapter 4 of this book.
134 See the paraphrase of the decree in Wen, above n 2, at 68. See the translation and discussion of this decree in Chapter 3 of this book.
135 See the recommendation, approved by the emperor, in *Qing Shizong shilu xuanji* [Selected Veritable Records of the Yongzheng Emperor] (TWWX167), at 12–13, "各番鹿場頗多閒曠，應聽各番租與民人墾種，陸續陞科". There is a small discrepancy in time (1724 and 1725), but the wording was identical.
136 Ka Chih-ming *Fantoujia: Qingdai Taiwan zuqun zhengzhi yu shufan diquan* (*The Aborigine Landlord: Ethnic Politics and Aborigine Land Rights in Qing Taiwan*) (Academia Sinica, Taipei, 2003), at 107–108, argues that on the basis of this recommendation, the Yongzheng government first imposed the registration requirement on Han settlers who "*pu*" aboriginal land. However the recommendation was discussing eight aboriginal villages in the Fengshan County and had limited application. The imperial decree, although issued on the basis of the recommendation, applied to the whole of Taiwan and deliberately omitted the wording on registration and tax.
137 *Dazu Diaocha*, above n 23, at 600–601. This notice is also discussed in Chapter 4 of this book.
138 See the memorial and the emperor's rescript in Taiwan Shiliao Jicheng Bianji Weiyuanhui *Ming Qing Taiwan dang'an huibian* [Collection of Historic Documents Concerning Taiwan During the Ming and Qing Dynasties] (Yuanliu, Taipei, 2004–2009), vol 13, at 286.
139 Ka, above n 136, at 287, argues that this 1730 memorial imposed the obligation of land registration on aborigines and brought *fan yehu* into existence. However as discussed here, the aborigines started registering their land before 1730, and the government did not impose such a mandatory requirement either before or after the 1730 memorial.
140 The Qianlong government's 1737 policy recognised the legality of land that had been sold to Han settlers and registered for tax; the 1738 policy to allow registration of aboriginal land was limited to those that had been sold to Han settlers (see Table 3.1). In both cases the lands were sold and were no longer aboriginal land.
141 "臺郡番地原無征賦之例 (*li*)". See the decree issued by the Taiwan circuit intendant, Zhang Ting, in *Sifa cankao*, above n 41, vol 1A, at 293. The subject of discussion was aboriginal land, no matter registration by settlers or aborigines. Ka, ibid, at 292–293, argues that Zhang was mistaken given his view that registration of land by aborigines had emerged in 1730. Regarding the intendant's decree, 例 (*li*) could mean "example" or "precedent", but it was also an important form of legislation, as discussed in Chapter 2. Here Zhang meant no law on aboriginal land tax, rather than no example.
142 Noted in Governor Liu's memorial in *Liu Zhuangsugong zouyi*, above n 117, at 303, "眾番所耕，概不完賦".
143 Linshi Taiwan Jiuguan Diaochahui *Taiwan sifa* [Private Law of Taiwan] (Chinese translation, Taiwansheng wenxian weiyuanhui, Taizhong, 1990, original first published in 1910), vol 1, at 207, is of the view that *fan yehu* was designed to protect aboriginal land rights. Shepherd, above n 1, at 293, argues that without registration the aborigines' claims to land were weakened.
144 Some aborigines leased their land in periodic tenancy (hence the large rent and small rent were not separated and both belonged to the aborigines), like the Pan family of the Anli village. It is likely that such land was registered. However small rent owners were not adversely affected by the land tax reform.
145 Ibid, at 305–307.
146 See discussion in Chapter 4.
147 *Liu Zhuangsugong zouyi*, above n 117, at 306.
148 Hui, above n 72, at 109.

149 This was not Liu's innovation. The Qing did the same thing with the previous government estates of the Ming at the beginning of regime, and with the government estates of the Zhengs in Taiwan at the beginning of annexation.
150 *Sifa cankao*, above n 41, at 191.
151 *Dazu diaocha*, above n 23, at 435–436.
152 At 435–436, 633 and 636.
153 *Liu Zhuangsugong zouyi*, above n 117, at 300. The record was 38,100 *jia* plus 3621.5 *qing*, which converted to about 70,148 *jia* in total.
154 At 318–319.
155 See Liu's decree in *Sifa cankao*, above n 41, vol 1A, at 191. Except the named official estate, the *Quanhe* estate, all official estates were dealt with separately.
156 See the list of villages and rent in *Dan Xin dang'an*, above n 48, vol 13, at 299–316 and 354–372. This included the 40% of rent which was ceded to small rent owners.
157 See in Liu's memorial of 1887 in *Fu Tai dang'an*, above n 96, at 262, "沿海八縣之地，所有土地，番居其六，民居其四".
158 See the statistics in *Dan Xin dang'an*, above n 48, vol 13, file No. 17212.13 and 17212.69; *Liu Zhuangsugong zouyi*, above n 117, at 303.
159 *Sifa cankao*, above n 41, at 336–337.
160 *Tai'an bingji*, above n 123, at 64–65. Also see discussed in Chapter 4 of this book.
161 Shepherd, above n 1, at 8–9.
162 Ka, above n 136, at 318, and Tables 11.2 and 11.3.

6 Japanese colonisation

New tenure under the modern law

Taiwan became Japan's first overseas colony in 1895, a consequence of Japanese victory in the Sino-Japanese war over Korea and the subsequent Treaty of Shimonoseki. Japan had followed the Chinese law in many aspects since the 7th century,[1] had been in a state of "substantial 'national isolation'" since the 17th century and in the 19th century suffered the same Western aggression as the Qing did. In an effort to revise the unequal treaties imposed by the Western powers and to achieve equal status with the West, Japan embarked on a journey to build a modern nation state. The 1868 Meiji Restoration marked the start of that modernisation process, as the government undertook political and legal reforms modelling on Western examples. In 1872 sale of land was permitted, in 1885 a cabinet system was established, in 1889 a constitution was promulgated, and in 1890 the first national election was held and the Imperial Diet was convened. The laws followed European models after intensive studies: the Criminal Code and the Police Law of 1881, and the Civil Code of 1890, were modelled on the French law; the Constitution of 1889 was modelled on the Prussian Constitution of 1850; the Court Organisation Law and the Commercial Code were modelled on the German Law.[2] The modern laws were so powerful and the Japanese emulation so successful that, within three decades, Japan became a coloniser itself and had the unequal treaties revised.[3]

This chapter examines how Japan's European-inspired administration guided its colonisation and land tenure reform in Taiwan. To highlight the contrasting legal concepts of the Qing and Japan, which underpinned their respective colonisation styles, this chapter first reviews the Mudanshe Incident, where Japan and the Qing government were engaged in lengthy negotiation about the aboriginal territories following the Japanese military occupation of southern Taiwan. The chapter then traverses Japan's administration of Taiwan; in particular, the treatment of the aborigines and their land, the reform of agricultural land tenure, the possession and use of the forest and unreclaimed land, and the establishment of aboriginal reserves.

From the early years of colonisation, the Taiwan *Sōtokufu* (總督府 Office of the Governor-General) employed modern legal institutions to methodically and progressively transform the land tenure in Taiwan. First it reformed rural land tenure in western Taiwan, which was mainly occupied and cultivated by the Han settlers. Agricultural reform in the western plains started with investigation of land ownership and cadastral survey, progressed to abolition of large rent rights and tax reform, and concluded with the introduction of the Western model of land registration. Upon taking over the island, the *Sōtokufu* declared government ownership over all unreclaimed and forest land in Taiwan, a category that was equivalent to the Qing's "wasteland", and gradually took control of the land and confined the aborigines to aboriginal reserves.

Japan's objectives in Taiwan, the legal instruments used, and its views of the legal status of the Taiwanese aborigines and ownership of aboriginal land had Western origins. Western concepts of international law and colonisation, and Western instruments regarding land tenure, marked Japan's departure from the Qing-style of expansion. Japan pursued an essentially Western colonialist strategy in Taiwan, making Japan a kind of surrogate Western imperialist state in Asia.

A clash of legal concepts: the Mudanshe Incident

Japan and the Qing's different attitudes towards expansion and colonisation, and the different legal traditions that supported their conceptions, were manifested in the Mudanshe Incident. The two conceptions clashed as the two empires debated over Japan's entitlement to occupy southern Taiwan. The Incident prompted the Qing government to abruptly change its policies towards the aborigine territories in Taiwan. It was the precursor to the Japanese colonisation of Taiwan that commenced in 1895. The Mudanshe Incident was one of the most important events in the history of colonisation of Taiwan, because it was the miniature display of the contrasting styles of the Qing's 200 years' administration versus Japan's 50 years' administration. It signified the approach of a new colonial era that was to come with the full power of the Western legal concepts and instruments.

Japanese ambitions in Taiwan

The Mudanshe Incident occurred only a few years after the Meiji Restoration. This first colonial attempt was covert and was not universally supported within the Japanese government, but it led to Japan's colonisation of Taiwan two decades later.

The incident was driven by Japan's growing ambitions relating to Ryukyu (*Liuqiu* 琉球, present-day Okinawa) as well as to Taiwan. In 1871 (Tongzhi 10), a Ryukyuan ship was wrecked off Taiwan's southeastern coast. Ryukyu was an independent kingdom and had been a vassal of the Ming and then the Qing Courts, but at that time it also paid tribute to Japan. The ship was on its return journey after sending tributes to the Qing Court. After the shipwreck, 54 crewmen were killed by the aborigines of the Botan (*Mudan* 牡丹) and Kusukut (*Gaoshifo* 高士佛) villages. Twelve surviving crewmen were rescued by a Han settler, who sent them to the Fengshan County government. From Fengshan they were sent to the Taiwan prefectural government, and then to the Fujian provincial government, which accommodated them while they waited for a ship to return home.[4] The Fujian government reported the incident to the emperor and proposed to punish the aborigines,[5] but as the matter unfolded this appeared to have not been carried out. The Fujian government eventually sent the survivors back to Ryukyu with financial assistance, as it had done many times before when Ryukyuan ships were wrecked in Taiwanese waters.[6] The matter appeared to have settled.

The 1871 incident was not the first time that the Qing government had to deal with an incident of this kind. Cases where the non-acculturated aborigines in the south attacked shipwreck survivors had been increasing since the 1860s because of growing presence of foreign ships in Taiwanese waters. There had been an attack on a British vessel (the *Doob*) in 1866, and attacks on another British vessel (the *Sylvia*) and a US vessel (the *Rover*) in 1867. The attacks had caused some international concern and diplomatic problems for the Qing Court, which in the eyes of the international community was responsible for preventing such attacks, but no serious consequences ensued.[7] The 1871 incident, however, coincided with Japan's growing ambition to expand. The events took an unexpected turn, bought the two empires to the brink of war, and had profound effects on the subsequent expansion of Japan, the "self-strengthening" activities of the Qing, and eventually the fates of the Taiwanese aborigines.

Japan was ready and eager to expand after the Meiji Restoration. The shipwreck incident provided the perfect opportunity to send an expedition to Taiwan in the name of retaliation, which served multiple purposes: to claim Japan's sovereignty over Ryukyu, to occupy the aboriginal territory of Taiwan, to realise national prestige and security, and to ease the mounting discontent among the ex-samurai and calm the domestic situation through an expansive expedition.[8] Against such a background, the idea of sending an expedition to Taiwan emerged within Japan in 1872.

The preparation was conducted in secret, for fear of intervention from the international community.[9] When it eventually became known, the Russian, US and British governments all took action to forbid or warn against involvement of ships or nationals of their respective countries in the expedition, assuming that it amounted to a declaration of war against the Qing. Pressure from the United States resulted in the Japanese government's decision to halt the expedition, but nevertheless the naval commander, Sagō Tsugumochi, had a steamship set sail from Nagasaki for Taiwan in late April 1874, arriving in the aboriginal territory in southern Taiwan early the next month.[10] The government's hesitation under Western pressure was soon to be dispelled and the ambition stimulated by the military's success.

Japan's pretext for sending the expedition was to punish the Mudan aborigines, but the preparation before and activities during the expedition all pointed to colonisation of Taiwan. As part of the expedition, livestock was brought and civil engineering material was sent.[11] During the six-month period of Japanese occupation, there was barely any "punishment" activity. Only one skirmish occurred after "provocation" by the Mudan aborigines, and one attempt was made to attack the Mudan and Gaoshifo villages, but in the latter case the villagers fled before the Japanese arrived.[12] The Japanese occupiers spent their remaining time on informing the neighbouring aborigines of Japan's "pacific design", trying to subjugate them, collecting information about the territory and the people, planting crops and making plans to colonise the territory. A spot for "permanent occupation" was chosen, and methods of political control were conceived.[13] The political situation in Japan and the circumstance surrounding the expedition also indicated that Japan's real intention was to colonise Taiwan.[14]

The Japanese army occupied southern Taiwan for six months until the two governments signed a treaty in October 1874, whereby the Qing agreed to pay a large indemnity to Japan, in the name of compensation for the families of the killed crewmen and the infrastructure that Japan built, and Japan agreed to withdraw the military presence.[15] Japan hence ended its colonial venture in Taiwan triumphantly, the result of employing international law theories on sovereignty with the backing of military power. Indeed sovereignty was the key issue that the two parties debated.

Sovereignty over the aboriginal territories: Japan's argument

Throughout the 1874 expedition, Japan maintained that it was justified in entering and occupying the aboriginal territory of Taiwan, because the Qing did not have sovereignty over the "savage" land. Japan's introduction of and arguments about the notion of sovereignty were entirely informed by international law doctrines. These doctrines and the theoretical justification for the expedition were provided by Charles Le Gendre, a former US consul to Amoy (Xiamen) turned Japanese advisor. Le Gendre was familiar with Taiwan's aboriginal territory because of the *Rover* incident in 1867, and he became the instigator, facilitator and advisor of the Japanese expedition.[16] Japan's use – or misuse – of European international law was itself a sign of Japanese modernisation.

Introducing the doctrines of discovery and conquest, Le Gendre argued that the Qing had no sovereignty over the aboriginal territories in Taiwan for lack of discovery or conquest. The evidence was that Qing maps did not show details of the eastern part of Taiwan, and the Qing had failed to subjugate the aborigines. Furthermore, the Qing had no intention to occupy the aboriginal territory; its abandonment of a temporary fort was a renunciation of intention. More importantly, the Qing had failed to exercise any de facto control over the aborigines and to perform its obligation to civilise the aborigines, which was essential for possession and sovereignty.[17] Le Gendre concluded that there was no fact of Qing discovery of aboriginal Taiwan, and no intention or fact of possession. These doctrines were European inventions to justify their possession of aboriginal territories. They had greatly facilitated European expansion, and were now advanced on behalf of Japan for its taking of the aboriginal territories of Taiwan.

Guided by Le Gendre's advice, and quoting international law experts such as de Vattel and Bluntschli, Japan argued that sovereignty came from possession, and actual possession required administrative acts. According to Japan, since the Qing failed to implement law (*fazhi* 法治), station officials (*sheguan* 設官), exercise political control and education (*zhengjiao* 政教), or bring civilisation (*kaihua* 開化) in the aboriginal territory or to the aborigines, the Qing had not exercised administration over the aborigines. Therefore the Qing did not have sovereignty over the aboriginal territory.[18]

In the eyes of Le Gendre and Japan, the aborigines were "savages" without a sovereign (*wuzhu yeman* 無主野蠻), and hence Japan was free to send an expedition against the people and occupy the territory.[19] Following "the enlightened opinions of European jurists",[20] Japan regarded the aborigines as having no status under the international law, and their land as terra nullius.[21] To this end they had to advance contradicting arguments. On the one hand, to disprove Qing sovereignty, Le Gendre acknowledged that the aborigines asserted "unlimited independence and absolute sovereignty" over their land. On the other hand, to justify Japan's occupation, Le Gendre argued that under the "law of nations" other nations could "seize upon the territory" which was "occupied by a wild race", and "hold it not only against the natives themselves, but against everyone".[22] Japan and Le Gendre clearly chose the arguments that served their objectives.

Not only did Japan regard itself as justified to occupy the aboriginal territories, Japan even asserted that the expedition against the aborigines was to "assist the cause of humanity for all nations", which the Qing had failed to perform.[23] Japan appeared to genuinely believe in social Darwinism[24] and was proud to perform the "great and glorious work" of colonising and "civilising" the indigenous territories and peoples of Taiwan.[25] Japan regarded its expedition as carrying out a great civilising mission and was eager to share the "white man's burden". In every aspect Japan's expansion bore the mark of European influence.

Japan applied the international law doctrines of discovery, possession and terra nullius as though they were the absolute truth, yet in the Western world there had been serious debates about and examination of these legal doctrines, especially in terms of justice towards the indigenous peoples. The terra nullius doctrine was the subject of debate as early as in the 17th century, and by the mid-18th century had stopped being applied in North America. Its later application in Australia was because of an initial misunderstanding that the continent was "an empty continent" because it was so sparsely populated; even so criticism of its injustice towards the indigenous peoples had arisen from inside and outside the government in Britain and Australia in the early 1800s.[26] Japan was either ignorant of the controversy about the doctrine, or chose to ignore it because it did not serve Japanese purposes. As a new member in the power game and lacking a philosophical and ideological basis to the international law doctrines, Japan simply adopted the doctrines that suited it.

Ancient theory of governance: Qing response

The Qing clearly did not grasp the legal implications of its own action and Japan's action in the same light, because the Chinese system under which the Qing still operated was different from the Western one.

Before the incident the Qing had recognised the aborigines' autonomy, and had no notion of sovereignty in the modern sense. After the incident occurred the Taiwan circuit intendant thought that the Mudan village was "the aborigines' territory" (*fanjie* 番界); as a result the Qing could not stop Japanese interaction with the Mudan aborigines, but could only monitor the situation for the safety of the western territory.[27] This was because the Chinese tradition had no notion that "savages" lacked legal status, or that their territory could be possessed by any civilised country at will. To fight the aborigines as an enemy and take their land was one thing, but to claim possession of the territory as though it was terra nullius was another. Neither was justifiable, but the two accorded quite different status to the aborigines, and represented different philosophies regarding expansion.

After a British diplomat's enquiry about whether the area where the aborigines lived was Chinese territory, the central government started to claim that the aboriginal territory was within China's realm.[28] Even so, when declaring the land to be China's territory, officials at the Foreign Affairs Office (*Zongli yamen* 總理衙門) still plainly conceded that the people were not subject to Chinese law.[29] Later, officials stated to Japanese delegates that although the state law did not apply to the aborigines, the aborigines were nevertheless subject to China's administration.[30] The changes indicated the process of Qing officials' gradual and partial understanding, and reluctant acceptance, of the modern notion of sovereignty as the scenario developed. It was under pressure from Japan and out of self-defence that the Qing government abandoned its belief in the aborigines' independence, and asserted sovereignty over the aboriginal territory.

The point is not whether the Qing had sovereignty over the aboriginal territory, the notion of sovereignty itself being a Western invention, but that the modern concept of sovereignty was unknown to the Qing. Instead, the Qing relied on the traditional Chinese theory of governance in responding to Japan's challenges regarding administration and civilisation. Quoting the *Book of Rites* (*Liji* 禮記), the Confucian classic that records the administration and rites of the Zhou Dynasty (1046–256 BCE), the Qing argued that its administration of the aborigines followed the long-established tradition of carrying out administration without requiring the peoples to change their customs or depart from what they were accustomed to.[31] As such, China exercised administration and implemented law according to the local situations and customs, and the lack of active administration over the aborigines was itself a form of administration. The Qing hence operated in a deeply Chinese legal and cultural framework.

The Qing also argued that it was a common reality, in China as well as in many other countries, that in the administration of a country "the law could not always be applicable, local offices and armies could not be stationed in all places, civilisation could not immediately show influence, and the qualities of the people could not be the same".[32] This proposition has been found to be true by contemporary scholars.[33] Even Le Gendre held the same view before he became a Japanese advisor. In an 1871 report to the US government, Le Gendre noted that the status of the mountain territories under the Qing was similar to that of the Indian territories under the US government, or the aboriginal territories in Australia and New Zealand under the British.[34] Hence he recognised Qing sovereignty over the aboriginal territory before he was employed by Japan. This recognition was confirmed by the US and British assumption that the expedition was declaring war against the Qing. However, the recognition did not serve Japanese interests, so Le Gendre withdrew it and painstakingly tried to prove that the Qing lacked sovereignty over the aboriginal territory.

Thus the two parties argued on different bases. Japan advanced the modern theories of nation state and sovereignty. The Qing held on to the Chinese tradition and claimed that it "distinguished between civilised Chinese and uncivilised barbarians in the administration" (*huayi fenzhi* 華夷分治). Unlike the notion of state sovereignty, there were no clear boundaries of the empire.[35] Against Japan's use of international law theories, the Foreign Affairs Office answered, quite rightly, that international law was compiled by the Western countries and did not reflect the Qing practices, and therefore was not a basis for the negotiation.[36] The problem was that both the Qing and Japan were busy contending for their rights over the aboriginal territories, and neither gave any consideration to the aborigines, who were their own sovereigns over their land. While Japan had the clear intention to colonise the aboriginal territory for its own benefit and explicitly denigrated the aborigines, the Qing was also capable of expansion and disregarded the aborigines completely if its interests were at stake.

The respective beliefs of the Qing and Japan about state sovereignty and empire building determined their attitudes towards the aborigines, and in turn towards aboriginal land. The Qing tradition provided a footnote to its policies regarding aboriginal land in the previous 200 years, while Japan's argument provided a guide for the Japanese policies when its time came. In other words two competing discourses and conceptions of law were at stake.

Colonising Taiwan

Not only did Japan attempt to justify its expansion through employing Western legal theories, Japan's motives and goals to acquire Taiwan in 1895, and the administration of Taiwan after that, were also largely informed by European examples.

Power and exploitation

Japan's motive to annex Taiwan was for "national eminence" and "international prestige"[37] as well as for exploitation.

Having Westernised its legal system and consequently having the unequal treaties revised, Japan was determined to follow Western examples further and to transform itself from the "bullied" to the bully. Japanese politicians celebrated Japan's performance in its first overseas colony as a proof of Japan's "worthiness to be admitted into the community of the world's great colonial powers".[38] The fundamental drive was to be like the other great colonial powers and to create "a new, European style empire on the edge of Asia".[39]

The European powers' exploitation of resources of their colonies also informed Japan's action. Although it was said that Japan did not have a clear idea what practical benefit Taiwan could bring when it acquired Taiwan,[40] Japanese officials were determined that Taiwan as a colony was to be exploited for the benefit of Japan. As soon as Japan took over Taiwan, the chief of civil administration (*minsei chōkan* 民政長官) recognised that a priority was to exploit the rich resources in the mountain territories, in particular camphor and timbers, but also mines and agricultural products.[41] This clearly shows that prestige as such was not the only goal – prestige and exploitation went together. As will be demonstrated later in this chapter, all Japanese actions regarding land had a clear objective of exploitation.

Law and administration

For the administration of Taiwan, Japan consulted Western advisors, managed it as a Western-style colony and governed it through a series of laws made in modern form, unlike the Qing which simply governed Taiwan as a prefecture within the ordinary administration.

After annexation, Japan considered two options recommended by two Western advisors, respectively – to follow the French model and treat Taiwan as "a prefecture of Japan", or to follow the British model and treat Taiwan as a "legally, politically, culturally and financially separate" colony.[42] Japan decided on a compromise of these two models, and treated Taiwan as a colony with an ultimate goal to integrate.[43] Taiwan was governed by a governor-general. The 1898 "Law concerning Laws and Regulations to be Enforced in Taiwan" (known as "Law 63") and its subsequent amendments and re-enactments granted the *Sōtokufu* the power to make ordinances, which had the same effect as laws of Japan, provided that they did not conflict with Diet-enacted laws or Japanese imperial ordinances already in force in Taiwan.[44] The governor-general presided over the Legislative Council of the *Sōtokufu*, and usually had the final authority over legislation. In effect, the governor-general exercised legislative, executive and judicial powers with a high degree of autonomy, and was the "virtual sovereign" of Taiwan.[45]

As a rule, Japanese laws were not enforced in Taiwan, unless it was the intention of the law or was provided by an imperial ordinance, and with modifications. The successor to Law 63, the 1921 "Law Concerning Laws and Regulations to be Enforced in Taiwan" (known as "Law 3") altered this approach, and made the application of Diet-enacted laws a principle, rather than an exception. However the legal system in Taiwan remained separate until the end of Japanese rule, and legal integration was never achieved.[46] Thus, throughout the whole period of Japanese rule Taiwan remained an unintegrated part of the Japanese empire.

Japanese administration nominally covered the whole island, but the administration and civilisation did not apply to all of Taiwan at first. The areas where the government had full control were the "regular administrative districts" (*putong xingzhengqu* 普通行政區), while the territories occupied and controlled by the mountain aborigines were the "special administrative districts" (*teshu xingzhengqu* 特殊行政區) or "mountain areas" (*shandi* 山地). Following the Qing classification of the aborigines, the Japanese government recognised that there were acculturated aborigines (*shufan* 熟番), semi-acculturated aborigines (*huafan* 化番) and non-acculturated aborigines (*shengfan* 生番). Acculturated aborigines lived in the regular administrative districts and had a "civilisation level equal to that of the Han Chinese". The acculturated aborigines were treated no differently from the Chinese, and they lost their status as "aborigines" under the Japanese administration.[47] Han Chinese who stayed in Taiwan after the Japanese takeover and the acculturated aborigines were both referred to as "natives" of the island (*bendao ren* 本島人, J. *hontōjin*).[48] The laws of the *Sōtokufu* and applicable Japanese laws applied to the natives, but they did not enjoy the constitutional rights of Japanese nationals.[49] One level down were the semi-acculturated aborigines and non-acculturated aborigines, who were "barbarians" (*fanren* 蕃人, J. *banjin*). The "barbarians" lived outside the regular administrative districts and government laws did not apply to them.

The category of semi-acculturated aborigines was fluid, as they had the potential to become imperial subjects once their civilisation level was advanced.[50] Similarly, the boundaries between the regular administrative districts and special administrative districts were imprecise. In 1903 the chief of civil administration clarified that the guard lines, which the Japanese inherited from the Qing and extended, were not the boundary markers of the mountain areas. Instead the Han Chinese's customary recognition of mountain areas was to be the guide for determining the mountain areas.[51] This situation to some extent resembled that, under the Qing, but unlike the Qing, the Japanese government in principle asserted authority over the aboriginal territory and ownership of the land.

Therefore, Japan's objective, administration and legal institutions concerning Taiwan were of typical Western style, although in practice, there was some continuity from the Qing arrangements regarding the aborigines. The continuity was superficial, as Japan's treatment of the people and land in aboriginal Taiwan formed a huge contrast to that of the Qing.

Land and people

Declaration of government ownership

As at the time of the Japanese takeover, land in the western part of Taiwan was densely populated and controlled by Chinese settlers, who had their own commercial and land practices. The mountain areas were controlled by the aborigines who had not been brought under the government control. Land tenure could not be changed immediately, but the government lost no time in declaring ownership over forest and unreclaimed land.

To achieve the goal of exploitation, a few months after the takeover, the colonial government issued an ordinance in October 1895, declaring that forest and unreclaimed land (*senlin yuanye* 森林原野) belonged to the government unless claimants could prove "ownership" through producing "land documents or other certain evidence",[52] or as the Chinese language version put it, "evidence from previous owners and land deeds".[53]

Under the Qing system, only farm lands were surveyed and registered, and therefore forest land or unreclaimed land would not have been on record. Land deeds were made when land transactions occurred. The aborigines would not have land deeds if the forest land was their ancestral land. In some cases the aborigines let Han settlers extract resources in return for a fee, but no land deed would be made if the agreements did not concern land per se. Therefore as could be anticipated, most land fell into the category of government land. The Ordinance was not followed by investigation of titles and survey of unreclaimed and forest land until 1911, and as such it was in effect a pre-emptive declaration by the government.

Apart from making forest and unreclaimed land government owned in law, the government also suspended new use of the forest land. The 1895 Ordinance provided that apart from those who held a licence issued by the Qing government before the takeover, no one was to cut timber, reclaim land or manufacture camphor. Those who held a licence issued by the Qing government had to apply to the colonial government for a new licence.[54] The Rules on Control of Aboriginal Territory 1898 further clarified procedures for entering and retrieving resources from aboriginal territory.[55] In 1900, an Ordinance on Occupation of Land in the Mountain Areas was made to exclude non-aborigines from occupying land in the mountain areas or to contract with the aborigines regarding use of the land, unless otherwise permitted by regulations or by the governor-general.[56] The Ordinance regulated not only forest land, but also forests. It had been customary under the Qing that the Chinese contracted with the aborigines for rights to extract resources from the forest, such as timber. In responding to a query from the Hengchun Administrative Branch (*banwushu* 辦務署) as to whether such situations were governed by the Ordinance, the Tainan County magistrate (*zhishi* 知事) firmly asserted that the forest belonged to the government and the situations were governed by the Ordinance.[57] The Japanese authority hence thoroughly denied the aborigines' property rights over the land and anything in it.

The declaration of ownership over unreclaimed land by the colonial government was fundamentally different from the Qing government's treatment of "wasteland" as government land. The Qing government's title over wasteland was in effect an administrative power rather than a proprietary right.[58] In contrast, the Japanese administration claimed property rights over all forest and unreclaimed land. In 1896 the *Sōtokufu* made ordinances and rules to lease forest land and sell forest resources, although the actual lease and sale were limited to land and resources in the regular administrative districts and did not extend to the mountain territories.[59]

In summary, soon after annexation, the government asserted proprietary ownership over all wasteland in Taiwan. It took control of the wasteland in the regular administrative districts and started to profit from the land and the resources. Before the mountain aborigines were subjugated, the government could not actually possess the forest land in the aboriginal territory, but to some extent it controlled the land through legislation preventing Han settlers and acculturated aborigines from using the land or having any contractual relationships with the aborigines. No legal justification was provided for the assertion of ownership, but the underlying assumption was that the aborigines did not have property rights over the forest and unreclaimed land. This was made explicit in the 1900s when the government was ready to take actual control of the mountain territories.

The aborigines' ability to own land

To justify the government's preconceived plan to control the aboriginal territories, the government argued that the aborigines did not have legal ability to own land, implying that the land was terra nullius.

Soon after the annexation, the editorial of Japan's most influential newspaper, *Jiji shinpō*, suggested that "in order to pacify the island and develop the rich resources with the hands of our Japanese people, the goal of managing Taiwan should focus solely on the land while ignoring the natives", and called for the authority to "[focus] on the land while ignoring the islanders . . . based on the notion of no-man's island".[60] Such was the conviction of the Japanese elite.

This was exactly the stance of Japanese officials. A legal affairs advisor stressed in a report to the *Sōtokufu* that the principal issue respecting the mountains and the mountain aborigines was land, as did a treatise by a judge of the Appellate Court of Taiwan.[61] As legal specialists, both set out to argue why the ownership over the mountains rested with the government, not the tens of thousands of aborigines who occupied the mountain territories.

The modern notion of legal personality was employed to deny the aborigines property rights. The argument was that the mountain aborigines did not have legal personality. According to the *Sōtokufu*, even though the mountain aborigines could be recognised as human in biological and sociological terms, they were merely animals in terms of international law.[62] Backtracking from Japan's 1874 argument that the Qing did not have sovereignty over the mountains, Japanese officials argued that since the Qing ceded the whole of Taiwan to Japan, Japan had sovereignty over the aboriginal territory. The aborigines lived on the government's land, but did not submit to the government's authority. Because legal rights were not inherent but were conferred by law, the mountain aborigines, who did not have a political organisation to confer legal rights and were not granted legal rights by the government, could not enjoy property ownership. The conclusion was that the aborigines' occupation of the land in the mountains was factual, but not legal, and the land belonged to the government.[63] The Western law once again provided justification for Japan's agenda.

Expediency and colonial interest were the driving forces for the previously mentioned arguments. Japan in the 19th century had turned from following the Chinese legal system to adopting the Western legal doctrines and instruments. The Taika Reform of the 7th century had borrowed the Chinese law to build its society, and it has been said that "the imported law was *a tool of modernisation*" without the philosophical underpinning.[64] The same can be said of the Japanese importation of the Western law. Japan followed the mechanism of Western expansion without the debates that occurred in the West. The legal arguments justifying the government's rights over the aboriginal territories were put forward in the early 1900s, many years after the government's declaration of ownership over all wasteland. The arguments were put forward at that time to justify the government's action in aboriginal management (*fanzheng* 蕃政, J. *bansei*), the objective of which being to take control of the land.

Aboriginal management

Although in theory the colonial government disregarded the mountain aborigines, in practice it could not ignore those aborigines who formed strong obstacles to the government's mountain enterprises. The government several times stressed that the purpose of aboriginal management was to develop aboriginal land, and that the development of aboriginal land was dependant on good management of the aborigines.[65] As the first chief of civil administration, Mizuno Jun, put it, camphor manufacture, forest management, land reclamation, agricultural outputs, mining and even the settlement of Japanese migrants were all dependent on successful management of the aborigines.[66] It was in terms of exploitation that the Japanese government recognised the importance of bringing the mountain aborigines under control.

The focus and strategy on aboriginal management shifted during the colonial rule.[67] In the first few years of the Japanese rule, the government was preoccupied by the Chinese guerrillas who opposed Japanese occupation of Taiwan. The policy towards the aborigines was mainly to conciliate. As such the government retained some of the late Qing institutions and avoided provoking the aborigines.[68] The government also invested in collecting information about the aboriginal peoples, their land and the resources, which essentially prepared for later action. This was a period when the government consolidated its control over the island and took a pragmatic approach towards the mountain aborigines.

Beginning in 1903, the government began to implement stricter and more coercive policies. It first extended the boundary guard lines, which had existed since the Qing time. The intention was to expand the area of government control and to restrict the aborigines' living space.[69] This was fundamentally different from the Qing's purpose, which was to segregate settlers and aborigines, to eliminate interaction and ultimately to reduce conflicts. By 1904 the guard lines were 480 kilometres long, an increase from about 80 kilometres at the end of Qing rule.[70] The number of guards was also increased from about 1,300 in 1898 to over 4,500 in 1905.[71] The fifth governor-general, Sakuma Samata (1906–1914), launched a "five-year plan on aboriginal management" (*lifan wunian jihua* 理蕃五年計劃) for the period of 1910–1914 (Meiji 43–47). Military attacks and raids were carried out against the aborigines.[72] During this period the guard lines continued to function, and landmines and electrified fences were used to control and force submission of the aborigines.[73] This was a period of compressing the living space of the aborigines through military coercion.

The struggle between the government and the aborigines continued, but with the government gaining the overwhelming advantage the electrified fences were abolished in 1924.[74] The Musha Incident (*wushe shijian* 霧社事件) of 1930 (Shōwa 5), where the aboriginal group of Seediq rebelled against the government and which resulted in the death of over 900 aborigines following the government's retaliation, prompted the *Sōtokufu* to re-evaluate its aboriginal policies and to focus more on conciliating the aborigines than on military campaigns and coercion.[75] The focus was yet again shifted during World War II, when the government tried to assimilate the aborigines and make them loyal subjects.

Whether concerning the land or the people, Japan followed Western examples in its colonisation of Taiwan and adopted legal instruments and international law doctrines in managing or justifying its management of the colony, especially the mountain territories. Possibly because the colonial theories and practices were a direct transplantation from the West, as opposed to being developed through experiment and debate, Japan's application of the practices was swift, forceful and directly linked to the objective of exploitation. The shifting strategies of aboriginal management coincided with the government's shifting focus on land projects, which started from agricultural lands in the western plains, progressed to the forest and unreclaimed lands in the regular administrative districts, and finally extended to the aboriginal territories.

Land reform: agricultural land

The colonial government's reform of land tenure in Taiwan started soon after the takeover. It used different methods to reform land tenure in different areas and progressed the reform at different stages. Before each reform, the *Sōtokufu* thoroughly surveyed the land. In addition, extensive surveys and investigations about the tenure, the people and their customary practices were carried out as part of the colonial governance. The *Sōtokufu* also sponsored anthropological study of the Taiwanese aborigines, including their social organisations, customs and laws, and languages. In 1901, an "Old Customs Investigation Committee" (*Kyūkan chōsakai* 舊慣調查會) was established for the purposes of better understanding the colony and the colonised. During its 18 years of mission till 1919, the Committee produced three investigation reports (nine volumes in total), plus a comprehensive work on the private law (essentially Chinese customary law) of Taiwan, another on the administrative law of the Qing state, and a number of reports on the aborigines.[76] As a "latecomer" among the colonial powers and having studied other colonial experiences, Japan well understood the importance of "scientific colonial knowledge" to good governance.[77] The land surveys and tenure reforms were one example that thorough knowledge led to successful colonial administration.

The degrees of settler occupation, the levels of land development, the extension of government control and the types of available resources differed regarding land in the plains and the mountain areas, and in the regular administrative districts and the special administrative districts. The *Sōtokufu* methodically dealt with the reform, starting from agricultural land, progressing to wasteland in the regular administrative districts, and finally to forest land in the special administrative districts. This section examines the reform of agricultural land, and the projects concerning the forest land are discussed in the next section.

The western plains were well-established farms when Japan annexed Taiwan. As discussed earlier, the Chinese customary practice of land tenure was sophisticated, but very imprecise and flexible. This was inconsistent with Japan's newly modernised land law regime. The colonial government imported Western property law, and systematically investigated land and land rights, tidied up the large rent system and established a land register. The reform modernised land tenure in Taiwan, ultimately severed the nominal and last link the acculturated aborigines had with their land, and facilitated Japanese acquisition of and investment in land.

Land cadastre

The land cadastre was a process to gain comprehensive knowledge about the western plains, and a first step to reforming land tenure.

The Qing "fish scale" land register in Taiwan was partly missing or incomplete after the transition of power in 1895.[78] Lacking the basis for land tax collection, the Taiwan Land Tax Ordinance 1896 was made to stipulate that land tax was to be collected according to Qing precedents.[79] Possibly because of the Chinese tradition that tax payment denoted the *yezhu*'s rights to collect rights, and the Taiwanese *yezhu* wished to establish their rights under the new regime, most *yezhu* paid the land tax, which totalled over 750,000 yen – not too much less than the government estimation of 879,086 yen.[80] Nevertheless the government commenced the cadastre to collect precise information about the land.

In 1898 (Meiji 31), the Ordinance on Cadastre and the Taiwan Land Investigation Ordinance were made to provide for extensive land surveys.[81] *Yezhu* were required to report the details of their land for the cadastre, and those who did not report would have their land confiscated, in addition to a fine.[82] The government then dispatched land surveyors to survey and verify each parcel of land. The land cadastre recorded 777,850 *jia* of land when it was completed in 1904.[83] Scholars have compared this number with the late Qing survey record of 432,009 *jia*, and attributed the increase to the modern technology and equipment employed by the Japanese government. In fact the classification of land, the organisation of the survey, and the recording and reporting of the survey result by the Japanese administration were comprehensive modern processes. These all contributed to the increase and the two survey numbers cannot be compared at face value.

The Japanese land survey was part of the extensive investigation of the colony, quite different from the late Qing survey which was directed at taxable land. The Ordinance on Cadastre classified land into six categories, including traditional Chinese productive land such as farmland and fish ponds; other productive land that the Qing government never regulated, such as forest and pasture land; and other land such as house sites, parks, railroad, rivers and river banks, other water channels, and miscellaneous land.[84] The classification encompassed every possible type of land, and the survey only excluded roads, rivers and river banks, other water channels, land used for sewerage systems, and those forest and unreclaimed land that were deemed unnecessary for survey at that stage (essentially the mountain areas which were still beyond the government's control).[85] Therefore the purpose of the survey extended beyond land tax to thorough collection of information on land.

After the survey, the government decided that only farmland and fish ponds were taxable, and these amounted to 633,065 *jia*.[86] The number was still significantly higher than the late Qing survey result of 432,009 *jia*. At least three reasons could be attributed to the difference. Firstly, the Qing statistics did not include official estates and fish ponds.[87] Secondly, new lands were reclaimed between the two surveys. Thirdly, the Japanese survey employed modern technology, such as trigonometrical and topographical methods, which the late Qing survey could not match. Therefore the survey statistics were the result of different administrative methodologies, of which technological advantage was just one aspect.

The survey was carried out by the Temporary Land Survey Bureau of Taiwan (*Taiwan linshi tudi diaochaju* 臺灣臨時土地調查局), which employed over 1,200 personnel at its busiest period in 1903 (Meiji 32), and investigated 1,647,374 parcels of land in total.[88] A Land Survey Committee (*Tudi diaocha weiyuanhui* 土地調查委員會) was established in each sub-prefecture (*ting* 廳) to determine disputes about land titles, boundaries and land categories.[89] The Committee was led by the local administrative chief, and consisted of six members appointed by the chief.[90] While the Committee functioned as a special judicial body, the Land Survey Bureau was the executive body of the survey project. This model was borrowed from Germany.[91]

Appeals against the Committee's decision could be made to the Land Survey High Committee (*Gaodeng tudi diaocha weiyuanhui* 高等土地調查委員會), whose decisions were final. The High Committee consisted of three judges of Taiwan, three high-ranking officials in the *Sōtokufu*, and three other people recommended by the Minister of Home Affairs for appointment by the Prime Minister.[92] Disputes usually centred on boundaries or titles. In particular, because the late Qing reform did not completely exclude large rent holders from registering as *yezhu*, 961 title disputes between large rent holders and small rent holders were reported.[93] In total 457 cases, concerning 4,007 parcels of land, or 2.4% of the total investigated land, were heard by the High Committee.[94] The low percentage of appeals could be because of the accuracy of the decisions by the Land Survey Bureau, and their successful mediation of disputes which prevented disputes from reaching the Committee and the High Committee.[95] Another contributing factor was the relatively low level of disputes about land titles under the Chinese customary system, which could operate well among people who observed the same norms, but would not have suited Japanese migrants who had come from a different legal background.[96]

The survey of land in the western plains took seven years to complete (1898–1904). After obtaining thorough knowledge about the land and ascertaining rights, the government proceeded to abolish large rent rights, with the purpose of simplifying the land ownership system and reforming land tax.

Abolition of large rent rights

Before reforming land tax, the *Sōtokufu* abolished large rent rights. In Taiwan about 60% of agricultural land was subject to large rent.[97] In the late Qing land tax reform, Governor Liu had intended to simplify the "split-ownership" system through abolishing large rent rights. Opposed by large rent owners, Governor Liu shifted tax responsibility to small rent owners who became registered *yezhu*, and allowed large rent owners to continue receiving 60% of the large rent without any obligations. The reform was thus incomplete, and it was the *Sōtokufu* that completed the last step.

Before abolishing large rent rights, the *Sōtokufu* first clarified land titles and ascertained details of large rent rights. In 1903 the Ordinance on Ascertaining Large Rent Rights was made.[98] This Ordinance required recording and publishing of large rent right details, including information on the right holder, location and registered number of the land, and the annual amount of large rent. Concerned parties could request correction of the records within 90 days of the publication. No new large rent rights or increase of rent was permitted after the coming into effect of this Ordinance.[99]

The ascertainment of large rent rights was followed by the Ordinance on Reforming Large Rent Rights 1904.[100] This Ordinance abolished all ascertained large rent rights. The government paid compensation according to the mount of rent each large rent owner received and the value of such rent.[101] The calculation method for compensation was complex, but the end result was that the value of large rent rights per *shi* of grain was about three to five times of the grain price per *shi* (as large rents were paid in grain), depending on the location.[102] That is to say, the government paid three to five times the annual rent to buy off the large rent rights. In total over 36,000 large rent holders received over 3.78 million yen of compensation, for the value of 1.07 million yen of annual large rent.[103] This means that on average each large rent holder received just over 100 yen of compensation, which was a very small amount. The compensation was paid in bond, which devalued to about 40–50% of its par value soon afterwards.[104] Thus in true value large rent holders received compensation worth about 1.5–2.5 times their annual rent, and lost their rent collection rights forever.

The process was carried out "peacefully" without strong reactions from large rent holders.[105] There were two possible reasons for the lack of protest. Firstly, the calculation of compensation had taken into consideration the market price of large rent rights and the market price of grain.[106] The low compensation to some extent reflected the low value of large rent rights. One Japanese newspaper even reported that the acculturated aborigines were pleased to sell their large rent rights to the government, because they had had difficulties collecting rent.[107] Although the Japanese report might be biased, this to some extent indicated the predicaments of the absentee large rent owners and the plains aborigines. Secondly, to ensure smooth implementation of the land reform, the *Sōtokufu* had built up a strong police system, which was ready for action against protests and was likely to have had intimidating effects on the large rent holders.[108]

Thus the abolition of large rent rights was provided by legal instruments, implemented with sophisticated administrative calculation, and backed by police force. It was well prepared and was carried out in an orderly manner, quite different from the late Qing reform which was forced to change the initial plan because of protests from large rent holders and was heavily criticised, not always justly, by Governor Liu's rivals in the imperial Court. The Japanese reform was a complete modernisation of tenure. It simplified the land ownership system and paved the way for land tax reform.

Land tax reform

After the land ownership system was simplified, the government set new tax rates. Qing tax rates for private land in Taiwan simply followed that of a particular place in Fujian, and they did not change for nearly 200 years, until Governor Liu's reform.[109] Liu's reform made adjustments to the calculation and collection of tax. It simplified, but did not make fundamental changes, to the tax system.[110] In contrast, the Japanese administration investigated land quality, productivity, small rent rates, price of rice and other agricultural products, values of the various currencies used in Taiwan, land price, loan interest and other factors relevant to agricultural productivity, before deciding on land categories and their respective tax rates.[111] The tax reform was a complete reform based on thorough knowledge of the land, productivity, market and landlord-tenant relations.

The tax rates were greatly increased. For most categories of land the new rates were about three times the Qing rates.[112] Land tax revenue increased from 752,698 yen in 1896 to 2,975,736 yen after the reform.[113] However in effect small rent holders' burden of tax and fees for most categories of land reduced slightly, because during the Qing period small rent holders needed to pay large rent (which accounted for over half of the total payment obligation) and an additional supplementary tax. Therefore the reform of tenure and tax was a redistribution of benefits from large rent owners to the government. With the increased tax revenue the government recovered the cost of large rent compensation in just over one year's time. A Chinese report sums it up by stating that "our country increased tax [burden] but tax [income] reduced; the Japanese reduced tax [burden] but tax [income] increased. The clumsiness or skilfulness of political manoeuvring ability are shown here".[114]

The agricultural land reform simplified the land ownership system, but the benefits were not as great as might have been thought. After the reform, large rent holders, many of them aborigines, were excluded from the land tenure system with little compensation. The impact on small rent holders was in effect minimal, since they had already enjoyed *yezhu* rights before the reform, and their tax and fee burden changed little – although large rent was abolished, government tax was increased. The only beneficiary was the government, which received large rent holders' share as tax and increased revenue. To further modernise land tenure, the government proceeded to establish a land registration system.

Land registration

As already stated, the Qing's land registers were for tax purposes only and were often inaccurate or not up to date. The *Sōtokufu* introduced Western-style land registration, which impacted on the substance of rights. The land registration system changed a number of times.

At first, the Chinese customary land practice was allowed to continue. In 1898, the Ordinance on Civil, Commercial and Criminal Matters provided that all civil law and commercial law matters among the natives of Taiwan and the Qing subjects were to be governed by existing law – that is essentially by Chinese customary law.[115] More specifically, all rights relating to land were to follow old customs (*jiuguan* 舊慣).[116] This was a pragmatic approach as the government was still at the stage of collecting information.

Once all lands had been surveyed and titles had been clarified and simplified, the government was ready to introduce a new land registration system. After considering the Torrens registration system and the earlier experience in making Japan's Law on Real Estate Registration (1886 and 1899),[117] the Taiwan Land Registration Ordinance was issued in 1905.[118] Clause 1 specified that for all land recorded on the land survey ledger, the creation, transfer, alteration or disposal of the rights of *yezhu*, *dian*, *tai* and *pugeng* were invalid without registration, except succession of such rights which, if not registered, was recognised in law unless challenged by third parties. This was the first time that land registration became final proof of title, in contrast to the Qing period when customary practice prevailed, and titles were primarily determined by transaction deeds and supplemented by land registration and evidence of other surrounding facts.

The provision of title by registration was similar to the Torrens registration, but it was applied only to a limited extent, since clause 1 did not address existing rights. Rights of *dian*, *tai* and *pugeng* that were created before the Ordinance came into effect had to be registered within one year after the Ordinance came into effect, otherwise they were not protected against third-party claims.[119] No similar requirement was made concerning existing *yezhu* rights. The provision, or lack of it, for the four kinds of rights implies that such existing rights were valid even without registration.[120] As a result, in the first six months after the Ordinance came into effect, only about 2.5% of the 1,647,374 parcels of land had *yezhu* rights registered, and the percentage increased to about 60% in 1911.[121] Therefore the new registration system focused on newly created, transferred, altered and disposed rights, and provided a mixed regime of new and old. This was probably a pragmatic approach, seeking to accommodate the old customs while gradually modernising land tenure.

The Ordinance also went beyond land registration and specified that the rights of *yezhu* were to be equated with ownership, *dian* with pledge, *tai* with mortgage and *pugeng* with tenancy, as defined in the Law on Real Estate Registration of Japan.[122] Although the customary concepts of those rights were analogous to the respective Western property law concepts as introduced by Japan, the customary concepts were much less defined and had wide-ranging applications;[123] the Western concepts were defined and clear-cut. Hence the equating of the two sets of concepts in effect changed the substance of the rights.

With the coming into effect of the 1921 "Law Concerning Laws and Regulations to be Enforced in Taiwan" in 1922, most substantive laws of Japan eventually became applicable in Taiwan. The application of the Civil Code of Japan in Taiwan from 1923 extended registrable rights to include rights of lease and easement. However, the fundamental change to the registration system was that the Civil Code provided that contracts gave effects to creation and transfer of real property rights, and registration of such rights provided only an additional protection against third parties.[124] The difference between the system adopted in Taiwan earlier and the one applied in Japan, then extended to Taiwan, signifies that Japan was still in the process of receiving different Western models and of modernising its legal system.

In summary, although the *Sōtokufu* implemented a modern land registration system, it was a process of gradual change and a mixture of various norms, including Chinese customary law, the Torrens system and Japanese land registration law which modelled on German and French examples. This reflects the pragmatic approach of the Japanese government, as well as the reality that Japan itself was in the process of modernisation. Land registration to some extent consolidated land titles and other real property rights, and provided greater certainty and clarity to such rights.

Effects

Following Liu Mingchuan's tax reform in the late Qing, hidden land was discovered and registered, small rent holders became *yezhu* and aboriginal land in the plains areas became subject to registration and alienation. However Liu's reform did not impact much on the system of land ownership. *Yezhu* was still a concept primarily for tax purposes,[125] land registration was still not final proof of title, large rent owners were still a class within the land tenure system and in some cases remained the registered *yezhu*, and land transactions were still carried out in the old format. Liu's reform prepared the ground for the Japanese land reform, but it was not essential for the Japanese reform. The two reforms were of different nature – Liu's reform made adjustments to the existing system, while the Japanese reform was a thorough modernising process.

The Japanese administration implemented a modernising system of land records, surveys and titles in much the same way as colonial powers attempted to do elsewhere. The reforms were part of the Westernisation of laws in Japan itself as well as in Taiwan. Scholarly views differ as to the extent to which these new systems benefited Taiwan.

One view sees the modernisation of the legal system, especially the property law regime, as "the best legacy of Japanese rule for the Taiwanese people".[126] This view rests on the assumption that the modern law was better than customary law. It is true that the modern legal instruments were more precise and could provide visible and applicable rules for land title holders, but the actual benefits for all parties concerned – except the government and capital investors – are yet to be explored. As already mentioned, the elimination of the large rent holder class was to the government's benefit alone. Further, the Chinese customary land tenure had developed over a millennium to suit practical needs. It provided great flexibility for use of land and accommodated various parties' rights and interests. Under the Chinese tenure, the plains aborigines retained some interests in land on the margin; this was eliminated under the tenure introduced by Japan. The modern law was never friendly to indigenous land systems.

A contrary view essentially argues that these changes served the interests of the colonial government and its own people, as they ultimately paved the way for the expropriation of land for the benefit of Japanese capital investment.[127]

This was also true to a certain extent. The Japanese government did intend to implant Japanese nationals as colonists, and had assisted them in acquiring land. In some cases the government, in particular the police force, coerced Chinese land owners to sell land to Japanese enterprises.[128] By the late 1930s, while the Japanese population was about 5.4% of the total population,[129] Japanese nationals held about 20–25% of the total cultivated land area, which was also land of better quality.[130] The Japanese land owners accounted for the majority of large land holdings. In 1921, among the large land holdings, 112 Taiwanese land owners owned 42,000 *jia* of land, while 24 Japanese land owners owned about 51,500 *jia*, averaging 375 *jia* and 2,146 *jia*, respectively. Monopolistic Japanese sugar companies owned 8.2% of the arable land.[131] This indicates that the principal beneficiaries of the reforms were, as intended, Japanese colonists.

Yet the result was probably not as grave as it might be thought. Due to the overwhelming number and percentage of Chinese farmers in the total population and their deep-rooted land holding, Japanese colonists were not able to change the land holding on a large scale. Chinese farmers accounted for about 95% of the total population of over three million. In 1921 there were 423,278 land owners, and 84.58% of them owned less than 10 *jia* of land.[132] The Japanese colonists, especially the sugar companies, found it easier to dominate the sugar export and influence the production through financing the farmers, rather than through controlling production by establishing their own plantations.[133] In this regard, although the land reform facilitated establishment of plantations by Japanese colonists, it did not occur on a large scale. Most land owners were not negatively affected in terms of land rights, although they might have been dominated in other ways.

Therefore, the land tenure reform in the settled areas was a process of accumulating colonial knowledge and of modernisation, and was intended to facilitate Japanese capital investments. However its effect was limited because the Chinese tenure was well established, and to a lesser extent, because Japan was experimenting with different models of land tenure.

Forest and unreclaimed land

Investigation and disposal of forest land

The work on the land cadastre, large rent rights and land registration did not extend to forest land or land in eastern Taiwan.[134] After the agricultural land tenure reform was completed, the government extended its attention to the forest land. Between 1910 and 1914 the government investigated forest and unreclaimed lands in the regular administrative districts, and in the next 10 years made detailed decisions regarding these lands. From 1925 to 1935 the government moved on to investigate and allocate lands in the aboriginal territory. As already mentioned, these categories of land had in 1895 been declared as government land as a matter of principle, unless valid written evidence of ownership could be produced; the work in the 1900s was to make use of the land.

The Investigation of Forest Land Ordinance 1911[135] provided a procedure similar to that provided by the Land Investigation Ordinance 1898. *Yezhu* were to report their rights to the government, and a time limit of 60 days was imposed. Following *yezhu* claims, the government carried out a cadastral survey and ascertained the areas and right holders.[136] At the conclusion of the survey in 1914, only 56,961 *jia* were recognised as privately owned. The government acquired ownership over 916,775 *jia* of forest land, including about 187,000 *jia* that was being used by private users who could not produce proof of ownership.[137] The overwhelming majority of forest land in the regular administrative districts thus fell into government hands through administrative power. Apart from those that were already in use, the government decided to retain control of 319,294 *jia* of land for security, public use or research purposes, and to "release" 398,540 *jia* to private enterprises. Of those to be "released", 266,398 *jia* were sold with a revenue of 5,892,398 *yen*.[138] Through this project the government took control of the wasteland in the regular administrative districts and gained financial benefits.

From 1925 to 1935 the government undertook the "forest planning project" (*senlin jihua shiye* 森林計劃事業), which focused on the use of forest land in aboriginal territory. The aboriginal territory occupied about 1.68 million *jia* of land, nearly two-thirds of the total forest land in Taiwan.[139] As this mountain territory had hardly been touched by settlers; after subjugating the aborigines by force the government took over the whole area as government land. Out of the 1.68 million *jia*, the majority was set aside for private investment (485,250 *jia*) and government enterprises (existing and planned, in total 568,149 *jia*), as well as educational (117,091 *jia*) and security (45,672 *jia*) uses.[140] The mountain area enterprise (*shandi shiye* 山地事業) became a focus of government enterprises, which mostly was camphor manufacture, forestry and timber, but also included development of farmland and mining.[141] Only a small amount was reserved for aboriginal use.

The investigations prepared for promotion of forest enterprises and programmed use of land. About 90% of forest and unreclaimed land, totalling over 2.26 million hectares, remained government owned. The government extracted revenue from sale of forest products and licensing use of land,[142] and provided private investors, mostly Japanese, business opportunities in the forest. The Japanese government was the most active actor in the taking of land, for its own benefit and the benefit of Japanese investors.

Aboriginal reserves and relocation of the aborigines

The aborigines occupied the land that the government planned to use. As part of its development programme, the government eventually established policies or practices regarding aboriginal reserves and relocation of the aborigines. Relocation began in the early 1900s, but the peak period was between 1919 and 1934.[143] The main purposes for relocating the aborigines were exploitation of resources and management of aborigines.

To facilitate Japanese enterprises, aborigines were removed to smaller areas that did not impede forest development. A few examples show that as the forest enterprises developed and the government became more confident in its policies, the aborigines received decreasing areas of land and of monetary compensation.

To start with, the government insisted on government ownership of all land and prescribed very little compensation. For example, in 1922 (Taishō 11) the government relocated the aborigines in the Quchi 屈尺area because the land had been granted to a Japanese enterprise, the Mitsui 三井. The aborigines comprised 110 households and 546 people, and occupied over 10,200 *jia* of land, including 236 *jia* of cultivated land and 1,031 *jia* of fallow land. The government decided that each aboriginal household was to receive an average of 7.5 *jia* of arable land after the relocation, based on the estimation of five people per household. The actual allocation was 819 *jia* of land, including 164 *jia* of cultivated land and 655 *jia* of fallow land. The company was required to pay compensation for the remaining cultivated land and fallow land, at the rate of 150 *yen* per *jia* and 50 *yen* per *jia*, respectively. In the end the total payment was about 2,384 *yen* for cultivated land and 9,033 *yen* for fallow land, which converted to about 16 *jia* of cultivated land and 180 *jia* of fallow land. This means that 9,185 *jia* of land, including 56 *jia* of cultivated land and 180 *jia* of fallow land, were not compensated for. The government rejected the aborigines' conception that the land was their ancestral land. Officials informed the aborigines that all land belonged to the government, and that the reserved land for the aborigines was due to consideration for their livelihood. The aborigines had to renounce any relationship with their ancestral land once they received compensation from the company. Further, in the future if the company needed to use any of the allocated land for infrastructure purposes, the aborigines could not refuse, and the compensation was to be for crops on the land only, and not any rights over the land.[144]

Even so, the treatment that the Quchi aborigines received was better than other aborigines who were relocated. In another case, the government granted Mitsui 1,050 *jia* of land for development into wetland, tea farms and forestation. Forty-seven households lived on the land. The company's plan to provide each aboriginal household with 0.3 *jia* of wetland, 1 *jia* of dry land, 1.5 *jia* of fallow land and 0.2 *jia* of tea land, in total 3 *jia* per household, was approved by the government. This amounted to 141 *jia* for the whole village. No monetary compensation was mentioned for any existing cultivated land, and the compensation for fallow land was 5 *yen* per *jia*.[145] This was a significant reduction from the compensation of 7.5 *jia* of land per household, plus 150 *yuan* per *jia* for cultivated land and 50 *yuan* per *jia* for fallow land in the Quchi case. The fact that this village was smaller and weaker perhaps contributed to the ill treatment it received.

By 1925 (Taishō 14), the colonial government tightened up the policies regarding relocation of aborigines. In a dispatch to the Takao Shū (高雄州 Kaohsiung district) magistrate concerning the relocation of seven aboriginal villages, the *Sōtokufu*'s chief administrator (*zongwu zhangguan* 總務長官) directed that the aborigines had to be relocated speedily, their land be opened up without obligations to the aborigines, and preferably no compensation needed to be paid to the aborigines for their cultivated land.[146] Clearly as the government became better established, it grew more confident in taking land and dispossessing the aborigines with minimal cost.

In the examples given earlier, allocation of land declined from 1.5 *jia* per person or 7.5 *jia* per household, to 3 *jia* per household, to an unspecified allocation. Compensation for the lost cultivated land also reduced, until at last the government decided not to require any compensation. The aborigines had to relinquish any further claims, and had only user rights over the reserved land. This shows the *Sōtokufu*'s total disregard for the aboriginal land rights and livelihood, and its unconditional support of Japanese investors.

In 1928, the government formally decided that reserved land for aborigines was to be based on three hectares per person.[147] The three hectares included 0.2 hectare for living space, 1.8 hectare for agriculture, 0.5 hectare for gathering wood and 0.5 hectare for livestock and other use.[148] The government's investigation recorded over 80,000 aborigines, and accordingly 261,618 *jia* were set aside as aboriginal reserves, a small fraction of what the aborigines used to have.[149] This number was an artificial calculation and reserves were marked on maps as a plan, rather than an actual allocation. In the implementation stage, some of the marked reserves were taken for forest enterprises, and in some cases it was found that the aboriginal population was bigger than estimated. The adjusted plan saw the average entitlement reduced to about 2.3 *jia* per person, but ranging from 1.47 to 3.03 *jia* in different areas.[150] The plans served as guides when land of individual aboriginal villages was taken for forest enterprises and the aborigines needed to be relocated, but they were not always adhered to.

In 1930 the government formally launched the "mountain development investigation" (*shandi kaifa diaocha* 山地開發調查), which included both the investigation of aborigines themselves and the land needed for accommodating aborigines. Prior to the 1930 Wushe Incident, most relocation was to areas within the aborigines' native territory. After the Incident, the government changed to relocating aborigines to the foothills, and on making the aborigines become subsistence farmers.[151] The government invested in infrastructure for agriculture, such as irrigation systems. Even so, in 1933 the average agricultural land that each aborigine possessed amounted to 0.86 *jia*, ranging from as much as 1.3 *jia* to as little as 0.18 *jia* per person for different aboriginal groups.[152] Statistics for the period between 1935 and 1940 show little change – ranging from an average of 1.09 *jia* to 0.95 *jia* in different years. This was far less than the planned 1.8 *jia* per person needed for agricultural purposes.

The intention of making aborigines engage in traditional style of intensive farming, apart from making them self-sufficient, was to transform them from vigorous mountain "savages" to submissive farmers and reduce the risks of resistance against the government.[153] This was part of a programme to "civilise" the aborigines. More importantly, the relocation of the aborigines coincided with the development of the forest land, in particular the camphor industry. As the forest enterprises advanced, the aborigines were removed.[154]

The Japanese approach to aboriginal reserves was different from the late Qing's approach in a number of aspects. The starting point was ownership. The *Sōtokufu* regarded all land as government land, including the reserves. In contrast, the Qing recognised aboriginal ownership over land. The second difference was the location of reserves. The Japanese administration established aboriginal reserves as part of a land use plan and the reserves had small or no investment value. Under the Qing, the reserves were on the aborigines' ancestral land and usually were closest to the village. For example, in Gamalan's case the reserves encompassed the villages. Thirdly, the amount of land reserved was different. The Japanese administration prescribed a strict quota of land for the aborigines, which was further diminished in the implementation. The Qing's only requirement of the aborigines was that they open for reclamation the land that they could not reclaim themselves; it ensured the reserves provided sufficient support to the aborigines. Fourthly, the government's role was different. The Japanese administration was involved in setting up compensation to the aborigines; under the Qing it was up to the settlers and the aborigines to negotiate the price of land use. The Japanese administration directly controlled the planning and use of aboriginal land, supported Japanese forestry enterprises, and gained revenues from leasing forest land and selling forest products. In contrast, the Qing government for most of the time maintained minimal intervention and was concerned only with making use of land to its potential and ensuring the aborigines' livelihood. The Japanese *Sōtokufu* was more active and aggressive, being the law-maker, the performer and the benefactor in one body.

The aboriginal reserves and allocation of land were similar to the Indian reserves and the land allotment in the United States in the late 19th and early 20th centuries.[155] This was because Japanese officials had studied the status of aborigines in various colonies around the world, and had decided that the approaches of the United States towards the American Indians were the most suitable for Japanese Taiwan.[156] In the actual implementation, there were differences. In particular, the allocation of three *jia* to each mountain aborigine was on paper only, and was subject to change. The aborigines did not have ownership over the reserved land,[157] and at least in some cases, the aborigines used the land collectively.[158] This shows that Japan was skilful in applying Western models to local situations, making adjustments where it was beneficial and expedient for the colonial cause.

European-style colonisation

Following the Meiji Restoration, Japan rapidly modernised its own legal system to emulate the West. The same desire drove Japan's colonisation of Taiwan, since possession and exploitation of colonies were European phenomena of the time.

The legal theories Japan used to debate with the Qing during the Mudanshe Incident and to justify its occupation of the aboriginal territory were all Western in origin. Further, Japan adopted Western legal instruments in carrying out its colonial administration, especially legal instruments relating to land and property.

Western advisors were consulted and Western experiences were studied. They were followed in both reforming the agricultural tenure and rearranging the forest land use, albeit with some adjustments to the local situation. These included German, French, British and US models. Japan's "forms of knowledge" about the colony and the colonised even exceeded that of other colonial powers.[159] Japan's conscious emulation of the West highlighted the distinctions between Qing and Japanese approaches in property matters, in particular those concerning aboriginal land.

If efficiency and economic growth were to be the only standards of judgement, Japan deserves to be commended for its success. Indeed a Japanese commentator of the early 1900s had celebrated Japan's ability in colonial administration.[160] However this success was built on a foundation of total disregard of aboriginal land rights. Aboriginal land was rapidly taken by the government, and aborigines were relocated and confined to small areas, while Japanese investors entered the mountains to establish capitalist enterprises. In the plains area, the government's ability to rearrange land ownership was limited, but the land survey, land registration and tax reform changed land owners' substantive rights. It was no doubt a modernising process, but the main beneficiaries were the government and Japanese investors. The distinctiveness of the plains aborigines was eradicated and their last connection with the land was severed through the abolition of large rent rights.

The different approaches Japan adopted towards the colonisation of the Ainu land, Ezo, before and after the Meiji Restoration provides an interesting parallel. The Ainu land became a fief of the Matsumae clan in the 1500s, and was under the jurisdiction of the Matsumae clan for most of the time, but was under the Bakufu (the central government) direct control during 1799–1821 and 1854–1868. The central government took direct control over Ezo for defence – because of threats of Russian penetration – rather than for exploitation.[161] Before the 1868 Meiji Restoration, the treatment of Ainu by the Japanese overlords was in many aspects similar to that of the Qing to the Taiwanese aborigines. The Matsumae government implemented a policy to segregate the merchant settlers (who were called "contractors") and the Ainu, tried to prevent oppression of the Ainu by the contractors, and otherwise maintained a "non-interference" policy. The government preferred a slow and gradual acculturation over forced assimilation, focusing on appeasement and guidance.[162]

After the Restoration, however, the Meiji government incorporated Ezo as Hokkaidō in 1869. A Hokkaidō Development Commission was established in the same year to investigate the land. A census was taken, and settlement was encouraged.[163] In 1877, an ordinance was made to declare the Ainu land state owned on the basis of terra nullius,[164] and the government subsequently allocated the land to Japanese investors.[165] Government policies before 1868 resembled Qing Taiwan policies in many aspects, because Japan had itself followed Chinese legal system until the 1868 legal reform. Government policies after 1868 were consistent with the Japanese approaches in Taiwan, both following European examples and utilising modern legal instruments. The effect of the different types of legal system on colonisation is profound.

Notes

1 See Carl Steenstrup *A History of Law in Japan until 1868* (Brill, Leiden, 1996), in general.
2 See Nakamura Kichisaburō *The Formation of Modern Japan: A View From Legal History* (Centre for East Asian Cultural Studies, Tokyo, 1962), in general; Marius B Jansen (ed) *The Cambridge History of Japan Volume 5: The Nineteenth Century* (Cambridge University Press, Cambridge, 1989), in particular, Marius B Jansen "Introduction" 1–49, Hirakawa Sukehiro "Japan's Turn to the West" (trans Bob Tadash Wakabayashi) 432–498, and Kenneth B Pyle "Meiji Conservatism" 674–720.
3 The treaties were revised in 1899, and finally abolished in 1912. See Nakamura, ibid, at 12.
4 See a memorial of Tongzhi 11 (April 1872) in *Jiaxu gongdu chaocun* [Documents Relating to the 1874 Incident] (TWWX 39), at 1–2 ("*Jiaxu gongdu*").
5 Ibid, "現飭臺灣鎮、道、府認真查辦，以懲强暴".
6 This occurred in every reign of the Qing Dynasty, as many reports are collected in various volumes of Taiwan Shiliao Jicheng Bianji Weiyuanhui *Ming Qing Taiwan dang'an huibian* [Collection of Historic Documents Concerning Taiwan During the Ming and Qing Dynasties] (Yuanliu, Taipei, 2004–2009).
7 Inō Kanori (trans Taiwan Historica) *Taiwan wenhua zhi* [A History of Taiwan's Civilisation] (Chinese trans revised ed, Taiwan Shufang, Taipei, 2011), vol 3, at 80–81.
8 Norihito Mizuno "Qing China's Reaction to the 1874 Japanese Expedition to the Taiwan Aboriginal Territories" (2009) 16 *Sino-Japanese Studies* 99, at 101–102.
9 Edward H House *The Japanese Expedition to Formosa* (Tokyo, 1875), at 15–16. House was an American journalist engaged by Japan to report on, and to justify, the expedition.
10 Ibid, at 18–22.
11 Fujii Shizue *Taiwan yuanzhumin shi: zhengce pian* [History of Taiwan Aborigines: The Policy Chapter] (Taiwan Historica, Nantou, 2001), at 1.
12 See House, above n 9. House recorded details of the activities during the whole expedition, and the two events were recorded at 74 and 115.
13 Ibid, in general, but in particular, at 62, 142, 151 and 155.
14 See Leonard Gordon "Japan's Abortive Colonial Venture in Taiwan, 1874" (1965) 37(2) *Journal of Modern History* 171–185.
15 See the text of the agreement in *Tongzhi Jiaxu ribing qin Tai shimo* [Documents on the 1874 Japanese Invasion of Taiwan] (TWWX 38), at 178–179 ("*Jiaxu shimo*").
16 For Le Gendre's role in the expedition, see Sandra Caruthers "Charles Le Gendre, American Diplomacy, and Expansionism in Meiji Japan, 1868–1893" (PhD diss, University of Colorado, 1966); Li Li and Zhao Guohui "Li Xiande yu Riben diyici qin Tai" [Le Gendre and Japan's First Invasion of Taiwan] (2007) 3 *Jindaishi yanjiu* 100–116.
17 Charles Le Gendre *Is Aboriginal Formosa a Part of the Chinese Empire? An Unbiased Statement of the Question* (Lane, Crawford & Co, Shanghai, 1874), at 2–6, 8–12 and 19.
18 Letter of the Japanese plenipotentiary Ōkubo Toshimichi in *Jiaxu shimo*, above n 15, at 144–146, 153–154 and 158–159.
19 See letters of the Japanese representative Yanagihara Sakimitsu in ibid, at 105 and 109. The term *wuzhu* could also mean terra nullius. Japan's arguments in effect asserted that the aboriginal territory was terra nullius.
20 Le Gendre's memorandum of 5 October 1874, quoted in Caruthers, above n 16, at 225.
21 The same line of reasoning was to be followed after 1895 in justifying the *Sōtokufu*'s assertion of government ownership over the aboriginal territory.
22 Le Gendre, above n 17, at 15.
23 House, above n 9, at 4.
24 For example, see *Riju shiqi yuanzhumin xingzheng zhigao* [Administration of Aborigines During the Japanese Period, Translation of *Ribanshikō*, Compiled by the Police Administration Bureau, Taiwan *Sōtokufu*] (Taiwansheng wenxian weiyuanhui, Nantou,

1997), vol 1, at 149, where the government official talked about the elimination or assimilation of "inferior races" ("*Xingzheng zhigao*"); Yosaburō Takekoshi (trans George Braithwaite) *Japanese Rule in Formosa* (Longmans, Green and Co, London, 1907), at 233, where the author trumpeted "the law of natural selection".

25 Takekoshi, ibid, at vii, "A Word to My Readers".

26 Stuart Banner "Why Terra Nullius? Anthropology and Property Law in Early Australia" (2005) 23 *Law and History* 95, at 95–97.

27 "牡丹社系屬番界，彼如自往剿辦，在我勢難禁止". See the intendant's letter to the Fujian-Zhejiang governor-general in *Jiaxu gongdu*, above n 4, at 5. The letter was not dated, but it was before the Japanese expedition and when Japan carried out investigation in the Langqiao area.

28 See Prince Gong's memorial to the emperor in *Jiaxu shimo*, above n 15, at 1, "臺灣生番地方，系屬中國版圖". As scholars have heatedly debated how "Chinese" the Manchu Qing was, and some have argued that the Qing was not China, it is worth noting here that throughout the negotiation the Qing used the term "China" 中國 to refer to the Qing Empire. Also see the same references in *Qing Muzong shilu xuanji* [Selected Veritable Records of the Tongzhi Emperor] (TWWX 190), for example, at 145, 148 and 149. William T Rowe *China's Last Empire: The Great Qing* (Belknap Press of Harvard University Press, Cambridge (MA), 2009), at 210, notes that the Qing referred to itself as China within decades of conquering China proper.

29 "其人雖不治以中國之法，其地究不外乎中國之土". *Jiaxu gongdu*, above n 4, at 11.

30 *Jiaxu shimo*, above n 15, at 38, "向未繩以法律，總屬中國管轄之人".

31 See the Qing government's dispatch to the Japanese Foreign Affairs Department (*waiwu sheng*外務省) in ibid, at 5, "即禮記所雲不易其俗，不易其宜之意".

32 Letter to Ōkubo Toshimichi in ibid, at 161. "法律不能盡繩，郡縣官兵不能遍設，文教不能即通，民質不能即齊，凡此皆治國之恒情", "且不獨中國版圖如此類者甚多，即各國所屬版圖，如此類亦恐不少".

33 For example, see Richard Boast *The Native Land Court Volume 2: A Historical Study, Cases and Commentary 1888–1909* (Thomson Reuters, Wellington, 2015), at 158 and 252–253, where the author discusses a similar situation in New Zealand and the Spanish Latin America. Also see Shiri Pasternak "Jurisdiction and Settler Colonialism: Where Do Laws Meet?" (2014) 29 *Canadian Journal of Law and Society* 145; Lauren Benton *A Search for Sovereignty: Law and Geography in European Empires 1400–1900* (Cambridge University Press, Cambridge, 2010).

34 Charles W Le Gendre *Reports on Amoy and the Island of Formosa* (Government Printing Office, Washington, 1871), at 45–48.

35 For a thorough discussion of the two different theories of nation states and empires, see Chang Chi-hsiung "Dongxi guoji zhixu yuanli de chayi: 'zongfan tixi' dui 'zhimin tixi'" ("A Comparison of Eastern and Western Principles of International Order: Suzerainty vs Colonization") (2003) 79 *Zhongyang yanjiuyuan jindaishi yanjiusuo jikan* 47.

36 "萬國公法者，乃近來西洋各國編成之物，殊無載我清朝之事，故不引此論為論辯之用". Quoted in ibid, at 67–68. Also see House, above n 9, at 195; Caruthers, above n 16, at 222. However it should be noted that occasionally the Qing also tried to quote international law.

37 Mark R Peattie "Introduction" and Mark R Peattie "Japanese Attitudes Toward Colonialism, 1895–1945" in Ramon H Myers and Mark R Peattie (eds) *The Japanese Colonial Empire, 1895–1945* (Princeton University Press, Princeton, 1984), at 10 and 82, respectively.

38 Takekoshi, above n 24, at 2. Takekoshi was a member of the Japanese Diet.

39 Japanese Foreign Minister Inoue Kaoru in 1887, quoted in Marius B Jansen "Japanese Imperialism: Late Meiji Perspectives" in Myers and Peattie (eds), above n 37, at 64.

40 George W Barclay *Colonial Development and Population in Taiwan* (Princeton University Press, Princeton, 1954), at 7.

41 *Xingzheng zhigao*, above n 24, vol 1, at 3.

42 Edward I-te Chen "The Attempt to Integrate the Empire: Legal Perspectives" in Myers and Peattie (eds), above n 37, at 249. Takekoshi, above n 24, at 25–38 also made detailed comparisons of various styles of European colonies.
43 Chen, ibid, at 241 and 269.
44 At 248 and 259–260.
45 Wang Tay-sheng *Legal Reform in Taiwan Under Japanese Colonial Rule, 1895–1945: The Reception of Western Law* (University of Washington Press, Seattle, 2000), at 39; Harry J Lamley "Taiwan Under Japanese Rule, 1895–1945: The Vicissitudes of Colonialism" in Murray A Rubinstein (ed) *Taiwan: A New History* (revised ed, Routledge, New York, 2015), at 222.
46 Chen, above n 42, at 153–254, 256, 266 and 269; also see discussions in Wang, ibid, at 44.
47 "開化程度達至同于漢人". *Xingzheng zhigao*, above n 24, vol 1, at 149 and 151.
48 Wang Tay-sheng *Taiwan falüshi gailun* [Introduction to the History of Laws of Taiwan] (4th ed, Yuanzhao, Taipei, 2012), at 109. In some cases "natives" include Han Chinese and all aborigines, to be distinguished from Japanese and foreigners. See Chan Su-Chuan "Taiwan pingpuzu de shenfen rending yu bianqian (1895–1960) – yi hukou zhidu yu guoshi diaocha wei zhongxin" [The Ascertainment and Evolution of the Plains Aborigines' Identity: From the Perspective of the Household Registration System and Census] (2005) 12(2) *Taiwanshi yanjiu* 121, at 135.
49 Wang, above n 45, at 174.
50 *Xingzheng zhigao*, above n 24, vol 1, at 151–152.
51 At 241–242.
52 Ordinance on Government-owned Forest Land and Camphor Manufacture 1895 (No 26) 公[官]有林野及樟腦製造業取締規則, cl 1, "無證明所有權之地券或其他確證之山林原野者，全部爲公[官]有". See the Ordinance in *Taiwan zongdufu dang'an zhongyiben* [Chinese Translation of the Administrative Files of the Taiwan *Sōtokufu*] (Taiwansheng wenxian weiyuanhui, Nantou, 1992), vol 1, at 62. Unless otherwise specified, the statutes referred to or quoted in this chapter are taken from Xu Guo-zhang (trans) *Taiwan zongdufu gongwen leizhuan: lüling shiliao huibian* [Official Documents of the Taiwan *Sōtokufu*: Legislation Collection] (Taiwan Historica, Nantou, 2012), vol 1 & 2.
53 Both language versions were published by the government. "上手證據及山林原野之地契", see quoted in Li Wen-liang "Diguo de shanlin: Rizhi shiqi Taiwan shanlin zhengceshi yanjiu" [The Empire's Forest: A Research on the History of Taiwan Forest Policies During the Japanese Period] (PhD diss, NTU, 2001), at 28, note 20.
54 Cls 2 and 3.
55 山地取締規則, Rule (*Furei*府令, executive decree) No 72, 1898.
56 關於佔有山地之律令, Ordinance No 7, 1900, in *Xingzheng zhigao*, above n 24, vol 1, at 125.
57 The magistrate allowed the customary practice to continue for the time being because of difficulties in implementation. See ibid, at 127.
58 As discussed in Chapter 3 of this book.
59 Li, above n 53, at 112–115.
60 The editorials of *Jiji Shinpō* of 14 August 1895 and 31 July 1896, as quoted in Chang Lung-Chih "From Island Frontier to Imperial Colony: Qing and Japanese Sovereignty Debates and Territorial Projects in Taiwan, 1874–1906" (PhD diss, Harvard University, 2003), at 166.
61 See the report and the treatise in *Xingzheng zhigao*, above n 24, vol 1, at 149 and 741–744, respectively.
62 At 150.
63 At 152–153, and 741.
64 Steenstrup, above n 1, at 34 and 39. Emphasis original.
65 For example, see Wen Ji *Taiwan fanzheng zhi* [A History of Aboriginal Management in Taiwan] (translated and adapted from Inō Kanori *Taiwan bansei shi*, Taiwansheng wenxian weiyuanhui, Taipei, 1957), at 629, 646 and 694.

66 *Xingzheng zhigao*, above n 24, vol 1, at 3; Wen, ibid, at 630.
67 See Wen, ibid, for an overview of the Japanese government's management of the aborigines. For a more recent discussion, see Fujii Shizue *Rizhi shiqi Taiwan zongdufu lifan zhengce* [The Aboriginal Management Policies of the Taiwan *Sōtokufu* During the Japanese Period] (Wenyingtang, Taipei, 1997), which focuses on the period 1895–1915.
68 *Xingzheng zhigao*, above n 24, vol 2A, at 5.
69 Wen, above n 65, at 693.
70 Takekoshi, above n 24, at 214.
71 Wen, above n 65, at 702.
72 *Xingzheng zhigao*, above n 24, vol 2A, at 5. For Sakuma's aboriginal management actions, see Wen, ibid, at 747–819.
73 Wen, ibid, at 709.
74 At 715.
75 At 868–882.
76 Wu Wen-hsing "Jingdu diguo daxue yu Taiwan jiuguan diaocha" [Kyoto Imperial University and the Investigation of Old Customs in Taiwan] (2007) 1 *Shida Taiwanshi xuebao* 29, at 30. Also see Timothy Y Tsu "Japanese Colonialism and the Investigation of Taiwanese 'Old Customs'" in Jan van Bremen and Akitoshi Shimizu (eds) *Anthropology and Colonialism in Asia and Oceania* (Curzon Press, Surrey, 1999), at 197.
77 Yao Jen-To "The Japanese Colonial State and Its Form of Knowledge in Taiwan" in Liao Ping-hui and David Der-wei Wang (eds) *Taiwan Under Japanese Colonial Rule, 1895–1945* (Columbia University Press, New York, 2006), at 42 and 45.
78 Cheng jia-ying *Taiwan tudi zhidu kaocha baogaoshu* [A Report on the Taiwan Land Tenure, 1914] (TWWX 184), at 22.
79 臺灣地租規則, Ordinance No 5, cl 1.
80 Cheng, above n 78, at 23.
81 地籍規則, Ordinance No 13, 1898; 臺灣土地調查規則Ordinance No 14, 1898.
82 Land Investigation Ordinance, cls 1 and 7.
83 Sheng Ch'ing-I, Wang Shi-lang and Gao Shu-fan *Taiwan shi* [History of Taiwan] (Taiwansheng wenxian weiyuanhui, Taizhong, 1977), at 517.
84 Ordinance on Cadastre 1898, cl 1.
85 Cheng, above n 78, at 28.
86 At 64 and 69.
87 Official estates, which amounted to 15,352 *jia*, were recorded separately. Fish ponds were not surveyed. See Liu Mingchuan *Liu Zhuangsugong zouyi* [Memorials of Liu Mingchuan] (TWWX 27), at 318 and 322.
88 Cheng, above n 78, at 40 and 49.
89 Taiwan Land Investigation Ordinance 1898, cl 5.
90 Rules on the Local Land Survey Committee 1898 (*Furei* No 92), recorded in Cheng, above n 78, at 39–40.
91 At 38.
92 Land Survey High Committee Ordinance (高等土地調查委員會規則), Ordinance No 15, 1898, cls 1, 2 and 4Cl 2.
93 Zhou Mao-chun "Rizhi chuqi Taiwan tudi diaocha zhi yanjiu (1898–1905)" [A Research on the Land Survey During the Early Japanese Period, 1898–1905] (Masters thesis, National Taiwan Normal University, 2011), at 62.
94 Cheng, above n 78, at 40.
95 Zhou, above n 93, at 64; Cheng, above n 78, at 41.
96 See Zhou, above n 93, at 62, where the author notes that one type of disputes was caused by different understandings about customary *yezhu* rights between the native and the Japanese parties.
97 Cheng, above n 78, at 57.

98 關於大租權確定之件, Ordinance No 9, 1903.
99 Cls 2, 3, 4 and 12. See the Ordinance in *Gaichi hōseishi* [Legislation of the Colonies] (Ministry of Foreign Affairs, Tokyo, 1990). A Chinese version is quoted in Yen Ai-ching and Yang Guo-zhu *Yuanzhu minzu tudi zhidu yu jingji fazhan* [Land Tenure and Economic Development of the Aborigine Groups] (Daoxiang, Taipei, 2004), at 177–178.
100 關於大租權整理之件, Ordinance No 6, 1904.
101 Cls 1 and 2.
102 See the calculation in Cheng, above n 78, at 59–62. The island was divided into three areas, the north, the middle and the south, and the ratio was 5.351, 3.798 and 3.064 times, respectively.
103 At 57 and 59.
104 Ka Chih-Ming *Japanese Colonialism in Taiwan: Land Tenure, Development, and Dependency: 1895–1945* (Westview Press, Boulder, 1998), at 60.
105 Ibid.
106 Cheng, above n 78, at 59–62.
107 Yen and Yang, above n 99, at 180.
108 Ka, above n 104, at 59–60.
109 See Lian Heng *Taiwan tongshi* [A Comprehensive History of Taiwan, 1918] (TWWX 128), at 191–192 for lists of land tax rates during the Qing period.
110 See discussions and the new tax rates in ibid, at 177–178, and 192.
111 See Cheng, above n 78, at 64–66.
112 See ibid, at 84–85, Table 8.
113 At 23 and 69.
114 At 69.
115 民事商事及刑事相關律令, Ordinance No 8, 1898, cl 1.
116 Ordinance on the Implementation of the Ordinance on Civil, Commercial and Criminal Matters 1898 (No 9) 民事商事及刑事相關律令施行規則, cl 1.
117 See Li Zhi-yin "Taiwan tudi dengji zhidu bianqian zhi yanjiu" [The Evolution of Taiwan Land Registration System] (LLM diss, Taiwan National Chengchi University, 2010), at 51. Torrens is the system of title registration pioneered by Robert Richard Torrens in South Australia. It has long been used in Australia, New Zealand and a number of other countries.
118 臺灣土地登記規則, Ordinance No 3, 1905. The Ordinance is available at Digital Taiwan website http://catalog.digitalarchives.tw. See Li, ibid, at 52–53 for relevant clauses in the Chinese language.
119 Cl 13. Also see Li, ibid, at 187.
120 See Wang, above n 45, at 151; Li, ibid, at 187.
121 Li, ibid, at 189–190.
122 Taiwan Land Registration Ordinance 1905, cls 4 and 5; Li, ibid, at 53.
123 After the late Qing tax reform, small rent owners became *yezhu* and the rights of a *yezhu* became close to ownership, but the land tenure had differences from the modern land ownership. In particular, in some cases, large rent owners remained as *yezhu*.
124 Li, above n 117, at 191.
125 Even though land ownership and tax obligations overlapped in most cases after Governor Liu's reform.
126 Wang, above n 45, at 183.
127 Yao, above n 77, at 48–52.
128 Ching-chih Chen "Police and Community Control System in the Empire" in Myers and Peattie (eds), above n 37, at 228; Samuel Pao-San Ho "Colonialism and Development: Korea, Taiwan and Kwantung" in Myers and Peattie (eds), at 372.
129 is Andrew J Grajdanzev "Formosa (Taiwan) Under Japanese Rule" (1942) 15 *Pacific Affairs* 311, at 316.
130 Ho, above n 128, at 372 and 373. However, Ka, above n 104, at 101, notes that in 1939 Japanese nationals owned 13.2% of total arable land in Taiwan.

131 Ka, ibid, at 101 and 146.
132 At 102, Table 15.
133 At 157–158.
134 Li, above n 117, at 75.
135 林野調査規則, Ordinance No 7, 1911.
136 Cls 1 and 2.
137 See Horng Goang-jih "Linxue, ziben zhuyi yu bianqu tongzhi: Rizhi shiqi linye diaocha yu zhengli shiye de zai sikao" [Modern Forestry, Capitalism and Frontier Management: A Reconsideration of the Investigation and Arrangement of the Forest and Unreclaimed Land in Taiwan During the Japanese Period] (2004) 11(2) *Taiwanshi yanjiu* 77, at 79. The users were allowed to continue to use those lands upon paying a fee to the government.
138 At 102.
139 Li, above n 117, at 75; Yen and Yang, above n 99, at 206.
140 Yen and Yang, ibid.
141 See the reports from each *shū* (州district) every year under the heading of "Mountain area enterprises" in *Xingzheng zhigao*, above n 24, vol 4.
142 See Horng, above n 137, at 134, Appendix 1.
143 Kondo Masami (trans Lin Shi-ting) *Zonglizhan yu Taiwan: Riben zhimindi de bengkui* [Total War and Taiwan: The Collapse of the Japanese Colony] (NTU, Taipei, 2014), at 272–276.
144 *Xingzheng zhigao*, above n 24, vol 4, at 305–306 and 426–428.
145 At 309–312. Both cases were reported in the 1922 section, but the first case was carried out in 1922, and the second case appeared to be a work in progress.
146 At 630.
147 Through a document "Relevant criteria for reserved areas of land for aboriginal use" (蕃人使用保留面積標準有關要件). See Yen and Yang, above n 99, at 205.
148 At 205–206.
149 At 206. The number was adjusted at times and varied slightly in different records. For example, Kondo, above n 143, at 270, records the number to be 243,665 hectare.
150 Yen and Yang, ibid, at 208–209, 212–214 and 216.
151 Lin Shu-Ya "Jie/chonggou Taiwan yuanzhu minzu tudi zhengce" (De-/Reconstructing the Land Policies for Indigenous Peoples in Taiwan) (PhD diss, NTU, 2007), at 77.
152 See Yen and Yang, above n 99, at 228, Table 4.13.
153 At 212.
154 See Lin Qiong-hua "Taiwan yuanzhumin tudi chanquan zhi yanbian, 1624–1945" [The Evolution of the Land Rights of the Taiwanese Aborigines, 1624–1945] (PhD diss, Soochow University, 1997), at 163–169.
155 See David H Getches, Charles F Wilkinson and Robert Williams, Jr *Cases and Materials on Federal Indian Law* (4th ed, West Publishing, St Paul, 1998), at 141–190 for Indian reserves and the land allotments in the United States.
156 See a 1918 report by an Aboriginal Affairs director (*fanwu kezhang*番務課長) in *Xingzheng zhigao*, above n 24, vol 1, at 722–726.
157 Only when the aborigines resided in the regular administrative districts and paid land tax – a symbol of their civilisation – did their land rights become recognised. See ibid, at 146.
158 See Yen and Yang, above n 99, at 217.
159 Yao, above n 77, at 41.
160 Takekoshi, above n 24, at vii and 2. Also see the preface by Gotō Shimpei (Chief of Civil Administration of Taiwan, 1898–1906), at vi.
161 Takakura Shinichiro (trans John A Harrison) *The Ainu of Northern Japan* (The American Philosophical Society, Philadelphia, 1960), at 9, 51–53, and 81.
162 See ibid, at 23, 38, 44–47, 55, 59 and 77.

163 Mitsuharu Vincent Okada "The Plight of Ainu, Indigenous People of Japan" (2012) 1(1) *Journal of Indigenous Social Development* 1, at 5.
164 Tomonori Sugimoto "The Yellow Man's Burden: The Politics of Settler Colonialism in Hokkaidō and Taiwan" (MA thesis, University of California, San Diego, 2013), at 25.
165 Okada, above n 163, at 5.

Conclusion

Land tenure, colonisation and legal tradition

This book set out to explore Qing policies towards land settlement and aboriginal land rights in Taiwan, and the effects of its legal tradition on policymaking and the transformation of aboriginal land tenure, with a comparison from the Japanese period, situated within the theoretical framework of colonisation and colonialism. Chapter 1 depicted the spread of land settlement by Han Chinese till the end of the Qing administration; Chapter 2 traversed the three stages of Qing policies regarding land settlement in Taiwan; Chapter 3 analysed the Qing government's recognition and protection of aboriginal land rights in Taiwan; Chapter 4 considered the influence of Chinese customary land tenure on Taiwan's aboriginal land tenure; Chapter 5 explored the aborigines' action and reaction concerning the advancing Chinese settlement; and Chapter 6 examined Japanese colonial land policies.

This chapter draws together the findings of this book. It comments on the transformation of land tenure and aboriginal society in Taiwan, reflects on the different styles of colonisation of the Qing and Japan, extends the comparison to Qing colonisation and colonisation by Western states where relevant, and considers the relationship between colonisation and the legal tradition.

Transformation of land tenure and aboriginal society

The transformation of land tenure and aboriginal society in Taiwan were incremental and limited in scale during the Qing period, but swift and complete during the Japanese period.

After over 200 years of Qing administration, the plains aborigines had lost their substantive land rights but still retained some large rent rights. They were mostly acculturated, but their distinctiveness as aborigines had not completely disappeared. The change of policy in 1874 did not bring much change to the mountains – neither to the people nor to the land.

The main land tenure changes were brought about by Han settlers through private transactions and cultural influences. The government played very little part in the transformation of aboriginal land tenure. There was no requirement that aboriginal land tenure be changed in any way. If anything, the government delayed the transformation by restricting settlement and protecting aboriginal land rights. Settler-aborigine land transactions attracted minimal government intervention, unless such transactions contravened government protective policies or caused complaints from the aborigines.

There are some similarities of Qing Taiwan with other frontier societies around the world. For example, in British colonies such as the United States, Australia and New Zealand, there was also land speculation and squatting, violence and chaos, and fraudulent dealings.[1] Native land title was recognised in New Zealand, Canada and part of the United States.[2] What was different was the government approaches towards frontier settlement and native title. In British colonies, governments were actively involved in extinguishing native titles, through various means such as Crown pre-emption, treaties with the indigenous peoples, legislation and the operation of Native Land Courts.[3] Even where there appeared to be a private land market in operation, the government influenced and regulated the market through the operation of law.[4] This resulted in speedy land loss by the native peoples in British colonies. In New Zealand alone, within 20 years of the signing of the Treaty of Waitangi, nearly two-thirds of Maori customary titles had been extinguished, and the remainder was either extinguished or converted to new forms of tenure in subsequent decades.[5]

In contrast, the Qing government protected aboriginal land rights, and was not involved in extinguishing Taiwanese aboriginal land titles. Qing recognition and protection of aboriginal land tenure was not as ineffective as scholars have believed. It is true that settlers found ways to evade government laws, and reclaimed the whole western plains notwithstanding government prohibition. However, government protective policies did slow down the spread of Han settlement, enabled many aborigines to remain as large rent holders for over 200 years and excluded more than half of the whole island from settlement.

The slow transformation of land tenure and the protective stance of the Qing government were quite different from Japan's disregard for aboriginal land rights, swift declaration of ownership over wasteland, methodical disposal of wasteland for the benefit of the government and Japanese investors, and thorough reform of agricultural tenure. Under Japanese colonisation, the government was the only active actor in transforming the native land tenure. There was no frontier society as in the early contact years in the British colonies, or in Qing Taiwan. The government's role was absolute. This was because Japan was a latecomer as a colonial power, and by that time colonial methods had been matured. Japan was able to draw on the experience of other colonial powers and chose the most advantageous methods.

Consistent with its minimal interference with land tenure, the Qing government rarely imposed cultural changes on aboriginal society. While the Western colonisers typically asserted the "white man's burden" of civilising indigenous peoples, and Japan saw its assumption of civilising the Taiwanese aborigines as a contribution to the international community, the Qing did not share the same mission. Although officials anticipated sinicisation of the aborigines, the process was expected to be and was indeed slow; there was very little "missionary zeal" and officials did not actively pursue any cultural transformation.[6] Even after the 1874 change of policy, the only requirements concerning culture were to shave heads in the Manchu style, a symbol of submission that the Qing imposed upon all Chinese, and the restriction on carrying weapons. This attitude helped the plains aborigines to retain their separate identity, even though they had become highly acculturated. It also allowed the mountain aborigines to maintain their culture and autonomy. The maintenance of a separate governing system for the aborigines and the minimal intervention approach especially helped to preserve the aboriginal community and hence their identity.

Japan criticised the Qing for not having civilised the aborigines. Chinese officials and literati preferred gradual transformation and often allowed one or two centuries for the aborigines to conform to Chinese civilisation, and for their land to be integrated into the empire. Japanese approaches were quite different. One Japanese politician dismissed the possibility of allowing a century to transform the aborigines, and argued this should be achieved within 10 or so years.[7] This did not preclude pacification and extermination if required. This was exactly what Japan did, with success.

The introductory chapter of this book considered the criteria for colonialism, which, among other things, require external manipulation and transformation of the aboriginal society and imposition of the colonisers' culture on the colonised. Qing policies on aboriginal land tenure and aboriginal culture show little manipulation, transformation and imposition by the government. Rather the manipulation, transformation and imposition were carried out by Han settlers. Colonialism was exercised by a people, rather than the government. Patrick Glenn has noted that Western expansion was often through the physical presence of settlers, and imperialism was often private rather than governmental in character.[8] Qing colonisation of Taiwan certainly bore these characteristics.

The critical distinction is that, in the case of Western expansion, whether rooted in the Common Law or Civil Law, settlers went with government support and the ensuing extension of law, especially the concepts of individualised property;[9] in Qing Taiwan's case, the settlers did not enjoy government support, there was no conscious extension of formal law regarding private property matters and the extension of law in other areas worked against the interests of the settlers.

Japan went a step further than many Western colonial states, in that the government initiated and organised the expansion and colonisation. Japan had just undergone the successful Meiji Restoration, revamping the political and legal system of the country, and bringing about a miraculous increase of national power and international status. This prompted Japan to follow Western examples with a clear intention and determination, bypassing the Western experimental stages.

The role of legal tradition

Qing Taiwan policies were not unique in the Qing Empire. The restriction of Han migration, the segregation of Han settlers and aborigines, and the protection of aboriginal land rights were the same in Taiwan as at other Qing frontiers, such as Manchuria, Mongolia, Xinjiang and southwestern China, although the timing and detailed operation varied depending on strategic needs. Measures of protection, such as demarcating settlers' land and aboriginal land, requiring return of encroached or illegally alienated land, and regulating pledges and loans to aborigines, were also consistent across the empire. The policy change in 1874 was consistent with the policy to encourage land settlement whenever the government needed to people the frontier for defence purposes. The common factor in play was Chinese legal tradition, particularly the constitutional framework and the nature of law in Chinese tradition.

Aboriginal land rights

The Chinese imperial constitutional framework was authoritarian. The empire was divided into the emperor (and his representatives), who had absolute authority, and the people, who were the "water" that either kept the "boat" of the imperial regime afloat or overturned it. This explains the government's preference for security and social stability over economic gains, and why Qing colonisation of Taiwan was basically non-exploitative. To achieve security and social stability, the government tried to maintain a power balance between different interest groups, which happened to be different ethnic groups in Qing Taiwan's case. Hence the government tended to suppress the perceived trouble-making Han settlers, and protected the disadvantaged aborigines.

In Western colonisation, there typically existed a two-sided relationship, that is, the European against the aborigines, the coloniser against the colonised. The government was the colonists' government and worked primarily for the colonists' interest. But in the case of Chinese expansion, the relationship was multi-dimensional. The emperor and his government presided over many different groups of people, and acted as the adjudicator between the colonists and the colonised. As a contributing factor, the Qing ruling house, itself a minority ruler, was inclined to suppress the Han and ally itself with the aborigines.

Traditional ideologies were also in play. The Confucian model of a sage king required managing the frontier only for defensive purposes, and not for territorial expansion – even less for exploitation. Further, traditional Chinese political thought favoured rule by moral example, and the reverse side of the absolute authority of the monarch was his moral obligation to treat the subjects as children. This dictated the paternalistic attitude of the emperor and officials towards the disadvantaged aborigines.

However, the government's overriding consideration of security meant that when security was at stake, the government was prepared to sacrifice aboriginal rights. This was demonstrated in the incorporation of Gamalan due to pirate trouble, and the "opening the mountains" campaigns because of foreign threats. Protection of aboriginal land rights was a means to an end, the end being social stability and security of the reign.

Land tenure changes

The European idea of improvement to land favoured investment of labour and capital in land and making the land productive, which was a powerful drive to the great land rush in the British colonies.[10] The Chinese, having been an agrarian society for millennia, had a similar, if not stronger, love for cultivation of land. Some Qing officials in Taiwan saw the potential of vast wasteland becoming productive farms, and felt it a pity that the aborigines were not good farmers. Yet unlike the governments in the British colonies, the Qing government did not seek to change aboriginal land tenure or to "improve" and individualise land title. This was largely because of the property law regime in imperial China.

The Qing inherited the Chinese legal tradition where formal legal processes were used mainly to maintain political control over the society and to deal with criminal offences and official misdeeds. This meant that the government rarely regulated property law matters. The government's place in the land tenure system was to exercise public powers to grant land and charge a tax, and its "ownership" over wasteland did not amount to proprietary rights. The neglecting of property law matters meant that the government was not inclined to transform aboriginal land tenure. This was especially so for the Manchus because they did not have highly developed individualised land tenure themselves.

British colonisers pursued individualisation of title and transformation of aboriginal tenures out of a tradition of upholding individual land title.[11] Private land ownership was created and guaranteed by the state, and transformation of aboriginal land tenure laid in the hands of the government. The Chinese legal tradition, however, left property law matters to Chinese customary practice, which was highly developed and dynamic. Private land ownership was well established, and land transactions had many flexible forms suitable for sophisticated commercial practices. Chinese customary practice was capable of transforming aboriginal land tenure without government involvement.

However the Chinese approach to property law could also mean that government attempts to protect aboriginal land tenure became ineffective. Most of the time the government played no role in regulating private land transactions. When the government did intervene, the methods were administrative and criminal in nature, and were not adequate to regulate the complex and dynamic practices among the people. The focus on cultivating good officials and the reluctance to make law also contributed to the inadequate response to land issues on the frontier.

Japan's style of colonisation and its land policies were also shaped by its legal traditions. The Japanese legal system followed the Chinese style from its inception in the 7th century till the Meiji Restoration in the late 19th century, and then turned towards Western law after that. A fundamental difference between the Japanese legal tradition and the Chinese legal tradition was that, in China, law was "ancillary to the Confucian state philosophy", but in Japan law was the tool of modernisation and civilisation.[12] Whether following Chinese law or Western law, this unique operation of Japan enabled it to rapidly revamp its legal system to serve immediate needs. After a swift transition to legal modernity during the Meiji Restoration, Japan embarked on a modernising journey, and emulated the West in its acquisition and management of overseas colonies. The role of the legal system is evidenced in the contrast between the Qing and Japanese administrations of Taiwan. What a change of legal system could entail is also highlighted in the contrast between Japanese colonisation policies in Hokkaidō before and after the Meiji Restoration.

Apart from settler presence with government support, Western expansion had two other essential concepts: the notion of the state and Western concepts of social organisation such as international law.[13] These concepts were both missing in the Qing administration of Taiwan. In contrast, Japan used these two concepts extensively. Other Western legal instruments concerning property law were also applied by the Japanese, including land titling, registration and surveying. The Japanese colonisation of Taiwan, in effect an example of the imposition of Western styles of colonialism based on Western legal concepts, illustrates the importance of law in the colonising process.

The Qing administration of Taiwan proves that Chinese legal tradition was less likely to favour expansion and colonialism, or to impose Chinese culture, including land tenure, on indigenous peoples. This was consistent with Glenn's observation.[14] It formed a contrast to Western legal traditions and to Japanese legal traditions.

Notes

1 For example, see John C Weaver *The Great Land Rush and the Making of the Modern World, 1659–1900* (McGill-Queen's University Press, Montreal, 2003), ch 7; Richard Boast *Buying the Land, Selling the Land: Governments and Maori Land in the North Island1865–1921* (Victoria University Press, Wellington, 2008), at 137 and 408–409.

2 Boast, ibid, at 25; Stuart Banner *Possessing the Pacific: Land, Settlers, and Indigenous People From Australia to Alaska* (Harvard University Press, Cambridge (MA), 2007), at 60.

3 For example, see Boast, ibid, 19–31 and ch 2; Banner, ibid, ch 3 and 7.

4 Boast, ibid, at 448.

5 At 26.

6 This finding is consistent with John Robert Shepherd *Statecraft and Political Economy on the Taiwan Frontier, 1600–1800* (Stanford University Press, Stanford, 1993), at 370 and 378.

7 Yosaburō Takekoshi (trans George Braithwaite) *Japanese Rule in Formosa* (Longmans, Green and Co, London, 1907), at 230.

8 H Patrick Glenn *Legal Traditions of the World: Sustainable Diversity in Law* (5th ed, Oxford University Press, Oxford, 2014), at 273–274.

9 At 273–274.

10 See Weaver, above n 1, at 81–87 and 360. Also see Richard Boast *The Native Land Court Volume 2: A Historical Study, Cases and Commentary 1888–1909* (Thomson Reuters, Wellington, 2015), at 249–250.

11 See Boast, above n 1, at 42 and 166.

12 Carl Steenstrup *A History of Law in Japan Until 1868* (Brill, Leiden, 1996), at 34 and 36.

13 Glenn, above n 8, at 275–276.

14 Ibid, at 355. Also see discussion in the introductory chapter of this book.

Glossary

ai	隘 guard posts along the aboriginal boundaries
aishou	隘首 head guards, a person who was responsible for organising the guard posts
aizu	隘租 rent that related to guard posts, especially rent paid to the guards
baojia	保甲 a household and neighbourhood registration system
bansei (fanzheng)	蕃政 aboriginal management
dazu	大租 "large rent"
di	地 land
dian	典 pledge
dian	佃 tenant
dou	斗 a measurement unit of approximately 10 litres
fan	番 literally "barbarians", referring to the aborigines
fandi	番地 aboriginal land
fanjie	番界 the aborigines' territory
fanjing	番境 the aboriginal territories
fantun	番屯 aboriginal colonies
fazhi	法治 "governing by law"
fengjin	封禁 "quarantine", the Qing's policy of making the aboriginal territories unavailable for settlement
geiken pi	給墾批 reclamation deed
guandi	官地 "government's land"
guanhuang	官荒 wasteland owned by the government
guantian	官田 "government land" (of the Zheng period)

guanzhuang	官莊 official estates
houshan	後山 "at the back of the mountains", eastern Taiwan
huafan	化番 aborigines who submitted themselves to the government but remained non-acculturated (Qing period); semi-acculturated aborigines (Japanese period)
huang ce	黃冊 yellow register
huangdi	荒地 uncultivated land, wasteland
huishu	回贖 redeem
huomài	活賣 revocable sale
jia	甲 a measurement unit of approximately one hectare
jianmin	奸民 Han "villains"
jienei	界內 "within the boundaries", the settlement area
jiewai	界外 "beyond the boundaries", the aboriginal boundaries
jingtian	井田 an ancient Chinese land system where land was divided into nine plots as in the shape of the character *jing* 井
juemài	絕賣 irrevocable sale
Junjichu	軍機處 Grand Council
kaishan fufan	開山撫番 open the mountains and subjugate the aborigines
kenhu	墾戶 reclaimer
kouliang	口糧 grain ration
li	禮 rite, propriety
li	里 a measurement unit of just over half a kilometre
li	例 precedent, regulations
lifan tongzhi	理番同知 aboriginal affairs sub-prefects
Lifanyuan	理藩院 Board for Governing Outer Territories
litouyin	犁頭銀 "plough-head money", the price paid by a reclaimer to the land permit holder for the right to reclamation
mài	賣 sale
minsei chōkan	民政長官 chief of civil administration
mu	畝 a measurement unit for land area, 1 *mu* is about 666 square metres
paohuang	拋荒 "left to waste", abandoned land

Pepo	平埔 literally “flat land”, referring to the plains aborigines
pu	贌 a form of lease
pugeng	贌耕 tenancy
pushe	贌社 village trade monopoly (of the Dutch period), tax farming (of the Zheng period)
puyin/pudi yin	埔(底)銀 “soil money”, the price paid for the “sub-soil” rights
qi	旗 banner, a Manchu system of organising soldiers and society
qi	契 deed, contract
qianshan	前山 “in the front of the mountains”, the western plains
qidiyin	磧底銀 bond, guarantee money for payment of rent
qing	頃 a measurement unit for land area, 1 *qing* is 100 *mu*
qishui	契稅 stamp duty
renzhi	人治 “governing by men”
sakoku	鎖國 national isolation
she	社 [aboriginal] village
shengfan	生番 non-acculturated aborigines
shexiang	社餉 [aboriginal] village tax
shi	石 a measurement unit for volume, 1 *shi* is just over 100 litres
shoutian	授田 “land grant”
shu	贖 redeem
shufan	熟番 acculturated aborigines
shuizu	水租 “water rent”
Sōtokufu	總督府 Office of the Governor-General
tai	胎 mortgage
Taiwan dao	臺灣道 Taiwan circuit intendant
tian	田 agricultural land
tianzhu	田主 field owner
tiandi	田底 “sub-soil”
tiandian	添典 price top-up for pledge
tianmian	田面 “top-soil”

tongshi	通事 interpreter (of aboriginal villages)
tongtu kouliang tian	通土口糧田 unregistered land which the aborigines held in collective at the village level
touxian	投獻 commendation (of land to the powerful or the privileged class)
tuishou ce	推收册 transaction register
tundi	屯地 a category of land, "company land", land that the government leased and used the rent to support the aboriginal companies
tuniu	土牛 "earthen oxen", aboriginal boundaries (of the Zheng period)
tunlian	屯練 militia
tuntian	屯田 a quasi-military-style organised land reclamation
wangtian	王田 "king's land" (of the Dutch period)
wuzhudi	無主地 "land without an owner", *bona vacantia*
xiaozu	小租 "small rent"
xiedou	械鬥 communal strife
xun Tai yushi	巡臺御史 inspecting censor for Taiwan
yangshan pudi	養贍埔地 "upkeep land", land that was allocated to aboriginal braves for their upkeep
yezhu	業主 literally "proprietary owner", the person who received the land grant wand was the registered taxpayer for the land
yintian	隱田 "hidden land", land reclaimed but not registered for tax
yingpan tian	營盤田 military colonies (of the Zheng period)
yuan	園 dry land
yuanhuang	原荒 "originally waste", virgin land
yuanzhumin baoliudi	原住民保留地 aboriginal reserves
yulin ce	鱼鱗册 "fish scale" register
zhaojia	找價 price top-up for sale
zhuandian	轉典 assigning pledge
zongbing	總兵 regional commander
zu	租 lease, rent

Appendices

Appendix 1

Land deeds quoted in Chapter 4

(1)

具稟人沈紹宏，為懇恩稟請發給告示開墾事。緣北路鹿野草荒埔原為鄭時左武驤將軍舊荒營地一所，甚為廣闊，並無人請耕，伏祈天臺批准宏著李嬰為管事，招佃開墾，三年後輸納國課；並乞天臺批發明示臺道，開載四至，付李嬰前往鹿野草草地起蓋房屋，招佃開墾，永為世業，須至稟者。

今開四至，東至大路及八撐溪，西至龜佛山及崁，南至抱竹及崁仔上，北至溪崁。

康熙二十四年十月　日。

墾荒，現奉上令，准速給照，以便招佃及時料理；候墾耕成熟之後，照例起科，照。

(2)

(原書第一行腐蝕，字劃不存)賦足民事。據墾戶詹陞請打貓梅仔坑寮口荒埔十餘甲，東至梅仔坑枋寮，西至溪，南至山，北至中溪仔。據通事謝章等查明無騐，合行給墾。為此，單給墾戶詹陞即便前往所請界址內開墾輸課，給此執照。

康熙四十七年四月　日給。

(3)

本衙馬鳴山莊地，　內給出水田一甲二分，付佃蔡贊亨前去開墾成田，初年、二年一九五抽，三年依例每甲納經風 搧淨乾好粟八石，車運到倉交納，不得短少，給批，付照。

業主　陳衙

雍正三年十月　日給

(4)

立招批業主簡琳芳，有明 賤 南大肚番愛箸魯霧莊園埔一所，今有林生亨願自備牛工種前來耕種，時約定每甲園埔願貼犁頭五十兩，以為開圳費用之資。其銀即日交訖；其園埔隨即丈明十甲，界址分明，議定每甲佃首年納租粟五石滿，次年納租粟八石滿，以後每甲納租粟八石滿，永遠定例。其租粟至收成之日，務要重風 搧淨，車運到鹿仔港交納，不敢少欠誤課；如有拖欠租粟者，任從業主起耕招佃。倘日後奉憲縣主到莊清丈，俱要照甲納租，佃人不得異言；但佃人要回家之日，先問明業主之後，任聽其脫替，工本業主不得均分。委係二家甘願，各無反悔，恐口無憑，立招批是實。

內分達皆弟名下園 埔三甲銀一十五兩正。

內分此沐姪名下園 埔二甲銀一十五兩正。

雍正七年(己酉)正月　　　　日立招批。

業主　□□□

知見人　陳紹慶

代筆人　林利壽

(5)

立招佃人業 戶李朝榮，明買有大突 青埔一所，坐落土名巴劉巴來，東至柳仔溝埤為界，西至大溝為界，南至入社大車路為界，北至黃邦傑厝後港為界，四至明白。今有招到李思仁、賴東、李祿亭、梁學俊等前來承 賤 開墾，出得埔銀六十五兩正，情願自備牛犁方建築坡圳，前去耕墾，永為己業。歷年所收花利照莊例一九五抽的，及成田之日，限定經丈八十五石滿門為一甲，每一甲經租八石，車運到港交納。二比甘願，日後不敢生端反悔，增加減少，亦不敢升合拖欠；如有拖欠定額，明官究討。口恐無憑，立招佃一紙存照。

即日收過埔銀完，再照。

雍正十年十月　日。

立招佃人　李朝榮

(6)

立合約大武郡社土官蚌肉等，有草地一所，北至水漆林為界，西至 吳宅往海 豐路為界，東至本莊熟園，南至溪為界；四至明白。因課餉無征，今招得丁作周前來出本開築坡圳，以作水田。今當 鄉保通事公議，雍正元年起，每年佃粟五十石斗，系舊斗，番人到莊車運，永遠定例，日後不得聽人唆使生端等情。倘佃人有短少租粟，以及為非等情，系丁作周之事，不干番人之事。此系二比甘願，不敢異言；今欲有憑， 立合約為照

雍正元年八月日

知見　葉伯選

　　　張 苑

立合約　蛤 肉

　　　　丁作周

代書人 李士 元

(7)

仝立合約人下淡水社土官阿裡莫、教冊施也落等，原有草地一所。自肆拾陸年因何周王招得□□□□□□□傳如鐸等開墾成頓物莊。後因本社番民與何周王爭訟，蒙前任縣主宋審斷，頓物莊租粟歸於番民完課。當日番佃面立合約，其築埤開圳費用工本俱係佃人自備，墾成水田業主□□□□□□□十五甲□□□□□□□□□□□□□□□□無異□□□□十餘□，歷年每甲納租七石送社交倉明白。茲因伍拾玖年本社番齒益眾，向佃議增租粟，至控縣主李審斷，加租貳石□□□□□案，番佃兩相允服。茲今頓物莊，各佃名下額租，並審斷所加之租，俱一足收，但今本社眾番，苦無應公，仍向頓物莊各佃借過粟共七百石，於完課供□□□斷□□情願允□□□歷年每甲扣除減租一石五鬥滿爲利。當日業佃面議，每年每甲實收租粟七石五鬥滿，佃人車運本社交倉，永爲定例。其佃人日後有別圖生業以及回唐者，其田底聽憑佃人頂退，抵還工本，業主不得再生枝節。（下略）

康熙陸拾年貳月仝立合約下淡水社土官阿裡莫 (餘略)

(8)

立典契字人下水仔莊陳周，有自己應份鬮分份下水田一段，址在旱溪底。大小三坵，東至園崁，西至添生田，南至添生田，北至番叔田；四至界址明白。今因乏銀別創，先盡問房親人等不能承受，外托中引就向與本宗陳玉麟出首承典，當日三面議定時 值價銀一百五十大員正。其銀即日同中交收足訖；其田隨即踏付銀主前去掌管起耕，招佃耕作，年納大租穀一石，又水租四鬥。其田限自甲子年起，至甲戌年終，聽周備足典契字內銀一足送還，取回原契字；如銀未備，任從銀主耕作，不得刁難。保此田係周應份鬮分物業，與房親人等無幹，亦無重張典掛他人財物，並無拖欠大租及上手來歷交加不明等情；如有此情，周一力抵擋，不幹

銀主之事。此係二比甘願，各無反悔，口恐無憑，立典 契字一紙，鬮書一紙，共二紙，付執為照，行。

即日同中收過典字 內銀一百五十大員正完足，再照，行。

其上手契連在別段，難以開折，再照。

嘉慶九年六月　日。

代筆人　(宗姪)希周
知見人　(胞兄)　起
為中人　葉圓
立典契字人　陳

(9)

立招耕給壓地契眉裏社番破難未 説、乾昆未說，同有承父鬮分熟園 二坵相連，坐落土名舊眉社崙仔下，東至伯巴難未 說 為界，西至蒲旱及陳縣園為界，南至六萬胡及小打晉巫仕園為界，北至車路及打晉巫仕園為界；四至界址明白。經同通土三面丈明三甲，歷年該帶園租粟十二石滿。今因離社窩遠，無力耕作，先盡問本社 內番親不能承耕，外托中招引與漢人楊從官耕作，先收過給壓地銀四百大員正。銀即日同中收訖；園聽楊從官前去翻犁耕作二十年。番 為業主，民為佃 戶，歷年備租粟十二石，付番社運去，不得短欠。限至已滿，未說原給壓地銀取回原契，不得刁難；如銀未還，付銀主再耕作，任從其便，不敢生端異言。保此園係巴難未說、乾

昆未 說兄弟承兄物業，並無叔兄弟姪爭執，及重張交關不明等情；如有不明等情，巴難兄弟自己出頭抵 擋，不幹佃 戶之事。今欲有憑，立招耕給佃契二紙，各執一紙，付執 為照。

即日同中收過給佃銀四百大員正完足，再照。

嘉慶三年十月　日。

代書　胡三重
再見伯　巴難未 說
知見母親　投大夷
為中　□□□
立招耕給壓地契番　巴難未 說
乾昆未 說

Appendix 2

"Land for water deed" 1723 quoted in Chapter 5 (Source: Wen (1957), at 432–434)

公仝立出合約字人，岸裡、搜拺、烏牛欄、舊社等社土官潘敦仔，[此處略去眾社番名]，緣敦等界內之地俱屬旱埔，播租五穀，無水灌溉歷年失收，無奈，眾番鳩集妥議，托中向懇通事張達京，有人能出工本，募工鑿圳，均分灌溉水田者，敦等闔社，愿將西勢南阿河巴之地，東至搭連溝（今罩蘭庄）直透石碑為界，西至山項頂，南至水堀頭（今拺東下堡）與貓霧拺草地分界，與岸裡社社東為界，西南至山頂貓霧拺分界，北至岸裡社社尾與崁頭至往牛頭横車路為界，此係敦等四社界內之地，併無侵碍他人界內旱埔，愿將此酧賞工本，付業主前去招佃開墾，該敦等眾番，日後子子孫孫不得異言，愿將此旱埔，懇托張達京代敦等，請到業戶張振萬前來擔承，自己出本銀九千三百兩開圳，分水與番灌溉，當日三面議定，張振萬開水定汴，私圳內之水定作十分，內八分歸張振萬灌溉自己田地，留二分歸番，灌溉番田，其阿河巴之草地照原踏四至界址內，付張振萬前去開墾，以抵開水工本，立戶陞科，永為己業，保此業係眾番愿割地換水，張振萬愿出銀開水，分番灌溉換地，兩相甘愿，日後子孫不敢言貼言贖侵越等情，保此地係敦等祖地，與他社無干，亦無重約他人，倘有不明，係敦等一力抵當，不干張振萬之事，每年張振萬粟二百石，聽敦等自己到庄車運，此係二比甘愿，兩無迫勒交成，恐口無憑，今欲有憑，公仝立出合約字二紙，各執一紙，存照。

即日批明，敦等四社眾番，寔收到字 內工本銀九千三百兩足訖，批照。

白番　阿打歪搭比　（下略眾番名）

代筆人 張金聲　通事　張達京

業戶　張振萬　土官　潘敦仔

雍正元年十月 日 公仝立出合約字人 岸裡 搜拺 烏牛欄 舊社等社土官潘敦仔、仕那搭比

Bibliography

Abbreviation:

TWWX – *Taiwan Wenxian Congkan* 臺灣文獻叢刊 [Taiwan Literature and Documents Collection] (Taiwan yinhang, Taipei, 1957–1975, 309 titles)

Adas, Michael "Imperialism and Colonialism in Comparative Perspective" (1998) 20 *International History Review* 371–388

Aldrich, Robert and John Connell *The Last Colonies* (Cambridge University Press, Cambridge, 1998)

Andrade, Tonio *How Taiwan Became Chinese: Dutch, Spanish and Han Colonization in the Seventeenth Century* (Columbia University Press, New York, 2008)

——— *Lost Colony: The Untold Story of China's First Great Victory Over the West* (Princeton University Press, Princeton and Oxford, 2011)

——— "Pirates, Pelts, and Promises: The Sino-Dutch Colony of Seventeenth-Century Taiwan and the Aboriginal Village of Favorolang" (2005) 64 *Journal of Asian Studies* 295–321

Atwell, William "The T'ai-ch'ang, T'ien-ch'i, and ch'ung-chun Reigns, 1620–1644" in Frederick W Mote and Denis Twitchett (eds) *The Cambridge History of China Volume 7: The Ming Dynasty, 1368–1644 Part One* 585–640

Azuma, Yoshio 東嘉生 "Qingdai Taiwan zhi tudi suoyou xingtai" 清代臺灣之土地所有形態 [Land Owning System in Qing Taiwan] in *Taiwan jingjishi chuji* 臺灣經濟史初集 [A First Collection of the Economic History of Taiwan] (Taiwan yanjiu congkan 25, Taiwan yinhang, Taipei, 1954) 86–102

Baker, John H *An Introduction to English Legal History* (4th ed, Butterworths, London, 2002)

Banner, Stuart *Possessing the Pacific: Land, Settlers, and Indigenous People From Australia to Alaska* (Harvard University Press, Cambridge (MA), 2007)

——— "Why Terra Nullius? Anthropology and Property Law in Early Australia" (2005) 23 *Law and History* 95–131

Barclay, George W *Colonial Development and Population in Taiwan* (Princeton University Press, Princeton, 1954)

Barclay, Paul D "An Historian Among the Anthropologists: The Inō Kanori Revival and the Legacy of Japanese Colonial Ethnography in Taiwan" (2001) 21(2) *Japanese Studies* 117–136

Bellwood, Peter, James J Fox and Darrell Tryon (eds) *The Austronesians: Historical and Comparative Perspective* (ANU E Press, Canberra, 2006)

Benton, Lauren *A Search for Sovereignty: Law and Geography in European Empires 1400–1900* (Cambridge University Press, Cambridge, 2010)

Blundell, David (ed) *Austronesian Taiwan: Linguistics, History, Ethnology, Prehistory* (revised ed, Shung Ye Museum of Formosan Aborigines, Taipei; Phoebe A Hearst Museum of Anthropology, Berkeley, 2009)

——— "A Century of Research: Austronesian Taiwan, 1897–1997" in David Blundell (ed) *Austronesian Taiwan: Linguistics, History, Ethnology, Prehistory* 3–44

Blust, Robert *The Austronesian Languages* (revised ed, ANU, Canberra, 2013)

——— "The Prehistory of the Austronesia-Speaking Peoples: A View From Language" (1995) 9(4) *Journal of World Prehistory* 453–510

Boast, Richard *Buying the Land, Selling the Land: Governments and Maori Land in the North Island1865–1921* (Victoria University Press, Wellington, 2008)

——— *For the Good of the Natives: Land and Society in the Pacific 1860–1940* (manuscript)

——— *The Native Land Court Volume 2: A Historical Study, Cases and Commentary 1888–1909* (Thomson Reuters, Wellington, 2015)

Boast, Richard, Andrew Erueti, Doug McPhail and Norman F Smith *Maori Land Law* (2nd ed, LexisNexis, Wellington, 2004)

Bodde, Derk and Clarence Morris *Law in Imperial China: Exemplified by 190 Ch'ing Dynasty Cases* (Harvard University Press, Cambridge (MA), 1967)

Borao Mateo, José Eugenio *The Spanish Experience in Taiwan 1626–1642: The Baroque Ending of a Renaissance Endeavor* (Hong Kong University Press, Hong Kong, 2009)

Campbell, William *Formosa Under the Dutch* (Kegan Paul, Trench, Trubner, London, 1903)

Caruthers, Sandra "Charles Le Gendre, American Diplomacy, and Expansionism in Meiji Japan, 1868–1893" (PhD diss, University of Colorado, 1966)

Chan, Su-Chuan 詹素娟 "Taiwan pingpuzu de shenfen rending yu bianqian (1895–1960) – yi hukou zhidu yu guoshi diaocha wei zhongxin" 臺灣平埔族的身分認定與變遷 (1895–1960) – 以戶口制度與國勢調查的'種族'分類為中心 [The Ascertainment and Evolution of the Plains Aborigines' Identity: From the Perspective of the Household Registration System and Census] (2005) 12(2) *Taiwanshi yanjiu* 121–166

Chan, Su-chuan and Chang Su-fan 詹素娟，張素玢 *Taiwan Yuanzhumin shi: Bei Taiwan pingpu zuqun shi* 臺灣原住民史: 北臺灣平埔族群史 [History of Taiwan Aborigines: The Northern Taiwan Plains Aboriginal Groups] (Taiwan Historica, Nantou, 2001)

Chang, Chi-hsiung 張啟雄 "Dongxi guoji zhixu yuanli de chayi: 'zongfan tixi' dui 'zhimin tixi'" 東西國際秩序原理的差異 – '宗藩體系' 對 '殖民體系' ("A Comparison of Eastern and Western Principles of International Order: Suzerainty vs Colonization") (2003) 79 *Zhongyang yanjiuyuan jindaishi yanjiusuo jikan* 47–86

Chang, Chia-ju and Scott Slovic (eds) *Ecocriticism in Taiwan: Identity, Environment, and the Arts* (Lexington, London, 2016)

Chang, Lung-Chih "From Island Frontier to Imperial Colony: Qing and Japanese Sovereignty Debates and Territorial Projects in Taiwan, 1874–1906" (PhD diss, Harvard University, 2003)

——— "From Quarantine to Colonization: Qing Debates on Territorialization of Aboriginal Taiwan in the Nineteenth Century" (2008) 15(4) *Taiwanshi yanjiu* 1–30

Chen, Bin 陳璸 *Chen Qingduangong wenxuan* 陳清端公文選 [Selected Writings of Chen Bin] (TWWX 116)

Chen, Ching-chih "Police and Community Control System in the Empire" in Ramon H Myers and Mark R Peattie (eds) *The Japanese Colonial Empire* 213–239

Chen, Chiu-kun 陳秋坤 *Qingdai Taiwan tuzhu diquan: guanliao, handian yu Anlishe ren de tudi bianqian 1700–1895* 清代臺灣土著地權：官僚，漢佃與岸裡社人的土地變遷 1700–1895 (*Taiwan's Aboriginal Proprietary Rights in the Ch'ing Period: Bureaucracy, Han Tenants and the Transformation of Property Rights of the Anli Tribe, 1700–1895*) (2nd ed, Academia Sinica, Taipei, 1997)

——— "Shijiu shiji chuqi tuzhu diquan wailiu wenti – yi Anlishe de tudi jingying weili" 十九世紀初期土著地權外流問題 – 以岸裡社的土地經營為例 [The Aborigines' Land Loss in the Early 19th Century – A Case Study on the Land Management of the Anli Village] in Chen Chiu-kun and Hsu Hsueh-chi (eds) 陳秋坤, 許雪姬（編）*Taiwan lishi shang de tudi wenti* 臺灣歷史上的土地問題 [Land Issues in Historical Taiwan] (Academia Sinica, Taipei, 1992) 29–56

Chen, Chiu-kun and Hsu Hsueh-chi (eds) 陳秋坤, 許雪姬（編）*Taiwan lishi shang de tudi wenti* 臺灣歷史上的土地問題 [Land Issues in Historical Taiwan] (Academia Sinica, Taipei, 1992)

Chen, Di 陳第 *Dongfanji* 東番記 [Accounts of the Eastern Barbarians, 1603] in Shen Yourong 沈有容 *Minhai zengyan* 閩海贈言 [Words of Praise From the Fujian Sea] (TWWX 56)

Chen, Edward I-te "The Attempt to Integrate the Empire: Legal Perspectives" in Ramon H Myers and Mark R Peattie (eds) *The Japanese Colonial Empire* 240–274

Chen, Guyuan 陳顧遠 *Zhongguo fazhishi* 中國法制史 [Legal History of China] (Zhongguo shudian, Beijing, 1988, facsimile copy of Shangwu yinshuguan, 1934)

Chen, Peigui 陳培桂 *Danshui tingzhi* 淡水廳志 [Gazetteer of Danshui Sub-Prefecture, 1871] (TWWX 172)

Chen, Shujun 陳淑均 *Gamalan tingzhi* 噶瑪蘭廳志 [Gazetteer of Gamalan Sub-Prefecture, 1852] (TWWX 160)

Chen, Wenda 陳文達 *Fengshan xianzhi* 鳳山縣誌 [Gazetteer of Fengshan County, 1719] (TWWX 124)

——— *Taiwan xianzhi* 臺灣縣誌 [Gazetteer of Taiwan County, 1720] (TWWX 103)

Chen, Zhe-san 陳哲三 "Qingdai Nantou xianjing de shuizhen kaizao guanfu yu minjian suo banyan de jiaose" 清代南投縣境的水圳開鑿官府與民間所扮演的角色 [The Roles of the Government and the Society in Opening Water Channels in Nantou County During the Qing Dynasty] (2007) 15 *Fengjia renwen shehui xuebao* 105–141

——— "'Shuishalian' jiqi xiangguan wenti zhi yanjiu" '水沙連'及其相關問題之研究 [A Research on Shuishalian and Related Issues] (1998) 49(2) *Taiwan Wen Hsien* 35–57

Cheng, jia-ying 程家穎 *Taiwan tudi zhidu kaocha baogaoshu* 臺灣土地制度考察報告書 [A Report on the Taiwan Land Tenure, 1914] (TWWX 184)

Chiu, Hsin-hui *The Colonial "Civilizing Process" in Dutch Formosa, 1624–1662* (Brill, Leiden and Boston, 2008)

Chuang, Chi-fa 莊吉發 "Qingdai Taiwan tudi kaifa yu zuqun chongtu" 清代臺灣土地開發與族群衝突 [Land Reclamation and Ethnic Conflicts in Qing Taiwan] (2000) 36 *Taiwan shiji* 3–31

Chuang, Chin-Teh 莊金德 "Qingchu yanjin yanhai renmin toudu lai Tai shimo" 清初嚴禁沿海人民偷渡來臺始末 [An Account of the Prohibition of Migration From Coastal China to Taiwan in the Early Qing Period] (1964) 15(3 & 4) *Taiwan Wen Hsien* 1–20 (Part 1), 40–62 (Part 2)

——— "Qingdai chuqi Taiwan tudi kaifa daoyan" 清代初期臺灣土地開發導言 [An Introduction to Land Reclamation in Taiwan During the Early Qing Period] (1971) 15 & 16 *Taipei Wen Hsien* 166–172

Chuang, Sung-lin 莊松林 "Helan zhi Taiwan Tongzhi" 荷蘭之臺灣統治 [Dutch Administration in Formosa] (1959) 10(3) *Taiwan Wen Hsien* 1–26

Cohen, Jerome Alan, R Randle Edwards and Fu-mei Chang Chen (eds) *Essays on China's Legal Tradition* (Princeton University Press, Princeton, 1980)

Cohn, Bernard S *Colonialism and Its Forms of Knowledge: The British in India* (Princeton University Press, Princeton, 1996)

Crossley, Pamela Kyle "Thinking About Ethnicity in Early Modern China" (1990) 11 *Late Imperial China* 1–35

Davidson, James W *The Island of Formosa: Past and Present* (MacMillan, London and New York, 1903)

Deng, Chuan'an 鄧傳安 *Lice huichao* 蠡測彙鈔 [Measuring the Sea With a Calabash, 1830] (TWWX 9)

Dennerline, Jerry "The Shun-chih Reign" in Willard J Peterson (ed) *The Cambridge History of China Volume 9 Part One* 73–119

Di Cosmo, Nicola "The Extension of Ch'ing Rule Over Mongolia, Sinkiang, and Tibet, 1636–1800" in Willard J Peterson (ed) *The Cambridge History of China Volume 9 Part Two* 111–145

——— "Qing Colonial Administration in Inner Asia" (1998) 20 *International History Review* 287–309

Ding, Yuejian 丁曰建 *Zhi Tai bigaolu* 治臺必告錄 [A Collection of Must-Read Documents on Governing Taiwan, 1868] (TWWX 17)

Ding, Zongluo 丁宗洛 *Chen Qingduangong nianpu* 陳清端公年譜 [A Chronological Biography of Chen Bin, 1825] (TWWX 207)

Elliott, Mark C. *The Manchu Way: The Eight Banners and Ethnic Identity in Late Imperial China* (Stanford University Press, Stanford, 2001)

——— "Review of Pei Huang *Reorienting the Manchus: A Study of Sinicization*" (2011) 54 *Journal of the Economic and Social History of the Orient* 584–588

Entenmann, Robert "Sichuan and Qing Migration Policy" (1980) 4(4) *Ch'ing-shih wen-t'I* 35–54

Eskildsen, Robert "Taiwan: A Periphery in Search of a Narrative" (2005) 64 *Journal of Asian Studies* 281–294

Fairbank, John K (ed) *The Cambridge History of China Volume 10: Late Ch'ing 1800–1911 Part One* (Cambridge University Press, Cambridge, 1978)

——— "The Creation of the Treaty System" in John K Fairbank (ed) *The Cambridge History of China Volume 10* 213–263

Fairbank, John K and Ssu-yu Teng "On the Types and Uses of Ch'ing Documents" (1940) 5 *Harvard Journal of Asiatic Studies* 1–71

Fan, Xian 范咸 *Chongxiu Taiwan fuzhi* 重修臺灣府志 [Revised Gazetteer of Taiwan Prefecture, 1747] (TWWX 105)

Fiskesjö, Magnus "On the 'Raw' and the 'Cooked' Barbarians of Imperial China" (1999) 1 *Inner Asia* 139–168

Fletcher, Joseph "Ch'ing Inner Asia c. 1800" in John K Fairbank (ed) *The Cambridge History of China Volume 10* 35–106

——— "The Heyday of the Ch'ing Order in Mongolia, Sinkiang and Tibet" in John K Fairbank (ed) *The Cambridge History of China Volume 10* 351–408

——— "Sino-Russian Relations, 1800–1862" in John K Fairbank (ed) *The Cambridge History of China Volume 10* 318–350

*Fujian shengli*福建省例 [Regulations of Fujian Province] (TWWX 199)

*Fujian Taiwan zouzhe*福建臺灣奏摺 [Memorials on Taiwan] (TWWX 29)

Fujii, Shizue 藤井志津枝 *Rizhi shiqi Taiwan zongdufu lifan zhengce* 日治時期臺灣總督府理蕃政策 [The Aboriginal Management Policies of the Taiwan *Sōtokufu* During the Japanese Period] (Wenyingtang, Taipei, 1997)

——— *Taiwan yuanzhumin shi: zhengce pian* 臺灣原住民史政策篇 [History of Taiwan Aborigines: The Policy Chapter] (Taiwan Historica, Nantou, 2001)

Gaichi hōseishi 外地法制志 [Legislation of the Colonies] (Ministry of Foreign Affairs, Tokyo, 1990)

Gao, Gongqian 高拱乾 *Taiwan fuzhi* 臺灣府志 [Gazetteer of Taiwan Prefecture, 1694] (TWWX 65)

Getches, David H, Charles F Wilkinson and Robert Williams, Jr *Cases and Materials on Federal Indian Law* (4th ed, West Publishing, St Paul, 1998)

Giersch, Patterson C *Asian Borderlands: The Transformation of Qing China's Yunnan Frontier* (Harvard University Press, Cambridge (MA) and London, 2006)

Glenn, H Patrick *Legal Traditions of the World: Sustainable Diversity in Law* (5th ed, Oxford University Press, Oxford, 2014)

Gordon, Leonard "Japan's Abortive Colonial Venture in Taiwan, 1874" (1965) 37(2) *Journal of Modern History* 171–185

Grajdanzev, Andrew J "Formosa (Taiwan) Under Japanese Rule" (1942) 15 *Pacific Affairs* 311–324

Guy, R Kent *Qing Governors and Their Provinces: The Evolution of Territorial Administration in China, 1644–1796* (University of Washington Press, Seattle, 2010)

——— "Who Were the Manchus? A Review Essay" (2002) 61(1) *Journal of Asian Studies* 151–164

Heuschert, Dorothea "Legal Pluralism in the Qing Empire: Manchu Legislation for the Mongols" (1998) 20 *International History Review* 310–324

Hirakawa, Sukehiro "Japan's Turn to the West" (trans Bob Tadash Wakabayashi) in Marius B Jansen (ed) *The Cambridge History of Japan Volume 5* 432–498

Ho, Ping-ti "In Defence of Sinicization: A Rebuttal of Evelyn Rawski's 'Reenvisioning the Qing'" (1998) 57 *Journal of Asian Studies* 123–155

Ho, Samuel Pao-San "Colonialism and Development: Korea, Taiwan and Kwantung" in Ramon H Myers and Mark R Peattie (eds) *The Japanese Colonial Empire* 347–398

Hoang, Peter "Law of Land Tenure in China: A Practical Treatise on Legal Ownership" (1922–1924) 1 *China Law Review* 90–96 (Part 1); 232–244 (Part 2)

Horng, Goang-jih 洪廣冀 "Linxue, ziben zhuyi yu bianqu tongzhi: Rizhi shiqi linye diaocha yu zhengli shiye de zai sikao" 林學，資本主義與邊區統治：日治時期林野調查與整理事業的再思考 [Modern Forestry, Capitalism and Frontier Management: A Reconsideration of the Investigation and Arrangement of the Forest and Unreclaimed Land in Taiwan During the Japanese Period] (2004) 11(2) *Taiwanshi yanjiu* 77–144

Hostetler, Laura *Qing Colonial Enterprise: Ethnography and Cartography in Early Modern China* (University of Chicago Press, Chicago, 2001)

House, Edward H *The Japanese Expedition to Formosa* (Tokyo, 1875)

Hsu, Wen-Hsiung "From Aboriginal Island to Chinese Frontier: The Development of Taiwan Before 1683" in Ronald G Knapp (ed) *China's Island Frontier: Studies in the historical Geography of Taiwan* 3–29

Hu, Chuan 胡傳 *Taidongzhou caifangce* 臺東州採訪冊 [Draft Gazetteer of Taidong Department, cir 1892–1895] (TWWX 81)

Huang, Fu-san 黃富三 "Anli she yu Hanren hezuo kaifa Qingdai Taiwan zhongbu de lishi yuanyuan" 岸里社與漢人合作開發臺灣中部的歷史淵源 [The History of the

Cooperation Between the Anli Villages and Han Settlers to Reclaim Central Taiwan During the Qing Dynasty] (1998) 16(2) *Hanxue yanjiu* 61–78

——— "Qingdai Taiwan yimin de gengdi qude wenti jiqi dui tuzhu de yingxiang" 清代臺灣移民的耕地取得問題及其對土著的影響 [The Methods of Acquiring Land by Migrants in Qing Taiwan and the Effects on the Aborigines] (1981) 11 *Shih-huo* 19–36 & 72–92

Huang, Huan-yao 黃煥堯 "Qingji Taiwan fanhuan shijian zhi benzhi tantao" 清季臺灣番患事件之本質探討 [A Discussion on the Nature of Aboriginal Attacks in Qing Taiwan] (1987) 79 *Taipei Wen Hsien* 129–206

——— "Qingling shiqi Taiwan de fanhuan fangzhi" 清領時期臺灣的番患防治 [The Prevention and Management of Aboriginal Attacks in Qing Taiwan] (1988) 32/33 *Gaoshi wenxian* 21–105

Huang, Pei *Reorienting the Manchus: A Study of Sinicization, 1583–1795* (Cornell University, Ithaca, 2011)

Huang, Shujing 黃叔璥 *Taihai shichalu* 臺海使槎錄 [Records of a Tour on Duty Over the Taiwan Seas, cir 1722] (TWWX 4)

Huang, Ying-kuei 黃應貴 (ed) *Taiwan tuzhu shehui wenhua yanjiu lunwenji* 臺灣土著社會文化研究論文集 [A Collection of Research Essays on the Society and Culture of Taiwan's Mountain Aborigines] (Lianjing, Taipei, 1986)

——— "Taiwan tuzhuzu de liangzhong shehui leixing jiqi yiyi" 臺灣土著族的兩種社會類型及其意義 [The Two Types of Taiwan Mountain Aboriginal Societies and Their Significance] in Huang Ying-kuei (ed) *Taiwan tuzhu shehui wenhua yanjiu lunwenji* 3–43

*Huangchao wenxian tongkao*皇朝文獻通考 [Comprehensive Collection of Important Documents of the Qing Dynasty, 1787]

*Hubu zeli*戶部則例 [Regulations of the Ministry of Households, cir 1865] (Chinese Text Project, www.ctext.org)

Hucker, Charles O *A Dictionary of Official Titles in Imperial China* (Stanford University Press, Stanford, 1985)

Hui, Tsun 惠邨 "Qingdai Taiwan zhi zufu" 清代臺灣之租賦 [Types of Rents in Qing Taiwan] (1959) 10(2) *Taiwan Wen Hsien* 91–147

Hung, Chien-Chao *A History of Taiwan* (Cerchio Iniziative Editoriali via Gambalunga, Rimini, 2000)

——— "Taiwan Under the Cheng Family: Sinicization After Dutch Rule" (PhD diss, Georgetown University, 1981)

Inō, Kanori 伊能嘉矩 *Taiwan banjin jijō* 臺灣蕃人事情 [Notes on Taiwanese Aborigines] (Taiwan Sōtokufu, Taipei, 1900)

——— *Taiwan Banseishi* 臺灣蕃政志 [A History of Aboriginal Management in Taiwan] (Taiwan Sōtokufu, Taipei, 1904)

——— (trans Taiwan Historica) *Taiwan wenhua zhi* 臺灣文化志 [A History of Taiwan's Civilisation] (Chinese trans Rev ed, Taiwan shufang, Taipei, 2011)

Jansen, Marius B (ed) *The Cambridge History of Japan Volume 5: The Nineteenth Century* (Cambridge University Press, Cambridge, 1989)

——— "Introduction" in Marius B Jansen (ed) *The Cambridge History of Japan Volume 5* 1–49

——— "Japanese Imperialism: Late Meiji Perspectives" in Ramon H Myers and Mark R Peattie (eds) *The Japanese Colonial Empire* 61–79

Ji, Yunfei 季雲飛 "Tongzhi jiaxu qian Qing zhengfu Taiwan yimin zhengce zhi tanxi" 同治甲戌前清政府臺灣移民政策之探析 [An Analysis of the Qing Government's Policies Concerning Migration to Taiwan Before 1874] (1998) 5 *Xueshujie* 64–68

Jiang, Yuying 蔣毓英 *Taiwan fuzhi* 臺灣府志 [Gazetteer of Taiwan Prefecture, cir 1689] (Taiwansheng wenxian weiyuanhui, Nantou, 1993)

*Jiaxu gongdu chaocun*甲戌公牘鈔存 [Documents Relating to the 1874 Incident] (TWWX 39)

Johnson, Denise R "Reflection on the Bundle of Rights" (2007) 32 *Vermont Law Review* 247–272

Jones, Susan Mann and Philip A Kuhn "Dynastic Decline and the Roots of Rebellion" in John K Fairbank (ed) *The Cambridge History of China Volume 10* 107–162

Ka, Chih-ming 柯志明 *Fantoujia: Qingdai Taiwan zuqun zhengzhi yu shufan diquan* 番頭家: 清代臺灣族群政治與熟番地權 (*The Aborigine Landlord: Ethnic Politics and Aborigine Land Rights in Qing Taiwan*) (Academia Sinica, Taipei, 2003)

——— "Fanxiaozu de xingcheng yu yanbian: Anli xinshe diyu shefan kouliangtian de zudian anpai" 番小租的形成與演變：岸裡新社地域社番口糧田的租佃安排 ("Formation and Transformation of Aborigine Small-Rent Land Tenure: Land Tenancy of Tribesman's Ration Plot in Anli New Territory") (2008) 15(3) *Taiwanshi yanjiu* 57–137

——— *Japanese Colonialism in Taiwan: Land Tenure, Development, and Dependency: 1895–1945* (Westview Press, Boulder, 1998)

Kang, Peter康培德 *Taiwan yuanzhumin shi zhengce pian: He Xi Mingzheng shiqi* 臺灣原住民史政策篇: 荷西明鄭時期 [History of Taiwan Aborigines: The Policy Chapter: The Dutch, Spanish and Zheng Periods] (Taiwan Historica, Nantou, 2005)

Kawaguchi, Choju 川口長孺 *Taiwan Zhengshi jishi* 臺灣鄭氏紀事 [Chronicles of the Zhengs of Taiwan, 1828] (TWWX 5)

Ke, Peiyuan 柯培元 *Gamalan zhilüe* 噶瑪蘭志略 [Brief Records of Gamalan, 1837] (TWWX 92)

Kim, Hyung I *Fundamental Legal Concepts of China and the West: A Comparative Study* (Kennikat Press, New York, 1981)

Knapp, Ronald G (ed) *China's Island Frontier: Studies in the Historical Geography of Taiwan* (University Press of Hawaii, Honolulu, 1980)

Knoblock, John *Xunzi: A Translation and Study of the Complete Works* (Stanford University Press, Stanford, 1988)

Kondo, Masami 近藤正己 (trans Lin Shi-ting) *Zonglizhan yu Taiwan: Riben zhimindi de bengkui* 總力戰與臺灣—日本殖民地的崩潰 [Total War and Taiwan: The Collapse of the Japanese Colony] (NTU, Taipei, 2014)

Kroker, Edward "The Concept of Property in Chinese Customary Law" (1959) Ser 3 Vol 7 *Transactions of the Asiatic Society of Japan* 123–146

Kublin, Hyman "The Evolution of Japanese Colonialism" (1959) 2 *Comparative Studies in Society and History* 67–84

Lamley, Harry J "Subethnic Rivalry in the Ch'ing Period" in Emily Martin Ahern and Hill Gates (eds) *The Anthropology of Taiwanese Society* (Stanford University Press, Palo Alto, 1981) 282–318

——— "Taiwan Under Japanese Rule, 1895–1945: The Vicissitudes of Colonialism" in Murray A Rubinstein (ed) *Taiwan: A New History* (revised ed, Routledge, New York, 2015) 201–260

Lan, Dingyuan 藍鼎元 *Dongzheng ji* 東征集 [Collection of Records of the Eastern Expedition, 1732] (TWWX 12)

——— *Luzhou chuji* 鹿洲初集 [First Collection of Lan Dingyuan's Writings] (Chinese Text Project, www.ctext.org)

——— *Ping Tai jilüe* 平臺紀略 [Brief Accounts of the Pacification of Taiwan, 1723] (TWWX 14)

Le Gendre, Charles *Is Aboriginal Formosa a Part of the Chinese Empire? An Unbiased Statement of the Question* (Lane, Crawford & Co, Shanghai, 1874)

——— *Reports on Amoy and the Island of Formosa* (Government Printing Office, Washington, 1871)

Lee, Robert HG *The Manchurian Frontier in Ch'ing History* (Harvard University Press, Cambridge (MA), 1970)

Lewis, M Paul, Gary F Simons and Charles D Fenning "Ethnologue: Languages of Taiwan", standalone report in the series of *Ethnologue: Languages of the World* (18th ed, SIL International, Dallas, 2015)

Li, Feng "'Feudalism' and Western Zhou China: A Criticism" (2003) 63 *Harvard Journal of Asiatic Studies* 115–144

Li, Gertraude Roth "State Building Before 1644" in Willard J Peterson (ed) *The Cambridge History of China Volume 9 Part One* 9–72

Li, Ju-ho and Chuang Chin-Teh (eds) 李汝和, 莊金德(編) *Taiwansheng tongzhi* 臺灣省通志 [A Comprehensive History of Taiwan Province] (Taiwansheng wenxian weiyuanhui, Taizhong, 1972) Vol 10

Li, Li and Zhao Guohui 李理，趙國輝 "Li Xiande yu Riben diyici qin Tai" [Le Gendre and Japan's First Invasion of Taiwan] (2007) 3 *Jindaishi yanjiu* 100–116

Li, Paul Jen-kuei 李壬癸 "Formosan Languages: The State of the Art" in David Blundell (ed) *Austronesian Taiwan: Linguistics, History, Ethnology, Prehistory* 47–70

——— "Taiwan pingpuzu de zhonglei jiqi xianghu guanxi" 臺灣平埔族的種類及其相互關係 [The Classification of Taiwanese Plains Aborigines and Their Inter-Relationships] in Zhang Yan-xian, Li Xiao-feng and Dai Bao-cun (eds) 張炎憲，李筱峯，戴寶村(編) *Taiwanshi lunwen jingxuan* 臺灣史論文精選 [Selected Essays on Taiwan History] (Yushan, Taipei, 1996) 43–68

——— *Xingang wenshu yanjiu* 新港文書研究 (*Studies of Sinkang Manuscripts*) (Academia Sinica, Taipei, 2010)

Li, Wen-liang 李文良 "Diguo de shanlin: Rizhi shiqi Taiwan shanlin zhengceshi yanjiu" 帝國的山林 – 日治時期臺灣山林政策史研究 [The Empire's Forest: A Research on the History of Taiwan Forest Policies During the Japanese Period] (PhD diss, NTU, 2001)

——— "Linye zhengli shiye yu dong Taiwan tudi suoyouquan zhi chengli xingtai, 1910–1925" 林野整理事業與東臺灣土地所有權之成立形態, 1910–1925 [The Forestland Investigation Project and Methods of Establishing Land Ownership in Eastern Taiwan, 1910–1925] (1997) 2 *Dong Taiwan yanjiu* 169–195

——— *Qingdai nan Taiwan de yiken yu Kejia shehui (1680–1790)* 清代南臺灣的移墾與客家社會 [Land Reclamation and Hakka Communities in Southern Taiwan During the Qing Dynasty] (NTU, Taipei, 2011)

Li, Zhi-yin 李志殷 "Taiwan tudi dengji zhidu bianqian zhi yanjiu" 臺灣土地登記制度變遷之研究 [A Research on the Evolution of Taiwan Land Registration System] (LLM diss, Taiwan National Chengchi University, 2010)

Lian, Heng 連橫*Taiwan tongshi* 臺灣通史 [A Comprehensive History of Taiwan, 1918] (TWWX 128)

Liang, Chih-hui and Chung Yu-lan 梁志輝，種幼蘭 *Taiwan yuanzhumin shi: Zhong Taiwan pingpu zuqun shi* 臺灣原住民史: 中臺灣平埔族群史 [History of Taiwan Aborigines: The Central Taiwan Plains Aboriginal Groups] (Taiwan Historica, Nantou, 2001)

——— *Taiwan yuanzhumin shiliao huibian di qi ji* 臺灣原住民史料彙編第7輯 [A Collection of Historic Records Concerning the Taiwanese Aborigines, vol 7] (Taiwansheng wenxian weiyuanhui, Nantou, 1998)

Liao, Ping-hui and David Der-wei Wang (eds) *Taiwan Under Japanese Colonial Rule, 1895–1945* (Columbia University Press, New York, 2006)

Lin, Chiou-mien 林秋綿 "Taiwan geshiqi tudi zhengce yanbian jiqi yingxiang zhi tantao" 臺灣各時期土地政策演變及其影響之探討 [The Evolution and Influence of Aboriginal Land Policies of Different Periods in Taiwan] (2001) 2 *Taiwan tudi yanjiu* 23–40

Lin, Qiong-hua 林瓊華 "Taiwan yuanzhumin tudi chanquan zhi yanbian, 1624–1945" [The Evolution of Taiwan Aborigines' Land Rights, 1624–1945] (PhD diss, Soochow University, 1997)

Lin, Shu-Ya 林淑雅 "Jie/chonggou Taiwan yuanzhu minzu tudi zhengce" 解/重構臺灣原住民族土地政策 ("De-/Reconstructing the Land Policies for Indigenous Peoples in Taiwan") (PhD diss, NTU, 2007)

Lin, Wen-kai 林文凱 "'Ye ping qi guan'? Qingdai Taiwan tudi yezhuquan yu susong wenhua de fenxi" "業憑契管"？清代臺灣土地業主權與訴訟文化的分析 ["Deed Determines *Ye*"? An Analysis on *Yezhu* Rights and Litigation Culture in Qing Taiwan] (2011) 18(2) *Taiwanshi yanjiu* 1–52

Lin, Yu-ju 林玉茹 "You yulin tuce kan Qingmo houshan de qingfu shiye yu diquan fenpei xingtai" 由魚鱗圖冊看清末後山的清賦事業與地權分配形態 [The Land Survey Project and the Pattern of Land Rights Distribution in Eastern Taiwan During the Late Qing Period as Seen From the "Fish-scale" Land Register] (1997) 2 *Dong Taiwan yanjiu* 131–168

Lin, Yu-ju and Wei Dong 林玉茹，畏冬 "Lin Shuangwen shijian qian de Taiwan bianqu tuxiang: yi Qianlong 49 nian Taiwan fanjie zixiantu wei zhongxin" 林爽文事件前的臺灣邊區圖像：以乾隆49年臺灣番界紫綫圖爲中心 [Frontier Areas in Taiwan Before the Lin Shuangwen Uprising: An Investigation Centering on the 1784 Purple-line Aboriginal Boundaries] (2012) 19(3) *Taiwanshi yanjiu* 47–94

Linshi, Taiwan Jiuguan Diaochahui 臨時臺灣舊慣調查會 *Taiwan sifa* 臺灣私法 [Private Law of Taiwan] (Chinese translation, Taiwansheng wenxian weiyuanhui, Taizhong, 1990, original first published in 1910)

——— *Taiwan sifa fulu cankaoshu* 臺灣私法附錄參考書 [Private Law of Taiwan Reference Book] (Taipei, 1910)

Liu, Ao 劉敖 *Xun Tai tuisilu* 巡臺退思錄 [Reflections on Being a Circuit Intendant in Taiwan] (TWWX 21)

Liu, Liangbi 劉良璧 *Chongxiu Fujian Taiwan fuzhi* 重修福建臺灣府志 [Revised Gazetteer of Taiwan Prefecture, Fujian, 1741] (TWWX 74)

Liu Mingchuan fu Tai qianhou dang'an 劉銘傳撫臺前後檔案 [Historic Documents Before and After Liu Mingchuan's Governorship in Taiwan] (TWWX 276)

Liu, Yi-chang 劉益昌 *Taiwan yuanzhumin shi: shiqian pian* 臺灣原住民史：史前篇 [History of Taiwan Aborigines: Prehistory] (Taiwan Historica, Nantou, 2002)

Liu, Ze-min 劉澤民 *Dajia dongxishe guwenshu* 大甲東西社古文書 [Historic Documents Concerning the Dajia East and Dajia West Villages] (Taiwan Historica, Nantou, 2003)

——— *Pingpu baishe guwenshu* 平埔百社古文書 [Historic Documents of a Hundred Plains Aboriginal Villages] (Taiwan Historica, Nantou, 2002)

Liu Zhuangsugong zouyi 劉莊肅公奏議 [Memorials of Liu Mingchuan] (TWWX 27)

Lu, Chih-chun 鹿智鈞 "Jin ershinian lai (1989–2009) baqi zhidu yanjiu de huigu yu taolun" 近二十年來 (1989–2009) 八旗制度研究的回顧與討論 [A Review and Discussion of the Research of the Eight Banner System in the Past 20 Years] (2010) 14 *Shiyun* 125–175

Luo, Dachun 羅大春 *Taiwan haifang bing kaishan riji* 臺灣海防並開山日記 [A Journal of Maritime Defence and Mountain Opening in Taiwan] (TWWX 308)

Mabo v Queensland (No 2) [1992] HCA 23 (High Court of Australia)
Manser, Martin H (ed) *Concise English-Chinese Chinese-English Dictionary* (2nd ed, Oxford University Press, Oxford, 1999)
Meng, Sen 孟森 "Baqi zhizhu kaoshi" 八旗制度攷實 [A Research on the Eight Banner System] (1936) 6 *Zhongyang yanjiuyuan lishi yuyan yanjiusuo jikan* 343–412
Mio, Kishimoto 岸本美緒 "Mingqing shidai de zhaojia huisu wenti" 明清時代的"找價回贖" 問題 [The Issue of Price Top-Up and Redemption During the Ming and Qing Dynasties] in Yang Yifan and Terada Hiroaki (eds) *Zhongguo fazhishi kaozheng disijuan bingpian* 423–459
Morrison, Wayne (ed) *Blackstone's Commentaries on the Laws of England* (Cavendish, London, 2001)
Mote, Frederick W *Imperial China 900–1800* (Harvard University Press, Cambridge (MA), 1999)
Mote, Frederick W and Denis Twitchett (eds) *The Cambridge History of China Volume 7: The Ming Dynasty, 1368–1644 Part One* (Cambridge University Press, Cambridge, 1988)
Myers, Ramon H and Mark R Peattie (eds) *The Japanese Colonial Empire, 1895–1945* (Princeton University Press, Princeton, 1984)
Nakamura, Kichisaburō *The Formation of Modern Japan: A View From Legal History* (Centre for East Asian Cultural Studies, Tokyo, 1962)
Ngati Apa v Attorney-General [2003] NZCA 117 (New Zealand Court of Appeal)
Norihito, Mizuno "Qing China's Reaction to the 1874 Japanese Expedition to the Taiwan Aboriginal Territories" (2009) 16 *Sino-Japanese Studies* 99–125
Okada, Mitsuharu Vincent "The Plight of Ainu, Indigenous People of Japan" (2012) 1(1) *Journal of Indigenous Social Development* 1–14
Osterhammel, Jürgen (trans Shelley L Frisch) *Colonialism: A Theoretical Overview* (Markus Wiener Publishers, Princeton, 1997)
Pan, Ying 潘英 *Taiwan pingpuzu shi* 臺灣平埔族史 [History of the Taiwanese Plains Aborigines] (Nantian, Taipei, 1996)
——— *Taiwan yuanzhu minzu de lishi yuanliu* 臺灣原住民族的歷史源流 [History of the Taiwanese Aboriginal Groups] (Taiyuan, Taipei, 1998)
Pasternak, Shiri "Jurisdiction and Settler Colonialism: Where Do Laws Meet?" (2014) 29 *Canadian Journal of Law and Society* 145–161
Peattie, Mark R "Introduction" in Ramon H Myers and Mark R Peattie (eds) *The Japanese Colonial Empire* 3–52
——— "Japanese Attitudes Toward Colonialism, 1895–1945" in Ramon H Myers and Mark R Peattie (eds) *The Japanese Colonial Empire* 80–127
Peng, Yuxin 彭雨新 *Qingdai tudi kaiken shi* 清代土地開墾史 [History of Land Reclamation During the Qing Dynasty] (Nongye, Beijing, 1990)
Perdue, Peter C *China Marches West: The Qing Conquest of Central Eurasia* (Harvard University Press, Cambridge (MA), 2005)
——— "Comparing Empires: Manchu Colonialism" (1998) 20 *International History Review* 255–262
Peterson, Willard J (ed) *The Cambridge History of China Volume 9: The Ch'ing Dynasty to 1800 Part One* (Cambridge University Press, Cambridge, 2002)
——— *The Cambridge History of China Volume 9: The Ch'ing Dynasty to 1800 Part Two* (Cambridge University Press, Cambridge, 2016)
Pyle, Kenneth B "Meiji Conservatism" in Marius B Jansen (ed) *The Cambridge History of Japan Volume 5* 674–720

Qinding Daqing huidian shili 欽定大清會典事例 [Imperially Approved Precedents of the Great Qing Institutes, 1886] (Chinese Text Project, www.ctext.org)

Qinding pingding Taiwan jilüe 欽定平定臺灣紀略 [Imperially Approved Accounts of Pacifying Taiwan] (TWWX 102)

Qingdai Taiwan dazu diaochashu 清代臺灣大租調查書 [Collection of Large Rent Documents in Qing Taiwan] (TWWX 152)

Qing Dezong shilu xuanji 清德宗實錄選輯 [Selected Veritable Records of the Guangxu Emperor] (TWWX 193)

Qing Gaozong shilu xuanji 清高宗實錄選輯 [Selected Veritable Records of the Qianlong Emperor] (TWWX 186)

Qing huidian Taiwan shili 清會典臺灣事例 [Great Qing Institutes, Precedents Concerning Taiwan] (TWWX 226)

Qing Muzong shilu xuanji 清穆宗實錄選輯 [Selected Veritable Records of the Tongzhi Emperor] (TWWX 190)

Qing Renzong shilu xuanji 清仁宗實錄選輯 [Selected Veritable Records of the Jiaqing Emperor] (TWWX 187)

Qing Shengzu shilu xuanji 清聖祖實錄選輯 [Selected Veritable Records of the Kangxi Emperor] (TWWX 165)

Qing Shizong shilu xuanji 清世宗實錄選輯 [Selected Veritable Records of the Yongzheng Emperor] (TWWX167)

Qing Xuanzong shilu xuanji 清宣宗實錄選輯 [Selected Veritable Records of the Daoguang Emperor] (TWWX 188)

Ramzy, Austin "Taiwan's President Apologizes to Aborigines for Centuries of Injustice" *New York Times* (Online ed, New York, 1 August 2016), Sinosphere

Rawski, Evelyn S "Reenvisioning the Qing: The Significance of the Qing Period in Chinese History" (1996) 55 *Journal of Asian Studies* 829–850

Reardon-Anderson, James "Land Use and Society in Manchuria and Inner Mongolia During the Qing Dynasty" (2000) 5 *Environmental History* 503–530

The Republic of China Yearbook 2015 (Executive Yuan, Taipei, 2015)

Riju shiqi yuanzhumin xingzheng zhigao 日据時期原住民行政志稿 [Administration of Aborigines During the Japanese Period, Translation of *Ribanshikō* Compiled by the Police Administration Bureau, Taiwan *Sōtokufu*, 4 vol] (Taiwansheng wenxian weiyuanhui, Nantou, 1997)

Rowe, William T *China's Last Empire: The Great Qing* (Belknap Press of Harvard University Press, Cambridge (MA), 2009)

——— "Social Stability and Social Change" in Willard J Peterson (ed) *The Cambridge History of China Volume 9 Part One* 473–562

Ruan, Minxi 阮旻錫 *Haishang jianwenlu* 海上見聞錄 [Things Seen and Heard Over the Seas] (TWWX 24)

Said, Edward *Culture and Imperialism* (Random House, New York, 1994)

Secher, Ulla "The Meaning of Radical Title: The Pre-*Mabo* Authorities Explained" (2005) 11 *Australia Property Law Journal* 179–208 (I) & 209–243 (II)

Sheng, Ch'ing-I 盛清沂 "Qingdai Taiwan Tong-Guang zhiji kaishan fufan shishi biannian" 清代臺灣同光之際開山撫番史事編年 [Chronicles of the "Opening the Mountains and Subjugating the Aborigines" Campaigns During the Tongzhi and Guangxu Years] (1979) 30(3) *Taiwan Wen Hsien* 1–26

——— "Xinzhu, Taoyuan, Miaoli sanxian diqu kaifashi" 新竹、桃園、苗栗三縣地區開發史 [The History of Reclamation in the Three Counties of Xinzhu, Taoyuan and Miaoli]

(1980) 31(4) *Taiwan Wen Hsien* 154–176 (Part I); (1981) 32(1) *Taiwan Wen Hsien* 136–157 (Part II)

Sheng, Ch'ing-I, Wang Shi-lang and Gao Shu-fan 盛清沂, 王詩琅，高樹藩 *Taiwan shi* 臺灣史 [History of Taiwan] (Taiwansheng wenxian weiyuanhui, Taizhong, 1977)

Shepherd, John Robert *Statecraft and Political Economy on the Taiwan Frontier, 1600–1800* (Stanford University Press, Stanford, 1993)

——— "Taiwan Prefecture in the Eighteenth Century" in Willard J Peterson (ed) *The Cambridge History of China Volume 9 Part Two* 77–110

Shi, Lang 施琅 *Jinghai jishi* 靖海紀事 [Records of Pacifying the Seas] (TWWX 13)

Shih, Tien-fu 施添福 *Qingdai Taiwan de diyu shehui: Zhuqian diqu de lishi dili yanjiu* 清代臺灣的地域社會：竹塹地區的歷史地理研究 [The Local Society in Qing Taiwan: A Research on the Historical Geography of the Zhuqian Area] (Xinzhuxian wenhua ju, Xinzhu, 2001)

——— "Qingdai Taiwan 'fanli bu'an gengzuo' de yuanyou" 清代臺灣'番黎不諳耕作'的緣由 [The Reasons Behind the Aborigines Being "Unskilful at Farming"] (1990) 69 *Bulletin of the Institute of Ethnology Academia Sinica* 67–92

*Shijing*詩經 [Book of Songs] (Chinese Text Project, www.ctext.org)

Shimizu, Akitoshi "Colonialism and the Development of Modern Anthropology" in Jan van Bremen and Akitoshi Shimizu (eds) *Anthropology and Colonialism in Asia and Oceania* 115–171

Simpson, Alfred W B *A History of the Land Law* (2nd ed, Clarendon Press, Oxford, 1986)

Song, Tsêng-chang 宋增璋 "Qingdai Taiwan fuken cuoshi zhi chengxiao jiqi yingxiang" 清代臺灣撫墾措施之成效及其影響 [The Consequences and Influences of the Qing's Land and Aboriginal Policies in Taiwan] (1979) 30(1) *Taiwan Wen Hsien* 142–156

——— *Taiwan fuken zhi* 臺灣撫墾志 [History of Aboriginal Management and Land Reclamation in Taiwan] (2nd ed, Taiwansheng wenxian weiyuanhui, Taizhong, 1997)

Spence, Jonathan D "The K'ang-hsi Reign" in Willard J Peterson (ed) *The Cambridge History of China Volume 9 Part One* 120–182

Steenstrup, Carl *A History of Law in Japan Until 1868* (Brill, Leiden, 1996)

Struve, Lynn A "The Southern Ming, 1644–1662" in Frederick W Mote and Denis Twitchett (eds) *The Cambridge History of China Volume 7: The Ming Dynasty, 1368–1644 Part One* 641–725

Sugimoto, Tomonori "The Yellow Man's Burden: The Politics of Settler Colonialism in Hokkaidō and Taiwan" (MA thesis, University of California, San Diego, 2013)

Sutton, Donald S "Violence and Ethnicity on a Qing Colonial Frontier: Customary and Statutory Law in the Eighteenth-Century Miao Pale" (2003) 37 *Modern Asian Studies* 41–80

Tai, Yen-hui 戴炎輝 "Qingdai Taiwan xiangzhuang zhi shehui de kaocha" 清代臺灣鄉莊之社會的考察 [An Investigation of the Local Society in Qing Taiwan] (1963) *Taiwan yinhang jikan* 198–228

——— "Qingdai Taiwan zhi daxiaozu ye" 清代臺灣之大小租業 [The Large Rent and Small Rent Rights in Qing Taiwan] 1963(4) *Taipei Wen Hsien* 1–47

——— *Qingdai Taiwan zhi xiangzhi* 清代臺灣之鄉治 [The Administration at the Town and Village Levels in Qing Taiwan] (Lianjing, Taipei, 1979)

Tai'an huilu bingji 臺案彙錄丙集 [Taiwan Document Collections Series C] (TWWX 176)

Tai'an huilu jiaji 臺案彙錄甲集 [Taiwan Documents Collection Series A] (TWWX 31)

Taiwan Guanxi Yanjiuhui 臺灣慣習研究會 *Taiwan guanxi jishi* 臺灣慣習記事 [Records of Customs of Taiwan] (Chinese translation, Taiwansheng wenxian weiyuanhui, Taizhong, 1984)

Taiwan lifan guwenshu 臺灣理蕃古文書 [Historic Documents Concerning Taiwan Aboriginal Affairs] (Chengwen, Taipei, 1983)

Taiwan Shiliao Jicheng Bianji Weiyuanhui 臺灣史料集成編輯委員會*Ming Qing Taiwan dang'an huibian* 明清臺灣檔案彙編 [Collection of Historic Documents Concerning Taiwan during the Ming and Qing Dynasties] (Yuanliu, Taipei, 2004–2009)

Taiwan Sōtokufu Banzoku Chōsakai 臺灣總督府蕃族調查會 *Taiwan fanzu diaocha baogaoshu* 臺灣番族調查報告書 [Investigation Reports on the Taiwanese Aborigines] (trans Academia Sinica, Taipei, 2007)

——— *Taiwan fanzu guanxi diaocha baogaoshu* 臺灣番族慣習調查報告書 [Investigation Reports on the Customs of the Taiwanese Aborigines (trans Academia Sinica, Taipei, 1996–2003)

Taiwan Sōtokufu Rinji tochi chōsakyoku 臺灣總督府臨時土地調查局 *Taiwan tochi kankō ippan* 臺灣土地慣行一斑 [Overview of Customary Land Tenure in Taiwan] (Taipei, 1905)

Taiwan zongdufu dang'an zhongyiben 臺灣總督府檔案中譯本 [Chinese Translation of the Administrative Files of the Taiwan *Sōtokufu*] (Taiwansheng wenxian weiyuanhui, Nantou, 1992)

Takakura, Shinichiro (trans John A Harrison) *The Ainu of Northern Japan* (The American Philosophical Society, Philadelphia, 1960)

Takekoshi, Yosaburō (trans George Braithwaite) *Japanese Rule in Formosa* (Longmans, Green and Co, London, 1907)

Tang, Qiyu 唐啟宇 *Lidai tunken yanjiu* 歷代屯墾研究 [A Research on Land Reclamation Through *tuntian* in the Various Dynasties] (Zhengzhong, Shanghai, 1947)

——— *Zhongguo de kenzhi* 中國的墾殖 [Land Reclamation and Colonisation in China] (2nd ed, Yongxiang, Shanghai, 1952)

Tavares, Antonio C "The Japanese Colonial State and the Dissolution of the Late Imperial Frontier Economy in Taiwan, 1886–1909" (2005) 64 *Journal of Asian Studies* 361–385

Teng, Emma Jinhua *Taiwan's Imagined Geography: Chinese Colonial Travel Writing and Pictures, 1683–1895* (Harvard University Asia Centre, Cambridge (MA), 2004)

Terada, Hiroaki 寺田浩明 "Tianmian tiandi guanli de falü xing: yi gainianxing de fenxi weizhu" 田面田底慣例的法律性 – 以概念性的分析為主 [The Legal Nature of the Customary Practice of Top-Soil and Sub-Soil Rights: A Conceptual Analysis] in Yang Yifan and Terada Hiroaki (eds) *Zhongguo fazhishi kaozheng disijuan bingpian* 344–422

Thompson, Laurence G "The Earliest Chinese Eyewitness Accounts of the Formosan Aborigines" (1964) 23 *Monumenta Serica* 163–204

Tian, Huan "Governing Imperial Border: Insights From the Study of the Implementation of Law in Qing Xinjiang" (PhD diss, Columbia University, 2012)

Tongzhi Jiaxu ribing qin Tai shimo 同治甲戌日兵侵臺始末 [Documents on the 1874 Japanese Invasion of Taiwan] (TWWX 38)

Tryon, Darrell "Proto-Austronesian and the Major Austronesian Subgroups" inPeter Bellwood, James J Fox and Darrell Tryon (eds) *The Austronesians: Historical and Comparative Perspective* 19–41

Ts'ao, Yung-ho 曹永和 *Taiwan zaoqi lishi yanjiu* 臺灣早期歷史研究 [A Research on the Early History of Taiwan] (Lianjing, Taipei, 1979)

Tsu, Timothy Y "Japanese Colonialism and the Investigation of Taiwanese 'Old Customs'" in Jan van Bremen and Akitoshi Shimizu (eds) *Anthropology and Colonialism in Asia and Oceania* 197–218

Tu, Jishan 屠繼善*Hengchun xianzhi* 恆春縣志 [Gazetteer of Hengchun County, 1894] (TWWX 75)

Tung, Yuan-Chao and Tseng Cheng-ming (eds) 童元昭, 曾振名 (編) *Gamalan Xilaya guwenshu* 噶瑪蘭西拉雅古文書 [Historic Documents of the Aboriginal Groups of Kavalan and Siraya] (NTU, Taipei, 1999)

Van, Bremen, Jan and Akitoshi Shimizu (eds) *Anthropology and Colonialism in Asia and Oceania* (Curzon Press, Surrey, 1999)

Wang, Dayuan 汪大淵 *Daoyi zhilüe* 島夷志略 [Brief Accounts of the Island Barbarians, 1349] (in TWWX 119)

Wang, I-shou "Cultural Contact and the Migration of Taiwan's Aborigines: A Historical Perspective" in Ronald G Knapp (ed) *China's Island Frontier: Studies in the Historical Geography of Taiwan* 31–54

Wang, Kaitai 王凱泰 *Fujian Tongzhi Taiwanfu* 福建通志臺灣府 [Gazetteer of Fujian, Taiwan Prefecture, 1871] (TWWX 84)

Wang, Tay-sheng 王泰升 *Legal Reform in Taiwan Under Japanese Colonial Rule, 1895–1945: The Reception of Western Law* (University of Washington Press, Seattle, 2000)

——— *Taiwan falüshi gailun* 臺灣法律史概論 [Introduction to the History of Laws of Taiwan] (4th ed, Yuanzhao, Taipei, 2012)

Wang, Wenjia 王文甲 *Zhongguo tudi zhidushi* 中國土地制度史 [History of Chinese Land Tenure] (Zhongzheng, Taipei, 1956)

Weaver, John C *The Great Land Rush and the Making of the Modern World, 1659–1900* (McGill-Queen's University Press, Montreal, 2003)

Wei, Hue-lin 衛惠林 "Taiwan tuzhu shehui de buluo zuzhi yu quanwei zhidu" 臺灣土著社會的部落組織與權威制度 [The Tribal Organisation and Power System in the Taiwanese Mountain Aboriginal Societies] in Huang Ying-kuei (ed) *Taiwan tuzhu shehui wenhua yanjiu lunwenji* 111–140

Wen, Chen-hua 溫振華 *Taiwan yuanzhumin shi zhengce pian: Qingzhi shiqi* 臺灣原住民史政策篇: 清治時期 [History of Taiwan Aborigines: The Policy Chapter: The Qing Period] (Taiwan Historical, Nantou, 2007)

Wen, Ji 溫吉 *Taiwan fanzheng zhi* 臺灣番政志 [A History of Aboriginal Management in Taiwan] (translated and adapted from Inō Kanori *Taiwan Bansei Shi*, Taiwansheng wenxian weiyuanhui, Taipei, 1957)

Wu, Mi-cha (ed) 吳密察 *Dan Xin dang'an* 淡新檔案 [Administrative Files of Danshui and Xinzhu Counties] (NTU, Taipei, 2006)

Wu, Qi-hao 吳奇浩 "You Dadushe zai tan Qingdai Taiwan zhi shufan diquan" 由大肚社再探清代臺灣之熟番地權 [A Discussion of the Acculturated Aborigines' Land Rights Through a Case Study on the Dadu Village] (2003) 20 *Taiwan shiliao yanjiu* 34–67

Wu, Tsong-min 吳聰敏 "Helan tongzhi shiqi zhi pushe zhidu" 荷蘭統治時期之贌社制度 [The *Pushe* System During the Dutch Period] (2008) 15(1) *Taiwanshi yanjiu* 1–29

——— "Pushe zhidu zhi yanbian jiqi yingxiang, 1644–1737" 贌社制度之演變及其影響, 1644–1737 [The Evolution and Reverberation of the *Pushe* System, 1644–1737] (2009) 16(3) *Taiwanshi yanjiu* 1–38

Wu, Wen-hsing 吳文星 "Jingdu diguo daxue yu Taiwan jiuguan diaocha" 京都帝國大學與臺灣舊慣調查 [Kyoto Imperial University and the Investigation of Old Customs in Taiwan] (2007) 1 *Shida Taiwanshi xuebao* 29–49

Xiao, Yishan 蕭一山 *Qingdai tongshi* 清代通史 [Comprehensive History of the Qing Dynasty] (Shangwu, Taipei, 1963)

Xu, Guo-zhang (trans) 徐國章(譯) *Taiwan zongdufu gongwen leizhuan: lüling shiliao huibian* 臺灣總督府公文類纂律令史料彙編 [Official Documents of the Taiwan *Sōtokufu*: Legislation Collection] (Taiwan Historica, Nantou, 2012) vol 1 & 2

Xunzi 荀子 [The Works of Xunzi] (Chinese Text Project, www.ctext.org)

Yang, Jingfan et al 楊景凡等 *Zhongguo falü sixiangshi jianbian* 中國法律思想史簡編 [A Brief History of Chinese Legal Thoughts] (Guangxi shifan daxue, Guilin, 1988)

Yang, Jun 楊軍 *Qingdai Xinjiang diqu falü zhidu jiqi bianqian yanjiu* 清代新疆地區法律制度及其變遷研究 [A Research on the Legal System and Its Evolution in Qing Xinjiang] (Minzu, Beijing, 2012)

Yang, Ming-tu "Going Back Into a Future of Simplicity: Taiwan Aborigines' Sustainable Utilization of Natural Resources" in Chia-ju Chang and Scott Slovic (eds) *Ecocriticism in Taiwan: Identity, Environment, and the Arts* (Lexington, London, 2016) 3–15

Yang, Yan-jie 楊彥傑 *Heju shidai Taiwan shi* 荷據時代臺灣史 [The History of Taiwan Under Dutch Occupation] (Lianjing, Taipei, 2000)

Yang, Yifan and Terada Hiroaki (eds) 楊一凡，寺田浩明(編) *Zhongguo fazhishi kaozheng disijuan bingpian* 中國法制史考證第四卷丙篇 [Research on Chinese Legal History Volume 4 Part 3] (Zhongguo shehui kexueyuan, Beijing, 2003)

Yang, Ying 楊英 *Congzheng shilu* 從征實錄 [Veritable Records of Zheng Chenggong's Expeditions] (TWWX 32)

Yao, Jen-To "The Japanese Colonial State and Its Form of Knowledge in Taiwan" in Liao Ping-hui and David Der-Wei Wang (eds) *Taiwan Under Japanese Colonial Rule, 1895–1945* 37–61

Yao, Ying 姚瑩 *Dongcha jilüe* 東槎紀略 [Records of My Appointment to the East, 1829] (TWWX 7)

Ye, Ruiping "Torrens and Customary Land Tenure: A Case Study on the Land Titles Registration Act 2008 of Samoa" (2009) 40 *Victoria University of Wellington Law Review* 827–861

——— "User Rights or Ownership: The Nature of Land Rights in Imperial China – Using Taiwan During the Qing Period as a Case Study" (2014) 20 *New Zealand Association for Comparative Law Yearbook* 169–198

Yen, Ai-ching and Yang Guo-zhu 顏愛靜，楊國柱 *Yuanzhu minzu tudi zhidu yu jingji fazhan* 原住民族土地制度與經濟發展 [Land Tenure and Economic Development of the Aborigine Groups] (Daoxiang, Taipei, 2004)

Yin, Zhang-yi 尹章義 *Taiwan kaifashi yanjiu* 臺灣開發史研究 [Research on the History of Land Reclamation in Taiwan] (Lianjing, Taipei, 1989)

Yongzheng zhupi zouzhe 雍正硃批奏摺 [Memorials With Rescripts of the Yongzheng Emperor] (TWWX 300)

Yu, Wenyi 余文儀 *Xuxiu Taiwan fuzhi* 續修臺灣府志 [Revised Gazetteer of Taiwan Prefecture, 1764] (TWWX 121)

Yu, Yonghe 郁永河 *Bihai jiyou* 裨海紀游 [Small Sea Travelogue, 1697] (TWWX 44)

Zelin, Madeline "The Yung-cheng Reign" in Willard J Peterson (ed) *The Cambridge History of China Volume 9 Part One* 183–229

Zhang, Jinfan 張晉藩 *Qingchao fazhishi* 清朝法制史 [Legal History of the Qing Dynasty] (Zhonghua shuju, Beijing, 1998)

Zhang, Junyue 張君約 *Lidai tuntian kao* 歷代屯田考 [Study of *tuntian* in the Various Dynasties] (Shangwu, Beijing, 1939)

Zhang, Yan-xian, Li Xiao-feng and Dai Bao-cun (eds) 張炎憲，李筱峯，戴寶村(編) *Taiwanshi lunwen jingxuan* 臺灣史論文精選 [Selected Essays on Taiwan History] (Yushan, Taipei, 1996)

Zhao, Gang and Chen Zhongyi 趙岡，陳鐘毅 *Zhongguo tudi zhidushi* 中國土地制度史 [History of Chinese Land Tenure] (Lianjing, Taipei, 1982)

Zhao, Rugua 趙汝适 *Zhufanzhi* 諸番志 [Accounts of Various Barbarians] (TWWX 119)

Zhou, Mao-chun 周茂春 "Rizhi chuqi Taiwan tudi diaocha zhi yanjiu (1898–1905)" 日治初期臺灣土地調查之研究 [A Research on the Land Survey During the Early Japanese Period, 1898–1905] (Masters thesis, National Taiwan Normal University, 2011)

Zhou, Xi 周璽 *Zhanghua xianzhi* 彰化縣誌 [Gazetteer of Zhanghua County, 1830] (TWWX 156)

Zhou, Yuanwen 周元文 *Chongxiu Taiwan fuzhi* 重修臺灣府志 [Revised Gazetteer of Taiwan Prefecture, 1718] (TWWX 66)

Zhou, Zhongxuan 周鐘瑄 *Zhuluo xianzhi* 諸羅縣誌 [Gazetteer of Zhuluo County, 1717] (TWWX141)

Index

Page numbers in italic indicate a figure and page numbers in bold indicate a table on the corresponding page

Sōtokufu 23, 182–3, 189–94, 196–8, 200, 203–5; *see also* governor-general

For Product Safety Concerns and Information please contact our EU representative GPSR@taylorandfrancis.com
Taylor & Francis Verlag GmbH, Kaufingerstraße 24, 80331 München, Germany

www.ingramcontent.com/pod-product-compliance
Ingram Content Group UK Ltd.
Pitfield, Milton Keynes, MK11 3LW, UK
UKHW011000180926
475701UK00004B/474

* 9 7 8 0 3 6 7 5 8 7 3 1 4 *